FutureWork

FutureWork

Putting Knowledge to Work in the Knowledge Economy

Charles D. Winslow
William L. Bramer

THE FREE PRESS
A Division of Macmillan, Inc.
NEW YORK

Maxwell Macmillan Canada
TORONTO

Maxwell Macmillan International
NEW YORK   OXFORD   SINGAPORE   SYDNEY

The Free Press
A Division of Macmillan, Inc.
866 Third Avenue, New York, N.Y. 10022

Maxwell Macmillan Canada, Inc.
1200 Eglinton Avenue East
Suite 200
Don Mills, Ontario M3C 3N1

Macmillan, Inc. is part of the Maxwell Communication Group of Companies.

Printed in the United States of America

printing number
1   2   3   4   5   6   7   8   9   10

Library of Congress Cataloging-in-Publication Data

Winslow, Charles D.
    FutureWork : putting knowledge to work in the knowledge economy /
Charles D. Winslow, William L. Bramer.
        p.   cm.
    Includes bibliographical references and index.
    ISBN 0-02-935415-3
    1. Industrial management.   2. Information technology.   I. Bramer,
William L.   II. Title.   III. Title: FutureWork.
HD31.W559   1994
658.4′03—dc20   94–15202
                                                                          CIP

CONTENTS

Part III: Preparing for Tomorrow

ABOUT THE AUTHORS

CHARLES D. WINSLOW is Andersen Consulting's Change Management Services managing partner for the Americas. He works with regional managing partners to ensure that the practice realizes appropriate challenges and opportunities. Mr. Winslow has been the primary sponsor of Integrated Performance Support within Andersen Consulting and in the marketplace. He earned an M.B.A. from the University of Michigan and an undergraduate degree in economics from Dartmouth College, Hanover, New Hampshire. He held a commission in the United States Navy and is a member of several professional and industry associations.

WILLIAM L. BRAMER is a senior partner at Andersen Consulting. He has held positions for Andersen Consulting in Pittsburgh, Chicago, Los Angeles, San Diego, London, World Headquarters, and is currently assigned to the Tokyo office. He has completed a number of national and international high-technology assignments, with emphasis on strategic planning, managing change, systems development, and computer center operations. Mr. Bramer led the development of Change Management Services and the conceptual framework of Integrated Performance Support from its earliest stages. He holds a B.S. from West Virginia University in Business Administration and Management.

FOREWORD

This book reflects a massive economic transformation in modern enterprise. No longer do huge capital facilities determine who wins and loses in competition. Managing intellect—knowledge-based assets and knowledge workers—has become the centerpiece for profitability in virtually all companies. Services—dominated by knowledge work—account for 79% of all employment and 74% of the value-added in U.S. Gross Domestic Product; 80% to 85% of all measured information technology (IT) investments are in services industries. Of the remaining 15% of IT investments, a large proportion supports "knowledge-based" work in manufacturing firms.

In a world where the economists' land, labor, and capital no longer explain wealth generation, we need new concepts to capture and harness the forces of economic growth. Intellect, intelligence, ideas are the substance of production. The essence of management now involves systematizing, supporting, and motivating these ephemeral forces. The old "worker and manager" paradigm has been effectively demolished elsewhere. Bramer and Winslow create an Integrated Performance Support environment—consisting of a Librarian, Coach, Coordinator, Historian, and Assistant—as the new integrated management unit. But these are not just cute terms. The authors call on a rich array of practical cases and results to bring their ideas to life. This work will be a reference for all pragmatic managers.

Knowledge, and knowledge work, dominate the value chains of virtually all companies—whether in services or manufacturing. Knowledge work includes research and development, process design, product design, logistics, market research, marketing, advertising, sales, distribution, legal, public relations, accounting, personnel, finance, health care, and so on.

During the 1980s, a number of books and articles recorded a lack of growth in the productivity of the white collar workers in their activities despite the massive information technology investments supporting them. So serious was the disparity between investment and apparent output that it became known as the "productivity paradox." Managers were often frustrated in their attempts to leverage their knowledge workers and intellectual assets with information technology. Although many books pointed to the benefits of IT use—that is, flatter organizations, more responsiveness, greater empowerment, and the capacity to manage highly dispersed systems—few offered useful insights on how to achieve these benefits effectively. *FutureWork* does just that.

Focusing on a "performance-centered workplace," Bramer and Winslow provide practical insights and thorough examples to tell us how managers can convert the highly disaggregated and constantly changing jobs of knowledge workers into a truly effective enterprise. They concentrate on the fundamental level at which work is performed. But they extend their commentary into the rarefied atmosphere of strategy as well. They even lace the work with historic quotations and words of wisdom that offer a timelessness rarely achieved in management books.

They focus on achieving optimum performance, every time. And they recognize that only the customer can determine what optimum performance is. Wisely, they make customer satisfaction, worker satisfaction, and profitability the triad of goals toward which managers must guide white collar performance. Research shows that when these three goals are optimized simultaneously, firms achieve six to 10 times the benefits of those seeking more simplistic, short-term financial targets. In their system, the organization continues to learn and to build—as well-designed knowledge organizations do—exponentially on their past successes.

A critical insight is their attention to "Integrated Performance Support" to allow both the workers and technology to synchronize most effectively. Their approach moves beyond solving today's problems to systems that can anticipate future performance needs and enable knowledge workers to handle challenging moments not yet anticipated. While consistent with current theories, this is no theoretical book. Nor is it a "how to" handbook designed for those looking for a quick fix. It consciously looks at "organizations in movement," the full dynamics of building, supporting, and leveraging knowledge workers. The authors look at not just improving present work, but at what sort of work workers should be performing in the new knowledge age, or "Infocosm," as they call it.

The book is energized by the knowledge and experience of Andersen Consulting. Andersen itself has been a leading innovator in linking and leveraging its own knowledge work through its AANET, stimulating and integrating 55,000 knowledge workers worldwide. The company has become a leader in both software and software management practices. Drawing on this rich resource, the authors go well beyond the popular concepts of "reengineering process" to the full dynamics of human-computer interaction. The computer becomes an extension of human capabilities—while the human extends machine capabilities in a symbiotic relationship to perform work that neither could perform alone. Symbols, metaphors, and zooming electronic lenses allow a new dimensionality for Integrated Performance Systems. Neither the knowledge worker nor the computer is a static system. Each starts with previously learned concepts and builds wholly new capabilities. This is the true power of Integrated Performance Support environments. The same concepts of interactive learning between knowledge workers and computers can extend to the interactiveness, changed symbols, and massive integration of complexity necessary to manage a modern refinery or distribution system. The entire approach of Bramer and Winslow anticipates and avoids resistance and builds a dynamic for future development.

This book is designed to use experience—not to replicate that experience, but to change the entire future dynamic of systems. If applied well, the book's concepts should avoid the productivity crises many companies have experienced in moving to knowledge work. These concepts are a flow of fresh mountain air into a stale realm that has often been too narrowly confined by technicians, too rigidly constrained by how-to-do-it tacticians, or dealt with in the rarefied hyperbole of futuristic dreamers. This book spans all levels and is useful beyond them all. This is truly an "Integrated Performance Support" book, in itself.

James Brian Quinn
Buchanan Professor of Management,
The Amos Tuck School,
Dartmouth College
January 21, 1994

INTRODUCTION

INTRODUCTION

In 1911, a race car driver named Ray Harroun won the first running of the Indianapolis 500 auto race. Today, if we put his car on a freeway or autobahn, he would barely be able to keep pace: his average speed was not quite 75 miles per hour. This is the fate of all machines and technologies as they are shaped by the hands of human genius and innovation: they get better, faster, more powerful. Changes are rarely dramatic in any given year. If you look at the list of winning times in the Indianapolis 500 since 1911, for example, improvements are rarely more than a couple of miles per hour. But when you add together those incremental improvements, you end up with the jawdropping, 200 mph speeds of today's cars.

The power of today's information technologies is similarly awesome. Indeed, computer systems and related technology, particularly in the workplace, appear to be outstripping the capacity of human beings to use them efficiently. Here the analogy to the racing car is again fortuitous. The modern racing engine is so powerful that it frequently strains to the maximum the ability of other components of the car—its tires, metal structure, braking systems, and so forth—to keep up. Finally, in fact, the speed potential of the car is so great that ways must be found to keep that power under control so that a human being can even drive it safely.

In the world of computers, safety is not as direct an issue, but *usability* is. If we look at the history of information systems over the past few decades, we see that the hardware itself has often outstripped the ability of the software to keep up with its power. In turn, the software has often outstripped the ability of people to use that software effectively. Again, the changes have come incrementally. But adding up those incremental changes, we find that knowledge workers today are challenged more than ever before to perform at the levels necessary to propel their organizations to success.

In a relatively brief period of time, computers and telecommunications have radically altered our world, and they promise to alter it even more in the coming years. The cycle of innovation-change-improvement has taken place rapidly in the world of information technology, and the modern organization, the modern workplace, is where the bulk of these innovations are first tested. For better

---

KEY MESSAGES: INTRODUCTION

- The focus of today's and tomorrow's successful organization must be on *workforce performance.*
- Powerful emerging information technologies will have an impact on workforce performance only if they are designed from a human-centered point of view.
- Integrated Performance Support, or IPS, is a strategy that links technology with workforce performance and productivity, and thus with overall organizational performance.
- IPS contains three primary imperatives: (1) focus at the level of knowledge worker performance; (2) support that performance on demand, at point of need; (3) integrate the performance support facilities into every system available to a worker.
- An IPS strategy can help organizations meet today's toughest marketplace challenges: time compression, tough standards for customer service, high-quality goods and services, worker proficiency and productivity, information overload, downsizing initiatives.
- An IPS strategy can also help organizations prepare for *tomorrow's* marketplace challenges: new workforce demographics, the need to respond to radical change, the ability of knowledge workers and consumers to take advantage of new technologies..
- Above all, Integrated Performance Support anticipates the next phase of the world economy: the movement from an information economy to a knowledge economy. Here, the basic economic resource will not be capital, nor labor, nor natural resources, but rather *knowledge.*
- In the knowledge economy, productivity of knowledge workers is the primary performance imperative. Integrated Performance Support aims to achieve for knowledge workers what Frederick Taylor achieved for manual workers in the industrial economy.

---

and for worse, the modern worker has been a participant in a grand experiment testing the effects of information technology on productivity, efficiency, and quality. The results of this experiment, surprisingly, have been mixed. When information systems have been introduced properly, with concurrent efforts to manage change in the organization, technology has done great things. It has enabled organizations to be more competitive, to do more in a shorter period of time. But for some organizations, the dramatic productivity improvements promised by information technology have eluded them.

We argue in this book that one of the reasons that productivity and efficiency have not always followed on the heels of technological innovation is that the innovation-change-improvement cycle has taken place at the level of the machines themselves. Efforts have been focused on making the *machines* faster, more powerful, and smarter. The results have been breathtaking, to be sure. Our point, however, is that unless those smart machines succeed in making an organization's *workers* smarter, the real potential of the machines may never be realized. We want to talk about the way in which technology can be directed toward *workforce performance;* we want to reach the subject of technology by beginning first with the people, the emerging class of *knowledge workers,* who are to use that technology. This is a deceptively simple point, one that has exceedingly powerful ramifications. Indeed, as others talk today about reengineering the organization, reinventing the factory, redesigning business processes, we want to talk about *reinventing the way we work:* The manner in which we support the people within our organizations to perform at their highest levels so that the entire organization can perform at *its* highest level.

Technology, in particular the information technology that forms the infrastructure of the modern business organization, must do two things to fulfill its promise:

1. Support the work we do *right now,* helping us to perform at higher levels of proficiency, by giving us access to advice, tools, knowledge, and training at the place we need it, at the time we need it, and in the amount and strength we need.
2. Support the work we will do *in the future* by creating a knowledge infrastructure within our organizations that will help us learn and grow and change in line with market demands.

This dual perspective—support us now, and help us prepare for the future— is the focus of this book. *FutureWork* reflects knowledge gleaned from countless conversations with executives and line workers, from our brightest colleagues and from academicians, from years of experience helping organizations find the right technological mix to meet their needs, and from similar years helping organizations change to exploit the technology they have chosen.

The primary enabler, the catalyst that can help organizations meet both short-term and long-term needs, we call "Integrated Performance Support,"™ or "IPS"™ for short. IPS is not itself a technology or an information system, though powerful new information technologies and computing architectures are its key elements. Instead, IPS is best understood as a strategy with three primary imperatives:

1. *Focus at the level of knowledge worker performance.* First, Integrated Performance Support is founded on a particular orientation toward the work of an organization. It involves a focus at the most important level for a business: a focus on the *performance* of people doing their jobs at every moment. IPS says that it is no longer sufficient for information technology to help workers process transactions; technology must now support workers as they transact their business. This support enables workers to apply their knowledge and increase it as a natural by-product of working: knowledge workers doing knowledge work.

2. *Support that performance on demand, at point of need.* Second, IPS involves *supporting* (not controlling) worker performance with the knowledge firepower of the entire organization whenever and wherever a worker needs support. Embedded within the IPS concept are unique and powerful approaches to the design of information systems so that advice, tools, reference, and training are provided to a worker at his or her work location at the moment of need.

3. *Integrate the performance support facilities.* Finally, IPS involves *integrating* that performance support into every system available to a worker, particularly the information systems of the organization. Technologically, this means a quantum leap forward in application design. Today's systems, for the most part, require the workforce to adapt to fit the needs of the system. With Integrated Performance Support we can construct systems that can themselves adapt to meet the needs of the workforce, continuously. With IPS we move beyond the conception of the employee as a "system user" to an employee who is a true "knowledge worker." With IPS we move beyond systems that merely teach and inform to systems that can anticipate performance needs and coach workers through particularly challenging moments. With IPS we move from a "one size fits all" system to a true *performance* system that knows the profile of the particular worker, and that provides support tailorable to that individual's work objective, background, ability level, preferences, and, indeed, the immediate task at hand. This task may never have been encountered before by the knowledge worker, but it must still be supported with knowledge and skill, and dispatched with speed and accuracy.

At a higher level than technology, however, the integrated nature of IPS means something much more important: it means that a focus on workforce performance and on performance support is integrated into the mindset of the organization. This mindset means that an organization is thinking both of today's needs and of tomorrow's.

WHAT IS INTEGRATED PERFORMANCE SUPPORT (IPS)?

Integrated Performance Support, or IPS, is both a high-level, organizational concept and a systems design strategy.

1. As a *concept,* IPS allows organizations to focus their attention on worker performance, on the moment of value as performance occurs for each person in the organization, from the CEO on down to the front-line clerk. IPS gains much of its power by linking individual performance to overall organization performance.
2. As a *systems design strategy,* IPS enables organizations to build performance systems. Unlike traditional systems that are built to process transactions around specific business functions, performance systems are built to transact business across multiple business functions. A performance system provides integrated advice, tools, reference, and training to the worker on demand, at point of need. With a performance system, support can be tailored to meet the needs of workers based on their experience and proficiency levels.

The benefits of Integrated Performance Support: more satisfied workers; more productive and efficient workers; workers who take a fraction of the time to reach basic proficiency levels and then higher proficiency levels; workers who can exceed customer expectations because the support they require to respond to a customer's needs is right there at the workstation; workers who, above all, meet or exceed the performance requirements of their jobs continuously. And the overall result: satisfied customers.

WANTED: PRESCRIPTIONS FOR THE WHOLE ORGANIZATION

One frequents the pages of business books to try to find an edge, that approach or theory that can make an organization more competitive and successful. Occasionally one may become frustrated at the bewildering variety of prescriptions provided. Are organizations supposed to concentrate at high strategic levels or at lower levels where new management techniques are frequently recommended? Are they supposed to look inside or outside their organizations for the answer? Are they supposed to take advantage of what is going well within their companies and only fix what's not working, or are they supposed to scrap everything and try to start from scratch? As in the old parable of the blind men and the elephant,[1] what is most often needed is an understanding of the whole elephant: everyone seeks an understanding of the *whole* organization—the whole business, or industry, or government entity. It's interesting to note in this light that the word "whole" is related to the word "health." Those who practice a "wholistic" approach to medicine, for example, argue that health is not traceable to any one particular aspect of the body, but is rather founded on the optimum workings of all elements, physiological and psychological. So it is with organizations. A bottom-line mentality does not begin to capture the fullness of what we mean; indeed, financial health is only possible when a higher state of wholeness or health is achieved.

The healthy organization runs smoothly. It is alert and responsible; it is always learning. Its internal synapses fire away efficiently, ensuring that communication occurs at all times, and that stimuli are processed and understood. External events may threaten it, and may even enter into the organization, but internal mechanisms exist that ward off harmful effects, or that ensure that a healthy state is achieved again quickly. The healthy organization renews itself each day: it changes, grows, and evolves.

Here we find again the perspective that says we must attend to today's needs as well as anticipate tomorrow's. Sometimes, like a human body, an organization may be sick; it may need prescriptions that can heal it quickly, that can overcome problems occurring right now. But neither organizations nor humans can go on for very long merely solving problems that come along; the problems will begin to overwhelm them. At some point, they need to ask what they need to do to *stay healthy.* As we age, change, and grow, what regimen must we follow to remain vigorous and vital?

The analogy to a healthy body is fortuitous here for one or more reason. No one can really measure the health of a person only at rest. We have to see that person in movement, as well—at work or at recreation, as part of a family or some other human network. So it is with organizations. We want to look at organizations in movement, which is to say, organizations *at work.* As one looks around at organizations at work, one can usually see what succeeds and what doesn't, organizations that are winning and others that are losing their competitive edge. There are no "miracle diet pills," no magic elixirs to regain that edge overnight. Integrated Performance Support represents, however, a powerful new way of thinking about the work that an organization and its people do, and a method by which technology can better support and empower the workforce to perform at its highest levels.

MEETING TODAY'S PERFORMANCE CHALLENGES

What is your organization's greatest internal asset? The right answer: the people who work for your organization. But the workplace and today's market pressures place great demands on that asset today. Here are some of the most important imperatives facing workers today:

1. *Provide higher-quality goods and services.* Quality programs are omnipresent today, as organizations are increasingly finding that quality goods and services are the key to long-term survival in the marketplace. But some companies *say* the right things about quality without simultaneously giving their employees the means or incentives to improve the quality of their performance.
2. *Serve customers better.* Excellence in serving customers has become another key to success in this decade. But ask yourself these questions: when you talk today to, let us say, a customer service representative, how positive are you that you've gotten the right answer? If you call back and talk to a different representative, do you think you'll get the same answer? As products and services have become more complex, many workers are becoming overwhelmed by the amount of information they must know or have access to in order to serve customers adequately.
3. *Perform tasks right the first time.* The demands placed on organizations because of time compression and quality standards dictate that workers be

---

TODAY'S TOP TEN WORKFORCE PERFORMANCE CHALLENGES

1. Provide higher-quality goods and services.
2. Serve customers more quickly and efficiently.
3. Perform tasks right the first time.
4. Perform a broader, more complex range of tasks.
5. Reduce costs of supervision and quality control.
6. Manage significant and continuous change in policies and processes.
7. Reach proficient performance levels quickly and then maintain them.
8. Be proficient in multiple product/service areas.
9. Maintain productivity with a smaller workforce.
10. Cope with the information deluge.

given the support to do things right the first time, rather than reach high performance levels slowly, over time.

4. *Perform a broader, more complex range of tasks.* The time when organizations could have many categories of worker, each becoming an expert in one area or small number of areas, is over. Workers must have diverse skills to perform diverse tasks.

5. *Reduce costs of supervision and quality control.* Employee-to-supervisor ratios are rising steeply. Workers must be given the power and the support to be self-motivated and self-directing.

6. *Cope with continuous change.* The pace of change in the marketplace continues to rise. Organizations must provide their workers with the means to assimilate change, or the entire organization will suffer.

7. *Attain proficiency quickly, and sustain it continuously.* On-going employee education and training are crucial to the success of an organization. Or at least that's what most people would say. But how effective is that training? Is it pertinent and timely? What percentage of workers within your organization receive it? Does your training occur as a separate event that takes your workers away from the place where the work is actually done? Is it linked effectively to their actual job tasks? How much do you suppose your workers remember and apply from that intensive and expensive training program they attended as they started their jobs? What programs do you have in place so that your workers at all levels are challenged to exhibit sustained proficiency and continuous improvement? Have you looked lately at the time it takes to get your workers to proficient performance levels? And then have you compared that figure to your average turnover rate? In some cases, organizations are losing employees faster than they can get them to proficiency.

8. *Be proficient in multiple products/service areas.* To stay competitive, organizations must expand their product and service offerings. Workers are thus challenged to stay abreast of these changes, and to have sufficient knowledge of them in order to serve customers optimally.

9. *Maintain productivity with a smaller workforce.* Layoffs continue to soar around the world. By mid-1993, permanent job reductions announced by companies in the United States alone had totaled nearly 400,000.[2] Organizations are getting smaller. Sometimes they have to reduce workforce numbers in order to survive; there are too many in the lifeboat. But will there be enough left behind to navigate and row the boat to safety? Other organizations are moving to leaner and flatter structures in order to improve efficiency. But leaner does not necessarily mean better-performing. How many organizations are coupling downsizing movements with efforts

toward changing the work and empowering the workers who remain behind? Statistics are showing that some organizations that downsized during the 1980s did more poorly than competitors who maintained their workforce numbers.[3] The reason: the workers who were left behind after the downsizing movement got buried by the avalanche of work that remained—the un-reengineered work, so to speak. Asking fewer people to do more work the old way is not exactly the best way to make lasting improvements in company performance.

10. *Cope with the information deluge.* The same workers who must cope with fewer colleagues and with more complex products and services to sell also face a bewildering onslaught of information from external sources. The mind reels at the figures: the amount of available information doubles every five years, we are told;[4] the average weekday edition of the *New York Times* contains more information than the average person in the sixteenth century encountered in an entire lifetime.[5] Information technology was supposed to take care of this, wasn't it? In fact, the amazing technological developments of the past decade or so have only intensified the problem as more information has been made available to the workforce. The line between working and living is blurring. In a global economy, with today's telecommunications capabilities, one could mix working and living twenty-four hours a day, seven days a week. Intense? Frightening? Perhaps. Computer systems make access to information easier than ever, but they don't tell our workers what to do *with* that information. At the rate that information is increasing, the system's ability to support the worker is not keeping up. Occasionally, a worst-case scenario occurs for today's knowledge workers: as information continued to deluge them, they simply ignore it.

Information technology has tried to address these performance challenges from its beginnings. But we believe that a machine-oriented point of view has reached the limits of its ability to help workers perform their jobs. To this point, an inadequate amount of attention has been paid to the knowledge worker; insufficient focus has been placed on the individual, the person, the workforce. Organizations developed the processes, automated them with new technology, and then "trained" the users a week before system conversion. At one time, this worked well enough. But as the workplace has become increasingly complex, the gap between what organizations want technology to do and what it really is doing, and the gap between optimal workforce performance and actual performance, have become deep and difficult chasms to bridge. Our work is dynamic and multidimensional; a machine-oriented approach to technology has resulted in systems that have been static and one-dimensional. We have ended up with organizations whose workers are systems users, not knowledge workers or system-enabled service workers.

Over the past few years, promising work from a number of different, though related, fields has been coming together to produce an approach to information technology that has the potential to revolutionize the workplace. The field of artificial intelligence began to develop so-called "knowledge-based" approaches to systems, creating systems with the ability to provide advice to a worker. The field of instructional design discovered the benefits of using computers to rework the approach to workforce training; it became apparent that training could now be delivered to workers at the point of need, at the moment of need, rather than taking them away to some separate classroom. And the field of systems design began to be influenced by thinkers advocating "user-centered" design—an approach that begins with the performance needs of workers, not with system functionality. These fields and a number of others are converging on what is now most frequently called "performance support." Here a variety of acronyms compete for attention: PSS, for performance support systems; EPSS, for *electronic* performance support systems. Our choice, Integrated Performance Support, is intended to connote the fact that we cannot begin with systems; we can only end there. The larger issue is the orientation toward performance, and with supporting that performance every moment of the day.

By whatever acronym, the initial thinking behind performance support was to give workers, at the moment they need it, a range of support resources, including:

- an "advisor" who would provide advice via expert systems and knowledge-based systems
- an "assistant" who would provide tools and on-line help
- a "librarian" who would make available a variety of reference and information databases
- a "teacher" who would provide computer-based training[6]

But it is crucial that this approach to systems technology fulfill its promise. One of the reasons why we felt there was a need for a book such as this was our concern that the idea of "performance support" was about to be buried under limited and limiting misconceptions. As we have worked with and listened to others explain performance support, we have noted a tendency to equate it merely with the instructional design viewpoint and to see it as just a new approach to training workers; others are speaking of performance support merely from the systems design perspective, calling it just the next generation of on-line help. When one looks behind the claims of some so-called performance support systems today, one often finds little more than a few modules of computer-based training and some context-sensitive help—that is, help that is linked to the action being done within a system application. Such systems do not necessarily solve the greater problem: technology and an approach to systems design that resolutely continues to treat workers merely as system users. Unless organizations can move beyond the system-centered orientation to a performance-centered orientation—to the idea of *supporting workers at work*—they will not reach the root of today's performance imperative.

What is that performance imperative? We believe it is knowledge worker and service worker productivity. These types of workers account for anywhere from 75% to 80% of the workforce in developed countries today, up from around 30% only forty years ago. As Peter Drucker writes, the productivity of these workers, not of those who make and move things, is the productivity of a developed economy.[7] The key today is to achieve the same breakthrough in knowledge worker productivity that people like Frederick Taylor achieved in manual work in the industrial economy. We believe that Integrated Performance Support is one of the keys to dramatic growth in the productivity of knowledge workers, and service workers, as well, in the knowledge economy.

It is important, then, to place the specific parts of performance support—training, help, systems design, expert systems, and so forth—in the greater context of the *new way of working* that Integrated Performance Support facilitates for knowledge workers. Think of it in this way: at the time of its invention, the automobile could have been considered just another, and better, mode of transportation. It got you from point A to point B faster and more efficiently than a horse and buggy. But in fact, the automobile radically altered the world. It made distant locations accessible and permitted easier movement and travel. It affected the way cities and towns developed. It affected economies and created a whole new economic infrastructure as people no longer depended on nearby providers of goods and services. We could use the example of computers themselves to make the same point. The original conception of these machines is embedded in their name: they were simply more efficient machines for computing, and some early analysts forecast that the entire world would never need more than a couple of them. We know what happened instead.

In much the same way, the new potential of information systems—of what we call "performance systems"—dramatically alters the way we should think about our work, simply because we *can* think about it differently. Suppose that technology has evolved to the point where it almost fades into the background—where it no longer dominates the stage but rather helps the real actors, the real *performers,* do their work. What if executives can begin with the

What Is a "Knowledge Worker"?

Since it was coined by Peter Drucker, the term "knowledge worker" has meant different things to different people. We know that Integrated Performance Support is geared primarily toward support for knowledge workers. But what are they, exactly?

Our working definition has been that a knowledge worker is "someone who interprets and applies information to create and provide value-adding solutions, and to make informed recommendations."

The definition intentionally does not attempt to place knowledge workers at any particular level in an organization, or in any particular industry. It is certainly incorrect, for example, to equate "knowledge worker" with "white collar worker." As a survey of the performance systems and prototypes in this book will quickly reveal, these systems support customer service representatives, workers who inspect water pipes, sales representatives, jet engine mechanics, consulting professionals, commercial lenders, service station owners, window salespersons, leasing agents, and venture capitalists. If you are reading this book *you* are probably a knowledge worker.

If our definition seems puzzling, perhaps it would help to contrast it with a definition of a "service worker." A service worker would be someone who interprets and applies information to complete assigned tasks correctly, and to make informed decisions. The creation of value-adding solutions is a crucial role for a knowledge worker, rather than simply completing an assignment from a supervisor. Making recommendations, instead of just making decisions, is also a crucial differentiator.

In any case, "knowledge worker" can sometimes be a rather cumbersome term to use frequently in a text. Hence, we use the simple term "worker" to refer to this new, important category of people in the knowledge economy.

simple but powerful question of *what sort of work their workers should be performing.* Suppose further that technology is now sophisticated enough to support work even when particular performance challenges are not known until the instant that the work must be done. If this is indeed a real possibility, then it must radically alter the manner in which all of us create organizations, go about business, and bring about change within our organizations. This book says that we *can* do this—that we can use state-of-the-market thinking and technology in order to meet state-of-the-market performance challenges organizations face today.

MEETING TOMORROW'S PERFORMANCE CHALLENGES

But this book also says something else. It says that Integrated Performance Support has the ability to prepare organizations for the challenges that they will be facing *tomorrow:*

- the need to make information systems easily accessible to customers, as certain processes are transferred directly to the consumer; and the need to make these systems easily usable by a workforce with varying abilities;
- the need to change quickly, to be resilient in the face of new technological and strategic developments, something that will require new methods of ensuring that change can be rapidly welcomed and absorbed throughout all levels of the organization;
- the need to ensure that knowledge can be captured, stored, and shared across an organization so that its knowledge base can grow;
- the need to support workers as organizations and people throughout the world find their environment changed by the coming universal networks, which will link nations and the world together into what we are calling the "Infocosm";
- an economy that will change in unpredictable ways as we enter the mature phase of the information economy, as *services* (rather than products) increasingly dominate the global economy, and as *knowledge* becomes the new means of production over capital and land.

We live not only at the turn of the century but of the millennium. The numbering of the years is a human invention, of course—a convenience. As we move inexorably toward the year 2000, no odometer in the sky will record it. Nature will not notice, nor will those cultures that do not follow the calendar of Western industrialized nations.[8] But for the rest of us, 2000 seems to beckon, seems to call for a response—of hope, fear, exhortation, prediction. We want to believe that something is ending, and that something new and hopeful is beginning. What would that something be?

The presumptions of the twentieth century—about society, education, nation-states, economics, families, business—are called into question almost every day. We have watched political boundaries change and nations vanish by both peaceful and bloodthirsty manners. In his book *The Work of Nations,*

Robert Reich predicts the end of the nation-state as any useful economic reality in the global economy. There will be no such thing as an "American" economy, a "German" industry, a "Japanese" product. (It is already clear, by tracking Direct Overseas Investment figures, that multinational corporations exert more financial influence than nations do in their collective foreign aid programs.) The very notion of a nation may change to one defined by logical boundaries and electronic communications more than by physical and geographical locations. As our alliances, partners, and competitors are increasingly located all over the globe, the work of nations will become the work of the world.

And what will that work be? Increasingly, the answer being given is that *knowledge* will be the basis of the work of the world. Peter Drucker argues that the world has crossed another great divide—has witnessed another transformation, and the creation of what Drucker calls the "post-capitalist" society. In this society, says Drucker, the "basic economic resource—the 'means of production,' to use the economist's term—is no longer capital, nor natural resources (the economist's 'land'), nor 'labor.' *It is and will be knowledge.*" Wealth-creating activities will not be labor, or the allocation of capital to productive uses, but rather the application of knowledge to work. "The leading social groups of the knowledge society will be 'knowledge workers'— knowledge executives who know how to allocate capital to productive use. . . . The *economic* challenge of the post-capitalist society will therefore be the productivity of knowledge work and the knowledge worker."[9] In the words of the subtitle of this book, the challenge is to put knowledge to work in the knowledge economy.

We find these predictions about the place of knowledge—of learning and of intellect—echoed in seminal business analyses everywhere.

- "Intellectual and service activities now occupy the critical spots in most companies' value chains—regardless of whether the company is in the services or the manufacturing sector" (James Brian Quinn, *Intelligent Enterprise*).[10]
- "The control of knowledge is the crux of tomorrow's worldwide struggle for power in every human institution" (Alvin Toffler, *Powershift*).[11]
- "In [the next decade], the newest and lowest-level employee will be expected to know more about the company that employs him or her than many middle managers and most supervisors knew about the company they worked for in the 1970s and 1980s" (Boyett and Conn, *Workplace 2000*).[12]
- "Success in the new economy is predicated on the ability to understand and utilize a loosely connected set of economic and social processes, including the following: scientific inquiry, invention, innovation, dissemination, net-

working, investment, commercialization, cumulative learning" (Anthony Patrick Carnevale, *America and the New Economy*).[13]

- "In the future, economic success will be determined not by the products a nation produces, but by its ability to organize and channel the information it possesses. . . . In the information age, the key [to wealth] is intellectual capital—knowledge and ideas."[14]

An attention to knowledge as the source of real economic activity has made its way into economic schools of thought, as well. Influential research is now being conducted by economist Paul Romer, for example, into what he calls the "economics of ideas." Romer holds that ideas are "the major engines of growth in the wealth of nations," and his goal is to move that notion to the core of economic theory. "Instead of just capital and labor and raw materials producing output, it is the ideas themselves and the economic incentives that lead to their creation and diffusion that are the fundamental determinants of economic well-being."[15]

One of the chief supporters of research into the knowledge economy is the Royal Bank of Canada. Chairman and CEO Allan Taylor notes: "We must understand that ideas, innovation, inventions, and entrepreneurship—supported by appropriate education and training—are the real engines of growth. . . . Renewed and sustained economic growth means investing in knowledge in the same way we have invested in machines. Investment spurs knowledge. Knowledge spurs investment."[16]

But what will companies be *doing* in the new knowledge economy? What will our *workers* be doing? What is the relationship between knowledge and workers? The most important differences between your organization today and your organization in ten years will not be found primarily in the products you make, the services you provide, or the equipment you use. The most important differences will be in the manner in which your employees will be working: the level of responsibility they will have, and the *ability and support they must be given to generate new applications, products, and services from knowledge—to effectively employ knowledge as a means of production.*

The technological and philosophical architecture resulting from Integrated Performance Support—the architecture that will allow organizations to meet today's performance challenges—will become the knowledge infrastructure that will permit knowledge workers to generate new products and services, to develop new realms of knowledge, and to discover new ways to create and grow businesses. Some are calling such an organization a "learning organization," but we want to up the ante here. Integrated Performance Support can create environments in which learning leads to productivity, innovation, and profit. We want more than organizations that can learn; we want organizations that can grow: that can effectively employ the results of learning to business success.

INTEGRATED PERFORMANCE SUPPORT CASE STUDIES

This is a practical book. Its emphasis is on people actually doing their work; we talk not only about theories, but about real on-the-job performance. We believe that the primary obstacles to business success today are problems related to doing, to performing, and that Integrated Performance Support offers a revolutionary breakthrough in the manner that we facilitate excellence in workforce performance. However powerful the ideas and concepts are at the heart of Integrated Performance Support, they are worthless unless they are able to be practically implemented in real-life business situations today. Thus virtually every chapter of this book builds upon actual companies and actual information systems designed with the Integrated Performance Support concept. Because these systems—which we call "performance systems"—are so new, many are still in the prototype stage, under consideration by companies as the basis for a fully implemented system.

Here are some examples of the cases discussed in this book.

- At McCaw Cellular Communications in Kirkland, Washington, and Rogers Cantel Mobile Communications in Toronto, Canada, customer service representatives work on-line at their workstations with new customers. The system coaches workers through the process and automatically performs a credit check on the customer. Total time for the process has been reduced from two hours to fifteen minutes.
- At Andersen Windows in Bayport, Minnesota, customers building or remodeling a home can work with a sales representative at a computer system and can design the window construction in real time. An image of the customer's home is created, and different window configurations can be manipulated so customers can see immediately how their choices will look. When final decisions have been made, the system generates and places the parts orders and construction orders.
- At a major aircraft engine manufacturing company in the United States, airline mechanics who must repair jet engines work with handheld computers, to which they download diagnostic information from a jet returning from a test flight. Based upon this information, the prototype performance system

advises the mechanic about the most likely reason for the engine fault, helps the mechanic isolate the problem, locates the necessary parts, and coaches the mechanic through the repair. During times when the mechanic would previously have been idle, the system can conduct multimedia training sessions, allowing the mechanic to practice repairs by actually manipulating graphical representations of engines at the computer workstation.

- At Connecticut Natural Gas in Hartford, Connecticut, new customer information systems presented a number of challenges to workers. Using the existing mainframe system, the new applications would mean that customer service representatives who previously used about 30 different computer screens would now use around 250 screens. This increased functionality presented a number of usability challenges. Without expensive investment in new hardware, Connecticut Natural Gas was able to build Integrated Performance Support functions into the system to permit workers to access the screens in a natural and intuitive manner, easing navigation through the system, and allowing workers to serve customers more quickly and efficiently.

- At North West Water, a large water and waste water organization in the United Kingdom, an Integrated Performance Support research project included the development of a prototype performance system called "Learning Manager." The system promises to deliver training in a powerful way to help workers cope with major process restructuring. Major new information systems are being developed within the company, and increased demands will be placed on workers to continue to provide high levels of customer service, even as they learn new jobs and new skills. With the prototype performance system, the entire workflow for tasks is presented to the worker, and supporting services—a Librarian, a Coach, a Coordinator, an Historian, and an Assistant—provide support for the completion of those tasks.

- Customer service representatives for Bell Atlantic were asked to become more sales-oriented as a result of strategic efforts to increase focus on customer satisfaction. In this new performance situation, increased demands were placed upon the representatives to keep up with product and service information. The answer for the company was a performance system that provided workers with supporting information and advice at their workstations. Based upon certain criteria entered into the system by the worker during a phone interview with a customer or potential customer, the system recommends the most appropriate product or service. The performance system has enabled workers to achieve impressive sales increases.

Although many of the performance systems and prototypes discussed later in detail are for U.S. companies, the Integrated Performance Support phenomenon is truly international. We have already mentioned the system in prototype stage in the United Kingdom. Other systems are currently in development in Canada, Sweden, Japan, Italy, Australia, and the Netherlands, to name just a few.

ONWARD TO A HUMAN-CENTERED TECHNOLOGICAL FUTURE

In his latest book, Donald A. Norman quotes the motto of the 1933 Chicago World's Fair: "Science Finds, Industry Applies, Man Conforms."[17] The motto is, in fact, a perfectly accurate summary of the prevailing attitudes toward science and technology that have endured for several hundred years. What we now call science was primarily a European invention of the sixteenth and, especially, the seventeenth centuries. One important analysis of the rise of modern science notes that science sprang from the belief, inherited from the late Middle Ages, that the avenue to truth was through an analysis of the nature of things, "which would thereby determine how things acted and functioned."[18] As scientific rationalism increased, and as observation, experimentation, and classification took over, the natural world for the first time came to appear ordered: it followed rules and immutable laws. There was nothing mystical or uncertain about nature, or about our methods for observing it.

As humans gained understanding about the natural world, they were also able to imitate some of its power, to harness energy in order to manipulate the natural world. It was a momentous development for humankind—one with both wondrous and unfortunate consequences. Science and technology have always had unintended consequences. During the European Renaissance, for example, the demand for wood by both the iron industry and the shipbuilding industry virtually decimated the natural forests of much of Europe. The industrial revolution of the late eighteenth century utterly transformed economies from a rural, agricultural focus to a town-centered, factory focus.

Above all, the rise of science and technology has been fueled by the belief that the chaotic and messy lives of real human beings will and must be brought under control by the marvelous order and power of machines. Only now are we able to see that control has also been the vain attempt of some developments in information technology. Again: science finds, industry applies, man conforms. Norman offers his own rewriting of this motto, one with which we concur: people propose, science studies, technology conforms.[19] Such thinking represents a truly human-centered approach to technology. It says that technology has no worth except as it supports the work of human beings and enriches their lives. Beneath the abstruse technology of computer systems and technical architectures, beneath the concepts and ideas of Integrated Performance Support is this great truth: technology must help us work better, learn better, and live better. If it does not, then all of us will have failed. Then we will be forced to admit that the machines we work with are more important than the people who work with the machines.

PART ONE

Basic Issues in Integrated Performance Support

CHAPTER 1

THE PERFORMANCE-CENTERED ENTERPRISE

What is the secret to business success and where is it to be found? Most organizations, whether they realize it or not, are prone to look outside for the answer: to new technologies, new people, new management techniques. But consider an ancient story: the gods are conspiring from on high about what to do about the wretched humans below them. The divines have in their possession the secret to human happiness, and it's important to them that humans never discover it, lest they try to become *like* gods. They are arguing about where to hide the secret. "Let's bury it deep beneath the sea," one of the gods says. "No," replies another, "for humans will learn to explore the oceans and they may find it one day." "Let's bury it on the highest mountain, then." "No," comes the same voice, "for surely they will also learn to scale even the tallest of the mountains of the earth." Several other suggestions are made and discarded until one of the gods comes upon the answer. "I know: we will hide it deep within their hearts, for that surely will be one place they will never look."

Where are business profitability, quality, efficiency, and productivity buried? The fact that we do not have an answer to that question is clear from the endless stream of prescriptive analyses of businesses and of the economy. Organizations and their executives are on a constant quest for the best way to be competitive, productive, efficient, cost-effective, profitable—successful. Some answers seem profound, but are vague and difficult to implement. Other answers are, mercifully, short-lived. Few of us, we suspect, would want to live again through that period in the 1980s when executives were reading about ancient Samurai sword fighting and Attila the Hun leadership secrets in an effort to be more competitive.

Most recently, information technology has been seen as a powerful way to increase productivity, efficiency, and quality. Knowledge will be the new capital of the twenty-first century, many now predict, and those who control knowledge will have the power and wealth that comes with it. Information technology, then, must be the answer, right? Well, yes and no. Yes, in that the world now is too complex, too competitive for organizations to be successful without powerful technological enablers. But no, as well, because the technological answer

---

KEY MESSAGES: CHAPTER 1

- Organizations today increasingly find their knowledge workers falling into the performance "gap": a disparity between ideal and actual performance.
- The key to avoiding the performance gap is to become a "performance-centered enterprise."
- The success of every organization is founded ultimately on the effective performance by workers at "moments of value": moments when they are deciding, doing, acting.
- "Performance" should not mean just doing something: it should mean doing something well. Performance is "an action or process accomplished with precision and completeness."
- Optimum performance depends on the answers to two question: (1) *Can* the individual do it? (2) *Will* the individual do it?
- Integrated Performance Support ensures that the answers to both questions will be affirmative. IPS-based systems, or "performance systems," provide advice, tools, reference, and training where and when they are needed to support the performance of knowledge workers in real time.

---

will truly work only if executives begin, as in the story of the buried secret, *inside* their organizations. The answer, so we argue, begins with the *work* itself— with real employees performing their work, and with supporting those employees and helping them perform optimally in the face of a complex technological and competitive environment. Anthony Patrick Carnevale has insightfully noted that the expansion of technology's role in the workplace has meant that new skill requirements have come into play. As technical complexity has increased, a job has demanded from a worker a greater *depth* of skills; as the job's scope of action has expanded, the job has required greater *breadth* of skills. To move beyond the workstation, the worker needs greater interpersonal and organizational skills; to cope with change and the demands of today's marketplace, the worker needs enhanced learning and problem-solving skills.[1]

We are at the end of one phase of information technology in the workplace, the phase that looked at workforce challenges and said, "Here's a system; do it this way and you'll be more productive." We believe that the end of this era can be seen in the mounting evidence that something seems to be wrong with the way in which workers are performing their jobs. The wording of that sentence is important. We might have said, for instance, that something is wrong with the workers themselves, or that something is wrong with the work that our workers are accomplishing. These problems, if real, are only subsets of the larger problem: something is wrong with the *way* workers are performing their jobs.

The problem is not limited to any particular industry, or to any particular part of the world. The inability of organizations today to understand the problem of working has several different roots. One is in the natural human tendency to ignore or rationalize problems, or to try to blame someone or something else for what is happening. If workers aren't being productive, or if quality is lacking, or if employee turnover is high, it's a social or environmental problem, right? Or it's because of the school system, or television, or the breakdown of the nuclear family. Another root of the problem is in the natural tendency to seek high-level, single-focus solutions: strategic planning, business process reengineering, new technologies, and system architectures. All of these are important, certainly. But we also have to move out of the war room and into the trenches. We must look at the obstacles faced every day by workers from the full range of abilities and skill levels of the workforce—from less committed and less talented workers all the way up to those who are committed and able.

Consider the following scenarios and what they have in common:

- Customer service representatives for a utility company are about to be trained to use two brand-new information systems. In their old manner of working, they used about 30 screens to do their jobs. With the new systems, they will use about 250 screens, each of which has to be accessed by a different four-digit code. "I've been working here twenty-five years," one representative says. "I've never had to use this many screens before. Do I have the same job, now? What am I supposed to be doing?"
- An assistant in a doctor's office is trying to help a patient with her bill. How should she pay? Should she pay before leaving and have the insurance company reimburse her, or will her company pay the doctor directly? It depends on whether her deductible has been satisfied, but the assistant has no way of checking on that. Is a copayment required? Does the policy cover the procedure she just had performed? Will the medications prescribed to her interact negatively with her other prescriptions? I'll have to check with the insurance company, the assistant tells the patient. I'll have to check with the pharmacist, I'll have to ask the doctor, I'll have to ask. . . .
- A customer service representative for a phone company has been charged with being more than a typical service representative. She is being asked to sell her company's entire range of products and services to her customers, based upon their current profiles and anticipated needs. During a single

phone call, she must now be able to diagnose a wide range of problems, as well as match that customer's needs to a list of over 60 possible service and product enhancement options. "It's not the new responsibility I mind," one representative says. "It's the fact that there's simply too much product information to remember, especially when we get changes to them every month."

- The president of a bank in Spain is examining two reports that have crossed his desk the same day. One report, from the head of Teller Services, explains that 70% of all turnover for his bank's tellers occurs in the first eight months after they are hired. The other report, from the director of human resources, notes that the time it takes a new teller to get proficient at the job is around nine months. With a grimace, the president now sees the cold statistical truth that he is losing tellers faster than he can develop them. At their next meeting, he asks his staff to consider which came first: is the time to proficiency period long because of employee turnover, or is employee turnover happening because it takes too long to become proficient?

- Like many in the defense industry today, contractors are having to make do with fewer employees and with fewer levels of management. But the planes still have to be maintained, tested, and repaired. The experience of one jet engine mechanic is typical: a plane has encountered some problems in flight. Back in the hangar, the mechanic looks at a print-out of diagnostic readings from the airplane. It has been several months since he has worked on this particular type of engine; he must sift through the print-out, locate the problem, and make the repair. The plane is scheduled for another test flight in several hours.

These scenarios are linked in several ways. In each case, the problem is not that management has been unclear about their expectations, or that the particular job tasks are vague. Nor is the problem that employees are not satisfied with or committed to their jobs. The problem, rather, is that there are built-in barriers in the *way* of working that are preventing workers from doing their jobs well. Their information systems or the manner in which they are trained may no longer be aligned with the demands of their work. They may face increasing demands for customer service or be forced to cope with an overload of information or a time-compressed working environment. These are not strategic problems, or technological ones. These are *performance* problems.

One well-known model by which to speak of performance in organizations today is the one proposed by Geary Rummler and Alan Brache in *Improving Performance: How to Manage the White Space on the Organization Chart.* Rummler and Brache describe three levels of deploying performance measures in an organization. One level is the people, those who are performing and being directed by a set of performance measures. A second level is the process, the series of activities that provide a product or service. A third level is the organization, which encompasses the performance at the other two levels.[2] Organizations must have performance measures at all three levels.[3] Our point, however, is that performance at the people level is the one type of performance that one can actually see happening. At any given moment of the day, customers will not care much about organizational and process performance. They will care a great deal, however, about the performance of people, so it is crucial to ensure that there is adequate support at each of those performance moments.

Are your people performing optimally, or have they fallen into what some have called the performance "gap,"[4] the disparity between ideal and real performance? Here are some phrases you may hear from those who have fallen into that gap: "I'm sorry, I'm new here; I'll have to ask my supervisor." "We don't handle that in this department; I'll have to transfer you." "Let me get back to you." "Please hold." The key to avoiding the performance gap for your workers is to become a "performance-centered workplace."

A PERFORMANCE-CENTERED WORKPLACE

No one could deny that this is a time of unprecedented change—politically, culturally, technologically, and economically. But we believe that successful organizations will be those that look beyond this change and see continuity; those that realize that the key to success has been, and always will be, the performance of the people who make up the organization. From this perspective, organizations can never change at their most fundamental level, as long as they are comprised of human beings.

We need, somehow, to be constantly reminded that the success of every organization centers ultimately on the effective performance of its workforce, from the CEO to the front-line clerk. More precisely, success is founded upon the effective performance at those moments when workers are deciding, doing, acting. We can call those moments "moments of value." Our colleague Rudy Puryear speaks of those moments of value as the times when the consumer and the provider come together, and the provider delivers value to the consumer.[5] Our use of the term opens it up to a broader realm. A moment of optimal performance by a worker is a moment of value. Each worker performs his or her job by moving from task to task, from moment to moment, from one moment of value to another. Far below the rarefied air of strategic thinking, underneath the advancements of technology and the challenges of regulation and competition, is where the real work of an organization takes place. Synergy is said to occur when the whole is greater than the sum of the parts. But the fact is, there wouldn't *be* a whole without those parts: the accumulation of multiple moments of value.

Few organizations are oriented in this way. If one looks back at the scenarios we presented earlier in this chapter, for example, each boils down to the performance of an important task, the task of the moment. But sometimes it is easy to rationalize and slide over performance that may be below par for a given task. After all, it's only one task. Or there may be a tendency to give in and just accept the fact that a certain degree of poor performance is inevitable. But suboptimal performances eventually add up for the organization as a whole. If truth be known, people rationalize or accept suboptimal performance more than they think, and it may be costing them big money.

But let us suppose that organizations can overcome their tendency to rationalize and accept suboptimal performance. Let's suppose that everyone can see the problem. Now what? The key here is not merely being able to recognize unacceptable performance levels. The key, rather, is being able to *enable competent performance.* Supporting and enabling competent performance at every moment of value for today's knowledge workers is the breakthrough of Integrated Performance Support.

WHAT IS PERFORMANCE?

What do we mean by "performance"? Like many concepts, it is easy to use in ordinary speech, but difficult to pin down precisely. ("If you do not ask me what time is, I know," wrote Augustine. "If you ask me, I do not know."[6]) The word comes to us already slightly watered down. "To perform" most often means simply "to do" something. A worker performs a task, an automobile performs well, a surgeon performs an operation. But the word has not always been so bland and neutral. Its original meaning, now almost lost, was "to carry through to completion; to complete or finish or perfect an action or product or process." Some traces of that meaning remain in the English language. For example, we speak of a symphony concert as a musical performance, and the musicians as performers. By that we mean that the music has been practiced and that a level of expertise has been achieved. The concert is a *perfected* action, something done thoroughly, competently, and completely.

Organizations must reclaim this understanding of performance: an action or process accomplished with precision and completeness. The goal today cannot be just doing things better; it must be doing the right things right, 100%

WHAT IS PERFORMANCE?

In the context of the workforce, performance is work that is accomplished with precision, to completion, and done correctly the first time.

Courtesy of Chicago Symphony Orchestra. Photograph by Jim Steere.

Performance is not just doing something; it's doing it well. Some of this meaning of the word can still be seen in the sense in which we think of a musical or theater performance: it's an accomplished piece of work, done to the full capabilities of the people involved.

of the time. But organizations, not focused properly on the moment of value, either do not see or too easily overlook those moments when performance does not match expectations. The consequences of poor performance moments are not always clear or are not always immediately apparent, but eventually, they add up. The late U.S. Senator Everett Dirksen once made a similar point about the government budget. "A billion dollars," he said, "isn't all that much money. But you take a billion here, and a billion there, and pretty soon you're talking real money." So it is with performance. One customer who gets bad service over the telephone, or one part poorly made on the assembly line, won't sink your business. But put several disgruntled customers together, several inferior parts, and pretty soon you're talking real, bottom-line problems.

True excellence in the next century will partly depend on being best in class at "delighting" the customer. Mere satisfaction will not be enough; the goal is to have customers delighted with the service rendered by a company. This notion of delight is the natural outcome of an orientation toward performance—work that is accomplished with precision and done correctly the first time.

Achieving optimum performance is a complex matter, as evidenced in the performance model[7] shown in the accompanying figure. The first question to consider in empowering workers to attain and sustain optimum performance is: *"Can* the individual perform the necessary tasks?" This question primarily involves matters of *ability:* the aptitude, knowledge, and skills of the workforce. The second question, however, relates to *motivation* as well: *"Will* the individual perform the necessary tasks?" Here an organization must concentrate on issues of the needs, values, and attitudes of the workforce. The third

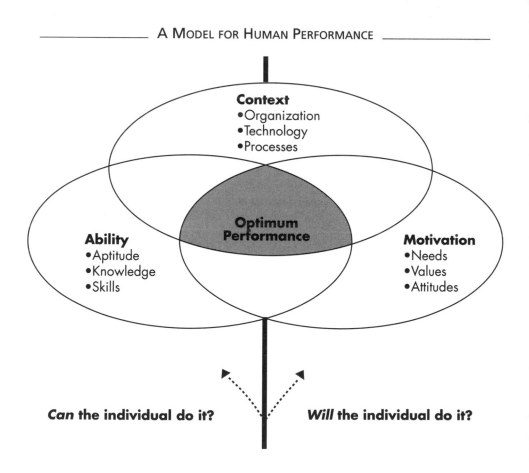

A MODEL FOR HUMAN PERFORMANCE

Context
•Organization
•Technology
•Processes

Optimum Performance

Ability
•Aptitude
•Knowledge
•Skills

Motivation
•Needs
•Values
•Attitudes

Can the individual do it?   *Will* the individual do it?

component of the performance model, *context* (or environment), spans both performance questions. An organization's self-understanding, its technology, and its processes should, first, ensure that adequate support is provided to the worker to ensure optimum performance. This is, of course, one of the breakthroughs of Integrated Performance Support. Another breakthrough, however, is in becoming a performance-centered workplace, an organization fundamentally oriented toward the moments of value of each individual worker. One cannot overestimate the motivational value of that orientation. The employees of a performance-centered enterprise are more satisfied, more fulfilled. Ingvar Petursson, CIO of McCaw Cellular Communications, notes that employee satisfaction is an important benefit of Integrated Performance Support. "Employees feel frustrated when they do not have supporting resources available to them when they need them. That frustration increases as they get into a more dynamic and fast-changing environment. And frustration leads inevitably to dissatisfaction."

TECHNOLOGY THAT SUPPORTS PERFORMANCE

The workplace has grown too complex for organizations to expect their workers to perform without technological support. But in turn, the technology has developed to the point where we must be far more cognizant than we have been about the kinds of support we provide. As we move to the next phase of information technology in the workplace, there will be a new starting point: not, "Here's a system, do it this way," but rather, "What are your performance needs? What do you want to do? Now, here's a system that will anticipate needs and coach workers toward their performance goals." Technology *can* be the powerful enabler to organizations that it promised it would be. It can, that is, if it is properly oriented toward the real performance needs of the workforce. It can if technology conforms to the needs of humans, not the other way around. Here is the sort of technology we mean:

Consider a system that gives a worker a more wholistic picture of the work to be done. Almost every task to be performed should be available within the worker's field of vision. Part of making this happen is to provide a basic interface—the primary screen that the worker sees—that makes the system intuitively understandable to the worker. No blinking cursors waiting for complex keystrokes, no memorized codes taking them into green-on-black computer screens full of poorly structured and overwhelming data. Workers could interact with this system naturally: in addition to the keyboard, they could talk to it, or gesture and point, or write.

But the interface is only part of what gives the worker a whole picture of the work to be performed. Everything within this system is designed from a performance-centered point of view. Every feature and function is designed to facilitate what workers actually need to do. This worker is a real person *at work,* not a "user" using a system.

The system "knows" this worker, or at least recognizes the class or type of worker. It knows the person's skills inventory, training history, job responsibilities, career path, and authority level. The system also recognizes that this is a dynamic individual. He or she changes over time: changes jobs, learns new things, gains new competencies. The system knows about the work that this person does. It contains a "knowledge base" (not a database), which holds job tasks, work flows, and performance standards. It knows what the critical success factors and key performance indicators are for each job or role and can track these, helping the organization ensure that they are constantly aligned with larger objectives. The processes and functions that accomplish strategic objectives can be linked, by working models and measurement criteria, with the strategic objectives they support.

Most important, this system contains powerful support features that are integrated within the application environment the person uses and are made available to the worker seamlessly under a common interface. These are available at point of need, either at the request of the worker or provided directly by the system. The support features include:

- *Advice.* Coaching provided by the system at particularly important moments in the work flow. This, too, may be requested by the worker or initiated by the system. Advice may include case descriptions of how experts and co-workers have resolved similar situations; it may also include diagnostic support, decision modeling, and suggestions on how to proceed with the support from other support services.
- *Tools.* A set of integrated and customized job aids for such things as project management, document creation, computation, and communication are available to automate or simplify routine tasks.
- *Reference.* Job-relevant information from an organization's internal knowledge base and/or from external sources.
- *Training.* Tutoring, examples, and practice that are delivered on demand, often interspersed with actual job assignments, and organized into task-specific chunks, or "granules." Workers "learn by doing," rather than having to remember information delivered as a separate training event, away from the job.

All of the support that the system provides is linked by a steering mechanism, which monitors and directs the workings of the integrated system. The system is not passive, not a tool, but a *proactive* operating resource representing the work to the worker and providing the support necessary to ensure that the work can be accomplished. In fact, the system has become so powerful that the workers can concentrate once again on doing their jobs, not just on using the system.

The result of this performance support environment? More satisfied workers. More productive and efficient workers. Workers who take a fraction of the time to reach basic proficiency levels and then higher proficiency levels; workers who can exceed customer expectations because the support they require to respond to a customer's needs is right there at their workstations. Workers who, above all, meet or exceed the performance requirements of their jobs continuously. And the overall result: satisfied customers.

We have described here not just a new technology, but a new approach to *using* technology. Ultimately it is a *new way of working,* a way we are calling "FutureWork." This way of working is not far off in the future; indeed, as the saying goes, "the future is now." Instead, FutureWork here implies that this is the way in which productive knowledge and service workers of the future will be working. We call the system that enables this way of working a "performance system," and the concept driving the system is called "Integrated Performance Support™," or "IPS" for short. The goal of IPS is to orient organizations toward the moments of value of their workers' performance and then to deliver a seamless and customized range of services to support and enable the performance of those workers.

Integrated Performance Support is not a system; neither is it a technology. More accurately, IPS is a particular orientation that organizations must have—a special kind of self-understanding. We are not after a system-centered workplace or a technology-centered workplace. What we're after is a *performance-centered* workplace.

TODAY'S WORKFORCE PERFORMANCE CHALLENGES

Certainly it is a challenge to understand all the components of the performance environment and the necessary interaction among those components. Organizations must go beyond partial solutions, integrating the performance measures from the organization level on down to the worker level. Most important to us, however, is that they must take a workforce-performance perspective, a performance-centered perspective. Without it, the growing complexity of work and of the workplace will create real performance challenges for employees, which in turn will create performance problems for the organization as a whole. In the Introduction, we named 10 of the primary workforce challenges organizations are facing today. Of those, the following are most crucial:

- Technology and information systems that force employees to become system users rather than job performers.
- Changing and increasing expectations on the part of customers for higher levels of service, levels which for some strange reason always seem to be available from competitors.
- The deluge of information in the workplace today, both from external sources and from the internal expansion of products and services.
- Difficulty in reaching and sustaining high worker performance levels, due in part to traditional modes of training that deliver too much information, too soon, to workers, and then deliver too little information, too late, when the need for knowledge intensifies.
- The need to do more with less—to increase productivity and innovation and to be self-managing, even in the face of downsizing and organizational restructuring.

Part II of this book is devoted to exploring each of these challenges in detail, looking at real organizations that are meeting the challenge with the help of an Integrated Performance Support strategy. But at the outset, let's look at each of them briefly.

TECHNOLOGY THAT SUPPORTS JOB PERFORMANCE, NOT JUST SYSTEM USE

The utility company service representatives we referred to earlier know all too well what happens when information system functionality begins to overwhelm the performance needs of a worker. Those 250 screens for the new customer systems probably pack in a lot of functionality. But how are workers going to remember how to access all of them?

A professor of industrial design at the University of Buffalo, Valerie Shalin, puts this challenge well: "The people who think they know everything [about technology] don't know everything, and they don't know much about humans. They don't understand human flexibility, and they don't understand how a human might try to use a tool in a way a designer doesn't anticipate." Shalin notes that some computing systems and programs are so difficult and complicated that they are the equivalent of requiring people to tune a piano every time they sit down to play.[8]

Part of the problem with technology and systems design today is the inertia of history and precedent. Systems get designed by experts, and experts don't need "friendly" systems. One story that circulated for a time was of a sign on the wall in one company's development lab: "It was damn hard to develop, and it damn well better be hard to use!" That, admittedly, is an extreme example, and rarely found today. But the bias toward experts still exists. Shalin argues that it is almost a tradition "to design for the hard sciences—the electronics, the electricity, the metals, the structures, the manly things of engineering."[9] Make no mistake: these aspects have to work correctly. But so does the individual using them, and enabling the work of that individual leads to the idea of performance-centered design.

Performance-centered design involves a focus at the opposite pole of expertise: a "right-to-left" approach that begins with workers at work and ends at the experts, whose role now is to design a system that the worker really doesn't notice. This is most often called transparent or ubiquitous computing: computing that is so natural, powerful, and pervasive that a person interacting with a system doesn't have to learn how to use it, doesn't have to wrestle with it every day, and so can concentrate on the performance of a job. In his book *The Design of Everyday Things,* Donald A. Norman puts the matter this way: "Design should make use of the natural properties of people and of the world: it should exploit natural relationships and natural constraints. As much as possible, it should operate without instructions or labels. Any necessary instruction or training should be needed only once; with each explanation the person should be able to say, 'Of course,' or 'Yes, I see'. . . . If the explanation leads the person to think or say, 'How am I going to remember that?' the design has failed."[10]

"User-centered design" is the phrase that Norman and others use to describe the concept at the heart of "transparent computing," computing that is so powerful that we don't notice it as much anymore.[11] But we want to take that idea one step further. We don't want workers to be thought of as system "users"; that makes the system itself the dominant focus. The focus, again, should be *performance*-centered. We want to enable workers to do their jobs, not focus on having to use a system. Only when actual performance needs are determined do we begin to design the system. As you will see later, the solution to the problem of the 250 computer screens was a classic example of performance-centered design: workers now access these screens not by typing in codes, but through a new primary interface designed around their actual job tasks—a solution that enables them to navigate naturally through the system.

The benefits of performance-centered systems? Ken Otis of Blue Cross/Blue Shield of Florida puts it well: "One of the powerful benefits of a performance system is that it really enables employees to be problem solvers and decision makers. Instead of being embroiled in the complexity of the system and in the heads-down inputting of data, all of a sudden we've got a powerful tool to do part of that, and our employees instead are positioned to make decisions and solve problems. I think that's very exciting."

HIGH-QUALITY CUSTOMER SERVICE

The doctor's assistant trying to help a patient through the bewildering world of contemporary health care knows the challenge of customer service today. As Joe Grantham of Blue Cross/Blue Shield of Florida puts it, "Our business has become exponentially more complex, and the amount of information that an employee must have to respond to a provider or customer has expanded greatly."

We will have much to say about the manner in which Integrated Performance Support enables workers to satisfy customers, because this is one of the biggest performance challenges organizations face today. A business puts its reputation on the line every moment one of its employees deals with a present or potential customer. What is the cost of poor service? Approximately 68% of lost customers can be traced to poor service.[12] And the most frustrating part of that statistic is that companies rarely find out the details of an incident of poor service: some 96% of customers who leave never complain directly to the company.[13] They do, however, tell their friends and business associates: the average dissatisfied customer tells nine other people about his experience.[14] And companies get a customer to replace that dissatisfied one only at great cost: an organization spends five times the amount to get a new customer as it spends to keep an old one.[15] On the positive side, the average happy customer tells five other people about his or her experience.[16] The service a company renders to its customers overwhelmingly affects the consumer's perception of overall quality of a company's goods and services.

But how does an organization improve the quality of customer service? Exceeding customer expectations can be difficult to achieve under the conditions most workers have to deal with to do their jobs. Too often, workers have only a partial picture in their heads of what their organization does and how it does it. The resources that workers need to answer a customer's question or meet a need are only rarely in front of them when they most need it. With a performance system, the medical assistant's job referred to earlier might go something like this: as a patient checks out, the assistant obtains via the system all of the information about her copayment, deductible, and insurance carrier's billing procedures. The system recommends the best method of payment and identifies the prescription that needs to be filled. At this point, the system advisor warns the assistant that the patient received a prior prescription, and that there may be a harmful interaction with these two drugs. The doctor can then reassess and represcribe. Based upon the information entered during this brief transaction, the system helps the assistant analyze the cost/payment options and suggests the best alternative for the patient.

As Grantham notes, customer service in the health care industry or in any industry "requires an interactive process with both the provider and the customer. The amount of information you can make available to your employees, and the ability to provide decision support for them, will be critical for success in the '90s and beyond."

COPING WITH THE INFORMATION DELUGE

A journalist, writing about the information age, captures its problems well: "If, through some miracle, one could turn information into a seething, visible, and living thing, it would look like a big, fast-moving river. It would be swirling and splashing and shifting all around everyone. And those who learn how to navigate in these waters and use them to achieve some end will do well. Those who don't will be pitched and tossed every which way, wondering all the time what is happening to them, why their job at the dress factory disappeared and turned up again somewhere on the Pacific rim."[17]

Most of us have heard the startling statistics about the amount of information being created and made available to us: that more information has been created in the past thirty years than in all of human history that preceded it. Though this fact is perhaps supposed to impress people, it probably just frightens them. At what point does information become so omnipresent that it ceases to have any value to us? By what criteria are we supposed to be able to sort this information, to determine what has value to us and what does not?

These questions are not necessarily new ones. At the invention of the telegraph, for example, inventors bragged, "Now, Maine will be able to talk to Boston." Yes, replied Ralph Waldo Emerson, "but will Maine have anything to *say* to Boston?" This is the problem of the Information Age: everyone is talking, but is anyone really *saying* anything? Moreover, there are some profound societal issues that arise as a consequence of the information deluge.

Robert Bellah and the other authors of the groundbreaking work *Habits of the Heart* speak, for example, about the withdrawal of many people from the realm of public policy because of its "invisible complexity."[18] That is, many people are giving up even basic civic duties such as voting because everything seems so hopelessly complex. This is the problem many organizations face with their workforce: if too much information is coming in, the natural tendency is to ignore it all.

Technology was supposed to ease this problem, but, of course, it has only exacerbated it. Harold Salzman of the University of Louisville's Urban Research Institute has conducted research on the impact of technology on the workplace. He notes that "the futuristic vision of access to instant information on everything has now become overload. People now need selectivity in looking at information. The real service industry in the future will focus on how to select information."[19] Selection is indeed the primary concern because, without it, workers can only operate by random selection or pure luck. "There is a tremendous amount of Information Available now," says David Gillespie, professor of social work at Washington University in St. Louis, "but I'm not sure we really know well how to make good use of it. It's like an avalanche, and very few of us have the tools to [maneuver] our way through that. We end up picking and choosing on what may be essentially a random process."[20]

Here again, one of the problems with the Information Age is based on inertia and precedent. Almost all the automation and database activity over the past decade has been geared toward making access to information easier, making more of it more readily available. Hence the explosion in its availability. Indeed, "explosion" is a perfect word to describe it: it's random, chaotic, frightening. We receive information today that appears untethered to any overarching sense of reality, unconnected to anything that could give that information context and meaning. We have unprecedented access to information, but what good is access unless we know what to *do* with it? How do we understand it? How do we fit it into our jobs? How do we use it to support our performance?

What we need is support for our workers, something that will turn chaotic information into *knowledge*—the accumulating result of experience in a form that is shareable. This accumulation occurs as feedback, as information is used and then passed on to others. What is needed, and what Integrated Performance Support can provide, is the feedback mechanism—the knowledge network or knowledge exchange that facilitates knowledge transfer.

The distinction between "information" and "knowledge" is a crucial one. Let us say that you have stumbled upon a new archaeological find, and you see inscriptions written on the wall of what appears to be a tomb. You do not know how to translate these inscriptions, yet you can recognize them as writing of some sort. Let's call what you see at this point "data." You find an expert to translate the words for you, and suddenly the inscriptions—the life story of an ancient Egyptian king—make sense to you. Now you have what we can call "information." But what good is this information to you unless you can put it into a context where it becomes useful? Who was this king? When did he live? What was the world like when he was alive? It is only with the answers to these questions and others like them that the inscriptions become knowledge to you.

The stock market figures provide another kind of example. If we open up the morning newspaper to the business section, we see columns of numbers about stocks on the exchange—mere *data.* All sorts of resources may be available to us to turn some of that data to *information:* the steep decline of a major retailer, for example, is explained by bad quarterly figures that were released yesterday morning. But what would connect that piece of information to some historical and contextual realm that would turn it into *knowledge?* Perhaps a customized listing of references about the company, itemized for a worker on the basis of his or her particular level of expertise and preferences. Or a bit of training, explaining the history of that company and its place within the industry. Or maybe even an advisory facility, which could examine similar movements of this stock, and recommend whether to hold or sell. If you've got that, you've got knowledge.

Information deluge problems can also be seen in such cases as the service representatives described earlier who are coping with product information. Petursson of McCaw Cellular notes that workers today face increasing complexity of product sets. "The telecommunications marketplace today is one where new products are coming out regularly. They come out every month, every week, every day. In order to deliver new products to the customer, the people who sell and support those products have to be made aware of them, and trained on them. To the customer, they have to look like experts at all times."

Systems enabled by Integrated Performance Support do more than provide information. They turn information into *knowledge*—into the accumulated experience of an organization, structured for and shareable by all workers.

ATTAINING AND SUSTAINING PROFICIENCY

The Spanish bank president who is losing tellers faster than he can develop them exemplifies the training challenge today. In today's marketplace, organizations cannot afford to have new employees spend months on training before they can begin working. After a basic orientation to the company, workers need to be at their jobs, getting training as part of the natural performance of their work; they need to be learning by doing. "We want our workers to learn about policies and procedures, new products, and basic skills while they are on the job," says Carol Krenek, Assistant VP of Field Human Resources at Avco Financial Services.[21] When jobs were stable year after year, training that occurred once, early in a new job or new responsibility, may have been sufficient. But as the work environment became more complex, as workers required a broader range of skills and the demands placed upon them intensified, traditional training ceased being an adequate form of performance support.

Think of traditional forms of employee training as a kind of old-fashioned "bucket brigade" approach to fire fighting. As new employees are hired, they are each given a bucket. During the first week or so, the bucket gets filled with water: as much information and training as the bucket will hold. But weeks and months go by before the employees get tested in actual duty. As time goes by, the water in the buckets begins to evaporate. Some buckets spring leaks, so we try to patch them up and put in new water. For others, the water sloshes out as the bucket gets carried from new task to new task. When the first real alarm comes in—maybe a customer problem, maybe the need for immediate expertise about an industry—the workers grab their buckets, race madly to the fire, aim the buckets at the flames . . . only to find that not enough water remains.

No one doubts that broader and deeper workforce education is crucial to business success. But getting a return on investment in employee training has been, for many companies, the impossible dream. In 1992, for example, American companies invested $40 billion in corporate education. That sounds like a lot of money. But a closer look at that spending reveals some alarming facts. Most of it was spent by a handful of giant companies. Eighty percent of it was spent only on managers.[22] And, most frightening, there was only a 10–15 percent retention rate of the information from that $40 billion investment.[23] Clearly, these buckets have bigger leaks than we thought.

But the problem really isn't with the buckets. The problem is with the way organizations have been filling them. For most organizations, training is either too much, too soon—or too little, too late. Too much training is made available to workers at the beginning of their jobs, when they cannot possibly place the training into the context of their actual performance. Then, as they become more experienced workers, too little training is made available to them to keep them abreast of changes within the organization and in the marketplace. The challenge for organizations today is to have their employee training programs integrated into the very structure of the work that their employees do every day. Certainly there may always be some sorts of training that take place in a traditional classroom format. But beyond the mere basics of the job, most of the training available to employees must be available on demand, and it must not take them away from the place where they do most of their work. Most important, it must be integrated with their overall job responsibilities so that the normal performance of their jobs becomes another mode of training. This is often referred to as "learning by doing."

The Spanish bank president in our earlier scenario asks an important question: are the costs for getting workers to proficiency high because of excessive employee turnover, or is there high turnover because organizations are not developing and supporting their workers adequately? We think the latter option is true more often than not. We destine workers to failure if we believe that a little upfront training can possibly prepare them for the demands of their jobs today. We also doom our organizations to low productivity if we cannot design employee training so that workers reach a level of proficiency faster. A key here is to align the supply of training with an employee's demand for knowledge and skills, and then to deliver that training when and where it is needed. (See graphs on the next page.)

For purposes of the traditional return on investment calculation, reduction in training costs is typically where organizations will find much of the discernible cost savings with performance systems. These systems reduce the time required for workers to reach and maintain proficient performance levels. (In fact, the ideal or logical outcome of Integrated Performance Support is to eliminate the need for training as we know it today.) More difficult to pin down or quantify are a number of other benefits of IPS: doing a job right the first time, satisfying a customer, keeping a competitor at bay, and maintaining a satisfied workforce—one cognizant of its worth to itself and, therefore, to the entire organization.

DOING MORE WITH LESS

As the jet engine mechanic found in our earlier scenario, the downsizing and "rightsizing" movements of the last decade have put additional strains on workers. Many organizations who reduced the size of their workforce did not think about changing the actual work for those who remained. For many companies, workers would be justified in recalling the story of ancient Egypt, where the Hebrew slaves who complained of their brickmaking quota had their allotment of straw reduced and their quota doubled.

Aligning Supply of Education and Training with Demand for Individual Knowledge and Skills

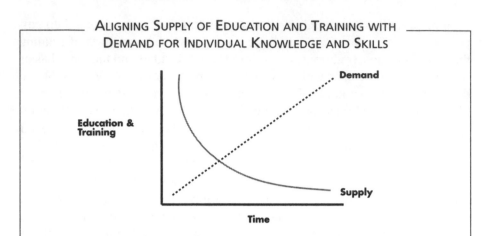

All too often, education and training are provided early in the cycle of a worker's new job assignment before the worker starts the work. As the individual grows in the job, there is very little support provided to meet the growing performance demands. In other words, the supply of education is not matched with the demand over time.

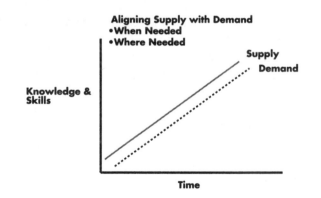

Integrated Performance Support principles provide the means for organizations to align the supply of knowledge and skills with demand, on the job, when needed, where needed. This will allow organizations to significantly improve their workforce performance and meet their strategic objectives.

But even organizations with the best of intentions for their workers find themselves in the position of having to do more with less, and having to do it better. Consider the example of one small factory that employs about a hundred workers manufacturing four varieties of cleaning and laundry solvents. Because of competitive pressures, the company has expanded their product line. Now these same hundred workers are being asked to manufacture *ten* products. Clearly, conventional information systems are not going to be able to support these workers. How are they going to be trained? And once they are trained, how are they going to shift these basic skills from one task to another? These workers require support for their performance directly at the point of need. They will not be able to rely on the expertise of supervisors, who will now be stretched beyond the limits of being able to monitor each task. And they may not have time to achieve expertise in every new task, particularly as they are moved from one to another more often. Greater leveraging of organizational expertise is vital to the survival of this company and others like it.

Demographic projections indicate that organizations will have to continue doing more with less for quite some time, as fewer workers enter the workforce. Organizations will no longer have the luxury of grooming workers to be highly trained specialists in one or two tasks. Workers will have to be generalists, and so they will need information systems that will support their performance in a variety of tasks for which they have not achieved expert competence. And even if competence is achieved in a particular area, it may go away tomorrow, and new ones may take its place—areas demanding new competencies.

Organizations will only be able to "do more with less"—indeed, will only be able to meet all of the performance challenges just discussed—if their information systems can capture and make available to their employees at all times the very best expertise and knowledge that the entire organization has to offer. The knowledge firepower of an organization must be at the fingertips of its workers if they are to do their best for the organization. The system must not only teach and inform; it must also anticipate and coach. It must enable real "performance" of workers—enable the completion of their tasks with precision and delight—by providing advice, tools, reference, and training on demand, at point of need. This is the goal of the performance-centered enterprise.

CHAPTER 2

PERFORMANCE SUPPORT AND INFORMATION TECHNOLOGY:

From Processing Transactions to Transacting Business

Our task in the previous chapter was to explain some of the philosophical background of Integrated Performance Support, and to begin to show how many of the workforce performance challenges today can be overcome through an IPS strategy. Our goal in this chapter is to trace the recent evolution of information technology as it has moved gradually toward what we are calling a "performance-centered perspective." To have begun with the technology discussion would have contradicted the primary message of this book: that technology comes into play only in service to what people are trying to accomplish in the workplace. One of the enduring truths of this technological age is that when organizations begin by speaking primarily in terms of *systems,* they will inevitably end up thinking of their workers primarily as *systems users.* Systems users are oriented, not toward the work they are performing, but rather toward the system on which they are working. Is this really what executives want—workers whose focus is on how to use the terminal or workstation sitting in front of them? We think it more likely that executives want their workers focused on the work they are doing and on the value they are providing. It is no longer sufficient for organizations to have powerful information systems that process transactions. Organizations now must have systems that allow their workers to transact business.

Many information systems today restrict the workers' vision of the work they are performing. Instead of providing an open window upon the work, systems often put blinders on the worker, allowing access to only one particular line of vision—one particular type of transaction or task. This is another example of what we have referred to as the "inertia of precedent": doing something the way it's always been done, or not doing something because it hasn't been done that way before. Until recently, most information systems have shared a number of limiting characteristics:

46

KEY MESSAGES: CHAPTER 2

- Traditional information systems only allow workers to process transactions. Today's systems must allow workers to *transact business.*
- Information systems evolved during the last decade from a product-centered perspective to a customer-centered perspective. Today, systems must be designed from the perspective of *knowledge worker performance.*
- Recent innovations in information technology have resulted in the concept of "performance support systems." These systems, driven by new architectures and more natural interaction with computers, have begun to alter the way workers interact with systems.
- The next step in performance support, *Integrated* Performance Support, represents the convergence of several current developments related to learning and technology, including user-centered design, knowledge-based systems, cognitive science, computer-supported cooperative work, and knowledge management systems.
- IPS-based systems, or "performance systems," are *proactive,* integrating support facilities under a common interface. With these systems, workers are *workers,* not just system "users."
- With IPS, organizations can begin with what their workers are doing and with what they need to do. Everything else about the system flows from that basic orientation.

- They were transaction-centered, rather than performance-centered.
- They required workers to adapt to the mode of work dictated by the system.
- They depended upon off-line support, such as training classes, manuals, help desks, and assistance from colleagues.
- They were designed around either products or customers, not around the work processes of employees.

SYSTEMS DESIGN: FROM PRODUCTS TO CUSTOMERS TO WORKER PERFORMANCE

Systems that trace their origins to the 1970s were mostly *product*-centered. An insurance company, to take one example, sold various kinds of policies, so it structured its systems around those products. With a product-centered point of view, the workers' perspective on their customers, and on the work they were performing, was fractured. To an insurance agent, the customers were *customer numbers;* to a claims processor, they were *claim numbers;* to an underwriter, they were *policy numbers.* In this environment, products and business functions developed their own systems, with little, if any, integration with other applications. This approach to systems design had two limiting consequences. First, it was complicated to share information among departments, so an organization's left hand often did not know what the right hand was doing. Second, customers became frustrated when they had to be transferred from department to department to get even a basic question answered.

Customer-centered system designs of the 1980s were a response to increasing customer demands for one-stop shopping or "one-point-of-call" service. These systems were the first attempt to share information about a customer; to a degree, they have been a significant advance over their predecessors. But here, too, there have been difficulties. First, workers became overloaded with information. Customer service representatives, for example, were now required to handle all aspects of the customer's business, so more data was presented to them. As it turned out, it was too much. Second, there were many technical barriers to these designs. It was extremely difficult to integrate applications, given the different manual systems and electronic tools and given the variety of hardware and software environments. The interfaces became more complex than the application.

Because of increasing demands placed on workers, and because of the technological barriers, isolated groups of systems designers began to dream of new ways that systems could be centered: not on products or on customers, but rather on the performance needs of workers.

At about that same time, three distinct, though related, developments were converging within information systems technology:

1. A new kind of processing, called "distributcd" or "cooperative" processing, based upon an architecture called "client/server."
2. An effort to make computer interfaces more "user-friendly" and to make interaction with the computer easier and more intuitive.
3. Computer software that was interactive and thus able to be used and experienced in different ways by different people.

Client/Server Architecture.   By the late 1980s, technology had evolved and matured to the point that systems could begin to mimic the manner in which human beings work. Few of us, after all, proceed through our days in a perfectly linear and logical fashion. We begin a particular task and then get interrupted, or an idea comes to us, or the phone rings. The traditional "dumb" terminals connected to mainframe computers forced workers into a linear manner of work. With the new client/server computing architectures, employees were given greater access to a variety of information sources within the company. Systems built upon the client/server concept meant that workers potentially had more freedom and greater control in accessing what they needed to do their jobs.

More Natural Interaction with Computers.   Led by the first Apple™ computers, systems became easier to learn, and the manner in which workers interacted with their computers became more intuitive. We have already spoken of the customer service representatives who had to access hundreds of different computer screens with distinct four-digit codes. This may sound daunting, but systems like that have been the rule rather than the exception. Computer users turning on their machines found a demonically simple interface staring at them: a "C" prompt and a blinking cursor. No wonder so many people have feared the Information Age: you had to be an expert even to perform the first task at the machine.

Several years ago, so-called "graphical user interfaces," or GUIs, began to appear. Macintosh™ systems first popularized these interfaces and Microsoft Windows™ software has now made them available to virtually everyone with an adequately powerful personal computer. When combined with a "mouse," the point-and-click device that is now an adjunct to the traditional keyboard, people could actually use their systems within minutes rather than days. Moreover, these interfaces made interaction with the computer more natural. If you were using word processing software, for example, and wanted to print a document, you could now simply point the arrow/cursor at a small graphical representation of a printer, click once, and walk over to your printer to retrieve the document.

Interactive Computer Software.   Computer software also began to appear (driven, most likely, by the video game craze of the 1980s) that was truly interactive. People could now navigate in different ways through the system; they could browse or tailor the software to their unique backgrounds and needs. "Hypertext"-based software appeared on the market—products like Hypercard™ and Supercard™—that enabled programmers to design systems with interactive capabilities. Hypertext linked different objects or procedures together so that users could request additional information. A number of different paths were available within the system, and users could now navigate their way through the system in unique ways.

Taken together, these three developments became a powerful driving force toward performance-centered systems design. Technology could now support workers as they searched for information specific to their needs; computers began to present a view of a worker's tasks more intuitively; and software was capable of being tailored to individual user requirements. When you combine these developments with an organization's need to do more with less, with the workers' needs to cope with more information, to satisfy customers, to reach proficiency faster and then maintain it, you arrive at the potential for new systems that are powerful productivity aids. These systems came to be called "performance support systems."

PERFORMANCE SUPPORT: THE GENIE IN THE LAMP

The powerful idea at the heart of a performance support system is to make a wide range of resources available to workers electronically, on demand, at point of need. Think of the countless ways in which most workers today are interrupted in the course of their work because they do not have a supporting resource to help them complete a task, a resource that may be the difference between an ordinary moment and a "moment of value" for a worker. Now imagine a system that would provide most of this support immediately, tailored to a specific performance need. Such a system takes the "information at your fingertips" concept one step further. This is *performance support* at your fingertips: not just information, but also assistance in knowing how to apply that information to the task at hand.

One could think of performance support as a kind of magic "genie in the lamp." There is a good reason, after all, why the classic story of Aladdin and his magical lamp has appealed to people for hundreds of years. That genie appeals to something deep within us as human beings. It's only human to dream of having a powerful genie at our beck and call, ready and able to meet our every need, to cater to our merest whim, to give us whatever we want whenever we want it.

Imagine what your organization could do with such a genie. (As the genie says in the Disney movie *Aladdin,* no funny business like wishing for more wishes is allowed.) Certainly he could help your workers solve any number of problems put to them. But more important, he could direct and advise them; he could provide ideas, suggest relevant resources and training, point them toward helpful job aids and tools. He could structure their basic tasks, freeing them to be more creative. He could keep track of novel and innovative solu-

A PERFORMANCE-CENTERED SYSTEM

With traditional information systems, workers must have system software knowledge—the knowledge of how to use a system as well as the business knowledge—to complete a task successfully. As a result, workers usually turn into system users: people conforming to meet the needs of the computer system rather than having a computer system that meets the performance needs of the workers.

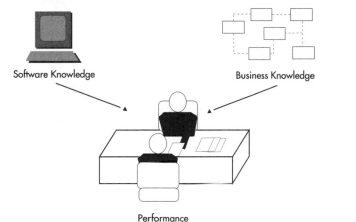

Software Knowledge

Business Knowledge

Performance

With performance systems, workers will focus on improving their business knowledge. They will also:

- Focus on business performance.
- Concentrate on completing the work, not just on using the system.
- Depend on just-in-time job support instead of off-line support.

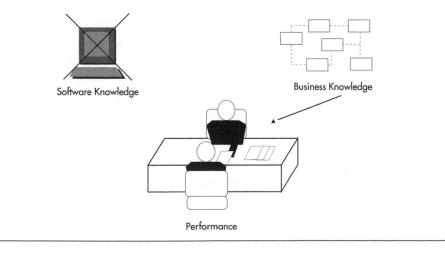

Software Knowledge

Business Knowledge

Performance

tions, captured at the moment of application, to be shared throughout the organization. Think of your workers every day who face the workplace challenges we have already described—situations where they do not have the support to enable their best performance, particularly at those moments when their jobs' demands are greatest. With the genie it would be a whole new story. Unsure of a certain procedure? Rub the lamp. New skill requirements? Rub the lamp. Want some advice about new ways of meeting customer demands faster and more efficiently? The lamp. For the first time, your workers would have at their fingertips the information firepower of the organization, organized to accommodate their individual needs, capabilities, and preferences.

With the genie of a performance support system, workers can access:

- job aids, which take routine job functions and replace them with macros and templates, and which provide easier access to various tools for document creation, computation, and communication;
- reference information, a facility that replaces traditional paper-based support such as periodicals, manuals, and memos;
- on-line help, which replaces the productivity-draining tradition of having to stop work to find information in a manual, or to ask a colleague;
- computer-based training, which replaces off-site, classroom training with a training approach specifically tailored to the experience level of the worker, and delivered in granules relevant to the particular task at hand.

But for all his power, the genie of performance support as it is often spoken of today still has at least two limitations:

- First, he's not really one genie, but several. That is, the performance support components are not actually integrated into the applications of the system to provide a unified sense to the performance support.
- Second, workers still must rub the lamp to get what they want—workers must always initiate the actions needed to get the genie's help. This means they have to know when they need help and then have to remember to ask for it. The system is passive; the performance support components have to sit there, awaiting the user's initiation before they can help the worker.

Moving beyond these two limitations is the breakthrough of Integrated Performance Support. To make this distinction between passive and proactive support facilities, we use the term "performance system" to describe this powerful human-centered technology.

CONVERGENCE OF DISCIPLINES

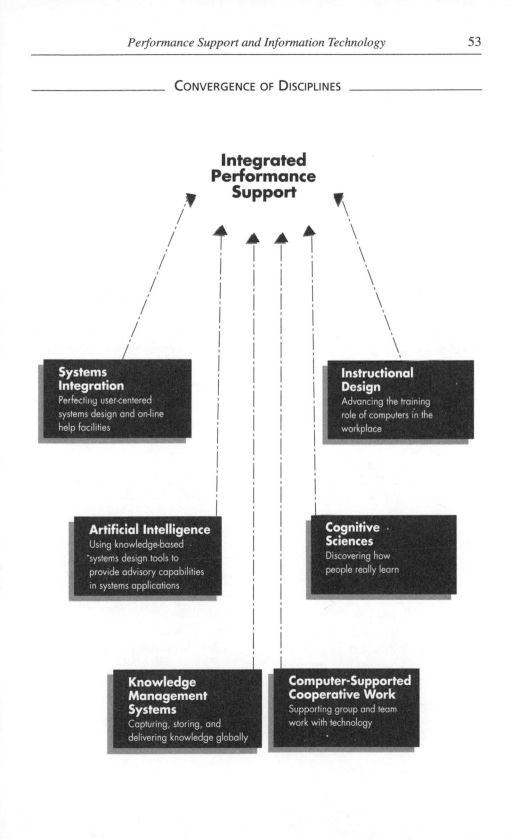

Integrated Performance Support

Systems Integration
Perfecting user-centered systems design and on-line help facilities

Instructional Design
Advancing the training role of computers in the workplace

Artificial Intelligence
Using knowledge-based systems design tools to provide advisory capabilities in systems applications

Cognitive Sciences
Discovering how people really learn

Knowledge Management Systems
Capturing, storing, and delivering knowledge globally

Computer-Supported Cooperative Work
Supporting group and team work with technology

Integrated Performance Support draws upon a number of exciting developments related to technology, learning, and group work. (See the figure on the previous page.) Instructional designers, empowered by new authoring tools and by emerging multimedia technology, are expanding the boundaries of computer-based training. Systems designers are exploring user-centered systems design (or, as we have recommended, "performance"-centered design), employing graphical user interfaces and client/server technology, and increasing the amount of embedded system training and on-line help. Knowledge-based systems designers from the field of artificial intelligence, empowered with new knowledge-based design tools, are developing applications that provide advisory capabilities. In the cognitive sciences, researchers are discovering the manner in which adult workers really learn and are making that information available to systems designers. Within the field of computer-supported cooperative work, designers are perfecting a category of software called "groupware" so that computers can more easily support group work. Designers of knowledge management systems are finding ways to capture, store, and move knowledge throughout organizations to workers located around the globe. These disciplines, together with their respective technological advances, are improving the design and expanding the field of Integrated Performance Support.

WORK, WORKER, SUPPORT: THE BASIS OF THE IPS MODEL

Let's begin with a "clean slate" question. Suppose you wanted to create the ideal performance environment for your workers. Forget about the system for a moment. If you had Aladdin's genie, what would you want him to know about your workforce, and what would you want him to help them do?

1. First, you would focus on the *work* that needs to be performed by your employees to transact your business. You would identify work flows, job tasks, the skills they require, and the desired outcomes of the work. You would look at the work through:
    - task analysis (a breakdown of the task structure and a description of individual tasks of which a job is composed); and
    - performance analysis (an analysis of performance aspects of tasks, such as performance goals, indicators, work-environment factors, cultural factors, and so forth).

You would want to align the tasks to be performed with the goals of your organization and with the performance capabilities of the workforce. You would also want to bear in mind that, once this alignment is complete, it will change. In today's changing work environment, tasks, workflows, customers, and workforce all change continuously. They change in response to external forces such as changing market needs, as well as to internal forces, as the workforce strives for continuous improvement.

2. Second, you would attempt to characterize the workforce required to do the work: individual *workers* (and work groups). You would identify the various levels of workers (managerial, professional, support, and so forth), their experience, the skills and attributes they currently possess and those they will need to possess in the future. You would want to take into account the worker's training history, experience, job responsibilities, and other attributes.

3. Finally, you would design the elements that would *support* the workforce during performance, given the unique configuration of work and worker that you have just ascertained. The sidebar summarizes this performance environment.

This understanding of work, worker, and support is the basis of the logical model of Integrated Performance Support. We will provide more details about the model in the next chapter, as we show a performance system in action. But note here the features that make a performance system *proactive*— that move the system beyond current restrictions to the point that it can anticipate a knowledge worker's needs and tailor a unique package of support services for that worker.

1. Two distinctive services of IPS—Work Profile Services and Knowledge Worker Services, which we describe in more detail in Chapter 3—contain information about the work and the workforce: about the individual worker (or workgroup) and the basic work for which that worker has responsibility.

2. Based upon the unique background and ability level of that worker, and based upon his or her work profile, the performance system tailors a unique set of support services to empower the worker to perform better:
   - Advice, provided by Advisory Services
   - Tools, provided by Job Aid Services
   - Reference, provided by Reference Services
   - Training, supplied by Training Services

3. The human-computer interaction layer of the model represents, first, a nat-

Work, Worker, Support

The work to be performed consists of tasks:

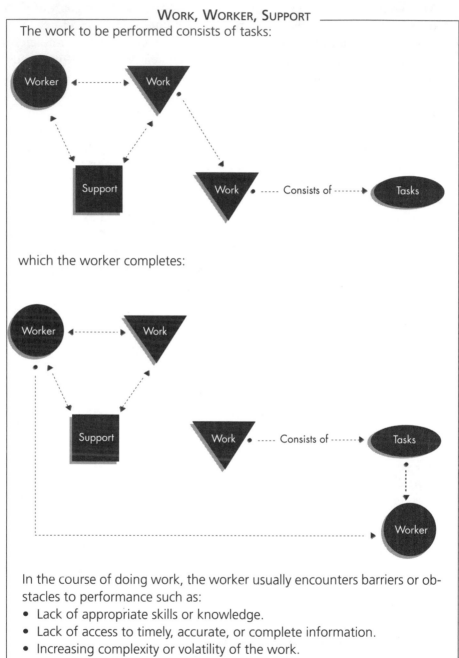

which the worker completes:

In the course of doing work, the worker usually encounters barriers or obstacles to performance such as:

- Lack of appropriate skills or knowledge.
- Lack of access to timely, accurate, or complete information.
- Increasing complexity or volatility of the work.
- Unavailability of an expert or experienced co-worker.
- Scarcity of suitable work tools.

Work, Worker, Support (*Continued*)

To overcome these barriers, the worker requires performance support resources which may be in electronic or nonelectronic forms, or a combination of both.

There are four categories to structure the support resources, namely

- Advice
- Tools
- Reference
- Training

Some support resources fall squarely into one of these categories, while others might fit into a range of categories due to the integrated nature of IPS. What is important, however, is the functionality of the support resources, not whether or not each resources fits neatly into a category.

A proactive performance system depends upon the ability of designers to make the support resources relate to the worker in unique ways:

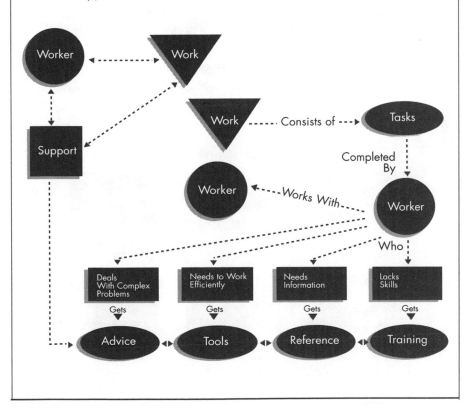

ural and intuitive interface that gives the worker a picture of the capabilities of the system and a representation of the work for which the person is

INTEGRATED PERFORMANCE SUPPORT; LOGICAL MODEL

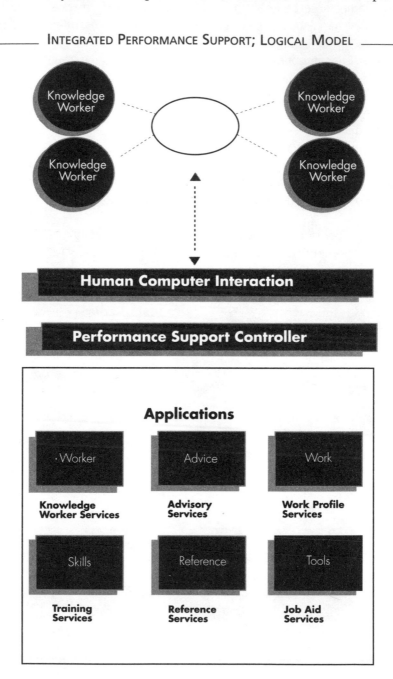

responsible or with which the person could interact. Second, this layer represents a natural mode by which the person navigates through the system and by which the system supports the performance of the worker on demand, at point of need.
4. The Performance Support Controller layer represents the manner in which the performance system provides a seamless package of support services. The person at the workstation is not aware that a certain support service is in operation. The Controller simply monitors performance requirements and provides support tailored to those requirements.

TRUE INTEGRATION: WHAT'S DIFFERENT ABOUT A PERFORMANCE SYSTEM?

The figures on the next pages compare the character of performance support in traditional transaction-based systems with its character in a performance system. Here we have represented worker activity as falling into either on-line activity or off-line activity. In some systems and with some applications, there is help available on-line (as part of the system), but this help is typically focused on providing screen or field-level support.

If additional support is needed, workers must exit the system, or "go off-line" to get performance support. As the diagram suggests, this off-line support is not connected to the business application system. Workers must search for information in paper-based reference manuals, access a particular computer-based training module, participate in training (paper-based or instructor-led), call up a tool, or seek advice from other external sources.

The power of a system enabled by Integrated Performance Support is that performance support services are integrated into the business applications. The performance support components discussed above—on-line help, reference, job aids, and training—gain an enormous amount of power because they are integrated into, or made available through, the application being used by the worker.

But more important, the additional services available in a true performance system—Advisory Services, Work Profile Services, and Knowledge Worker Services—make the system:

- uniquely tailorable to the knowledge worker, and
- proactive, moving beyond the "teach and inform" paradigm of traditional systems to an "anticipate and coach" paradigm.

SUPPORT FOR A USER OF A TRANSACTION-BASED SYSTEM

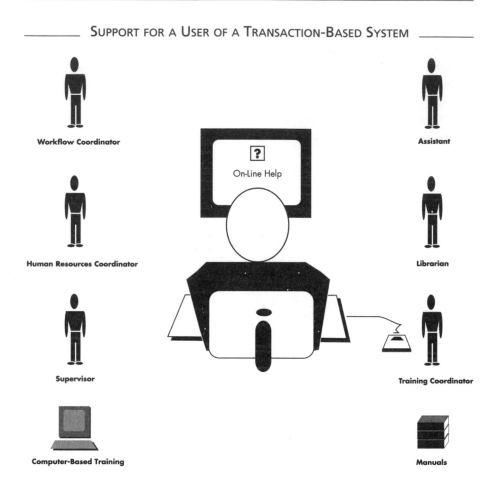

Again, we emphasize that Integrated Performance Support is about *support for* the workers, not *control of* the worker. Knowledge workers are always in control of their performance. IPS enables them to do their jobs better under *their* control. We will have much more to say about the performance support services in the next chapter.

The integrated capability of a performance system is founded upon the performance-centered principles of systems design of which we have already spoken. Because the nature of performance systems differs so much from that

SUPPORT FOR A WORKER AT A PERFORMANCE SYSTEM

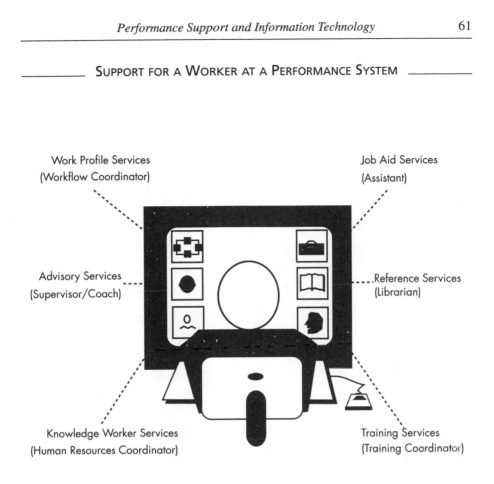

Work Profile Services
(Workflow Coordinator)

Job Aid Services
(Assistant)

Advisory Services
(Supervisor/Coach)

Reference Services
(Librarian)

Knowledge Worker Services
(Human Resources Coordinator)

Training Services
(Training Coordinator)

of traditional transaction-based systems, designing and developing them requires a significantly different approach as well. Traditional transaction-based system design focuses on how business data is structured and processed inside the system. Performance-centered system design focuses more on how data and processes can be applied to enhance the worker's work performance, factors that lie outside the system. The shift in design approach is illustrated in the figure on the next page.

Traditional transaction-based systems are designed with an emphasis on process and data modeling. In a way, they are designed *inside-out*. The user interface modeling is derived from the process and data structures. For example, the layout of screens is often a reflection of a record structure, and the menus of the system reflect the functional structure.

THE "OUTSIDE-IN" DESIGN OF PERFORMANCE SYSTEMS

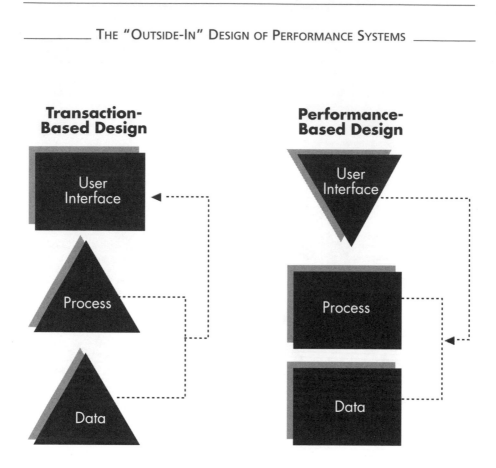

Performance systems are more interactive, and more oriented toward actual work circumstances. Thus, these systems need to be designed from the *outside-in.* The character of process and data modeling in itself does not change so much, but the (outside) user interface modeling drives the (internal) process modeling and data modeling.

In simpler terms, begin with what your workers are doing, with what you want them to do, and what support they need to be successful. Everything else about the system flows from that basic orientation.

LEVELS OF
INTEGRATED PERFORMANCE SUPPORT

IPS is not an "all or nothing" proposition. Although the ideal implementation of IPS is in a fully integrated environment, the IPS concept can be applied in many ways with a range of dimensions. Three basic levels apply here: (1) IPS functions (one, several, or all) can be implemented as a "stand-alone" application; (2) the functions can be "added-on" to existing applications; or (3) IPS functions can be "built-in" or fully integrated into one or all systems. The type of IPS implementation appropriate to an organization will depend in part on the answers to the following questions:

1. *What is the desired level of functionality?* This level may range from a simple look-up table listing the type of support available to an extensive set of functions for accessing and using integrated support services.
2. *What data will be required?* The amount and structure of data may range from a limited list of specific facts to an extensive knowledge base originating from multiple sources.
3. *What level of integration is required or possible?* Integration refers to the extent to which IPS services, data, media, applications and various technologies are seamlessly integrated under a common user interface. Here, organizations will need to decide among the stand-alone, added-on, and built-in options.
4. *What is the span of work to be covered?* Support can be targeted at different levels of work. The scope of support can range from specific task support, to full job support, or to the support of a whole business function or process.
5. *To what extent will the support be customized to the workforce?* Customization refers to the extent to which support is tailored to the specific needs of workers or workgroups, based on their profiles. Customizing support could be based on distinguishing between novice, experienced, and expert workers.
6. *What is the migration strategy for the organization?* If the organization has begun with a stand-alone or added-on implementation, particularly with their legacy mainframe systems, when and how do they intend to migrate to the more powerful client/server environment?

Thus far we have discussed the theory behind Integrated Performance Support and its place in the natural evolution of information systems from a transaction processing paradigm to one in which the actual business of an organization is transacted. IPS changes the orientation of designers from a control system to a support system. It's time now to look at one of these systems in action so that the various services of IPS can be seen more clearly, and so that the remarkable power of these systems can be made more apparent.

CHAPTER 3

A PERFORMANCE SYSTEM IN ACTION

A TALE OF TWO WORKERS

You are a top level executive for a major international organization. It could be in any industry, in any country in the world. Let us say, though, that you are the president of Elite Bank. You have been with the bank for twenty years, and your shelves and credenza are filled with mementos from colleagues representing projects undertaken and goals attained during your career. One of your most prized possessions, however, is a small lucite cube commemorating your bank's conversion to an Integrated Performance Support environment. As the president of the bank, you had gone out on a limb for this system. Now, as you walk through the bank, observing your commercial lenders at work, you can see the fruits of your labor and the payoff on this gamble each day. In fact, when you watch these lenders at work, you sometimes imagine giving a speech entitled "A Tale of Two Workers."

The first tale would be of a young commercial lender who started with the bank in the mid-1970s. The lender is you: fresh out of graduate school, confident, self-assured, filled with your learning about the world of finance. You did well and progressed steadily in seniority at the bank. But each year, in spite of your success, you knew that you could have done better. You knew in your heart about the questions that went unanswered, the risks that you had taken without even knowing about them: you knew that occasionally you had been lucky. Perhaps you had missed opportunities to close a deal or had miscalculated risk—sometimes losing money, other times missing out on the opportunity to make money.

For a time, you and your co-workers would blame yourselves when your performance wasn't as good as you would have liked. With understandable frustration, you could often vaguely and guiltily remember being told something about a particular task when you began the job, or when you completed a new phase of training. But the information at that point had been only an abstraction, not tied to real job performance. Without actual experiences to reinforce the knowledge, you were never really able to take ownership of it, and

_____ KEY MESSAGES: CHAPTER 3 _____

- The conceptual or logical model of Integrated Performance Support is built upon the basic framework of *worker* (the unique person who is performing), *work* (workflows, job tasks, desired outcomes), and *support* (the necessary advice, tools, reference, and training needed for optimal performance of work by that worker).
- *Human-Computer Interaction* is the "window on the work." It ensures natural interaction between the worker and the performance system so that the worker is not reduced to a mere "system user." Through an intuitive and transparent interface to multiple applications and knowledge sources, workers at a performance system can focus on completing tasks, rather than focusing on how to deal with the technology itself.
- *Knowledge Worker Services* is the "human resources coordinator," containing information about workers or workgroups (job responsibilities, training history, skills inventory, and so forth). This facility permits the performance system to tailor a unique package of support services for particular workers and workgroups.
- *Work Profile Services* is the "workflow coordinator," identifying workflows, job tasks, specific procedures, skills required, and other work-related information to provide customized support to knowledge workers.
- *Advisory Services* is the "coach" or advisor, providing advice, reminders, and assistance. It suggests support options and helps the worker examine alternatives, make effective decisions, and solve problems.
- *Job Aid Services* serves as the "assistant," providing automated tools and techniques to simplify routine and repetitive tasks.
- *Reference Services* is the "librarian," structuring and presenting timely, job-relevant information from internal and external sources.
- *Training Services* is the "tutor," providing task-specific training on demand, delivered in small portions (granules) at point of need, and constructed around the paradigm of "learning by doing."
- *Performance Support Controller* is the "orchestra conductor" of the system, monitoring, coordinating, and controlling the IPS services so that seamless support is provided as needed to the knowledge worker.

it gradually faded away. "When I need help," you thought, "I'm always sent somewhere else, or to some past training event for support. But when I need something, I need it *now*. And I need it right *here*."

At other times, the sheer amount of information inundating you had prevented you from using it optimally. So many times you would recall reading something about a particular company in the business journals, or about a particular industry trend. But by the time the research department had located that item for you, the moment to capitalize on it had often passed. There were other times when you could have used the immediate advice of one of the industry experts located in other offices of the bank. But it always seemed that this person was out of town, or in a meeting. How did management know if you were making a right decision? You couldn't begin to estimate how many times you had to tell clients, "Let me get right back to you on that."

You had prided yourself on your ability to build and maintain excellent relationships with customers. But even there, you remembered times when banking procedures had almost undermined your best work. You recalled especially one promising young company that you had watched grow steadily over the course of a couple of years. You felt honestly that you had helped the company to grow. One week, though, the company had made a miscalculation and had sent a payment to an important supplier that resulted in their account being overdrawn. Without consulting you, someone had bounced the check! The supplier halted their next shipment, and the company missed a deadline. The call you received that day from the company president was maybe the low point of your first five years as a lender. "If only" you thought, "I could have known about this immediately. One phone call could have prevented all this!"

Based upon that experience and others like it, you had been at the forefront of the movement in banking toward "relationship managers," where a single lender would take charge of all the banking needs of a customer. But this was a huge task in those days. It seemed that the majority of your time was spent on internal administration duties and you didn't have time to spend on really understanding your customers' business. How could anyone have at their fingertips all the knowledge and skills needed to cope with the varying regulations and policies for hundreds of different financial instruments? When you became a vice-president, that was the task given to you: find a way to get that expertise to our lenders whenever they need it. It's not enough to have it available to them only if they know where to find it. Get it to them now; and if they don't know enough to ask about it, find a way to tell them that they *should* be asking about it.

The second part of your "tale of two workers" speech would describe the way in which your commercial lenders work using the bank's performance system. The system is called "Total Information Management," or "TIM," for short.

THE POWER OF A PERFORMANCE SYSTEM

PART 1
HUMAN-COMPUTER INTERACTION: THE "WINDOW ON THE WORK"

Sue Peters has been a commercial lender at Elite Bank for almost three years. It's Monday morning, around 7:00 A.M., and Sue is getting ready to have breakfast at home. Her laptop computer is still on the table, where she had been working the night before. "Good morning, TIM," she says. The system comes awake: on the screen appears a graphical representation that mimics her desk at work. An in/out box and an address file sit on the desk. Binders on the shelf to the right contain the following:

- Personal information
- Organizational information
- Research tools
- Product cross-selling tool
- Industry information tool
- Deals in process
- Loans

In addition, a toolbox on the shelf below the binders contains various kinds of software, such as spreadsheet programs, a word processing program, and graphics programs. Sue can also take advantage of the calendar function and a notepad tool that can dynamically attach notes to various files according to her instructions.

"TIM," Sue says to her workstation, "tell me the events for the week."

"Monday you have a luncheon meeting with Jenna Kristin of McCormick Natural Gas," says a voice from her computer. "Tuesday you have a meeting with Albert Butzer in the morning. Wednesday you have the Ryerson Steel presentation in the afternoon. Friday you have a breakfast meeting with Jonathan Stewart."

Sue pours herself a cup of coffee and sits down, asking TIM to open the "Research" binder. She selects a business publication from the list of options, and it appears on her screen. She scans the headlines and then requests a particular search: "McCormick Natural Gas." In a moment, the system tells her there are no references to McCormick in that publication. Sue widens her search: she requests any references to McCormick in her predetermined list of business periodicals over the past month. This brings up eight articles. Sue could read them right there on screen, but this time she sends them over her modem to her office printer. She may want to take the articles with her to look at on the way to her lunch appointment.

With her mouse, Sue clicks on her in-box, and the system shows her the incoming mail. She has several voice and electronic mail items and one video update from Jonathan Stewart, the bank president. She selects this item, and a full-motion video clip from the president explains a new strategic direction for the bank. Color graphics and charts outlining the bank's new direction accompany the message. Sue responds quickly to a couple of other voice and electronic mail items in her mailbox.

"TIM, show restaurant list," Sue says. A listing of restaurants in the area appears on her screen. Sue selects her favorite, enters the necessary information about time of reservation and number in the party, and the system sends a fax to the restaurant for her, making the reservation. The restaurant will confirm her reservation by return facsimile or voice mail.

Sue sees on screen that it's just before 7:30. She gathers up her things and heads for the office.

TIM'S DESKTOP INTERFACE

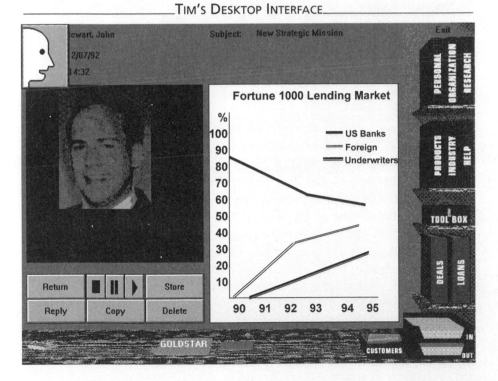

TOTAL INFORMATION MANAGEMENT AND THE BANKING INDUSTRY

The goal of commercial lending is to maximize profits and revenues, which contributes to the bank's success. Today's commercial lender helps achieve this goal by delivering and managing good customer service as well as managing business deals and loans. Obviously, managing risk while delivering quality services to customers is vital to survival and profitability. Improving risk management means improving knowledge worker skills to make better business decisions.

In addition, the speed at which customer questions are answered can make the difference between losing and keeping a customer. The type of service that lenders provide to their potential and existing customers is important. Customers want to be treated with respect and courtesy and receive personalized attention. A customer that is treated well will tend to stay with the bank, maybe even when the loan terms are not quite as favorable as they would be at another bank.

Lenders have a large amount of information to manage. They must keep research and track potential customers to increase their likelihood of giving a loan to that customer. Once a loan is made, the lender must monitor it and make sure that all the conditions and terms are being met. Lenders must be proactive about monitoring their customers' business developments and looking for business changes. They must have access to late-breaking news and information about their customers and about their customers' industries. Personal information about customers—new promotions, for example—must also be tracked to maintain a personal relationship.

A conventional information system could not begin to support these complex tasks of the average commercial lender. But a performance system, which knows the particular lender's background and experience, and knows the job responsibilities of the lender, can tailor a dynamic package of support capabilities to empower the lender.

To demonstrate the viability of Integrated Performance Support, a prototype system—Total Information Management, or "TIM"—was designed by Andersen Consulting to support commercial lenders throughout the loan process, from prospecting to deal closing and loan servicing. The system provides assistance ranging from offering advice on how a task should be completed to tools designed to simplify the lender's job. For example, if the lender is interested in a particular client, TIM can dynamically create a company profile, reducing research time. If a lender is uncertain about

TOTAL INFORMATION MANAGEMENT AND THE BANKING INDUSTRY *(CONTINUED)*

an aspect of a deal, TIM can retrieve past deals that are similar, allowing the lender to learn from the experiences of others.

TIM brings specific, real-time performance feedback to the desktop. Lenders have immediate access to past evaluations and performance trends and can see how their performance compares with that of their peers. The lender can review personal training history and commence new training. The lender has access to the corporate mission, policies and procedures, the organization chart, and executive profiles.

The first thing you notice about the scenario thus far is the ease with which Sue is interacting with the system. Indeed, it is more correct to say simply that Sue is interacting with her working environment: she is *performing*. The system itself is facilitating and enabling her work, not forcing Sue into a predetermined work path. The mode of interaction is natural: Sue can speak directly to TIM and TIM will respond by voice as well. But voice, of course, is not always going to be appropriate for all types of environments or even for all kinds of work that any one lender wants to do. All interaction with the performance system can take place with mouse, keyboard, or other input devices. The most important thing is that each lender can choose the manner in which he or she prefers to interact.

The basic interface—the primary screen of the computer system—is performance-centered: a graphical representation of the actual work environment of a lender. Interface designers will often speak of the "desktop metaphor," and this is the model here, quite literally. The purpose of the primary screen design is not just to be colorful or clever; its purpose is to make the system intuitively understandable even to a first-time user, and to provide access to various applications and information in a common fashion. But the interface is also tailorable to individual needs and preferences. As lenders become more proficient, they may opt to go into so-called "expert mode," eliminating the desktop graphic, if they feel that would make them more efficient. Or, a "virtual interface" capability of the system would permit lenders to design their own interface to better suit their understanding of their work. Sue likes the desk, though. For her, it continues to represent the rich content, functionality, and flexibility of the system, and it helps her focus on her own job performance.

The interaction with TIM also gives her a number of ways with which to communicate. Phone, voice mail, electronic mail, facsimile, and video-conferencing can all be made available to her from her workstation. The multimedia aspects of TIM seen to this point reveal an important fact about the future of multimedia in the workplace: it has to add value. In the message from the president, for example, the video medium was appropriate and effective; the new strategic direction for the bank needed the tangible, personal presence of the bank president to reinforce its importance to a wide, geographically separate audience. The color animated graphics that accompanied the clip helped illustrate the basic principles of the new strategic direction. Video is not always necessary, nor is animation. In many instances, text may be the preferred means of communication; in other instances, voice alone may be the best. Photos, images, sound, and other multimedia elements should be used only if they add value to the communication itself. *The mode by which information is presented must be a good match for the function of the information.*

Human-Computer Interaction in the IPS Model. The first layer within the logical view of the Integrated Performance Support model is the human-computer interaction (or "HCI") layer. The major functions of this layer are:

- to manage data and information *presentation;*
- to facilitate efficient *navigation* through the system; and
- to provide for effective *manipulation* of information within the system.

Presentation. The primary interface or primary screen presents a performance system to the worker as a tool to support work performance, rather than as a cumbersome system that must be negotiated with in order to work. Powerful and effective interfaces provide an appropriate simulation of the overall picture of the work, represent access to multiple sources of information with a common look and feel, and provide a picture of the entire capabilities of the performance system. TIM is a good example of work in this area. The advent of graphical user interfaces, or GUIs, as well as new multimedia technologies, has greatly enhanced the usability and impact of systems. A graphical interface uses symbolic representations of familiar objects to represent more complex capabilities of the system. For example, most workers would be familiar with the process of getting telephone numbers from a Rolodex or cardfile, so the TIM system uses the symbol of a cardfile to indicate where the worker's personalized list of names, addresses, and phone numbers can be found.

Effective interfaces use *metaphors* to present the system options to workers. TIM's primary interface is a good example of the "desktop metaphor," but other metaphors are used as well. Not every metaphor is appropriate for every work environment. Not all people, for example, work at a desk. A "process metaphor," by contrast, might show maintenance workers at a factory a schematic drawing of the entire facility, allowing them to access important information about the facility by pointing and clicking at the various components. The "human metaphor" is often given as the umbrella term for effective human-computer interaction. That is, one of the ways to help people interact with a computer is to mimic the type of interaction we would use with another human being. TIM's voice capability is an example of this. The voice and graphic picture of a human figure is called an "agent," and becomes a personal assistant to the worker using the system.

One of the most important aspects of the interaction within performance systems is that all of the IPS services—Advisory Services, Reference Services, and so forth—are presented seamlessly to the worker, without a distinction among the types and forms of support. The workers don't notice or care which service is at work; all they notice is that they can do their jobs efficiently and productively.

Navigation. How does a worker discover and then take advantage of all the capabilities, all the functionality, of the information system? If you use one of the major word processing software packages, for example, ask yourself what percentage of the full options of that software you are familiar with. If, like most people, that percentage is small, ask yourself why. The answer: because it is difficult to "navigate" through the application and find everything that you are able to do. Options are not dynamically presented in the context of what you are trying to accomplish, and there is no feedback to let you know you have successfully performed an action. There is little or no advice provided to you to help you perform; icons and menu options are grouped or labeled in a way that makes it difficult to locate and understand information; and the cost of changing or standardization to a new application package is significant.

The traditional response of organizations to these design problems has been user training. But traditional training is costly, time consuming, and takes the worker away from the job. Performance systems respond to this problem by making navigation through a system more natural and intuitive. Context-sensitive help and advice from these systems coach workers through their tasks and point them toward additional system functions that can support their work.

Manipulation. How does a worker work with data and information and move that information around? Until the advent of graphical interfaces, manipulation of data was a labyrinthine process. Consider the amount of effort necessary with older word processing programs to do a simple task: copy a document from the computer's hard drive onto a diskette. When Apple revolutionized the marketplace with their graphical interfaces, the process became intuitive and obvious: an icon, or symbol, of a piece of paper represented the document; it was located in a file, represented by an icon of a file folder. With the handheld mouse, users pointed at the file, clicked on it, "dragged" it over to another icon representing the diskette, and *voila!* It was done.

A considerable amount of exciting work and research is being done all over the world in Human-Computer Interaction and Human-Computer Interface design. Under the direction of our colleague Carlos Cervantes, Andersen Consulting has developed an HCI Usability Framework and a series of straightforward HCI Usability Engineering Rules. The purpose of the framework and the engineering rules is to provide a planning and implementation tool for delivering excellent graphical user interfaces for systems projects.

PART 2
KNOWLEDGE WORKER SERVICES:
THE "HUMAN RESOURCES COORDINATOR"

Sue gets to her office shortly before 8:00. She wanted to come in a little early today: she is due for a performance review, so she wants to look at how her performance compares to her peers in the commercial lending department. She also wants to look at previous reviews to familiarize herself again with the review process.

"TIM, show personal evaluations," she says. On the screen, TIM displays summaries of her past performance evaluations. "TIM, show performance." In another window, she gets real-time information in the form of a graphic representing her fee generation for the current year. Next to the graphic showing her performance are graphics showing the high, the low, and the median performances for her group for that year. She sees that she is slightly above median. Part of her annual review will discuss her training to this point in her career, and her training plan for the coming year, so she needs to be sure she's up to date: "TIM, show training," and a summary of the courses she has taken appears. Finally, she asks TIM to show her general profile, and a total summary of her basic responsibilities, level of authority, and current status appears.

TIM gives Sue the ability to see a snapshot of her status with the bank at any time. The system "knows" Sue—her responsibilities, authority level, inventory of skills, training history, even her basic preferences for how she wishes to interact with the system. But TIM also knows that Sue is dynamic: her responsibilities and competencies change over time, and so TIM has the ability constantly to upgrade and enhance her status according to tasks mastered and training completed.

Knowledge Worker Services in the IPS Model.   The Knowledge Worker Services facility of a performance system profiles an organization's workforce—its human capital and its capacity to perform work. This component can be rich and deep, or it can be as simple as a listing of all the jobs or positions that the organization recruits for or staffs.

Knowledge Worker Services provides functions to support both individual performance and workgroup performance. Information provided by this IPS service allows performance support to be customized to the unique capabilities and needs of workers and workgroups. Knowledge Worker Services may include information related to:

- Job responsibility and authority level
- Current career profile and expected future career path
- Training history
- Skills inventory
- Performance feedback
- Preferences for interaction with the system (for example, different ways of grouping information, color selection, icons, menu choices)

PART 3
WORK PROFILE SERVICES: THE "WORKFLOW COORDINATOR"

Sue's co-workers are beginning to come in as the time nears 8:30. Lights are going on in other areas around her, and she hears the usual noises of greeting and socialization. A few people stick their heads inside her door to say good morning and to ask about her weekend. One co-worker asks Sue about the message from the president and suggests getting together later to talk about customer prospects based on the new bank strategy. Grabbing another quick cup of coffee, Sue gets down to her regular business.

"TIM," Sue says, "tell me the events of the day."

"You have a luncheon meeting with Jenna Kristin of McCormick Natural Gas. You are conducting a new employee orientation at 3:00."

"TIM, tell me what's most important."

"The Smith account is overdrawn."

Sue grimaces. "TIM, show that item."

The system displays at Sue's workstation a detailed look at the account of one of Sue's clients, Smith Manufacturing. An image of the overdraft check is shown, along with a detailed look at the history of the account over the past few months. The TIM system has made a recommendation to Sue that she not authorize the bank to cover the overdraft. By clicking on the question mark near the recommendation, the system displays its reasoning behind this recommendation. Sue sees that this is the third overdraft in the Smith account in the last couple of months—not a good sign. Based upon her personal knowledge of the customer, she reluctantly agrees with the advice and elects not to have the bank cover the check.

The message from the president that Sue reviewed earlier had spelled out a new strategic marketing direction for the bank. Sue decides to do some prospecting to look for potential customers in the midmarket. Sue clicks on her "Customer" card file, and the system shows her personalized list of customers and potential customers. Searching through the list, Sue selects the Goldstar Printing Company and begins the preparation of a customer binder for Goldstar.

Work Profile Services in the IPS Model.   The Work Profile Services facility of a performance system represents the structure of the work that is being completed by the knowledge worker—workflows, job tasks, specific procedures, and other work-related information. It works in conjunction with Knowledge Worker Services to provide the right level of support to meet the performance needs of the knowledge worker.

Work Profile Services has three primary functions. (1) It identifies the work to be performed and the steps required for a given job. (2) It links the appropriate support services available to the task at hand. (3) It provides task structuring support by incorporating the steps associated with tasks into a given sequence.

- *Maintaining Work Data.* Work Profile Services maintains data regarding the work *content* and work *context.* Work content includes the task descriptions associated with the work and the sequencing of those tasks within the workflow. Work context includes the skills profile necessary to complete the work and the key performance indicators associated with the work.
- *Linking Available Support.* Work Profile Services provides a basis for linking the tasks to the support granules, the discrete "chunks" of support available to workers when they experience performance problems, or when the system anticipates problems. For example, if a worker is continually completing an invoice incorrectly, support can be provided to show the worker an example of a correctly completed invoice. In this case, the support service is directly linked to the task of completing an invoice.

- *Task Structuring.* Work Profile Services can provide the basis for structuring a task for the worker. Task structuring involves including the steps or procedures associated with each task. For example, procedures can be presented in the form of checklists to track what is and is not completed for a given task. Checklists may also list the specific equipment or parts needed to create a product or achieve a certain result.

The performance system should be designed so that the workflow and task structure can be represented within the system's interface. For example, in the Total Information Management system, a lender's key tasks involved in preparing a deal are structured and presented in a matrix form showing the completed and pending deals, as well as the status of various deal proposals. In another example we will see later, a system supporting workers in the petrochemical processing industry, the interface is designed to reflect the workflow of an oil refinery process.

Work Profile Services and Knowledge Worker Services represent an important development for performance support, for they permit the information system to be proactive rather than reactive. The system knows the work to be done and knows about the person performing the work. With that knowledge, the system provides support tailored to that individual's unique needs and responsibilities.

PART 4
REFERENCE SERVICES: THE "LIBRARIAN"

Having selected Goldstar Printing Company as a potential customer, Sue needs to do some research, both on the company itself and on the printing industry in general. Sue clicks on the "Research" binder on her bookshelf, and chooses the "News" option. Sue types "Goldstar" in one search field, and "1992+" in another, and asks that all sources be searched. The system locates several items for her, and Sue reads these directly on-line. There is also a video clip about Goldstar available from a local TV station report, and Sue watches this as well.

Now Sue electronically accesses the "Industry" binder from her shelf. Because she has little previous experience with the printing industry, she wants to get some overview information. Sue takes about an hour browsing through this research material, organized in what is called an "Ask System." (See Chapter 10 for an example of an Ask System called "ORCA.") This type of system, pioneered by the Institute for the Learning Sciences at Northwestern University, allows a worker to simulate having a conversation with an expert.

The system is developed by gathering hundreds of stories—"war stories," as it were—from others with experience on a particular topic. Questions are grouped by category, and Sue can ask any question she wants by moving it into the middle of the screen. An explanation, answer, or story may be given in a variety of media—text, animation, video, and so forth.

Because the president's initiative specifically targeted the midmarket industry, Sue begins with questions about that segment of the industry. Because Gold-star is a printing company, she is most interested in examples of a midmarket printing industry. To gain more general knowledge of printing, Sue asks about the major processes used for printing. Here she receives a brief presentation about the printing industry, complete with full-motion video, graphics, and text.

Having completed her research on the printing industry, Sue glances at her watch. It's time to prepare for her luncheon engagement.

Reference Services in the IPS Model.   The Reference Services facility of a performance system serves as the librarian or, perhaps, the historian of the system. It structures and presents job-relevant information from an organization's internal knowledge base and from external public- or vendor-supplied databases. Reference Services is particularly powerful in the manner in which it can provide context-sensitive knowledge. That is, when desired by the worker, Reference Services provides information relevant to particular tasks being performed by the worker. Reference Services moves beyond the mere presentation of random information, to the presentation of applicable knowledge.

Many different kinds of information are provided by Reference Services:

- Product descriptions
- Policies
- Diagrams
- Pictures
- Information about the organization
- Industry-related information
- Research information
- Historical information

Reference Services may be used to browse, search and retrieve, and to communicate.

- *Browse.* Reference Services enables the knowledge worker to browse through the repository of the organization's knowledge capital by producing information in various formats, including text, graphics, full-motion video, digitized images, and audio. In the Total Information Management prototype, for example, a commercial lender can use the industry research tool to browse across various industries.

- *Search and Retrieve.* Reference Services allows knowledge workers to access a topic index (for example, the Help Menu on various software packages) or to select context-sensitive support. For example, in one performance system for the cellular telephone service industry, customer service representatives can quickly access and listen to representative sounds made by telephones that are not working properly. When a customer has a problem, the agent can play the sounds associated with the customer's model of telephone in order to diagnose the problem quickly and to provide a remedy to the customer.
- *Communicate.* Reference Services can be used to maintain structured, catalogued, or indexed information that is frequently updated and provided at the point of need. For example, organizations can have a "What's New" knowledge base to communicate the latest revisions to ever-changing policies and procedures. In this way, communication between knowledge workers is facilitated through the knowledge base.

In addition, Reference Services can be used to facilitate the information exchange between workers. For example, using an electronic mail package, a knowledge worker wanting information can post a question regarding a specific process. Workers with expertise on the subject can answer the question, and the new question/answer is catalogued in the knowledge base. Increasingly, this type of "conversation" is being seen as an important part of the workplace.

PART 5
ADVISORY SERVICES: THE "COACH"

Sue returns from lunch in a terrific mood. During her lunch with Jenna Kristin from McCormick Natural Gas, Sue received the final financial reports needed to complete the $1 million loan presentation package to expand one of their facilities. Over lunch, Sue had used TIM to present financials to Jenna in a graphical format that was easy to understand and modify.

"TIM, show McCormick Deal—Financial Analysis," Sue says. On screen, TIM opens the McCormick Deals binder to the financial analysis section, where Sue can now input the final financial reports. One of the powerful functionalities of TIM, provided by Work Profile Services, is its representation of the entire process that a commercial lender goes through to initiate, evaluate, and close a deal. In another binder, called "Deals," TIM keeps track of all the deals she has in progress. Her current customers are listed, along with the stage that each deal has reached. Although Sue's work is structured, she has the flexibility to decide how she wants to work.

Having received the last piece of information she needs, Sue is now ready to submit the McCormick loan package to the loan committee for approval. Before she does, though, she completes a deal evaluation on the McCormick presentation by initiating TIM's Deal Evaluation Tool. This function offers a system assessment of the probability of the deal being accepted by management. This is obviously an important system capability for Sue, permitting her to make sure that a customer has passed a certain standard before the deal is submitted. It reduces the number of resubmissions and improves the loan approval turnaround time.

To Sue's dismay, TIM forecasts that her deal may not be accepted. She asks for detail on the forecast, and a matrix appears showing the criteria used in the evaluation. Using a technique called "case-based reasoning"—reasoning based upon similar instances or cases—the system can show the basis for the conclusion, helping Sue improve the areas of the presentation that could cause a rejection by management. As you might expect, Sue has some mixed

ADVISORY SERVICES AT THE WORKSTATION

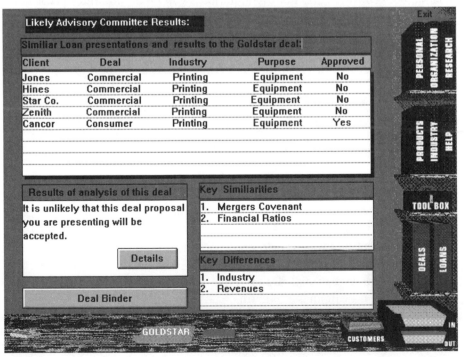

feelings about the system's conclusion. She knows she has some more work to do before she can submit this deal for evaluation.

Advisory Services in the IPS Model. The Advisory Services facility of a performance system acts as the coach—or perhaps the advisor or counselor—to the worker. Advisory Services provides advice and assistance and suggests support options to help the worker examine alternatives, make effective decisions, and solve problems. From a higher point of view, Advisory Services can help a complex organization learn and grow in accordance with management's policies. Support from Advisory Services may include things like:

- Support in diagnosing problems
- Case descriptions of how experts and co-workers have resolved similar situations
- Decision modeling with simulations to help workers make tactical and strategic decisions
- Guidance to identify the appropriate support services

Advisory Services can provide both minor and major services. It can prompt workers, reminding them of certain rules or procedures that must have to be followed. In one performance system, for example, plant workers shutting down a facility are warned about specific safety procedures that must be followed, then walks the workers through these procedures.

But Advisory Services can also support workers in more complex work such as decision making and problem solving. Performance systems can help workers with decision modeling and with pattern recognition—things that machines can sometimes do better than humans. These more complex advisory functions become relevant in situations with one or more of the following:

- Large number of variables
- Many decision rules
- High degree of task complexity
- Inconsistent or conflicting data
- Unpredictable conditions

PART 6
JOB AID SERVICES: THE "ASSISTANT"

As Sue prepares to do the loan overhead calculation for the McCormick deal, TIM alerts her about a new method that the bank has adopted for doing this calculation. She realizes that this new accounting method is going to have implications for several other deals she has pending. She doesn't have time to look at each one right now, but she wants to make sure she remembers the new procedure the next time she looks at those customer files.

"TIM, show Note Pad," Sue says. On screen appears TIM's Note Pad tool. On the pad, Sue types, "Recheck loan overhead calculation." Clicking on the "File" button, Sue can now attach this note to any or all files she wishes. In this case, she attaches it to all deal-pending files. For those customers, the next time Sue opens their file, this note will remind her to recalculate the loan overhead.

Job Aid Services in the IPS Model.   The Job Aid Services facility of a performance system provides automated tools and techniques to simplify routine and/or repetitive tasks. Job Aid Services acts as the worker's "personal assistant," automating or simplifying all or some part of a task. Ideally, the job aid will be context-sensitive and integrated with the task at hand. The following are some of the functions of this service.

- *Messaging and Communication.* Job Aid Services can route information quickly and efficiently through use of electronic mail, faxing, and other data transmission devices. Early in the morning, when Sue sent a fax to make a restaurant reservation, she was taking advantage of Job Aid Services. A performance system also facilitates the distribution of messages to several individuals, both inside and outside the organization. Messages could be enhanced using multiple formats, including text, graphics, and video.
- *Computation.* Job Aid Services can aid in the computation of numerical data. With the TIM system, for example, a lender must price a potential loan to determine how profitable it will be, and must produce a sample income statement. Job Aid Services can provide a pricing worksheet, into which all parameters of the loan can be entered, which will produce a sample income statement.
- *Document Creation and Report Generation.* Job Aid Services can assist with generating documents and reports. Templates can speed the creation of letters and memos. With the TIM system, loan documents can be automatically created from variables entered by the lender.
- *Scheduling.* Job Aid Services can track a knowledge worker's schedule and automatically alert him or her to upcoming events. This function becomes increasingly useful for workers with excessive demands on their time.
- *Data Representation.* Data representation refers to the ability to quickly change the look of data based on the preferences or needs of the worker. For

example, a tool that shows profit and loss statements may use various types of charting techniques (for example, graphs and tables) that display numerical data in different formats. Also, the table may allow for quick restructuring, depending on the type of work performed.

Many information systems now in operation have some sort of job aid for the user. Word processing software, for example, has spell checking, a thesaurus, grammar checking, and on-line help. But job aids within performance systems are integrated. As with the notepad tool in the TIM system, a job aid connects the current task with the relevant information, and so could be thought of as "intelligent job aid." It is proactive rather than reactive, active rather than passive, providing the exact job aid that is needed, exactly where and when it is needed.

PART 7
TRAINING SERVICES: THE "TUTOR"

TIM also alerts Sue that training on the new accounting method is available, and she elects to take this training now. The session begins with an overview of the new loan calculation method, comparing it to the old method. Sue wants a little more explanation at this point, so she clicks on the "Huh?" button at the bottom of the screen. Here she gets more detailed information. By clicking on the "Background" button, Sue views a video clip of a lender speaking from experience about how the old accounting system was preventing the bank from being competitive in the small and midrange markets. By clicking on the "Why?" button, Sue can watch a technical explanation from the head of the commercial lending department about why the change was made.

Following the video, Sue calls up another screen with several graphs explaining the effects of the accounting change. As she begins to understand this new method, she clicks on various colored regions of the graph, and a short tutorial provides an explanation of each of the graph's components. On another screen, the tutorial shows Sue examples of loan income statements before and after the change. The screen illustrates how the accounting change will increase the yield of small loans and decrease the yield of larger loans and then shows actual income statements from loans the bank has made.

Sue takes full advantage of this training, trying her hand at calculating overhead under the new system from several different examples TIM provides her. Finally, she thinks she's got it, and she accesses the "Try It" option. TIM asks Sue several questions, each time asking her to type in her answer and match it to several choices TIM gives her. Sue answers each question correctly, and

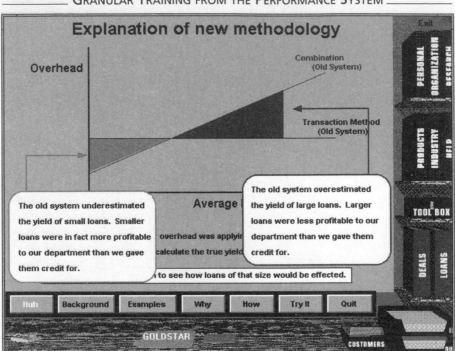

TIM informs her that she has successfully completed the training. When Sue next accesses her Personal binder, she will see that her completion of this lesson has been noted.

Thanks to the training she has gotten on this new accounting method, she thinks that she can solve the problem with the McCormick deal. "TIM, show McCormick Deal," she says, and on she goes.

Training Services in the IPS Model.   The Training Services facility of a performance system plays the role of a tutor, a personal instructor. The parallel with tutoring is important here, because training within a performance system is a one-on-one, tailored event, unlike traditional corporate and schoolroom education, and unlike most approaches to computer-based training (CBT). Like a competent tutor, Training Services provides relevant knowledge, examples, and practice opportunities to help the worker gain additional skills.

• *Training Services delivers training in a "granular" manner.*   Traditional corporate training, even computer-based training (CBT), has been structured hierarchically and sequentially, according to some overall instructional strategy and approach. For example, many courses consist of a number of modules that are sequenced beginning with orientation, and then moving through presentation and exercises on to a final test. The focus of CBT has been directed, for the most part, at providing modular training programs outside of the job context.

The approach to training with an Integrated Performance Support strategy brings training close to the real work at hand, integrating training with current tasks. It is structured in small chunks or "granules" and is provided as an integral part of the work environment. Training can be delivered on the job, where a worker completes training while performing tasks.

- *Training Services emphasizes "learning by doing."* We all learn best when we can immediately apply our new skills on the job. If we do not use learning soon after it is acquired and then reinforce it experientially, it will fade from our memories quickly. A performance system provides task-specific training on demand, rather than relying on off-site classroom training or on a separate "training event."
- *Training Services provides immediate feedback.* A performance system presents essential information with built-in practice exercises and immediate feedback relevant to the task at hand.
- *Training Services supports the adult learner.* Traditional training is instructor- or trainer-controlled. Adult learners in particular must have training tailored to their unique needs, training that they can access in ways that best suit them.

PART 8
PERFORMANCE SUPPORT CONTROLLER; THE "ORCHESTRA CONDUCTOR"

We almost have to "sneak up" on the last part of the Integrated Performance Support model, because it's the part that the worker at a performance system doesn't—and shouldn't—notice. Performance Support Controller, or PSC, is the steering or coordinating mechanism of the performance system. Like an orchestra conductor, it ensures that all parts of the system deliver an optimum "performance." PSC monitors, coordinates, and controls the delivery of performance support.

- *Monitor.* PSC provides mechanisms to monitor the states (the worker's responsibilities, for example), the events (the general job being done), and the activities (the specific tasks) that determine the context of the work and the worker. This contextual information is then used to deliver the right support at the right time. The determination of what should or should not be monitored is vital to the success of the performance system.

For system-initiated support, the PSC may only monitor vital contextual information to invoke performance support functions automatically. For example, the type and frequency of errors that create barriers to performance may be monitored through an error detection mechanism. For worker-initiated support, the PSC may monitor the context in which the worker initiates the support request and provide support functions from which the worker may choose. Regardless of whether the support is system-initiated or worker-initiated, the appropriate support resource should be given to the worker based on the work being performed. Most important, the worker— not the system—is in control at all times.

• *Coordinate.* By identifying appropriate contextual information, the PSC can coordinate the services of the performance system. To do this, the PSC could obtain the context for the support request and identify which support resources are available.
• *Control.* The PSC may provide various degrees of control functions including: (1) the control of the context within which support is offered; (2) the control over access, entry point, and/or navigation through support resources that may consist of confidential or sensitive information; and (3) the control over required or optional functions. In general, if the support is system-initiated, it should be unobtrusive, and workers should have the option of ignoring it without interrupting their current activities.

Sue's performance system has propelled her into the era of "FutureWork." The system's ability to teach and inform her *when* she needed it, *where* she needed it, is only part of the power she has accessed. The full power had come, rather, with the system's ability to *anticipate* her performance needs and to *coach* her—to advise Sue, to suggest specific actions, and to recommend particular procedures and resources that would support her work. Everything she needed, she received: right at her workstation, tailored to her background and to her level of experience. The performance system became an active partner with her in the performance of her work, rather than a passive tool or, worse, an impediment to what she wanted to accomplish.

Most important, Integrated Performance Support ensured that the support services were delivered to her seamlessly. Sue didn't necessarily realize, or care, that some support was coming from Reference Services, others from

Training or Advisory Services. All she knew was that she was able to perform her job in ways unimaginable only a few years ago. Her performance at every moment of value was connected to the performance of her entire organization. And it was the integration and proactive nature of that support that represented the real breakthrough for her and for her organization.

So ends your "Tale of Two Workers." Or not quite: because as the day is ending, as lights come on in the city below you, you have the chance to send over the network to Sue Peters a copy of the following mail item that you received a moment ago from the head of the bank's Advanced Technology Group:

> Following the successful implementation of the Total Information Management system within the bank's commercial lending department, we are recommending that we extend the range of Integrated Performance Support concepts throughout the bank's full range of services. We are appointing a task force to begin this multiyear project, and recommend that Sue Peters be appointed as the representative from the commercial lending department.

Back in her office, Sue is packing up to go home when TIM alerts her: "You have a new high-priority message in your In Box."

WHAT IPS IS—AND IS NOT

IPS IS		IPS IS NOT	
Is	A conceptual design strategy focused on supporting workforce performance.	**Not**	A system or a technology, nor is it a strategy to *control* performance.
Is	Focused on helping workers or workgroups do the work.	**Not**	Focused on helping workers or workgroups only to use an application.
Is	Focused on explaining the functions and features of a business solution, product, or service.	**Not**	Focused on explaining the functions and features of software applications.
Is	Focused on providing advice to help workers make decisions.	**Not**	Focused on building systems that make decisions for workers.
Is	Enabled by various technologies (e.g., client/server, multimedia, image).	**Not**	A new technology in itself.
Is	About transacting business.	**Not**	About processing transactions.

PART TWO

Meeting Today's Challenges

CHAPTER 4

MAKING TECHNOLOGY WORK

The scene fades in to show two workers in an office. Apparently owners of a small business, they are setting up a new computer. The room is a mess: boxes and manuals of systems documentation are everywhere. The person at the computer is pecking at the keyboard and muttering: "C, colon, backslash. . . ." The other person, brow furrowed, is hunting through a manual. A co-worker comes through the office, eyebrows raised: "Are you still working at that computer?" "We're trying to set it up so it's just right for us," one of the workers says defensively. "Yeah," says the other, "so we can be more productive." "If you're any more productive," the co-worker mutters, walking out of the office, "we'll be going out of business."[1]

The scene is exaggerated for dramatic purposes, for it is that most exaggerated of communications—a television commercial—but the point is well taken: we know that systems have more functionality in them than ever before, but how can the average worker tap into that functionality quickly and easily? How can we use information technology more effectively, more powerfully in the workplace? In the 1980s, in the United States alone, businesses invested a trillion dollars in information technology. But not everyone is happy about it. Some companies have begun to say things about technology that would have been heretical only a few years ago. General Electric's vice-president for business development notes that they have, in some cases, begun to take automation out of factories. "We have found," he says, "that in many cases technology impedes productivity."[2]

The debate about the technology-productivity link is controversial, mostly because productivity measurements are inevitably somewhat subjective. We have seen countless examples of productivity improvements through technology when efforts were also made to:

- reengineer processes rather than simply automate existing processes; and
- help the workforce manage the change that accompanied the new technology.

Because many organizations did not adequately engage in process reengineering and change management, one can certainly find statistics to support the contention that productivity gains sometimes proved elusive. According

91

- The key to increasing productivity gains from technology in the work-place is the right kind of approach to the design, implementation, and use of information technology so that it serves the larger purposes of the work that knowledge workers are to perform.
- The IPS approach to information technology results in a workforce that *knows* more, that can *do* more, and that *will* do more.
- Various factors can cause workers to resist certain forms of technology: resistance can be based on a worker's culture, age, educational back-ground, and habitual ways of working. A performance system can anticipate and overcome these kinds of resistance.
- Interaction with technology must be natural to the worker. This means several things in a performance system: (1) the primary interface gives the worker a picture of the work that is to be done and a picture of the entire functionality of the system; (2) the support services are provided seamlessly to the worker, almost without being noticed; and (3) all features of the system are designed from a performance-centered point of view.

---

to some figures, the services sector saw only a 1% rise in productivity in the 1980s, despite an $800 billion investment in technology.[3]

In fact, however, productivity gains are starting to be seen now: one analysis of 400 large companies from 1987 to 1991 shows the return on investment in information systems to be 54% in manufacturing and 68% for all businesses surveyed.[4] In part, these new gains are grounded in the combination of advanced information technology and new management structures. Just as important to these productivity gains, however, are the initiatives we noted in Chapter 2 that have converged into the concept of Integrated Performance Support.

The key to seeing further productivity gains from technology in the workplace, we believe, is the right kind of approach to the design, implementation, and use of information technology so that it serves the larger purposes of the work we do. Work precedes technology; performance needs should drive the design of information systems; people propose, technology conforms.[5] Technology has, of course, done startling and marvelous things, and life for most of us would be inconceivable without it. A bumper sticker we have occasionally seen on U.S. highways—"If you liked the good old days, turn off your air conditioning"—points only to the most mundane example of how certain kinds of technology have enriched our lives.[6] Thomas Hobbes' famous seventeenth century description of human life as "nasty, brutish, and short"[7] is a stark reminder of what life was like before modern sanitation and medical advancements. Nevertheless, technology often has unintended consequences. Modern medicine helps us live longer, only to present us with insoluble moral dilemmas in our old age as our still-functioning bodies house ever-failing minds. Automation makes us more efficient, only to put increasing numbers of people out of work.[8] Computer systems become so rich in functionality that new attention must be paid to supporting people as they use the systems and, more important, supporting people as they do their jobs.

The right approach to information technology in the workplace results in systems that have the ability to help people work better and smarter. The Integrated Performance Support approach to the design and implementation of performance systems results in a more competitive workforce:

- One that *knows* more, because advice, tools, reference, and training are delivered to them when and where they need them.
- One that *can do* more, because the systems are designed from a doing, or performance, point of view.
- One that *will* do more, because the traditional change barriers associated with new technology and new processes have been removed or lessened.

The larger issue addressed in this chapter is how to help your workforce perform better, by *making your technology work*.

UNEXPECTED RESISTANCE TO TECHNOLOGY

Technology can face resistance in unexpected ways. Take the case of one company in the petroleum refinery and distribution business which was developing a powerful new information system, one that would link not only office workers, but also maintenance crews and tanker drivers. All was proceeding smoothly until the testing phase, when the truck drivers resolutely refused to use the keyboards on their computers.

Many of us have seen similar examples of resistance. We know of one executive, for example, who resisted using his voice mail when his company adopted it and had an assistant transcribe every message he received. A technical writer for another company recalls the time only ten years ago when her supervisor refused to give the writing staff their own personal computers because of the fear that the writers would then be perceived only as support staff. Companies sometimes stumble, or find their workers stumbling, over other technological pitfalls that were not anticipated. We are now long past the time when we could introduce technology to workers and expect them to be immediately enthralled and dazzled by it. What technology experts think of as terrific innovations can often face resistance from a significant number of workers. Technology represents change to them, which in turn creates apprehension, and organizations must anticipate resistance and help their workers cope with change.

Take something as simple as the mouse—the handheld adjunct to the computer keyboard. The mouse came into being after an enormous amount of research into more natural interaction with a computer. But those who have used a mouse every day for years need to remember that workers may need time to adjust even to "natural" things. Some workers have real trouble adjusting, and it doesn't do any good merely to tell them that the mouse is better than a keyboard. Most innovations take time before they are accepted. If you're not used to a keyboard, it's foreign to you; if you're used to a keyboard, a mouse is foreign to you.

The introduction of any technology into the workplace must be accompanied by a sensitivity to its impact on the real human beings who use it. This is a simple truth that is now gaining increased recognition. The actual design of system interfaces and interaction procedures is the most obvious challenge one thinks of here, and we will get to that aspect in a moment. But there is a more important, higher-level challenge here: the manner in which computers have changed the very way we think about our work.

Consider, if it is even possible, what our work was like before the computer. We came to our jobs, to our offices or factories, and worked. If we worked at a desk, the various things on it were nothing more than tools to help us do our jobs. The telephone helped us find out things and talk to people without having to wait for postal deliveries or telegrams. The typewriter helped us (well, some of us) write faster and, at the least, made our correspondence look neater and more professional. But our minds were focused on the overall goals of our work: the sales quota for the month; x number of customer service inquiries; so many products manufactured per day.

For better and for worse, the computer altered that understanding of our work. The computer made those things we did more efficient, but it also put blinders on us: no longer could we look at the whole picture of our work, but only that slice of it that a particular system application let us see—sort of the Frederick Taylor method automated. Little did we know at the time how troublesome that limited view would turn out to be. The computer turned out to be far more than a neutral tool, far different than a window upon our work. It altered, and sometimes distorted, the very work we did.

Only now that computing technology has advanced beyond the mainframe/dumb terminal model are we able to return to our former, more natural notions of working. With earlier technologies and applications, companies told their workers to do their jobs within the constraints of whatever the system allowed them to do. The sequential chunks of batch processing were a good example of altering our work form to accommodate the computer. We know that people do not think or work in batch mode. Subsequent transitions in computing technology—from on-line to real-time, and now to client/server architectures and cooperative processing—have eased the return to a more natural form of human work. We're still not quite there, but the starting point for systems design is correct: today we start with an analysis of *the work to be done*. Then we design a system that lets workers perform in that mode, and that also gives them the flexibility to change their mode of performance as the work, workplace, and marketplace change.

VISION OF WORK WITH TRADITIONAL SYSTEMS

VISION OF WORK WITH PERFORMANCE SYSTEMS

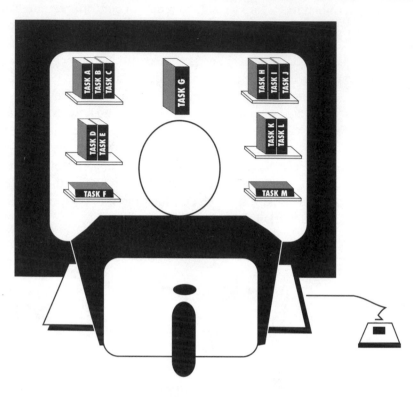

We thus began several decades ago with systems that restricted our vision of our work; gradually the blinders have been opening up, allowing us to see more. The goal now—what some are calling "ubiquitous computing"—is a system operating almost totally at the periphery of our vision: the window on our work will be so large we will forget we are even looking through a window.

TYPES OF RESISTANCE

The resistance that technology can provoke in workers takes many different forms. In some cases, workers bring with them certain concerns or limitations that represent barriers to their understanding of technology. In other cases, the technology itself can have embedded within it some limitations that prevent even the most earnest workers from performing their jobs properly.

CULTURAL RESISTANCE

The example of the truck drivers who wouldn't use keyboards is an example of cultural resistance. In cultures where divisions of work by gender continue to dominate, we will continue to see resistance to some technological innovations, at least by older workers. Sometimes, if old dogs cannot be taught new tricks, they can be taught to encourage the young dogs. We recall visiting one corporate headquarters in Tokyo some years ago and seeing a computer terminal conspicuously displayed on the chairman's desk. He was just learning to use it himself, he told us, but it was there for his management team to see; he wanted to send a message to them that they needed the vision, and he had to set the example for the workforce. A high-tech company needs high-tech leadership.

The larger issue here is the fact that someone's cultural context—are you male or female? what nationality? what socioeconomic class? how much formal education?—inevitably instills an orientation toward one's work and the technology that is a part of that work. This orientation is reinforced through the educational system, the social system, and the economic system. What one leading thinker on organizational change has written about corporate culture in general, we could also say about an information system: that it "must necessarily be at least *minimally* consistent with the societal culture from which it is derived."[9] More than that, an effective system, a performance system, should be *tailorable* to these different cultural orientations.

GENERATIONAL RESISTANCE

A recent newspaper cartoon effectively shows what we mean by generational technology resistance in its depiction of a father and his young son staring at a TV and VCR. Says father to son, "How do I program the VCR to record something later?"

"Well, let's see," the son replies. "You start by pressing several of the buttons on the front at random. Then you slowly toggle the power switch on and off for about a minute. Then you take a blank tape and put it in upside down. Then you pick up the remote control and just kind of stare at it for a while."

"Correction," says the father. "How *should* I program the VCR to record something later?"[10]

The adage that the child is father to the man has never been more true than with current technology. Organizations witness every day the fact that their older employees have difficulty with technology that younger co-workers take for granted. It does organizations no good to be impatient with those who don't

THE IMPORTANCE OF CULTURAL CONSIDERATIONS IN THE DESIGN OF TECHNOLOGY

Human-centered design must be sensitive to the ways people from different cultures can interpret aspects of the design. Even something as simple as a color choice must consider the different symbolism of colors around the world. Tailorability of interface design, within certain restrictions, is thus an important feature of human-computer interaction principles of Integrated Performance Support.

Below are some different cultural associations of color.

	RED	BLUE	GREEN	WHITE	YELLOW
China	Happiness	Heavens Clouds	Ming Dynasty	Death Purity	Birth Wealth Power
Egypt	Death	Virtue Faith Truth	Fertility Strength	Joy	Happiness Prosperity
France	Aristocracy	Freedom Peace	Criminality	Neutrality	Temporariness
India	Life Creativity		Prosperity Fertility	Death Purity	Success
Japan	Anger Danger	Villainy	Future Youth Energy	Death	Grace Nobility
United States	Danger	Masculinity	Safety	Purity	Cowardice

Source: "How Fluent is Your Interface? Designing for International Users," Patricia Russo, Steven Boor at INTERCHI 93. Noted in "The GUI Guide": Minimizing the Risk of the Graphic User Interface," Andersen Consulting, 1993. Copyright 1993, Association for Computing Machinery, Inc.

get it as quickly; this is not a matter of intelligence but rather of environment—not nature, but nurture. Those born after 1960 grew up in the space age, in the age of computers, and have been immersed in technology in ways older workers were not. If, as researchers in the physiology of the brain tell us, the mind becomes predisposed, based upon its experiences, to a particular view of the world,[11] we can easily see how older workers have difficulty adjusting to the breathtaking pace of technological change.

But again, why shouldn't a system be adaptable both to older workers and to younger? Why shouldn't a system have the capability to ease the "can't-even-program-the-VCR" kind of worker into the system gradually?

HABIT RESISTANCE

A U.S. bank is reengineering its processes for handling customer trust funds. One of its newest systems incorporates imaging technology so that workers will no longer have to sift through mountains of customer correspondence. Customer service representatives will work with scanned images of documents that they can access from their workstations. In the initial phase of the project, designers noticed a strange phenomenon. Workers were calling up the scanned image of letters on their computers, printing out a paper copy on their printers, and storing the copy in their desks. All that money for a new system, and workers were doing it the old way after all.

Habits become barriers to change. New technologies often encounter the inertia of old ways of doing things. When the microwave oven was a new phenomenon, comedians called it an expensive way to heat a cup of water for coffee—because that was the extent of its use for many people unaccustomed to its capabilities. The computer is only just beginning to overcome its own inertia for many people. In the United States, for example, only about 27% of the 92 million households own a home computer.[12]

But even those accustomed to computers will cling to old systems at the expense of productivity. Clearly there are larger issues of organizational change at work here, issues we will discuss later in this book. But even at this level, the level of basic interaction with the computer, workers will usually opt for the known over the unknown. We spoke earlier of the customer service representative who resisted the graphical user interface of a new system, opting instead to continue using the old green-on-black screens of her character-based system. A similar example of resistance occurred years ago in one specialty store that converted to a computerized inventory control system. The individual merchants, however, kept their black books, the record of their commitments and deliveries, and posted them by hand, so they could compare them to the computer. Some readers may recall those people who checked up on their new handheld calculators when they first became available, doing the arithmetic by hand and then comparing it to the answer from the machine.

But the resistance of habit becomes easier to overcome if organizations merely take the obvious and simple step of being sensitive to it. To a worker, the choice is often between two paths: the old, well-traveled performance path may be long, but it is safe and well known; the newer path is shorter but is unfamiliar and will appear treacherous at first. Long and safe wins out almost every time. A performance-centered perspective in this case would first find out what performance paths already exist for workers; then it would design a system that would not only improve existing paths, but would also make the new ones more enticing.

A sensitivity to old ways can be important because it takes advantage of existing mental models, of what workers already know. When McCaw Cellular Communications was developing a performance system for its customer service representatives, for example, the primary icons, or graphical symbols, of the interface (signifying where access could be obtained to reference information and training) were lifted directly from the manuals the workers had been using. This provided an effective link with earlier work, while at the same time it transformed that work into new processes. At another company, customer service representatives were accustomed to figuring out bills by hand on a desktop calculator. Under the new system, the software figures the bills automatically. But system designers included, in the primary interface of the system, an icon by which workers could access a calculator. The icon was merely transitional, but it gave an important nod toward the past, as well as bringing workers sensitively toward the future by building upon things they already knew.

EDUCATIONAL BACKGROUND RESISTANCE

A global organization is challenged, and will continue to be challenged, by a workforce with different backgrounds and varying degrees of education. Not all countries have the same sorts of problems in this respect, but more than a few are finding functional illiteracy to be increasingly common. In the United States, for example, more than 27 million people, over 9% of the population, cannot read or write well enough to meet the basic requirements of a job. In 1992, *The Wall Street Journal* reported on the growing use of computers by illiterate workers. Some critics contend that systems are exacerbating this problem by making it easier for illiterate workers to operate a system. (Fast-food restaurants whose cash registers have pictures of products on them are frequently cited in this regard.) The *Journal* article quotes a spokeswoman for Laubach Literacy Action: "Companies, instead of working to enhance the literacy skills of their employees, are dummying down the equipment."[13] We cannot agree with this assessment. The larger issue, again, is making any kind of technology *performance-centered,* and part of this mindset is to make systems usable by people with a broad range of skills. At its best, technology elevates a person to a performance level that could not have been attained without it.

We will have more to say later about the power of performance systems to overcome certain kinds of educational deficiencies. But educational barriers are encountered even by intelligent, well-educated workers. One of the problems here is that many organizations seem to work on the basis of an old, now discredited theory about the relationship between technology and worker skills. According to this theory of "deskilling," advanced by Harvard's James Bright in the late 1950s, advanced skills would be required at the introduction of a new technology, but once the technology matured, the skills needed to operate it would decline. In fact, as more recent analyses suggest,[14] jobs of the future will require *more* skills, not fewer, and more complex skills at that. Thomas Bailey of Columbia University writes that "increased international competition, changes in both consumer demand and industrial structure, and the facility of technology to help firms meet these challenges [are] largely preventing firms from using technology to reduce skills."[15]

Systems technology of the future will thus be forced to be adaptable and tailorable to many different educational backgrounds and geared toward supporting a greater variety of complex tasks. The point is not to exacerbate the problem of illiteracy; the point is to solve workforce problems by ensuring that even less literate workers can do their jobs, given an environment over which businesses have no control: workforce shortages combined with growing illiteracy.

SYSTEMS DESIGN RESISTANCE

Design barriers are, in one sense, a sort of "habit barrier" as well—but this time, they represent the habits of information systems designers. Here are just a few of those habits:

- The "here's the data, now you know what to do with it" habit: I'm a designer; let the training people take care of the workers who can't figure out this great system I designed.
- The "data retrieval is expensive" habit: pack as much information on a single screen as you can. Sure it's hard to read and cumbersome to work with, but the user is just going to have to get used to it.
- The "react when you have to" habit: we can't possibly anticipate everything; if it doesn't work, we'll fix it in the next maintenance cycle.
- The "one size fits all" habit: one public school system in the eastern United States found that the information system it had developed was appropriate for some school districts in the state, but not for others. Because the smaller districts were most in need of the new system, designers with the best of intentions had assessed the information needs of these smaller districts when building the system. But when the resulting system was then man-

dated for the entire state, the larger districts found their needs over-whelming the system. Ultimately, several districts were forced to imple-ment something totally different to give them the capabilities and functions they required.

Integrated Performance Support represents a breakthrough for systems de-signers precisely because it draws from many disciplines, systems design be-ing only one of them. As we noted in Chapter 2, performance systems draw their power from leading-edge research in such areas as instructional design, cognitive sciences, computer-supported cooperative work, and artificial intel-ligence. In our own experience, we see systems work energized by cross-func-tional development teams, drawing expertise not only from the technologists, but from professionals trained in change management and in a wide variety of other skills.

For each of the kinds of resistance to information technology we have just mentioned, the answer is the same: a system that supports—indeed, facili-tates—performance by centering itself on the needs of real workers. We do not focus on some composite profile of the average worker; rather, we antic-ipate the range of backgrounds, education, abilities, and needs of all workers and create a system that will adapt to these different profiles. We put the work-ers in the driver's seat: we give them the capability to choose the manner in which they will interact with the system. The system can adapt continuously to support their needs as these needs change.

HUMAN-COMPUTER INTERACTION, PART I: THE INTERACTION OF SUPPORT SERVICES

We have already noted that the idea of system design that is centered around the system user has been around for some time. User-centered design em-phasized the needs of the system user, above the needs of the system. Donald Norman lists four important facets of user-centered design:

- Make it easy for the user to know which actions are possible at any moment.
- Make visible to the user such things as the entire conceptual model of the system, the alternative actions, and the results of actions.
- Make it easy to evaluate the current state of the system.
- Make natural to the user the manner in which intentions are linked to re-quired actions, as well as the link between actions and results, and between the visible information and the interpretation of the state of the system.

In short, simply make sure that users can figure out what to do, and that they can also track easily what is going on at any given moment.[16]

As we have said, our change to the phrase "performance-centered" design bespeaks an important new emphasis on the *worker at work.* A performance system is oriented toward *doing*—toward, if you will, the human in movement rather than the human at rest or in some existential state. Norman writes elsewhere about the need to keep technology subservient to the goals of the person using the computer. "In the future," he writes, "I want less emphasis on 'interfaces,' and more on appropriate tools for the task. More on user-centered design. Less emphasis on technology; more on people, and groups, and social interactions. And tasks."[17]

Exactly right. *But:* if we are truly after performance-centered design and not just user-centered design, we must add to Norman's list above several additional points:

- Make sure that the system can identify the person using it, and that it can adapt itself to the unique needs and goals of that person.
- Make sure that the system can identify the work to be performed by this person, and that the person can alter the basic work profile in response to changing conditions.
- Make support services—advice, tools, reference, training—available whenever the person needs it, and deliver it right there, at the point of need.
- More important, make the system anticipate the performance needs of the worker by offering proactive advice and assistance.
- In general, make available to workers everything they need to *perform*—to accomplish their tasks to completion with excellence—and if they don't know it's available, tell them so.

With these points, we move beyond the limitations of a passive information system, waiting for the user to initiate; instead, we achieve a true performance system—one that is proactive rather than reactive. Here, then, we have the first perspective—one often overlooked—of what defines "human-computer interaction." In the context of the performance-centered workplace, this interaction is the *interaction of the support services of the system,* so that support is provided to the worker seamlessly. A worker is never aware that one particular service is providing support; support is not separate from the system but integrated within every application. With a system designed to deliver seamless support to meet the performance needs of the person at the workstation, worker and system interact properly—which means simply that they work together to get the job done.

HUMAN-COMPUTER INTERACTION, PART II: PERFORMANCE-CENTERED DESIGN

The human brain is built to make sense of things. With just a little bit of help it can explain, reason, and understand.[18] But we are confronted every day by objects that seem to defy and mock that natural sense-making ability. All of us have examples of things—usually electronic things—that make us despair of ever using them adequately or efficiently: VCRs, microwaves, watches, stoves, washing machines, phone systems. Anyone who spends any time with different types of rental cars knows the frustration of trying to figure out how to get a station on the car radio without causing a major highway accident.

"Well-designed objects," writes Donald Norman, "are easy to interpret and understand. They contain visible clues to their operation. Poorly designed objects can be difficult and frustrating to use. They provide no clues—or sometimes false clues."[19] Nowhere is this basic design problem more apparent than in the contemporary computer and the traditional ways we interact with it. We could find some examples of inadequate design even with the rather sophisticated word processing software we are writing with at this very moment. This may seem a mundane example, but it is something many of us are familiar with. Consider what must happen, for example, to get a fairly simple and often-used character: a dash. Typists are used to typing two hyphens (--) for a dash, but we're more sophisticated desktoppers these days, and we know that we should be able to get a solid character (—). There is no character on the keyboard for it, so the software has to take care of it for us. But how do we find out how? Well, let's select the "Help" feature of the software. We could look it up in the manual, but that's what we're trying to help people avoid, right?

Here's the answer. Make sure Number Lock is on; hold down the ALT key and, on the keyboard's number pad, type 0151. At first we don't believe that information (sometimes computer software recognizes the regular numbers the same way as the number pad), so we hold down ALT, followed by the numbers across the top of the keyboard. The computer beeps at us: wrong, buster! Okay, we look for Number Lock. There it is, but with this brand of laptop computer we have to hold the function key down while pressing that button. At the bottom of the screen, the word "NUM" appears: apparently we've been successful. (That's good design: always let the person know when an action at the system has been successful.) Then, again because of this brand of laptop, the keys have to double up for us. M is the "0," J is "1" and so forth. We hold down ALT and begin to type; but the "I" key, which doubles as the "5" key, looks like a 1 on this keyboard, so we accidentally type the wrong number. We back up, type 0151, and the dash appears:—. Then, when we continue to type, we get th5s k5nd of sentence, beca4se we've f6rg6tten to deact5vate the NUM key. Even discounting the normal kinds of mistakes first-time users of systems make, we count seven keystrokes to make a single character.

How could this same simple function be achieved from the perspective of performance-centered design? As an experiment, we asked several friends and colleagues to think of a better way. Most of them simply pointed out to us that we could set up a macro on the very software we are using. (That is, word processing software has some miniprograms, or macros, that will permit you to set up a complex function and then access it with only a couple of keystrokes.) But we wanted something more. Only one person came up with what we felt to be a better solution: the software could easily have been written to recognize two hyphens next to each other and automatically convert those two hyphens into a dash.

This sounds simple, but the solution has built into it the basics of performance-centered design: the solution built on something that the average typist already knows—two hyphens make a dash—and solved the performance problem in an intuitive way.

HUMAN-COMPUTER INTERACTION, PART III: THE INTERFACE

We come finally to the most obvious facet of human-computer interaction: the primary interface of the system. To a worker at a computer workstation, the interface may be the most important part of a system; indeed, to most workers, the interface *is* the system. When the computer gets turned on, and the first screen appears, it tells the worker—or, more accurately, it *should* tell the worker—all the basics of the system: how to communicate with the system, what the worker should be able to do at the system, and how to reach optimum productivity while working with the system. At a higher level, the interface should give workers an accurate picture of the work for which they are responsible.

COMMUNICATING WITH THE SYSTEM: SYSTEM "METAPHORS," "SIGNS," AND "SYMBOLS"

We have noted that an unintended consequence of traditional systems design has been to alter the natural manner in which people do their work. One of the important reasons for this alteration is that the basic interaction—the manner in which a worker communicates with the computer—is generally unnatural. What is a "natural" interaction with a computer? Increasingly, the answer to this question will be: one where we hardly notice that interaction is happening at all. Our colleague Hugh Ryan writes that to be acceptable to people, computing has to be transparent. "To the extent a computer is noticeable," he writes, "it is objectionable."[20] And if human-computer interaction is to be unnoticeable, it must increasingly pattern itself after the way real humans interact with each other. This, says Ryan, is a new metaphor for such interaction: the "human metaphor." The model for successful computing is the human; thus, one implication of the human metaphor is that "if you want to foresee the shape of computing at the end of the decade, you need only look at the person next to you."[21]

One could easily misunderstand the human metaphor, however. The point is not to make the computer into a human being, or to imagine that a human being is living inside your piece of hardware. The point, rather, is that the computer becomes an extension of our human capabilities; human and machine enter into a symbiotic relationship in order to perform work more powerfully. This is, after all, how we use other sorts of tools all the time. Say we want to pound a nail into a board. Our own natural human resources (at least for those of us who do not know karate) are incapable of such a task, so we grab a hammer. And no one has to teach us the functions of a hammer. It clearly is to be grasped a certain way and used for a particular purpose. Its use is entirely natural to us. Alas, workers and their performance have often been hampered by designs that seem deliberately *un*natural.

Metaphor has become the word of choice for describing how the computer interface communicates with the worker, and vice versa. Why has this word escaped from college literature courses and entered the realm of systems design? To understand, we have to step back and think about the way humans communicate with each other, and the way we think about our world. Humans communicate through the exchange of signs and symbols—representations, things that stand for something else. Certain groupings of sounds come to stand for words that are signs for the real thing; certain groupings of markings come to stand for those sounds. "Semiotics" is the science that studies such things, and "visual semiotics" is the study of visual signs. Signs and symbols in the graphics of a system interface create expectations on the part of workers using that system. It is essential that there be a good match between the expectations created and the functions offered. It is also vital that the signs communicate quickly and effectively. (See the sidebar, "Icons and Actions," for an exercise to see how effective certain signs or icons are.)

THE CENTRAL METAPHOR

Communication between human beings is filled with metaphorical references. "The way we think, what we experience, and what we do every day is very much a matter of metaphor," two linguists write in their book *Metaphors We Live By.*[22] Consider the manner in which we think of arguments as a kind of "war": "Arguments have *sides* that can be *defended* and *attacked.* Facts can be *marshaled* to support one's *position; strategies* can be employed. If a position is *indefensible,* one can *retreat* from it. Arguments can have *weak* points— they can even be *destroyed;* arguments can be right on *target;* arguments can be *shot down.* "[23] Speech built upon metaphors is the rule, not the exception.

As with speech, so with our visual world. Metaphors function as common and natural models, which allow us to extend our familiarity with concrete objects and experiences to the level of abstract concepts.[24] The central metaphor of the system interface is the most crucial one for systems designers, one that must be selected with particular attention to the performance-centered perspective of which we have spoken.

The most common central metaphor now in use in graphical user interfaces is the "desktop" metaphor. According to this metaphor, the basic visual of the system application symbolizes the desk of the system user. Icons on the screen stand for items commonly found on the user's desk.

Some designers have overestimated the usefulness of this metaphor, at least as it has been most commonly applied. A user coming to these screens for the first time must usually be told that he or she is seeing a verisimilitude of his desk—it is not intuitively clear. One important reason for this is that the primary interface lacks *dimensionality.* The interface is two-dimensional and thus does not immediately present itself as a representation of the worker's three-dimensional world.

Far more effective here are the three-dimensional interfaces that take the "desktop" metaphor seriously. (See, for example, the sidebar on page 111 about an insurance industry prototype.) The effectiveness of these interfaces stems from two basic principles:

1. The interface gives the worker a better picture of the work to be performed.
2. The interface suggests intuitively the manner in which the worker is to navigate through the system.

Also important here is the fact that the interface is tailorable to the preferences and the level of expertise of the person at the workstation. Such things as color

An Interface Using a Desktop Metaphor

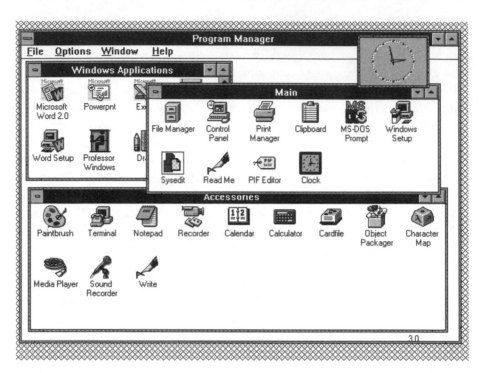

and placement of icons are at the discretion of the worker. Experts or so-called power users can elect to zoom in, past the graphic of the desktop, if they have reached a level of competence where the interface is impeding their productivity rather than enhancing it.

System designers should be cautioned against assuming that they are limited to the desktop metaphor. New user interface technologies such as bit-mapped displays and multimedia have turned the computer into a chameleon that can emulate virtually any information-rich object in the real world. The computer interface can closely emulate a magazine, airplane cockpit, classroom, social situation, shopping mall, or countless other artifacts with which humans are readily familiar. The computer has become a "metaphor machine." By building interfaces around metaphors of everyday objects, system designers use the plumbing that humans already have in their heads to virtually eliminate training requirements. For example, an electronic home shopping system built around a three-dimensional model or a shopping mall (see Chapter 9) is immediately usable by the majority of the population who know how to nav-

ICONS AND ACTIONS

Andersen Consulting's TIS-Scandinavia office has published a booklet entitled *The GUI Guide: Minimizing the Risk of the Graphical User Interface.* In their discussion, the authors note that icons and other pictures are often used in graphical user interfaces for several reasons:

- Two icons are usually more different and thus easier to distinguish from one another than two words.
- Icons and pictures can carry more information in less space than words.
- Pictures make metaphors visible.
- If a worker is only partially familiar with a system application, icons help him or her remember functions and select them quickly and accurately.

Icons are not meant to be self-explanatory all the time, though there must be a good match between sign/symbol and the function it represents. As a test, look at the icons below, and see if you can determine what actions within a word processing program they are intended to represent. See the next page for one set of possible answers.

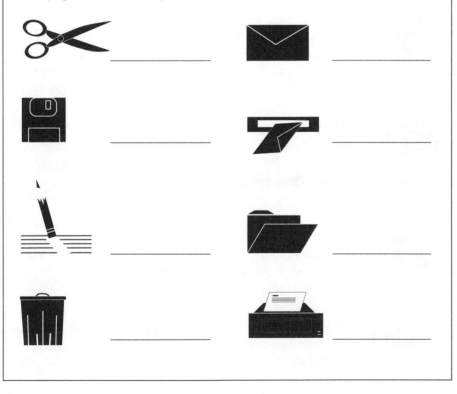

Icons and Actions

 Cut. Clear and straightforward. The scissors are open, connoting that an action is taking place.

 Save File. Not quite as clear. Can you save only to a diskette, or also to a drive? Might the icon be confused with the action of formatting a diskette? The icon is partially familiar, however; the match between icon and action must be learned, but is not counterintuitive.

 Erase. A good icon. Often, as some studies have suggested, an icon that includes both an object and an action will be more successful than one with only the object. (That is why the diskette icon is unclear.) But icons with three elements (if a hand, say, was holding the pencil) have been shown to be less successful.

 Throw Away. A clear icon. But is this action reversible? What if someone throws something away and later wants to retrieve it? With one software package, the waste basket bulges to show you have thrown a file away. But emptying the basket requires another action. Reversibility is a crucial feature of good interface design.

 Format an Envelope. Again, the object is clear, but the action unclear. Print an envelope? Send mail? Check mail?

 Send Mail. Object plus action works well here.

 Open File. Could easily be made more clear by adding a small arrow, indicating that an opening action is taking place. Without the arrow, the icon could also mean create a file.

 Send File to Printer. By having a piece of paper coming from the printer, the action is made more clear. Without it, there are any number of actions relating to a printer that this icon could represent.

___ INTEGRATED PERFORMANCE SUPPORT FOR THE INSURANCE INDUSTRY ___

We have noted that Knowledge Worker Services and Work Profile Services are the key facilities that enable a performance system to provide proactive, rather than reactive, support. One interesting prototype performance system that demonstrates this capability well was developed as a proof-of-concept system for a major insurance company. The system supports insurance underwriters as they analyze policies submitted by agents and determine whether to approve them. In the following brief description of this prototype, note how the system advises the underwriter, and lets him or her know of available support, without being intrusive or overly controlling.

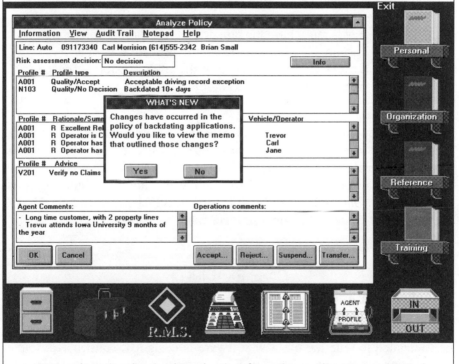

The underwriter begins by selecting from the work queue a particular policy for analysis. Immediately, the performance system provides the underwriter with a warning. Based on the worker's profile, he or she may not be aware of recent changes to company policy about backdating applications. Going on, the worker is later prompted about a possible Resident Student Discount for this family. One of the children has matched certain

---

INTEGRATED PERFORMANCE SUPPORT FOR THE INSURANCE
INDUSTRY (*CONTINUED*)

criteria embedded within the system for this discount, but the underwriter must first provide the name of the university so the system can calculate the distance from the school to the student's home. In this case, because the student qualifies, the policy and premium will be adjusted to account for the discount.

The underwriter accepts this policy and the system then reminds the worker that this customer has been doing business with the company for quite some time. The underwriter then has the ability to go directly into a word processing application to send a personalized letter to the customer. With the hectic pace of today's business environment, insurance under-writers and agents rarely have the time to notify customers of good news like a rate reduction, or to simply send a letter of thanks. The performance system in this case supports the worker in this crucial customer service ac-tivity with a minimum of time involvement.

---

igate a real shopping mall. With a well-executed metaphor, workers don't have to learn new concepts; they simply make use of concepts they already know. The ultimate realization of the human metaphor is a portfolio of systems pop-ulated by metaphorical versions of useful objects with which humans are al-ready familiar. One of the many useful metaphors that go beyond the desktop is the agent or guide metaphor described in the next section.

CASE EXAMPLE:
EAGLE TECHNOLOGY ADVANCED DEVELOPMENT

Eagle Technology Advanced Development is an Andersen Consulting initia-tive intended to redefine the way software is designed, constructed, imple-mented, and maintained. In addition, Eagle is seeking ways to embed principles such as usability, tailorability, and global applicability into packaged or cus-tom solutions. Having successfully built proof-of-concept models, Eagle is now working with other Andersen Consulting groups to bring processes, tools, and techniques to our practice and clients as quickly as practical.

Integrated Performance Support plays a crucial role in the overall goals of Eagle Technology. One of the most visible features of prototypes that have come out of the Eagle initiative thus far is *advanced usability.* Great care has been taken to depict information in the workers' natural, visual language. These systems use meaningful icons to portray objects or concepts: for example, graphical card files help organize the large amount of information that users need to review. The prototypes also allow users to access information in its most appropriate form—text, audio, video, or graphics—and enable users to move from task to task by seamlessly launching concurrent applications.

Eagle Technology places a strong emphasis on the human-computer interaction features of performance systems. One of the innovative features being explored is the presence of "guides." The guides metaphor first emerged from the Advanced Technology group of Apple Computer, Inc., as an interface metaphor for educational software. With certain educational applications, researchers found themselves naturally tending toward a narrative-like presentation of information. Because of this, they began looking at the use of characters and of human figures to suggest a story-like structure. This would get the person involved in searching for relationships among the various pieces of information.[25] The human figures "guide" the person through the material—in a similar way that a tour guide might take visitors through the Louvre or through the U.S. Capitol building—providing additional information if they have it, whenever the person requests it. One of the benefits first noted from the use of guides is that the person in a learning situation is not overwhelmed with the entire cognitive map of the application. This can become important in the design of interfaces that can be tailored to the ability levels of learners. Beginners, for example, could make frequent use of guides; experts would not need them.

As adapted by the Eagle Technology team, the guides signify the different kinds of interaction—which imply different kinds of interaction "protocols"—that can take place within the system. This concept builds upon our natural understandings of the different ways we interact with people in our daily lives. Suppose that you want some help from someone at your office to help you use your computer software. You would expect that your interaction with that source of information would be different from your interaction with a reference or technical librarian, or with your boss. Within Eagle Technology, software support is provided through a slightly different avenue than, say, librarian support, and the guide is a mental cue to help crystallize this dissociation in the mind of the worker. A different guide represents a different kind of interaction; the choice of a particular guide by the designers is intended to induce the natural categories—the inherent mental models—that already exist in the mind of the worker.

The concept of "natural categories" was made popular by noted psychologist Eleanor Rosch in the 1970s. The phrase refers to the fact that there is a natural level of categorization for all things that people commonly interact with. For example, people are much more likely to categorize an armchair at the basic level of "chair" than at the level of "furniture." Guides help the worker by bringing to mind the appropriate natural categories. This in turn causes what psychologists refer to as "priming." Building on the software versus librarian example just discussed, when we think of software, we think in terms of such things as commands, operations, and files. When we interact with a librarian, we think in terms of things like authors, subjects, and titles. By using guides as the first line of interaction, the person is "primed" to think in terms of the natural categories that that guide brings to mind. This helps to make the navigation through the information more intuitive.

The six guides are "anthropomorphic"—that is, human-like—but are much more than cartoon figures that change expressions. Each figure is a "performance support avenue": the figure provides the metaphor that becomes the

GUIDES IN THE EAGLE TECHNOLOGY PROTOTYPE

starting point for the definition of the interaction protocol between the performance system and a knowledge worker. In a supportive application, much more information must pass between the system and the worker than in traditional, transaction-based systems. The increased amount of information is the support that will allow workers to perform their jobs optimally. The guides within Eagle Technology provide the following functions:

- The Software Guide provides the worker with help related to the system and the application software.
- The Task Guide gives the worker task-specific advice.
- The Domain Guide also provides task-specific advice, but it does so at a more theoretical level.
- The Librarian Guide maintains all the references that pertain to the worker's job, such as on-line manuals, related articles, and wire-feeds from news networks.
- The Historian Guide maintains historical data such as previous purchases, interpretation of company policies, and trends. Whereas the Librarian uses internal and external information sources, the Historian provides internal historical company/policy-related information.
- The Work-Queue Guide manages a worker's tasks and manages all communication such as electronic, voice, and video mail systems.

One of the difficulties frequently encountered in designing support services for system applications is how to provide active support for a worker without being intrusive. In this respect, interaction with a computer is no different from interaction with a human. Imagine yourself making a presentation at a meeting. The first time that a colleague interrupts to make a suggestion you might welcome it. The second time would be less welcome. And beyond that, the collegial relationship itself might be put at risk.

So how do you actively support a worker without being intrusive? The answer for Eagle Technology is to provide, not just support, but a *supportive environment*. An application that has support isn't enough; workers need a *supportive application*. The Eagle Technology guides are one manifestation of this concept. They are active, but unobtrusive. The guides have several basic "states" of support, each represented by a slightly different version of the basic cartoon figure. When the guide has no support to provide at the moment, it looks away from the worker, or "sleeps." When the guide has information that *might* help, it looks alert and ready to respond. The worker need not stop and seek that information at that point; here, too, the performance-centered perspective realizes that not every work context is amenable to interruption. When the person has time, he or she selects (clicks on) that guide, and the relevant information is presented. However, when the guide has information that is vital to the performance of a task, it signals an alarm, telling the worker that he or she had better ask the guide for some support.

GUIDES AND AGENTS

Guides provide a natural transition to what is referred to as an "agent." An interface agent is a character in a computer-based environment, visually represented as a drawing or as a photo of a human-like character, which is able to perform actions on behalf of the worker. Agents can perform a variety of tasks: they can schedule, or conduct customized information searches.[26] In performance systems, these agents provide more sophisticated skills, such as providing advice and monitoring the performance of a worker and suggesting ways to work better. You have already seen one version of an agent in the Total Information Management prototype discussed in Chapter 3. "TIM" can monitor, suggest, and advise in a proactive manner.

At their best, agents should act as a primary *guide,* aiding workers in the performance of their work by facilitating the interaction with the computer system and with the outside world. But organizations must attend to the dangers of this metaphor. It would be misguided for workers to personify their computers, to conceive of their workstations as human beings. As we have said, this is a misunderstanding of the human metaphor. A guide or agent should act as another resource—just as a worker would turn to a colleague or supervisor, or to an outside expert. Again, the focus must be on human performance, and thus on making the technology work *with* the person to accomplish the performance objective.

CASE EXAMPLE:
AUTOMATED REFINERY INFORMATION SYSTEM (ARISE)

The Automated Refinery Information System, or ARISE, is a pilot system integrated by Andersen Consulting for a major refinery and chemical company. The pilot system was developed partly on site at a refinery, and engineers and other subject experts from the company assisted with several aspects of the system design. The goal of system designers in this case was to demonstrate the power of Integrated Performance Support within the process industry, and then to develop a system that could be modified to be effective in other types of environments, including the utilities industry.

ARISE was designed to provide all types of refinery employees with universal access to many types of data: documents, spreadsheets, real-time process control data, maintenance information, procurement status, process design, and so forth. The system assists process refinery engineers and operators to gather and analyze data; it also assists maintenance workers in performing routine maintenance, troubleshooting, and system repairs. The functionality of ARISE, as well as its primary visual metaphor, was refined through a series of iterative, application design focus group meetings with representatives from all workers in the refinery: process engineers, operators, maintenance workers, and plant managers. This method of piloting the design not only encouraged design contributions from the workers, but showed the workers how information was used throughout the plant, beyond the walls of their department.

If you have ever been to a refinery, you know that it is an extremely complicated working environment. Equipment is complex: distillation columns, furnaces, pumps, extensive networks of piping. Products move through the system continuously, undergoing processes that are potentially dangerous. Constant monitoring must take place of such things as temperature, flow rates, pressure, and vibration. Plant operators at the refinery are responsible for ensuring that the entire process is working properly. Refinery engineers monitor the efficiency of the processes and are responsible for redesigning processes when necessary. Maintenance workers ensure that the equipment is sound at all times. Each type of refinery worker has unique performance challenges.

Performance, we have said, links the higher-level objectives of a company with the specific performance objectives of its workers. The challenges to performance at both these levels is particularly evident in the process industry. These organizations are challenged to comply with the Clean Air Act, ISO 9000, API 1910, and other regulations governing hazardous processes and materials. Safety is the primary concern, not only for the management and workers in the plant, but for the surrounding communities as well.

What are the specific performance problems faced by a refinery worker? Existing information systems often create significant inhibitors that prevent workers from effectively carrying out their job responsibilities. These inefficiencies include:

- Cumbersome process control systems used for monitoring and adjusting the refining process.

- Laborious processes for retrieving data from a myriad of legacy computer systems and analyzing data in an appropriate tool (a spreadsheet, graph, and so forth).
- Excessive amounts of time spent gathering, validating, and organizing information dispersed throughout the organization.

In short, process engineers felt that they knew how to do their jobs well, but were constrained by inefficient ways of getting at basic information about the current state of the refining process. Early in the integration project, team members accompanied a process engineer during a typical workday, noting the kinds of information used, how that information was organized, how it was validated before use, and how easily the engineer's steps could be repeated. The project team discovered that the engineers spent over 75% of their time tracking down the latest version of documents, requesting that the IS organization download data from a legacy system into a spreadsheet, and manually keying the data from one system to another. The significant impact of ARISE is in its ability to provide workers with immediate access to many sources of plant information such as current and historical process instrumentation measurements, lab analysis, maintenance scheduling and status, CAD drawings, process flow diagrams, safety documents, and financial operating data for the unit. By automating the arduous tasks of gathering data, the engineer was able to focus on analyzing the data in the appropriate tools, capitalizing knowledge by organizing documents in a secure document vault, and building new types of information in the form of documents with dynamic links to legacy data.

This performance system supports the process industry's business objectives and commitment to safety, environment, and profitability. ARISE supports these priorities by:

- Increasing safety awareness and availability of safety information.
- Increasing environmental awareness by providing feedback on how output compares to environmental regulation.
- Increasing productivity by providing workers with job performance support on demand and at the point of need.
- Organizing, storing, sharing, and capitalizing on data in a document vault.
- Providing a repeatable, auditable trail of data gathered for a particular business or technical initiative.

During the refining process a number of measurements are taken at critical points to provide the refinery engineers with the data required to adjust processes and to plan for future modifications. Temperature, pressure, flow rate, torque, power consumption, vibration, and chemical composition are some common measurements. This performance system supports the critical actions of the refinery workers, ensuring that there is:

- Intelligent monitoring to warn of possible problems and to identify errors and omissions.
- Reference and decision support on environmental and governmental regulations.
- Worker-specific training and decision support on job activities such as equipment troubleshooting and repair.
- Immediate access to safety information relevant to specific processes and tasks.
- Integrated tool sets, including spreadsheet packages, to help the worker analyze information more efficiently and to perform job tasks more productively.

A REFINERY ENGINEER'S INTERFACE, BASED ON A PROCESS FLOW DIAGRAM

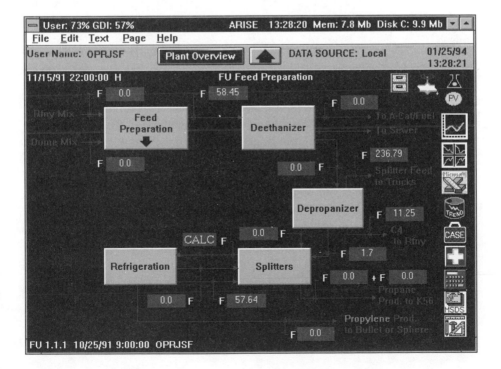

The visual metaphors for this system are particularly interesting. The worker begins with a high-altitude view of the entire plant. The engineer we will follow, in this example works in the Fractionation Unit of the plant, so by selecting, or zooming down to, that part of the diagram, the worker then gets a detailed schematic of that unit of the plant. To those of us who are not process engineers, this screen looks somewhat complex. In fact, however, it is a process flow diagram, just as the engineer thinks about it. Far from being cumbersome or complex, the interface has engendered considerable excitement from engineers who have worked with ARISE, because they are able to gather information and monitor the refinery exactly as they visualize it. This is an important point about the interface of a performance system: the goal is not necessarily to make the interface natural and intuitive to *anyone* looking at the screen for the first time. In many cases, the goal is to make the interaction and interface natural, based upon the capabilities and performance needs of a particular class of worker. It is, however, advantageous to choose a visual metaphor that many different kinds of workers can relate to. Unlike traditional systems, graphically oriented systems tend to require greater design effort on the presentation of the data than on the storage of the data. If the visual metaphor is designed to serve many different types of users, the presentation layer of the system can be extended and reused, thus reducing the overall system cost and simplifying the training of workers.

To the right of the screen are a number of icons representing job aids available to the worker, including several third-party software tools that support the analysis of data. The use of these existing tools was an intended aspect of system development. There is not necessarily a need to recreate software in a performance system; the added value of performance-centered design is to integrate these existing tools to support worker performance, and to make these tools work seamlessly, so that the worker never even notices the shift in software applications. This integration is powerfully accomplished in ARISE.

For example: the engineer selects several data points from the diagram and then exports the data into Microsoft Excel™ by clicking on the Excel icon on the right of the screen. The application wizards will then walk the worker through the graph preparation, asking for the time range and for the graph's title. Without the aid of the performance system, finding the relevant process data, generating the necessary reports, and preparing a graph previously required participation from three different people and manual data entry taking four to five hours. Now it can be done in a matter of seconds.

ARISE is equally powerful in its support of maintenance workers at the refinery. Here, the basic visual metaphor of the system is tailored to the performance needs of a maintenance worker. For example, ARISE maintains constant monitoring of the refinery, looking for exceptions in normal operating conditions. When an exception occurs, the system notifies the worker by giving a warning sound and by flashing on the computer screen that component which is problematic. By clicking on the warning sign, the operator receives useful information about the gauge, including the out-of-range reading, the expected readings, and possible actions to be taken. The system will suggest likely causes of the problem, help the worker determine the exact cause, and then even give the worker an estimate of the labor involved, a list of required parts and their location, and any relevant safety information involved with the repair.

In another example, a plant operator is blending a tank of gasoline. However, a lab sample run on an intermediary blend indicates that the blend does not match the specifications. The operator questions what should be done and prompts the system for help. The system provides a decision tree that guides the operator through the decision process. The decision tree specifies conditions and the corresponding corrective actions. For example, if the sample indicates low volatility or a high octane level, the decision tree indicates which component should be added to alter the blend.

ARISE ensures compliance with safety regulations through the Reference Services and Advisory Services capabilities of the performance system. For example, take a plant operator about to shut down a tank. Before it can be shut down, certain procedures must be followed on the system. When the system recognizes that the operator is performing a shutdown, it intervenes and presents a list of mandatory safety precautions. The operator must check off each item before continuing with the shutdown procedure. This is a good example of the proactive capabilities of a true performance system.

In this example of a performance system, note that the interface really *is* the information system for the refinery worker. Most services of the performance system are accessible, or prompt the worker, from the central interface—the logical view of the refinery. From the basic interface, the worker can access context-sensitive help and context-sensitive reference about aspects of the refinery. For example, a plant operator monitoring a pump on the system determines that the readings for the pump are out of range. The operator decides it would be useful to examine the maintenance history for the pump. By clicking on that particular pump and then switching to support mode, the operator can access any available reference, including maintenance history.

Also available for the refinery worker is context-sensitive training—that is, small units or granules of training specifically designed to support the performance of the relevant task. (This approach to training, inherent within Integrated Performance Support, is discussed in more detail in Chapter 7.) For example, a maintenance worker has been assigned to perform a maintenance procedure. Although he received initial instruction about the procedure, the maintenance training has been updated to reflect manufacturers' changes, mandated safety requirements, and plant-specific changes. From the primary interface, the worker clicks on the particular piece of equipment and then accesses training within ARISE from the same workstation, rather than hunting down the sometimes checked-out and often out-of-date paper-based training materials. He then is presented with that piece of training, including auditory learning cues, actual video, or photo-CD images. After taking a self-check, the worker proceeds to do the particular procedure. Training within ARISE is particularly important due to OSHA requirements for training and certification of refinery workers. Insurance companies are particularly impressed with the system's ability to present sight and sound experiences before placing the worker in a hazardous (and often costly) actual work environment. As the worker completes training, the training date, score, and version are recorded in the human resources system. This will assist plant management in demonstrating employee competence to investigators and inspectors.

We began this chapter by saying that information technology has often faced resistance from workers when their unique performance needs have not been taken into account. This is certainly true in the process industry, where legacy mainframe systems and restrictive software designs have prevented employees like these refinery maintenance workers and process engineers from getting access to timely and relevant performance support. ARISE is an excellent example of human-centered technology: a performance system that visualizes what the worker visualizes. ARISE gives workers the ability to access, analyze, organize, store, and share information through a familiar, meaningful navigation metaphor.

CHAPTER 5

SATISFYING THE CUSTOMER

The main character and narrator of Fyodor Dostoevsky's short novel *Notes from Underground* begins his story by speaking of his background as a petty Russian bureaucrat: "I was a nasty official. I was rude and enjoyed being rude. Why, since I took no bribes, I had to make up for it somehow. . . . When petitioners came up to my desk for information, I snarled at them and felt indescribably happy whenever I managed to make one of them feel miserable. Being petitioners, they were a meek lot. One, however, wasn't. He was an officer, and I had a special loathing for him. He just wouldn't be subdued. He had a special way of letting his saber rattle. Disgusting. For eighteen months I waged war with him about that saber. I won out in the end, and he stopped the thing from rattling."[1]

Why does this nineteenth century description of customer service within a Russian civil service bureaucracy sound so frighteningly contemporary? For many years, organizations have been able to get by with less than adequate service to customers. Because of industry monopolies, and because of the dominance of certain companies in many other industries, organizations didn't need to make customers a priority. Where else were they going to go? Well, they've got a lot of places to go now—anywhere in the world. It's the rare organization today that doesn't feel the heat of a competitor touting an edge in its ability to serve customers. And it's a rarer organization that is not aggressively developing programs to serve customers better and more efficiently.

Organizations can talk all they want about their commitment to quality, to service, to making the customer the center of their work. But unless they can give their workers, at any moment of the day, the resources they need to be *able* to satisfy the customer, the quality commitment will never move beyond words in a brochure, a credo, or a vision statement. Customer service is more than just talk. In this chapter, we will outline some of the ways in which performance systems can revolutionize the workplace by making an organization's knowledge capital, product and service information, and best practices available to all employees whenever they need it, so they can serve customers effectively. When workers are empowered to serve the customer, a number of things follow: worker productivity and job satisfaction increase, customers are retained, and the organization as a whole is more successful.

_____ KEY MESSAGES: CHAPTER 5 _____

- Good customer service today means *exceeding* customer expectations. It means nothing less than delighting the customer.
- Customer good will is a crucial intellectual asset of a company, and organizations must see each customer as a lifetime asset, not just someone making a transaction on one particular day.
- Among the challenges to meeting today's customer demands is the fact that workers often feel they do not have enough support—knowledge about products, services, company guidelines, and so forth—to deal with customers adequately.
- Several real performance systems supporting customer service representatives today are already bringing enormous benefits to their companies by speeding up processes, and by giving representatives immediate access to information and the support to know what to do with that information.

WHAT *IS* GOOD CUSTOMER SERVICE?

A customer is describing why he buys the same brand of luxury car year after year: "I had every intention this year of trying something different for a change. But then something happened a few weeks ago. The motor that drives the power antenna on the car went out on me. I happened to be driving by the dealership about twenty minutes before five one weekday, and stopped in, just to make an appointment to get the motor fixed. The service guy said, instead of coming back, why not wait a few minutes and see if they could fix it. Within thirty minutes I had a new antenna motor, the car was washed and vacuumed, and there was a box of chocolates waiting for me on the front seat. Guess what kind of car I'm buying next?"[2]

In the context of the experience of this satisfied customer, what is good customer service? We think it is *meeting and exceeding customer expectations*. Both parts of this definition are important. "Meeting" customer expectations is certainly the minimum requirement for organizations today. "Good customer service," one retail consultant says, "used to be politeness, friendliness. But today, with the lack of shopping time, good customer service is getting what you want when you want it."[3] But the "giving the customers what they want" mentality cannot be enough anymore to differentiate organizations in an economy where consumers have more choices than ever before. Customer service, as we have said, is "delighting" the customer—and that means *exceeding* their expectations whenever and wherever possible.

Consider a customer service representative for a telecommunications company at her workstation, using a system designed with Integrated Performance Support principles. Part of her job is to take incoming calls from customers. But this performance system has the facility to monitor the level of current incoming calls. Having determined that the load of incoming calls is low at this point in the day, the system prompts the representative with information about a customer: the particular calling package that the customer now has is not quite right, and they could save money on their monthly bill by switching to a different package. When the representative is ready, the system even places the call to the customer. Imagine what this conversation would sound like to the customer: "Hello, Mrs. Smith, we've been looking at your monthly bills and have discovered that you could save $12 a month by switching to a different calling package. Would you like some more information about this different service level?" *That* is exceeding customer expectations.

Why exceed expectations if you don't have to? Why go beyond expectations if it costs you money? Because the short-term investment generally pays off in the long run with repeat business. Consider one tailor who makes custom suits for a particular businessman. Toward the close of the sale, the customer's wife points out a beautiful tie that would go with one of the suits. "Here, take it with my compliments," says the tailor. Exceeding expectations may also prevent a customer from going elsewhere with business. A friend once told us the story of taking his car back to a quick oil change business to complain because the car had been leaking oil since the company worked on the car the day before. After a quick inspection, the manager returned to the customer: "We're sorry for this inconvenience, but you shouldn't have any more trouble now. At no charge to you we've installed a new kind of oil plug into your car, one that will make it easier for us to change your oil next time." In both these cases, exceeding the expectations of the consumer created a subtle but palpable feeling of *debt* on the part of the consumer—a debt to be repaid with return business. In the latter case, the company was able to retain a customer who might otherwise have been lost.

Organizations today are increasingly getting the message that customer goodwill is a crucial intellectual asset of a company. Customer goodwill may be one of the most important intangible assets of a company, and service failures thus become one of the most wasteful mistakes that organizations can make. The first step toward improved customer service is to take the long view of a customer's worth to an organization. One retailer, for example, considers each customer to be an investment: not just someone who may walk in and spend a hundred dollars in one day, but someone who may spend as much as $50,000 in a ten-year period.[4] This attitude toward customers is called "customer intimacy": the willingness to put increased time, effort, and money into building and maintaining a customer's loyalty, based upon the customer's *lifetime* value to the company.[5]

There are at least four primary challenges for organizations that want to reach a point where they are consistently exceeding the expectations of their customers:

- Keeping abreast of what customers expect and how the competition is attempting to meet and exceed those expectations.
- Getting enough reports back from *un*satisfied customers so organizations can learn about and correct the problem.
- Changing the outlook of all workers, from upper-level management on down, so that the customer is first on their list of priorities.
- Providing workers at all levels of the organization, particularly those dealing directly with customers, the support they need to serve the customer adequately.

WHAT DO CUSTOMERS EXPECT?

Who is a customer, and what does that customer expect? Increasingly, successful organizations are beginning to treat as *customers* all those people who are the object of services rendered. Within an organization, for example, the customers of the information services group are those workers who use the computer system. Whether internal or external to an organization, customers increasingly expect to be treated as individuals, with unique needs. They expect goods and services tailored to them, not to some abstract notion of a mass market; they expect a variety of products to choose from; they expect services to be rendered in a timely manner; and they expect convenience—they no longer assume that they must go to the business, but increasingly expect the business to come to them. In short, customers expect a lot more than they did in the days when Henry Ford is purported to have said that customers could have any color car they wanted, as long as it was black. Organizations can no longer think of an abstract category called "customer," or even a group of people called "customers." Now, there is only *this* customer, this one right here who expects the best from me and from my organization. If organizations don't meet or exceed the expectations of this customer, he or she will go somewhere else, to a competitor more willing to indulge that customer's personal tastes.[6] Customization extends even into manufacturing circles, where the notion of "Lot Size 1" describes the move away from standardized assemblies to customized lots. This has, of course, broad implications on the set-up process and on inventory management.

The lesson of the "customer's market" has been very hard to learn, particularly for companies that grew up in the post–World War II days when demand exceeded supply for most consumer goods. Producers had the upper hand, and customers simply took what they could get. The result was a move toward the lowest common denominator and a general drift toward mediocrity. If the industry was competitive, such mediocrity was quickly weeded out through loss of customers. But many organizations grew lazy because they knew customers had few other places to turn. And customers frequently lowered their expectations and stopped demanding better service. When this happened, there was no incentive to improve service quality. Because organizations set their standards by looking at their competitors, the result was a steady erosion of service throughout entire industries. Organizations and customers alike came to accept low standards without questioning them.[7]

The Pacific Rim changed all that in the 1970s and 1980s. When Japanese companies in particular entered the market with higher-quality goods at lower prices, and with high levels of service, those traditional companies mired in mediocrity could not compete. The standard of customer service has been raised and it cannot be lowered. Customers have been treated to caviar and they are unlikely to return willingly to crackers and cheese. Organizations that do not understand the new customer-buyer relationship won't have to worry for long: there won't be any customers left for them.

Information systems were supposed to meet the need to serve customers better by helping workers access the information they need to meet anything customers threw at them. But here again, most systems today do not have the flexibility, or the proactive nature, to help *this* worker deal with *this* customer, this one here on the phone or on the sales floor. Instead, the system is geared toward the generic customers that systems designers anticipated being out there; the system was designed to gather information to serve the company, not to provide support to service the customer. When the system cannot answer workers' questions, or prompt them to the appropriate resources, that customer may be lost forever.

HOW DOES AN ORGANIZATION FIND OUT WHEN ITS CUSTOMER SERVICE ISN'T MEASURING UP?

Here is an alarming statistic to companies wanting to reengineer their customer service processes: 96% of customers who abandon a company because of bad service never complain directly to the company.[8] Human psychology plays a crucial role here. In general, people shun unpleasant confrontations and would rather simply go somewhere else than confront a rude salesperson or an incompetent service representative. And if they are dissatisfied, and can quickly find a matching product or service from a competitor, why should they take the time to write a letter or make a phone call?

Some innovative means have been developed by companies to overcome this information vacuum. Chemical Bank in New York, for example, has given customers an economic incentive to let management know when service has been unsatisfactory. The bank instituted a policy that rewards customers for letting the bank know if they received bad service—if a teller was rude, for example, or if a customer service representative could not help them in a reasonable amount of time. For your constructive complaint, they would deposit $5 into your account.

Other companies have their senior management actually spend a certain number of hours per week dealing with customers themselves. Senior vice-presidents at Procter & Gamble, for example, have the goal of spending three hours a week answering their company's toll-free telephone number to answer questions and hear complaints personally. Other companies like Wal-Mart have management spend time at the stores, making personal contacts with customers. British Airways set up booths at Heathrow Airport where passengers could have their grievances videotaped to be reviewed later by managers.[9]

These efforts underscore the problem of measuring quality in a service-oriented business. Many readers will be familiar with the monthly movement of the Consumer Confidence Index, a leading economic indicator in the United States. The University of Michigan Business School has developed a methodology for compiling a National Quality Index and has piloted the program in Sweden. The program is led by B. Joseph White, dean of the Business School and a leading expert on quality. White believes that quality benchmarking will become a competitive tool in the global economy.

Nevertheless, there is an undeniably subjective dimension to the "quality" of service. Quality relies on such intangibles as convenience, timeliness, and rapport between server and customer. Because of this intangible quality, there is often a tendency to focus too much on related tangibles that end up being poor measures of customer service: things such as revenues generated, numbers of customers served, and costs of providing the service. We might call these measures "false quantifiers"—measurable performance indicators that are acceptable, but that do not yield true enhancements of service. False quantifiers can cause organizations to look good without actually being good.[10] They can also cause workers to be subjected to false standards, which leads them to be overworked and underappreciated because they are not given the support to perform their customer service roles adequately.

The primary goal of true performance systems is to support the worker during the relationship with a customer so that exceeding customer expectations can become a matter of course. But properly designed, these systems can also incorporate feedback for workers and management to track the satisfaction of customers. If key performance indicators were not met, the work profile and the support services for the position can be updated to minimize future instances of less than ideal performance.

HOW CAN ORGANIZATIONS MAKE CUSTOMER SERVICE THE PRIORITY FOR ALL EMPLOYEES?

It would be pleasant if customer service deficiencies could be solved merely by having senior management exercise their leadership to push a commitment to customer service down through the organization. Unfortunately, the problem of poor customer service is sometimes rooted *in* senior management. One study has found, for example, that executives are prone to rationalize customer expectations and excuse complaints, transforming these in their minds into other kinds of problems—problems which, of course, are out of their control or are someone else's responsibility. If turnaround is bad, it's because demand has been fluctuating; if there aren't enough workers to handle customers, it's because of vacation scheduling. There is a clear reluctance to look at these issues as *quality-productivity* issues that must be dealt with now, and then dealt with more comprehensively on a long-term basis.[11]

These rationalizations are similar to what Gloria Gery, writing on the subject of performance support systems, describes as the symptoms of organizational "denial"—the failure to face up to performance problems within an organization. The contributing strategies of denial, Gery writes, are:

- Selective perception
- Avoidance of information or circumstances depicting the problem
- Explaining data or problems away with a "yes, but . . ." response
- Deliberate dismissal of acceptable information
- Superficial review of information without appropriate diligence[12]

Satisfying customers will not come without: (1) a commitment by top management to the policy of exceeding customer expectations and (2) a commitment from the same top management to support their employees in their efforts to serve customers. The capability to exceed customer expectations must be developed systematically, beginning at the top of the organization. As Atok Ilhan, CEO of Philips Malaysia, recently stated in a presentation to government officials, management must "dirty the hands" if they expect their organizations to be effective in delivery services. But management, under time pressures and screened from customer contacts, often have difficulty getting a customer perspective. It is significant that companies known for exceptional customer service often have senior executives who maintain their own contacts with customers and mandate such contacts for all management. Bernard Marcus, CEO of Home Depot, is known as someone who will walk through stores and mingle with customers. "Every customer," says Marcus, "has to be treated like your mother, your father, your sister, or your brother."[13]

There are some cultural issues at work here, as well. If one compares, for example, American and Japanese firms, one can clearly see a different set of priorities for serving the various constituencies of any business. Profit-maximizing American firms will state that shareholders come first, with customers and employees following. Customers are important merely to the extent that they contribute to the goal of maximizing shareholder wealth. On the other hand, Japanese firms will reverse this order: employees are first, customers second, and shareholders third.[14]

The exceptions to these generalizations are instructive, because that is where we will find many of the most successful companies operating today. Wal-Mart is the most obvious example here. Sam Walton's philosophy came very close to the Japanese model just described. In his autobiography, for example, Walton wrote, "the way management treats the associates is exactly how the associates will then treat the customers. And if the associates treat the customers well, the customers will return again and again, and that is where the real profit in this business lies."[15]

Other retailers are not only following suit, but are creating training programs to instill a customer focus into their employees. At Target stores, for example, every new employee, from manager to stockperson, goes through a half-day program at Target University, a spinoff of Disney University. One Target store manager explains that Target's goal is to be "the Walt Disney of retailing"; accordingly, employees learn Disney's tenets that patrons are guests and employees are hosts. And, just as Disney taught his employees to think of themselves as "cast members," Target workers are taught to think of themselves as being "on stage" whenever they are at work. The result is not only better service, but more satisfied employees. Employee turnover has dropped to 40%—down from 180% turnover prior to the customer service training initiative.[16]

Or consider the case of one upscale retailer that has changed the job titles of its employees to reflect the fact that the only reason they have a job is to serve customers: cashiers are now "Customer Service Representatives: Cashier"; sales associates are now "Customer Service Representatives: Sales Floor." While critics and cynics might counter that these changes constitute mere semantic differences, they are actually a powerful way to instill a customer focus into workers—if, that is, the words are followed up with policies and rewards to reinforce the change.

But how does one teach good customer service? As we have said, good service results from innumerable intangibles. There is inevitably a *narrative* feel to explanations of good service. First this happened, and then I said this, and then this happened. As such, it really cannot be captured except in its primary form *as story*. Roger Schank, Director of the Institute for the Learning Sciences at Northwestern University, is perhaps the world's leading expert in "case-based" learning—on learning from previous relevant examples, especially narrative examples. His authoritative work, *Tell Me a Story,* focuses on the power of storytelling through the ages as a primary learning mechanism. Many of the innovative learning programs of the Institute for the Learning Sciences are described throughout this book.

The subject of customer service lends itself extremely well to story-based learning. There are no "rules" that will apply 100% of the time. Performance systems have the facility to capture this narrative dimension of customer service and to present it to workers in an innovative way. These stories in turn may do more than inform: they may inspire as well.

- "I must have spent close to an hour with this customer, showing him sample after sample of our carpeting. Everything was going extremely well, but he was unwilling at the end to take the plunge, saying he wanted to shop around a little more. Three weeks later, though, he was back in, asking for me by name, and I made a $2,500 sale. That time paid off in the end, but you have to remember to take the long view."

- "One busy Saturday morning a customer came up to me in the grocery store—she saw my manager's badge—angry because she was going to have to wait in a long line just to buy a bag of hot dog buns. 'This is a real busy morning, ma'am,' I said to her. 'But I'll tell you what. If you promise not to let anyone know I'm doing this, you give me the 65 cents plus tax for those hot dog buns, and I'll put them in a bag for you.' I must see that customer twice a week now, and every time she makes some joke to me about hot dog buns. The jokes may get stale, but not her repeat business."

One innovative feature of some performance systems that captures this storytelling mode of information sharing is the "Ask System," an example of which we have already seen in Chapter 3 in the description of the Total Information Management (TIM) prototype. Lenders at the TIM workstation are presented with a grouping of questions, organized onto file cards. By selecting (clicking on) a particular question—for example, "How do I handle customer complaints?"—another series of questions related to that one appears on the screen. From those, the worker can refine and focus the question—perhaps down to "What should I do when a customer makes an unreasonable request?" Then, a possible answer to this question will appear in one of a variety of presentation modes, from mere text to a multimedia presentation with full motion video. The clip would perhaps show someone telling a relevant "war story" about an instance when an unreasonable customer was dealt with successfully.

HOW CAN ORGANIZATIONS SUPPORT WORKERS SO THEY CAN SATISFY CUSTOMERS?

Lurking behind all the words about quality and serving the customer is the seldom-acknowledged fact that few organizations know how to turn the words into reality. And organizations may be diverted by flavor-of-the-month management fads, as perhaps evidenced by the company that recently told a business reporter that it had "converted from Total Quality Management to the Learning Organization."[17] Organizations may have read all the right books and attended all the right seminars, but unless they give their workers the capacity and capability to allow them actually to *deliver* quality goods and services, their efforts will result in a temporary benefit at best.

Make no mistake: the customer interface is enormously complex, and it is a daunting task to be the primary spokesperson for an entire company. Employees dealing with customers:

PERFORMANCE SUPPORT FOR SALES REPRESENTATIVES

An interesting and powerful prototype performance system has been developed by Andersen Consulting's Tokyo office to support the sales force for a large food production company. Based upon the initial prototype, the concept is now being expanded to support sales forces in other industries such as software, banking, and insurance.

The system supports the sales representative throughout the sales process, including:

- planning strategies to expand sales and acquire new customers;
- developing proposals;
- reporting, monitoring, and managing productivity.

The system also captures experience and know-how in a knowledge database, so that less-experienced or less-skilled personnel can refer to it and improve their productivity.

The menu bar across the top of the system screen shows the components of sales activities: "Sales Planning," "Customer Call Scheduling," "Customer Call Preparation," "Activity Reporting," "Sales Status Reporting," and "Sales Management/Monitor." When a sales representative selects an activity from the menu bar, the system displays the flow and descriptions of the tasks to be completed by the representative for that activity. In addition, icons needed for task completion are provided in the lower left corner. Boxes across the second top line, called Tool Bar, show support tools that are available regardless of the activity option selected: Customer Information, Product Information, Idea Box (real cases), Procedure Manuals, and Software Packages.

The prototype system also provides detailed descriptions of each task, as well as use guidelines for related tool bar functions. The tasks to be accomplished for "Sales Planning" include "Compare Plan/Actual," "Plan Sales Promotion," "Select Target Customers," and "Finalize Sales Target." In this case, the sales representative is required to conduct "Plan Sales Promotion." The system displays the steps necessary to acquire related information. For example, when selected from the tool bar, "Idea Box" provides examples of effective sales and competitors' activities. This information is updated through daily sales activity entries into the system by sales representatives. In this way, the sales representatives are supported by actual, real-time information.

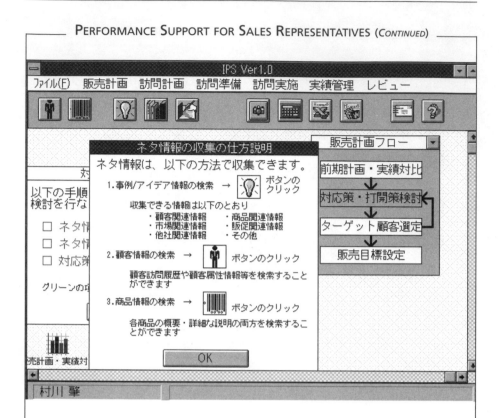

The following is a summary of the performance support functions to be addressed by the prototype system:

- sharing information about sales techniques and other know-how collected through a bottom-up approach, and then using a knowledge database to enable productivity improvement of less-experienced and less-skilled personnel;
- integrating functions such as word processing, procedure manuals, and reference information, to minimize non-sales-related activities;
- incorporating the functions for supervisors/managers to review sales representatives' activities, to eliminate additional work such as sales target and daily activity reporting;
- incorporating the procedure manuals for sales activities into the actual application screens for effective training and quality improvement.

- Must be competent enough to represent the range of the organization's products and services, by themselves or by fast referral;
- Must be able to tailor that range in unique ways to meet the unique needs of each customer;
- Must serve as a good listening ear and information gatherer to collect customers' expectations and deliver them to the right place in the organization;
- Must supply all the traditional services of customer interaction: being prompt, competent, personable, and dependable.[18]

Customer service is a challenging job. From the customer's perspective, that representative *is* the company. The phone company representative *is* the phone company; the bank teller *is* the bank. Ensuring adequate job performance here is a crucial task for organizations today, particularly in the service industry where, as one analysis has it, companies spend over 35% of their operating costs redoing work that was done wrong the first time.[19] And the costs of a lost customer are high: it costs five times more to obtain a customer than to keep one[20]; the cost of losing a customer is equal to five times the annual value of that customer's account.[21] On the other hand, studies indicate that even a 5% increase in customer retention can improve an organization's profitability by anywhere from 25% to 85%.[22]

What are the usual pitfalls that customer service representatives encounter within many organizations today? Among the most important are:

- *Inadequate access to information.* Relevant information is often not available to a worker when it is needed, nor is the worker able to receive advice about how to apply information to the customer request of the moment. With many information systems, a customer service representative may not even have information from a customer's bill formatted on the screen in a manner consistent with the bill itself. If the customer wants to ask about the figure in line 4, the representative has no way of knowing what that figure is.
- *Inconsistent responses.* Customers today have become wary that an answer received today from one representative may not be the answer received tomorrow from another representative.
- *Difficulty in receiving updated news about products and services.* Updates are usually passed along by memos, by word of mouth, or by training sessions where workers' actual job performance must be interrupted so they can attend a session.

- *Lengthy calls.* Representatives must often put customers on hold to ask a colleague a question, call a supervisor, or look something up in a manual. Often, routine tasks such as figuring a customer's bill must be done manually, by calculator.
- *Inadequate training.* As with many workers, customer service representatives often receive too much information too soon, when it has little or no relevance or applicability, and then too little information when the job demands get greater.

The case studies that follow show how some companies are using performance systems to empower their knowledge workers to satisfy customers.

CASE EXAMPLE:
McCAW CELLULAR COMMUNICATIONS AND ROGERS CANTEL MOBILE COMMUNICATIONS

One of the most exciting growth fields in the marketplace today is cellular communications. Barely a decade old, the cellular industry finds itself growing at the rate of 7,000 new customers a day in the United States alone. Business has become extremely competitive; two carriers are active in each market, and companies are constantly trying to expand their product and service offerings. Various kinds of interconnections and alliances among cellular companies are becoming increasingly common, as companies seek new resources to build the kinds of networks that customers want.

One rather long-standing alliance is between McCaw Cellular Communications, located in Kirkland, Washington, and Rogers Cantel Mobile Communications, located in Toronto, Canada. Both young and aggressive firms, McCaw and Cantel joined together in the late 1980s to create the North American Cellular Network (NACN), a network that ensures that customers will receive seamless cellular coverage as they travel between the United States and Canada. This alliance has led to other important joint initiatives.

Entering this decade, both McCaw and Cantel faced a number of business challenges characteristic of the workplace today:

- The accelerating pace of change
- The rising cost of getting workers to a proficient performance level
- Increasing pressure to produce quality results
- Increasing need to provide instant access to information

- Training that could be kept current, that would be available whenever needed, that would accommodate differences in learning styles, and that would be based on the fact that most learning happens for a worker while on the job.

With the cellular telecommunications industry growing and changing at such a pace, customer service was an especially important concern of cellular executives. Jim Barksdale, president of McCaw, tells of an incident that occurred shortly after he joined the company. The company mistakenly hotlined the phone of a valuable business customer—that is, programmed it so he could only reach the McCaw customer service office—"partly because the information system, our people, and the procedures we use to collect from our customers are not always the same ones we use to service them." Clearly, thought Barksdale, the company had an opportunity to improve service and the way they did business.

In 1991, McCaw embarked on an ambitious project to streamline their business processes in order to meet and exceed customer expectations. Following a reengineering and modeling of their best processes, they began development of a new customer system, called "Axys." Independently, Cantel had begun a similar initiative, and the two companies entered into a joint venture to design and develop the Axys performance system in 1992. As Todd Kutches, Manager of Instructional Design for McCaw, recalls, the project did not begin with some sort of rallying cry to develop a performance support system; rather, it began with a vision of what a system should be able to *do*. "The Axys project started with a team of five individuals putting together a conceptual design of what a new customer information and billing system should look like and what its functionalities should be. This document, visionary as it was, never mentions performance support by name. But if you read it now, you can see that it's full of ideas that we would now call performance support. The problem was that, at that point, few people had come across the idea of performance support as an operational concept. So merely saying that phrase wasn't going to get you very far."

One of the crucial points made by developers of the Axys system is that is is an ongoing, iterative project. The Axys project began in 1991 and different phases of the project were rolled out in 1992 and 1993. Current plans are for the project to continue through at least 1997. "It has been extremely helpful," says Kutches, "to manage Axys as an iterative development project. This has not been an attempt to go out and gather all the requirements, develop all the functionality, and deliver the whole 'enchilada' in one massive thrust. Functionality is being done incrementally—it's being prioritized and then delivered."

At both McCaw and Cantel, the functional requirements of the system were driven by clearly defined "to be" workflows, or redesigned business processes. This is a crucial step in the design and implementation of performance systems. Frances Bowles, Manager of Performance Support for Cantel, says, "We discovered quickly that it's too easy for workers to do something the way it's always been done, and too easy to design a system that only supports that old workflow. If you truly want a performance system, you have to ensure that system functionality is based upon the real informational, educational, and advisory requirements of workers who need to perform optimally. In that respect, change management—something that's usually done only after a system has been designed—has to be a part of the process of defining functional requirements. If you can do that, you'll have a performance system through and through. But overcoming old ways of building systems is a challenge."

One of the first steps designers took was to break down the companies' customer contact systems into three separate functions:

1. Customer acquisition—all contacts until the time a person becomes a customer; marketing, sales, credit checking, enrollment, and activation;
2. Customer care—all contacts involved with retaining a customer;
3. Rating and billing—all aspects of customer accounts that happen behind the scenes.

Beginning with the customer acquisition function, the project team developed a prototype of the Axys workstation. The prototype software was a fully functioning, or fully mimicking, stand-alone work environment that allowed the representative to navigate menus, select actions, enter information, and retrieve data, using a dummy database of customer, product, and network information. The goal of the prototype was to delve into just a few well-chosen areas of the business office, and to show what the primary user interface might look like. The team experimented here, trying things on for size, with the goal of narrowing in on the look and feel of the future performance system.

During this process, comments and suggestions from representatives trying out the prototype were crucial to the team as it zeroed in on the best possible implementation. In fact, Axys development was led by two active steering teams. The Executive Steering Team was responsible for:

• Creating and maintaining a high priority for Axys development within McCaw and Cantel;
• Setting high-level directions and helping to prioritize projects;

- Resolving key strategic business issues;
- Identifying decision makers and key participants; and
- Reviewing and approving major milestones.

The User Steering Team, on the other hand, was responsible for:

- Defining success criteria, and being accountable for working with field management to achieve those criteria;
- Reviewing and approving functional directions and standards;
- Making decisions on issues and directions;
- Communicating information and decisions to the field;
- Driving subcommittees or task teams as needed for issue resolution or research; and
- Assuming management of existing steering groups and absorbing them as they see fit.

The Axys project also included a number of dedicated users to work directly on the development team.

Usability testing was crucial to the successful implementation of the system. The team videotaped a number of different workers—customer service representatives, sales people, workers in accounts receivable—as they interacted with the prototype system. As Bowles notes, "We used a technique that had been tried with a great deal of success at Microsoft. We asked each worker to speak out loud as he or she was working at the prototype system; for every action the worker would say, 'Now I want to do such and such, so I'm going to try this.' By videotaping them, and then having them speak and explain why they were performing certain actions, we could see quite easily what was working and what wasn't."

Kutches notes that the first version of the system took everyone by storm. Version 1.0 of the Axys system "really turned some heads, really shocked some people who were expecting just some form of electronic on-line help. In a sense, that first iteration *was* just context-sensitive reference, integrated with splices of training. But because we drove it from a business focus, from the focus of what our workers really needed to support their performance, we delivered far beyond anyone's expectations. That initial success really helped us. An impressive prototype, showing rich functionality, would help any organization wanting to develop a performance system. If you find yourself having to sell the idea internally, you're not going to get very far unless you can show something that works. You can talk in the abstract all you want, but everyone, especially senior management, wants to see it *happening*."

AXYS IN OPERATION

What was the point-of-sale process like for McCaw and Cantel before the implementation of Axys? The process was a good example of how many companies have traditionally focused on collecting information to serve the company's interests, rather than providing support to serve the *customer's* interests. Furthermore, sales people were constrained because no part of the job was automated. Some locations had workstations for product inventory and service information, but the sale took place as a paper-based process. Sales representatives took down customer information on a form. Then they would go to the phone and dial the company's service bureau and wait for a credit check—which also went through channels. Then they faxed the form to a central office where another worker did nothing but enter new customers into the customer information database. Total time for the process: over two hours.

With a process and system redesigned to serve the customer, that process now takes about fifteen minutes. A customer walking into a point-of-sale location with Axys sits down at a workstation with the McCaw or Cantel employee, and the two work together to complete the process. Note that the primary interface follows the basic function here. With customer acquisition, the worker is primarily concerned with gathering information, so the interface uses a basic "form-filling" metaphor. Even here, though, the performance system offers important features. Everything the worker sees on the screen, for example, is in English, not in complex numeric codes. The system also gives the worker important feedback during the entry of customer information. Required fields in the form are colored blue and change to white when the needed information is entered. The customer credit check cannot be run until all required fields are completed. This feedback mechanism was designed following an early testing phase, when workers would occasionally wonder why the system wasn't allowing them to perform a credit check. The answer was that they hadn't completed all the fields, but the first versions of the system did not let workers know the status of their work.

When the customer and employee have stepped through the entire process together, the worker selects the "Run Credit Check" facility. An advisory window comes up on the screen, telling the worker that customer permission is needed to perform this function. When permission is granted, the check goes out to the service bureau via the system, and an answer returns, on average, *in eighteen seconds.*

Several support features are available to the worker at the Axys system. The "Information Resource" facility permits the worker to access context-sensitive information about fields on the screen and about the work being done. One of the features of excellent customer service is the ability of work-

___SUPPORT FOR A CUSTOMER SERVICE REPRESENTATIVE AT THE AXYS SYSTEM___

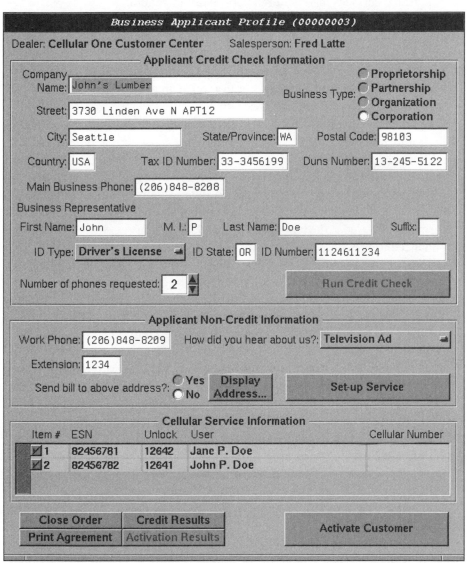

ers to answer questions that may be unrelated to the actual work at hand. Customers frequently have a "by the way" question for a service representative: "Oh, by the way, while I have you on the phone, can you tell me. . . ." The Axys system allows workers to access a glossary of services, and a speed search function brings up the needed information for the worker instantaneously. Training modules embedded within the system give workers the ability to receive more detailed knowledge about system features, about existing products and services, and about the company in general.

A number of benefits of the Axys system come from the fact that the customer and the salesperson work at the system together during the sales process.

- First, many customers are enjoying the experience of participating as the system is in operation—seeing the graphical interface, and watching the screens change as the process proceeds.
- Second, because the gathering of information is done on-line, it is now being validated as it's entered. Many data entry errors are avoided, and the manual checking of forms is eliminated. The credit check, as we noted, cannot be activated until all required fields are completed.
- Third, a frequent source of customer complaint—the initial bill—is anticipated by allowing customers to see what that bill will be, based on the information entered at the workstation. In version 1.1 of Axys, the system was enhanced to provide advice and information on how to educate customers before they walk out the door. Perhaps 65% of customer complaints up to that time were from "bill shock." With an advisory capability, representatives can anticipate that shock and handle it at point of sale.
- Fourth, the sticky matter of the credit check is made less confrontational for the worker. Prior to Axys, the results of the credit check would come back to the employee by phone, and the pressure was on the worker to have to tell the customer that the credit check came up negative. Cantel and McCaw employees appreciate the fact that now they are sitting at the workstation with the customer when the credit check results come back in. If it's negative, the system now tells the customer, not the sale representative. Plus, a negative result comes with some supporting information if the customer wants to follow up: a tracking number, information about who made the credit decision, and a phone number to call.

LESSONS FROM THE AXYS PROJECT

McCaw and Cantel systems development personnel have learned, and continue to learn, valuable lessons about the design of performance systems and about the implications of Integrated Performance Support. These lessons include:

1. Both Kutches at McCaw and Bowles at Cantel stress that development of a performance system should not begin with technical questions. Begin instead with the process you want to automate, and make sure that process is exactly right. Only then should you turn to questions of system design.

2. If you have to sell the concept of performance support internally, try to do so in terms that your audience feels comfortable with. Developers are familiar with context-sensitive support; Integrated Performance Support is much more than that, but there is nothing wrong with speaking in those terms and then delivering something that far exceeds that person's expectations. Systems people will often hear about Integrated Performance Support and reply that it's nothing more than just good systems design. IPS is much more than that, but let the eventual performance system speak for itself.

3. Don't try to do everything at once. IPS can be an evolutionary development process, and the most effective approach is an iterative one. For a time, it will be a rare situation where systems people can simply say, "Let's build a performance system," and then have everybody nod their heads and say, "Let's go." But interest builds when people see what can be delivered at relatively low cost. Then, when savings start coming in—savings generated by reducing the time it takes to get a new worker to proficiency, for example—senior management starts to think, why not take this a few steps further?

4. Because development of a performance system will most likely be an iterative process that crosses functional boundaries within the organization, it is vital to develop standards early and then document them. And this documentation, as Bowles notes, "needs to be living, ever-green material, not something gathering dust on a shelf. Because the idea of performance support is so new, organizations will most likely be creating new methodologies as they proceed. These have to be documented, both for the sake of the project at hand and for future projects."

5. Begin with functionality, and take a vertical slice, if necessary, through the basic IPS model. The IPS model shows the capability of a full-blown, powerful integrated performance system. But taking a performance-centered perspective means that not all services may be relevant to every particular situation—at least until performance systems become the rule rather than the exception. "Depending on a particular project," says Kutches, "you may need to take a vertical slice of the full spectrum of Integrated Performance Support, saying 'What are the services and features that relate to the needs of *these* workers and *this* project in particular.'" (On this point, see the discussion of levels of IPS at the end of Chapter 2.)

6. Easy navigation and intuitive interaction are the keys to interface design and to the design of the entire performance system. One of the keys to successful interface design, says Bowles, is to build in enough flexibility

so that the system can meet the needs of novices as well as more advanced knowledge workers. "For novices, the focus of the performance system should be on providing guidance when the workers are confused and require assistance. Generally they will have one basic question: 'What do I do now?' You don't want to overload such a worker with multiple path support; instead you want to build in a layer of guidance."

In version 2.0 of Axys, for example, the novice interface has only two support icons: "How Do I?" and "Business Reference." Whenever the novice is confused about a task, he or she goes to "How Do I?" and the next screen will provide some task support as well as additional information about getting to a more detailed supporting level. As the representative becomes more familiar with the available support, the system has the facility to allow workers to customize the interface so they can have fast, direct access to support areas. For experienced sales reps at Cantel and McCaw, the system allows them to customize the interface according to their most frequently performed tasks. The worker selects from a palette of icons—"Policies," "Procedures," "Training," and "Equipment," for example—and these then become important supporting services that are unique to that particular knowledge worker.

7. Organizations undergoing an Integrated Performance Support initiative may find themselves redefining what they mean by "training." As McCaw and Cantel workers have discovered, training takes place at many more levels than they may have assumed, especially since they now have a great deal of business reference material available to them at the touch of a button. As Kutches asks, "Doesn't easy access to context-sensitive reference eventually become a kind of training? What is 'just-in-time' training, anyway? In the context of IPS, it's a lot more than just computer-based training, I'll tell you that much, and the only way we found that out was by doing some CBT on our own."

Bowles emphasizes the radically different way that companies must look at training from a performance-centered perspective. "Computer-based training has traditionally proceeded by building modules. When the concept of 'granularity' came along—that is, providing only the small piece of training relevant to a particular task—some people felt that you could just cut those modules into smaller splices, reuse them, and call the result performance support. I think that's no longer good enough. If you sign up for Integrated Performance Support, you need to forget about that old linear CBT approach. You actually have to take the opposite view: now that we have these granules of context-sensitive training, how might we join them together into a cohesive lesson and build some longer piece of training that could be a good overview from a new learner's perspective? In terms of the way most people look at training, this is truly a sea change."

8. Systems designers are excited about the good design aspects of IPS, but they may need to be reeducated. There are far more tools available now to help those who want to engage in true performance-centered design. A systems person who says that IPS is "really just good systems design" may be right, but only partially so. That person may not be taking advantage of all the latest thinking. "Are you taking advantage of all the latest tools?" asks Kutches. "Probably not. Are you considering instructional information as just another piece of data that you can deliver at the touch of a mouse click? I don't think so, because a systems designer has always looked at training as something separate—as something to bring in after the system is already built."

9. Keep in mind, however, that trainers may need to be sold on the IPS concept, as well. There may be some initial resistance in some cases, but organizations need to stress the benefits of IPS not only from the employees' perspective, but from the trainer's perspective as well. As Bowles says, "Trainers get much more satisfaction from doing skills training for workers—training that really has an impact on performance—than they do by merely providing information. Trainers frankly are tired of giving the same information over and over: here's how you do this, here's how you find that. With IPS, trainers can work individually with people on their skill sets, or they can help design the system so that skills training is available to everyone at the time and at the point of need. They finally have a chance to move beyond the status of information givers to become real coaches and mentors."

   Some existing aspects of training will probably remain, though, according to Kutches. "The need for some classroom training never goes away—contact with a human being is important at certain times in the learning process—but we think we can cut it way down. And we should: our orientation classes for new employees range anywhere from four to six weeks. They could be shorter."

10. Compared to traditional transaction-based systems, performance systems pose fewer technology assimilation problems, even for those workers with little computer background or those tied to paper-based systems. "We found with our workers," says Kutches, "that only about 20% of them had no experience with computers. Most of them had a computer at home, or had used one before, so they were much better equipped than I had really anticipated. The resistance to the system was much less than we had ex-

pected. Even those starting from scratch found the system easy to use, in part because of the graphical interface."

11. Performance systems eliminate the problems of "versions." Training and employee education costs are high: organizations put a lot of money into developing educational materials, manuals, guides, classes. "And yet," says Kutches, "if you look at anybody's desk, they may not even have the latest version of the materials. Paper-based maintenance is unwieldy. All you need is one overworked manager, one weak link in the human chain, and your education maintenance, in effect, doesn't exist. Our Axys system allows us to have one person, literally, keep 6,000 people updated with the latest, most pristine, and appropriate knowledge about our products and services. That's big savings: you pay for development up front, but the savings on the back end are tremendous."

12. Increased employee satisfaction and employee development can follow directly from a performance system. "Our very first business goal," says Kutches, "is to hire and develop great people. And once they're hired, then we have a chance really to develop them. Old training methods focused on the training, not on the person. With Axys, finding information and giving excellent customer service comes quickly. That means that now we can focus on the more important thing: really developing excellent employees."

13. Change management is a crucial ingredient to the design and effective implementation of a performance system, "I cannot see performance support at this point being introduced without change management," says Kutches. "One thing I would do differently next time would be to suggest that the whole development project and all individuals involved go through a reengineering process with change management support. All of us are evolving by necessity; we're all going through the school of hard knocks together."

Bowles echoes this support for active and early change management efforts. "Change management has to be more than lip service. It has to be integrated into the project from the beginning, and has to be a part of defining the functional requirements. Without defining the future workflows—how you ultimately want workers to perform—you will be unable to build a performance system. These 'to be' workflows have to be the basis for the analysis and design phase of the project. In fact, the optimal way to go would be to have the overall project manager lead and be accountable for change management, reengineering, and performance support. This would ensure that the final product would truly be a performance system."

14. Not only can IPS improve customer service, it might eventually reduce the number of workers needed to provide that service. "Many people don't realize that performance support can even be offered to the end-user— that is, to the customer.[23] As we envision future iterations of Axys, we see the support being developed and extended right out to the customer. We might dramatically reduce the resources necessary for traditional customer service, because we can go right to the customers and educate them, provide performance support for them, maybe over the phone."

15. IPS allows organizations to dream beyond the mediocre. Says Kutches, "I think organizations today spend incredible amounts of energy and money to make people mediocre. It takes a lot of investment time to have a mediocre employee: someone who *might* be able to answer your question, if you're lucky; someone who *might* be able to get back to you some time with an answer if they can find it; someone who *might* only have to transfer you to two other people when you call. Organizations invest a lot in that, and then they're proud that they're just as mediocre as the next guy. We're aiming a lot higher than that. We think we can blow the lid off of this industry in terms of providing customer service that exceeds anyone's expectations."

CASE EXAMPLE:
BELL ATLANTIC

As recent events have made clear, Bell Atlantic has moved beyond regional Bell company status and is positioning to become a major player in the interactive, multimedia, ubiquitous computer networking of the future. (See Chapter 12, "Working and Living in the Infocosm.") Yet accompanying the grand technological visions that are driving Bell Atlantic into the next stage of the information age is this important and quieter thought from their most recent annual report: customers don't buy technology, they buy service. The challenge and the commitment at Bell Atlantic continues to be providing high-quality customer service during a time when competitive pressures dictate fast response to customer needs and frequent changes to product and service lines. In this environment of rapid change, how can customer service representatives at Bell Atlantic continue to provide high-value solutions to customers?

The workforce at Bell Atlantic faces many of the same challenges that we have discussed at length: information overload, increasing job complexity, the need to reach proficient performance levels quickly and then to sustain that performance continuously. Customer service representatives, who number over 7,000 and are located in over 60 different offices, each typically require from sixty to ninety days of upfront training before they can perform optimally on the job. Time to proficiency may take as long as one year. Within this already challenging environment, Bell Atlantic undertook in 1991 several major new initiatives to transform and augment the role of customer service representatives for the company. Bell Atlantic's commitment was to transform the role of a customer service representative from passive to active mode. That is, representatives were no longer to be mere resource people, answering questions and solving problems. Instead, each contact with a Bell Atlantic customer was now to be viewed not only as an opportunity to provide value within the customer's current condition, but also as a potential sales opportunity, a chance to suggest new and enhanced products and services offered by Bell Atlantic. In short, representatives would go from being fire fighters to being sales representatives. Certainly this put an added burden on the upfront training of representatives and presented challenges to ongoing training and support. Occasionally, following the introduction of a new product, representatives felt they could not sell it adequately because they didn't have enough detailed information about the product. Instead, they would continue to push products with which they were more familiar.

Expansion of products and services, and a strengthening commitment to customer service, also began to strain the company's existing or legacy systems. Many of the existing systems had been developed on mainframes fifteen to twenty-five years before. At that time, all that representatives needed to do was to enter data into a few fields on the screen. But over the years, as optional products and features grew, these screens got more and more crowded. Systems designers were squeezing data in, using more codes for certain functions, and the screens naturally became complicated. And, because representatives had to memorize all the codes, as well as the right fields in which to enter them, errors in data entry inevitably grew. At one time, for example, some customer service locations required two workers to concentrate solely on correcting data entry errors.

SALES SUPPORT FOR CUSTOMER SERVICE REPRESENTATIVES

The technological innovations that addressed these customer service challenges grew out of a larger initiative at Bell Atlantic, called "Systems 2000," which was nothing less than a total reengineering of the way Bell Atlantic conceives of and operates its business. As part of the reengineering effort, the workflow for the customer service representatives was redesigned from a sales point of view; the support system that followed this reengineering therefore follows a sales process. Although system designers did not originally conceive of their effort as a project in Integrated Performance Support, we can see retrospectively that performance support, particularly in the area of advisory services, was a driving force in the design of a new sales system.

The system is called SSNS, for "SaleService Negotiation System." One part of the system supports representatives in their contacts with residential customers; another part provides support for contacts with small- and medium-sized businesses. The primary innovation of Release 1 of SSNS is a SalesCue™ model that supports the representative during a customer conversation. As the representative listens to the customer, he or she can click on certain lifestyle characteristics summarized on the screen. These criteria are then used by the system to provide advice as to what products and services to recommend to the customer. For example, sales clues may identify the presence of teenage children in the home, or may note that the customer works at home, or is a member of a profession that requires taking calls away from the primary work location. SSNS identifies certain products and packages relevant to this customer's needs and then provides additional supporting information to assist with the sale. The system has been enormously effective, with customer service representatives showing impressive increases in sales.

Bell Atlantic is now using an iterative approach to develop full Integrated Performance Support features within SSNS. As part of this iterative approach, Andersen Consulting has developed a prototype performance system for Bell Atlantic building on features already present within SSNS, called "Business Marketing with Integrated Performance Support," or "BMIPS." Certain features of the prototype system are scheduled to be incorporated into future releases of SSNS.

BUSINESS MARKETING WITH INTEGRATED PERFORMANCE SUPPORT

BMIPS is an impressive, leading-edge example of the power of performance systems to support knowledge worker performance with an integrated set of services. It is also a good example of the link between IPS and process reengineering: that is, the development of a performance-centered system can be a stimulus to process reengineering. In fact, reengineering and the development of the system really occur simultaneously, as the freedom of systems design in a client/server environment lets management think in new ways and helps them brainstorm with their workers to ask what the best mode of work really is, what tasks should be done when, and what kinds of performance support might be necessary to reach high proficiency levels quickly. BMIPS developers began with task analysis of the work of the Bell Atlantic customer service representatives, decomposing their jobs and deciding that the primary division of performance was between work done on-line with a customer and work done off-line. Developers then designed two virtual desktop interfaces.

The primary system interface is designed to support the basic performance needs of the representative. On-line work in a customer contact mode primarily involves receiving and inputting information, so the interface metaphor is a form-filling metaphor. Options are available to the worker to customize certain parts of the screen, including the color scheme of the interface. (This sounds like a minor detail, but customer service representatives at Bell Atlantic were thrilled even with that relatively minor gesture. To be able to choose their own screen colors meant that, within limits, they could put some of their own preferences and tastes onto the screen they look at several hours a day. Their pleasure at this gesture is perhaps a testament to how rarely worker desires have been accommodated in traditional systems design.)

The BMIPS system can track the experience level of the representative and support work performance at the appropriate level. Three different support modes, for example, are available to the worker: novice, informational, and expert. In novice mode, the interaction with the customer is scripted for the worker. In informational mode, the supporting information is pared down to the level of a basic outline. In both cases, the information is lined up directly opposite the place on the screen where customer data is being entered. In expert mode, both types of support scripts disappear.

Color coding on the screen lets representatives know which fields are optional and which are required. Dynamic data entry in the novice mode allows the new worker to enter the customer information into the script but then automatically replicates it in the areas that will be used when the worker becomes more experienced. As the representative is working, Reference Services (the "Ask Me" facility of the system) provides supporting information about any field on the screen simply by double clicking on that field.

After the representative enters the basic customer information, including the customer's business identification number or social security number, the system supports the representative during the rest of the sales interview. The worker selects the type of industry represented by this company, and the system tailors an interview protocol for that type of business. The representative asks for and then enters basic information: size of company, numbers of locations and of employees, type and number of hook-ups desired. When all information is gathered, the system analyzes the customer profile and recommends the best options for that customer. It also brings up detailed descriptions of the products, their benefits, and costs.

SUPPORT FOR A NOVICE REPRESENTATIVE FROM THE BMIPS SYSTEM

The representative can access the system for more detailed information about why a certain product or service recommendation was made. If a customer has heard of a certain service through a particular advertisement, the worker can review on-screen an image of the actual ad to which the customer is referring. If the customer has heard of a product or service from a competitor or from a phone company in another state, the representative simply enters the name of that item and the similar product or service offered by Bell Atlantic will be displayed. The system also ensures compliance with the many regulations governing the telecommunications industry by prompting workers that certain information must be given to the customer.

When the interview is over and the customer has placed an order, the system performs the credit check. After the conversation with the customer is complete, the system customizes a confirmation letter to the customer, which the worker can scan and change if necessary. Through the workstation, the representative sends the completed, formal order through the system and returns to the primary desktop interface.

The second support mode for a customer service representative is the off-line mode. It also gathers together, within the primary interface, the basic services that workers might need when they are not directly interacting with customers. Here, a number of features are available that both enhance the workers' environment and increase overall productivity for the company. For example, the basic "in box" available to the worker contains electronic mail, memos, videos, images of new advertising campaigns, and voice mail. Also available are a note pad, a to-do list, a bulletin board, and a personal calendar. In one video message shown in the prototype of the system, a Bell Atlantic executive in a video message announces a new product and lets the workers know that training is available on the system to help them sell this new offering. In another example, the manager of customer service compliments the entire staff on exceeding their sales quota for the month and invites everyone to stop by the conference room for refreshments to celebrate. Today, getting information to the entire customer service staff often involves having to shut down all or most of the facility to bring the representatives together, a drastic sacrifice of productivity.

The off-line mode of the BMIPS system is an innovative way to compensate for worker downtime. Today, in order for Bell Atlantic to provide the highest levels of customer service, they may have to overstaff to accommodate the maximum number of customer inquiries in any given day. This overstaffing may mean that representatives occasionally spend a certain amount of time waiting for the next customer call. Here the system supports the workers in two primary ways to use this time productively:

First, training is available to the representative, and the system may even prompt workers, alerting them that a certain piece of training has not been completed and asking if they would like to take it now. Using the "Ask Me" facility of the system, the representative can access a training program on a new product rollout, for example, and then take a self-check to certify that the training has been completed.

Second, the system may alert the representative that the incoming volume of calls is low, and that this would be a good time to place a proactive sales call. The system presents the worker with an analysis of a customer's calling pattern over the past few months and indicates that this customer could save money by switching to another calling package. After the representative has examined the basic information, the system places the call and continues to support worker performance during the subsequent conversation with the customer.

One of the powerful features of this system is its ability to support performance in a manner that mimics the typical workday for a representative: that is, there is never a set pattern of what a day will be like. Any one mode of work can be interrupted by another. In the prototype demonstration, for example, a worker is interrupted during a training session by a customer calling in to disconnect an optional service. At the touch of a button, the representative can pull up billing history for this customer, as well as a record of the various contacts with the person over the past few months. Today, that worker would not really have the information resources to turn this customer contact back around into an opportunity to make a sale. With BMIPS, however, the worker can find out the reasons for the disconnect; based upon these answers, the system will recommend another, different service that might be better suited to the customer's needs. The system supports the representative in efforts to turn a potentially dissatisfied customer around and to make a sale.

"The ultimate response to competition," writes Bell Atlantic CEO Raymond W. Smith in a recent annual report, "is to out-innovate, out-smart, out-market your adversaries—in short, to constantly find new ways to *add value* to the lives of your customers and your communities." SSNS and future enhancements to that system driven by Integrated Performance Support concepts will play a major role in ensuring that all representatives of Bell Atlantic can add value to their customers.

CHAPTER 6

TURNING INFORMATION INTO KNOWLEDGE

Consider the following puzzle, the type that many people have been seeing since they began working years ago with kindergarten workbooks. You are to look at the items below and choose the one that doesn't belong.

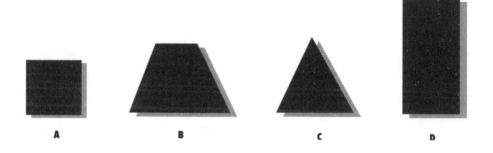

A　　　　B　　　　C　　　　D

The answer: C, most people would probably say. It's the only one that's not a quadrilateral, a four-sided polygon. But the answer is not necessarily that apparent. Suppose a teacher has been talking about squares, rectangles, and triangles, and then asks you to circle the odd figure. The answer: B. Or suppose the lesson for the day is: "things that are tall," or "things that are small." The figures that don't belong: A and D, respectively.

The point is that we are asked all the time to take actions based upon information in front of us. But unless we have the proper context for that information, and unless we are given some sort of direction, we won't know what to do. Lacking context and direction, the human mind will do one of two things: either take actions based upon assumptions that may or may not be valid, or simply ignore the information entirely.

There are probably countless examples of this problem in the workplace. Consider a customer service representative for a utility company. A customer phones in, wanting to know why the latest monthly bill was so high. There are a number of different variables here, and with experience, a representative will eventually be able to master the procedures for analyzing and isolating the relevant factor for this customer. But what is the worker supposed to do, and what is the company supposed to do, in the meantime?

Information technology today has given workers unprecedented access to information. But to this point, it has rarely been able to help workers *act* upon that information. The answer, again, is not just technology, but the right *approach* to technology: an Integrated Performance Support strategy resulting in performance systems that give workers not only the ability to gather and analyze information, but also the ability to act based upon that information. In this chapter, we examine one of the most powerful features of performance systems: the ability to help a worker turn information into *knowledge*.

THE INFORMATION CRISIS

"Water, water, everywhere," Coleridge wrote in "The Rime of the Ancient Mariner," "nor any drop to drink." We swim in a sea of information, yet cannot drink any of it: it is too coarse, too salty. It also lacks the elements that might nourish us and quench our thirst: meaning, analysis, history, context. After a while, we learn to ignore most of it because it is not relevant to us. It all looks the same, and we don't even know what differences might make a

---

KEY MESSAGES: CHAPTER 6

- Information anxiety in the workplace has both internal and external causes. From external sources, more information is available to workers than ever before. From internal sources, product and service lines are expanding, and workers face the challenge of keeping abreast of these developments.
- Now that information technology has given workers unprecedented *access* to information, it must do more: it must turn that information into *knowledge*.
- Knowledge is more than just knowing something. It is also knowing *that* you know, knowing *why* you know, and knowing what to *do* with what you know.
- There are at least six characteristics of knowledge. It is: (1) applicable or practical; (2) contextual; (3) experiential; (4) historical; (5) communal or social; and (6) individual.
- Performance systems, by providing proactive support services, help workers gather, analyze, and use information, thereby turning it into knowledge.

difference to *us*. Our workforce feels the stress of this strange "absent presence" of information in today's workplace—it's there, but it's not there. There
is always another survey to take, another market analysis to do, another article or book to read, another voice mail to hear.

This external sense of information anxiety is bad enough; coupled with internal information overload, it becomes almost unbearable. In today's markets, information about a company's service and product lines may change
weekly. How can anyone keep up? In the last chapter, we saw a hint of what
performance systems can do to overcome the problem of information anxiety: recall the fact that a single employee of McCaw Cellular or Cantel can
now keep all workers updated, through the Axys performance system, with
the most recent information from the company. But this is only part of what
an IPS strategy can do to turn information into knowledge, and to transform
an information processor into a *knowledge worker.*

What *is* information exactly? And what is knowledge? Several years ago
someone coined the word "factoid." The Cable News Network channel, for
example, will put a factoid up on the screen when breaking for a commercial:
75% of people will own a dog at least once in their life; the average family
spent $124 a week in the grocery store last year; 54% of women surveyed in-
dicated that their favorite color was yellow.[1] The newspaper *USA Today* does
similar things in print: colorful boxes with "filler" information or attractive
charts that are, at best, tangential to anything else on the page. So why tell us
these things? What do these statistics have to do with us, with our work, or
with the world in general? For most people, absolutely nothing. Why should
we remember them? We don't need to. That's the whole point: they're just
factoids, the fast food of the information age.

What's the difference between a "fact" and a "factoid"? The suffix is important: if you add "oid" to a word, it means something that resembles the
specified object. A humanoid isn't human, it just looks like one. Thus properly understood, factoid is a perfect word to describe how information inun-
dates us these days, and how difficult it is now to incorporate that information
into the structure of our lives and our workplace. We have fewer and fewer
"facts" and more and more things "resembling facts"—fake bits of wandering
and unrelated data, totally untethered to any overarching sense of reality. There
are a lot of these factoids floating around out there: more new information has
been produced in the last thirty years than in the previous 5,000 years of human civilization,[2] and the amount of existing information doubles every five
years.[3]

Information, we have said, is a step above "data"—it's a representation that
has at least some syntactical meaning. If we did a survey asking people what

pets they have had in their lives, we would get back a lot of data—but it wouldn't make any sense at first glance. If we analyzed and ordered that data, we would have a representation of something: we would get "information." Seventy-five percent of people will own a dog sometime in their lives. I understand the sentence—but why is that information important? What does it have to do with my work or with my life? More important, what am I supposed to do *with* it? Information that carries with it the answers to these questions is what we mean by "knowledge." Knowledge is more than just knowing; it's also knowing *that* you know, knowing *why* you know, knowing what to *do* with what you know—and then *doing* it.

Not everyone would agree with this data-information-knowledge distinction. William J. Clancey, of the Institute for Research on Learning, writes, for example, that it is not quite accurate to say that workers have "too much information." Instead, he says, what is meant is that people have too much data, more descriptions than they know what to do with. They have "too much data and not enough information."[4] But as the amount of information available to our workforce has grown exponentially, information has come increasingly to resemble data once again. Unless information can be given context and applicability, no one knows what to do with it. Having this information, being able to fit it into a larger structure of experience and community, and then knowing how to apply it in practice—this is what we mean by "knowledge." Understood in this way, knowledge is viewed, as Clancey writes, "not as a storehouse of facts and procedures that can be inventoried, but as a capacity to interact, to reflect, to innovate."[5] We will have more to say about the nature of knowledge in the workplace in a moment.

THE PROBLEM OF ACTING ON INFORMATION ALONE

The last decade has brought with it exciting developments in information technology. The advent of cooperative processing and client/server architectures has broken down many barriers within organizations, allowing workers access to much more information at the moment and at the point of need. But there have been problems with these developments, as well—far-reaching secondary effects that threaten the productivity of those very knowledge workers that the technology was supposed to support. Shoshana Zuboff argues in her book, *In the Age of the Smart Machine,* that the new information technologies will be counterproductive for workers unless they are taught

Data, Information, Knowledge

Elsewhere we have given a number of examples to make clearer the distinctions that separate data from information, and information from knowledge. Here is another way to think about it. Consider a number:

70

"70" is intelligible to us (in contrast to say, "^*\"). But the number alone is mere data, and virtually meaningless in itself. Now consider the following phrase:

70 % chance of rain

Here we have information. But that information would only be helpful to us if we were aware of it exactly when and where we needed it. Suppose we had a small wristwatch-sized device enabled by knowledge technology. One of the many things it monitors is the weather. The device alerts us as we head out the door that there is a 70% chance of rain today.

This information affects our behavior: it is experiential. It causes us to grab a raincoat and an umbrella. We have applied that information now; we have done something we might not have done otherwise, because information has been delivered to us at the moment of performance. Knowledge is the value gained from having applied or used the information. In a sense, knowledge is knowing the value to be gained from using the information based on the experience of having used it before.

new skills that will prevent them from becoming mere cogs in a huge technological wheel.

When organizations decide to automate all or part of a business function, the goals are usually to improve employee productivity and to centralize control at the highest management level possible. While the focus may be on automating a process, an enormous amount of previously unavailable data is also created. This information can be used to improve the business function itself. Zuboff coins the word "informating" to describe the process of using machines to create additional information about a business function. For example, the automating portion of technology in the banking industry is used to computerize transaction processing. The informating part is the ability to use the database to provide value-added information services: automatic account transfers, overdraft protection, automatic bill payment, all for which the bank can now charge fees. Automating often uses technology to routinize, fragment, or eliminate jobs. Informating, on the other hand, uses technology to increase the intellectual content of work across organization levels.[6]

The Total Information Management prototype from Chapter 3 is an excellent example of this development; increasing the intellectual content of work is not only a natural outcome, but an *intended* outcome of Integrated Performance Support. Performance systems do not seek to deskill the workforce through automation; rather they create an environment in which workers can discover and create knowledge, and then use that knowledge to support and facilitate their work to meet and exceed customer expectations.

Zuboff addresses the far more common occurrence of automation that deskills the workforce. Automation, Zuboff writes, can have an extreme impact on workers—not only on job function, but on performance and employee state of mind. Consider the example of a pulping plant. Before automation, employees were out in the factory—turning dials, pulling levers, and wading through pulp that had overflowed from the vats. It was strenuous, dirty work, but the employees always had a mental model of the process, one derived through physical contact with the pulp. After automation, the physical contact with the process was removed and replaced with numbers and symbols on computer screens. Performance of the process controllers dipped when their mental model was stripped from them, and their stress increased as well. Management was holding them responsible for productivity in the manufacturing process, but they were not given the tools they needed to perform their jobs effectively.

When the true potential of information systems is realized in a performance system, however, employees have more time to think about the process itself: how it operates, what models are beneath it, and how both model and process

────── THE INFORMATION POWER OF CLIENT/SERVER ARCHITECTURE ──────

Traditional processing has "host" computers (mainframes or minicomputers) that perform all the processing and contain all the data for their own set of "dumb" terminals. Users in this environment can only access the information contained in that one host, and only in the manner programmed into the applications.

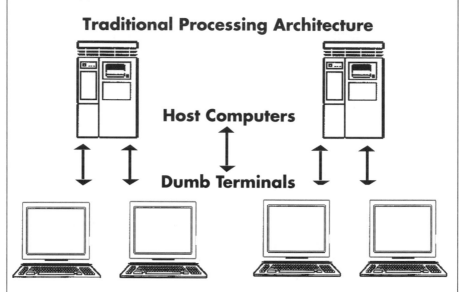

Traditional Processing Architecture

Host Computers

Dumb Terminals

In a "client/server" architecture, client machines (PCs, notebook-size computers, handheld devices, and workstations) can connect to a wide range of "servers" (voice mail boxes, image files, electronic mail boxes, enterprise-wide databases, and so forth). The client requests service, and the server provides it.

Processing can be divided among these machines, with the choice of the appropriate architecture hinging on cost and the ability to manage complexity. The power of client/server comes from putting this breadth of electronic information at people's fingertips. Integrated Performance Support principles, however, let organizations turn that information into knowledge for their workers.

An Integrated Performance Support strategy reaches its full power within a client/server environment. However, organizations can begin IPS implementation with existing systems and architectures, and then eventually migrate to client/server as they outgrow their mainframes and their legacy systems.

THE INFORMATION POWER OF CLIENT/SERVER ARCHITECTURE (CONTINUED)

Client/Server Architecture

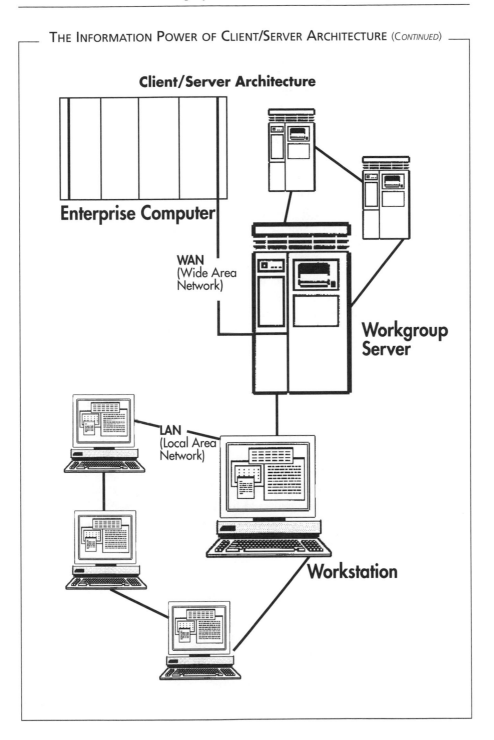

Enterprise Computer

WAN
(Wide Area
Network)

Workgroup
Server

LAN
(Local Area
Network)

Workstation

might be improved. Informating the workplace, to use Zuboff's term, can el-
evate the workforce above the routine job functions (which the system now
should handle) to the role of thinker and improver, customer service provider,
knowledge worker. However, not all workers come to the job with those innate cognitive skills, and organizations must be attentive to methods that can
bring workers up to that level.[7]

With the additional process data provided by informating strategies, says
Zuboff, workers' thinking becomes more abstract. They shift from thinking
of products as material objects to thinking of products as conceptual innovations. Workers now manipulate symbols, not things, and this change redefines
the job's basic skills.[8] The ability to generate this symbolic representation is
known as an "intellective" skill. An intellective skill is the power of knowing, and then knowing that you know—something different than the power
to will something or to feel something. It is the capacity for highly-developed
rational thought. Employees must understand the theory behind a process (and
how the automation systems work) in order to form a symbolic representation.
The opportunities offered by an informating technology cannot be exploited
without new intellective skills in the operating workforce. If knowledge workers cannot rise to this level (or are prevented from doing so), their functions
will be eliminated by automation instead of being elevated by information
systems, and a valuable opportunity will be missed. We are thus at a critical
juncture in the evolution of technology in the workplace. Zuboff suggests two
basic scenarios depending on which way we go. In one scenario, intelligence
becomes the domain only of the smart machine, and the human capacity for
critical judgment and creativity begins to atrophy. The majority of jobs in offices and factories become isolated, routine, and perfunctory. In the other scenario leaders within organizations realize that new kinds of skills and new
forms of knowledge will be needed to exploit the true power of today's information technology. They then direct their resources toward creating a
workforce that exercises judgment and creativity as it manages the information systems that enable their knowledge work.[9]

CASE EXAMPLE:
MAJOR AEROSPACE INDUSTRY COMPANY

Performance systems, we have said, are proactive. Because they know about
the worker and about the work to be accomplished, they can adapt a unique
package of support services for that worker. The system not only teaches; it also

anticipates needs and coaches the worker through an advisory facility. But the system does not control performance; it supports it. At all times, the knowledge worker is in the driver's seat, empowered to accept the advice of the system or to ignore it, based upon the unique performance circumstances of the moment.

But an advisory facility can be a powerful performance aid. One of the early performance system prototypes was developed in 1989 for a defense contractor in the United States to demonstrate how to assist maintenance technicians as they diagnose and repair jet engines. Like many industries, the aerospace industry takes part now in an increasingly competitive global environment in which increased productivity from its workers will be vital. The industry is facing a steady increase in operating costs—particularly in maintenance and logistics. Aircraft around the world are aging; new aircraft being designed and built will be much more complex, putting a burden on skilled workers, who are becoming more and more scarce.

Engine testing is dependent on the skills of these maintenance technicians. If a problem is detected by a pilot in flight, the technicians must identify potential problems—often on an engine they have not seen in some time, or perhaps have never seen—locate parts, and make the repair. Prior to the development of the performance system, these repairs could take hours—even days. The goal of the system developers was to enable technicians to make most repairs *within thirty minutes.*

To accomplish this, the system must support the performance of the technicians on the job in real time. After a potential engine problem arises, the maintenance technician interfaces with the aircraft's onboard systems using a handheld device called a Personal Maintenance Aid computer, or PMA. Based on the information downloaded from the aircraft, the system identifies possible faults. From these possibilities, the technician chooses the most probable fault candidate. The Advisory Services component of the prototype then suggests possible reasons for that failure, the probability of each reason, and the techniques needed to confirm the failure. When confirmation has been established by the technician, the system identifies the tasks required to perform the repair. Prior to and during the repair, the technician can access a list of equipment and tools needed, as well as past repair activities and the location of spare parts. Note the symbiotic relationship between worker and system in this example. Neither machine nor human acting alone could have accomplished the task. The machine enhances the power of the worker, but does not thereby diminish the person. The worker works; the machine supports.

Because of the Knowledge Worker Services facility of Integrated Performance Support—because, that is, the system identifies the capabilities of the person using the system—a performance system can provide different kinds of advice, based upon the background and experience of that worker. An inexperienced worker would receive the advice appropriate for that proficiency level, advice different from that provided to a worker at a higher proficiency level. For certain critical procedures, however, the performance system might prompt workers regardless of their experience level. In the example of the McCaw Cellular Axys system, for example, every worker is prompted to ask the customer for permission to run a credit check. This permission is a legal requirement, and even experienced workers forget. The system simply will not run the check until the worker has responded to this prompt.

Mandatory prompting from a performance system may also be crucial in heavily regulated industries and in environments with strict safety requirements. We have seen in the example of the Automated Refinery Information System (ARISE), for example, that the performance system will intervene when a refinery plant operator is shutting down a tank. The system then prompts the worker through the mandatory procedures to be followed in this case.

KNOWLEDGE AS THE PRECONDITION FOR DECISION MAKING

Albert Einstein was once asked what he would do if he knew he only had one hour to cope with a catastrophic, life-threatening problem. His answer: 90% of that hour would be spent collecting information; 5% on weighing alternative courses of action; the final 5% on making the decision.[10] In theory, the percentages sound wonderful. The problem is that for most of us, there is more information available than could possibly be processed and brought to bear upon the decision. Many decisions today seem conditional and are perhaps made with a certain resignation that there may be some information out there that could change our minds.

Information has no value to a business organization unless it is *practical* and *applicable;* information must support workers during the performance of their jobs, and it must support executives in decision making and in setting corporate direction. IPS, we have said, turns information into knowledge— and "applicability" is the first characteristic of what knowledge means. The other characteristics flow directly from that characteristic. Knowledge is:

- Applicable or Practical
- Contextual
- Experiential
- Historical

- Communal or Social
- Individual

KNOWLEDGE IS APPLICABLE

Knowledge is information that carries with it the characteristics of having been applied before. One writer discussing the importance of creativity in the workplace makes a similar point: that while "creativity" is the thinking process that generates an idea, "innovation" is the application of that idea toward doing things better.[11]

KNOWLEDGE IS CONTEXTUAL

Recall the puzzle from the opening pages of this chapter. One of the reasons that knowledge can be applied practically to our tasks is that it also carries with it context. It's not information floating out there for its own sake—like a "factoid." Knowledge presumes that there is a broader range of learning and experience—knowledge with a capital "K," we might say—into which a particular *piece* of knowledge fits appropriately.

KNOWLEDGE IS EXPERIENTIAL

One does not read books on how to fish and then claim to be a fisherman. The young engineer or lawyer or doctor fresh out of school may have passed a state licensing exam, but he or she then has to apply the book learning over time to become a true professional. Knowledge is obtained by actually working with information, and by testing and refining it in the fires of real life. Knowledge is the result of engagement in practice. It doesn't exist in the world out there in a pure form, nor does it become stored in our minds in that form. Knowledge comes from observing, participating, and acting.[12] This fact is a crucial component of the Training Services and Reference Services facilities of Integrated Performance Support. IPS reinforces the principle of "learning by doing," holding that workers understand and perform best when they can learn through real job tasks—or through simulations if risk of failure may produce unacceptable consequences.

The fact that knowledge is experiential also means, however, that doing must be accompanied by reflection. Reflection is, in fact, another *kind* of doing—a mode of thought from which inventiveness is most likely to arise. William Clancey writes that improving the learning process in business "requires granting people the uniqueness and openness of experience. People must have the freedom, when appropriate, of saying, 'I am not a machine, I am always doing something new. I am creating.' " We inhibit our workers' ability to learn when we view people as machines and force them to justify their work only in terms of previously articulated plans. "We don't properly evaluate human work because we have obscured the inherent unplanfulness and inventiveness of every action. . . . We must give people the right to acknowledge that they are constantly reperceiving and reorganizing their work." To manage this process, writes Clancey, is to manage learning.[13]

KNOWLEDGE IS HISTORICAL

One of the things that distinguishes knowledge from mere information is that knowledge has been refined over time. Robert Bellah and the other authors of *Habits of the Heart* have such a concept in mind when they characterize a true community: such a community is a "community of memory." It has a history; it tells narratives about its formation and about significant occurrences from the past.[14] Knowledge, we might say is "information with memory"—it has a history, a sense of the manner in which it has been developed and debated over time.

KNOWLEDGE IS COMMUNAL OR SOCIAL

The communal aspect of knowledge can be seen every day in our businesses. Managers are most prone to make mistakes, for example, when they run a project in a dictatorial manner, ignoring the need to cast an idea into the community of the workplace. A project, an initiative—even a book such as this one—ideally should be refined by so many different hands that it truly becomes a community effort. The Institute for Research on Learning calls these social learning environments "communities of practice." "United by a common enterprise, people come to develop and share ways of doing things, ways of talking, beliefs, values—in short, practices—as a function of their joint involvement in mutual activity. We call such informal aggregations 'communities of practice,' because they are defined not only by their membership, but by shared ways of doing things." People are enabled to enter and participate in these communities because of the way learning takes place within the community: learning becomes an act of membership, "not just the activity of a sole individual, but the primary engagement with others. . . . The key to enhancement and motivation in learning lies in the intimate connection between

---

REMOVING INFORMATION BARRIERS AT ICA HANDLARNA

For many organizations today, critical information is ignored because of the traditional barriers that inevitably develop between departments. Such a problem often requires reengineering the business processes so that information can be shared in a timely manner, and so that customers can be served better.

This information barrier problem has been faced and overcome by ICA Handlarna, Sweden's largest and most successful retailing group. ICA Handlarna and its wholesale subsidiary, ICA Partihandel, consist of 2,600 independent food retailers and 2,800 stores. They operate through over ten distribution facilities, providing groceries for up to 80% of Sweden's eight million people.

Torsten Engevik, ICA Partihandel's Director of Administration, recalls that by the late 1980s, the company had evolved into three separate distribution companies operating in three distinct regions of Sweden. "Each company had its own CEO, its own set of rules, and its own MIS department. Each distribution company acted independently, with its own set of item numbers and different methods of purchasing and shipping goods." ICA's top management decided that to compete effectively in the 1990s, the group would have to unify and coordinate operations under a single umbrella organization. In this new environment, Engevik explains, "it was very important that ICA's new information system remove existing barriers and obstacles to our unification as an organization."

Designed and built using Andersen Consulting's FOUNDATION® integrated tool set, ICA's new information system for ICA's logistic process allows the three previously separate distribution companies to operate as a seamless logistic network. Two other systems at ICA, merchandising and sales, were specifically designed to incorporate Integrated Performance Support principles. The graphical user interface, for example, uses metaphors such as radio buttons and icons to give the worker control over the applications and to enhance productivity. Training Services are available in the system, either as CBT modules or as context-sensitive granules of training provided at point of need. Reference and Advisory Services are also available, with over 50 user procedures supporting the workers using the systems.

the desire for participation and the role of new knowledge in enabling that participation."[15]

Within an organization that is a true community of practice, acquiring and exchanging knowledge through conversation becomes crucial. Some are arguing today that conversation is an important form of work in the new economy. Conversation becomes the mode by which workers discover knowledge within their peers and within themselves. Conversation helps create the relationships that define an organization.[16]

KNOWLEDGE IS INDIVIDUAL

Finally, however, knowledge must become a part of the individual, altering the manner in which the person perceives the world and the manner in which the person takes action in that world. The acquisition of knowledge through learning has both social and individual aspects, and the social aspects usually come first: learning occurs *in activity,* in interaction with people in a community. But finally, knowledge must make a difference in the lives of a worker performing on the job. With customer service, we said there is no longer some idea of the generic customer, but rather *this* customer. With Integrated Performance Support and performance-centered design, there is no longer the idea of generic workers—only *this* worker enabled with the knowledge to do what he or she needs to do, right now.

CASE EXAMPLE:
ANDERSEN WINDOWS

Those of you who have ever built your own home, or had remodeling done, know about the complex and generally clumsy way in which options are explored and decisions made. The contractor will present you with a long list of options: What would you like this room to look like? What about this wall? What window and door configurations would you like?

"Well," you answer, "I'm not sure. Can you show me some pictures?"

"Yeah, sure, here's all the catalogs. Why don't you look through these and get back to me."

Several weeks later: "We like what we see in this picture here. But what would it look like in our house?"

Taking out a notebook and a piece of paper, the contractor says, "I'm not a very good artist, but I can give you a sort of sketch of it."

You wait for the drawing. Even looking past the amateurish sketch, you can see it's not quite right. You think you might like, instead, an arch over this one window, and you want to change how this other window looks a little bit. "How much would it cost to do that?"

"Well," replies the contractor, "I hope I have the most recent price listings here. But you know, that wouldn't help much, because you want a custom job. Let me call a couple of the window companies and see about that. I'll get back to you."

And so on. One of the most critical problems today for retailers and for contractors like our friend above is that product lines have been expanding rapidly to meet the needs of the marketplace. As we saw in the last chapter, customers have become much more demanding. They expect products and services tailored to their particular needs and desires, not off-the-shelf solutions. And they do their homework, too. They know what the competition is doing and are much more apt to shop around for the best deal. Product lines expand to meet customer needs, but this expansion means, in turn, an explosion in the amount of information with which workers must cope.

Andersen Windows, the leading manufacturer of windows and patio doors in the United States, faced the challenge of product information explosion and of business process change several years ago when they began to offer more customized window solutions to customers. New strategies meant a radical change in one of the company's most basic business processes. In addition to manufacturing make-to-stock items, they would now be assembling window configurations to order. Retailers would work with the customer to design unique looks, and Andersen Windows would assemble that order.

That change in the business process, combined with an out-of-date information system, caused the entire mechanism to break for the company. As Mike Tremblay, Manager of Information Systems for Andersen Windows, recalls: "In 1991, we went to the annual meeting of the salesforce and had to announce that we couldn't make any more new products, because the system couldn't handle it. That was the real trigger point for us. The entire process had become information constrained: from the retail selling point, through the distribution channel, back into the main office, and even back through the supply chain. There were people who were starting to drop our line because they almost literally needed a two-wheel dolly to carry in all the information about our products and about all the various options."

Andersen Windows began a multiphase project to redesign their order fulfillment process and, with it, the information technology that could make that process happen. Now, several years later, the company is on the last phase of what will be a powerful process to sell, manufacture, and deliver Andersen

Windows products. One important piece of this new process, and certainly the part most appealing to customers at the retail level, is the company's Window of Knowledge System.

Window of Knowledge™ is an interactive performance system that allows retailers and contractors to work directly with the customer to design unique window configurations for that customer's home. As Tremblay recalls, "The system began when our management said that we have to rethink how people are going to sell products, and we have to straighten out the quotation end of things. At the point in 1991 when we announced a moratorium on new products, our discrepancy rates on shipments were at their highest level ever. One out of every five containers had an error in it. You can imagine the relationship problems that caused us with our customers, who could no longer necessarily rely on the accuracy of any shipment. That figure today is down to one in every 500 containers—about 0.2%. And we honestly think there's no reason why we can't get it to zero."

At the retail level, the new marketing strategy—to permit custom design and order fulfillment—had not been accompanied by the support structure to allow their workers to implement that strategy. Andersen Windows customers came back to the company and said they couldn't do it anymore—either they were forced back to selling old make-to-stock items, or they were forced to make errors in the way they estimated time and costs for the custom jobs. From this problem came the Window of Knowledge System.

THE WINDOW OF KNOWLEDGE SYSTEM IN OPERATION

Typically, the Window of Knowledge System is found as a separate kiosk in a retailer showroom. There, customer and salesperson sit together to begin the design process. The salesperson can construct on screen a graphical representation of the customer's home or of the particular wall where the new window configuration will be built. From a list of options, the customer can select windows with which to experiment. The salesperson can select those options, place them in the appropriate locations on the wall, and then let the customer see immediately what this configuration would look like. Full motion video of certain outdoor landscapes plays behind the windows as the salesperson puts the windows in place, giving the customer the added feel of what it would be like to sit in that room and look out the window.

But the interactive design capability is only the most obvious part of the system functionality. The system will also, based upon the choices made on screen, generate a parts list with prices. It will compare that price with ones from other configurations. As the salesperson changes the dimensions and redraws units to customer specifications, the system automatically adjusts the price. Salespeople don't have to worry about pricing something for a customer that can't be manufactured by the company: the system will not allow salespeople to draw or create a unit that cannot be made. The system's Design Tool provides all the necessary dimensions to place an order, as well. The real selling advantage with these new products is being able to produce an accurate estimate with graphics to illustrate the many combinations of products available. Customers appreciate being able to see their ideas "installed" in a mock elevation of their home. And they also appreciate the accuracy of the price quote that accompanies the drawing.

To say the least, this system capability has revolutionized the manner in which retailers operate when they work with customers on Andersen Windows products. According to Glen Murduck, vice-president of Berea Pre-Hung Door, a customer of Andersen Windows, the Window of Knowledge System is not only a welcome addition to their stores, but also makes an important impression at trade shows. "People at the trade shows love the Window of Knowledge System," says Murduck. "They enjoy watching how it's used, and they like being able to visualize their ideas and get them on paper.

GENERATING AN ORDER AT THE WINDOW OF KNOWLEDGE SYSTEM

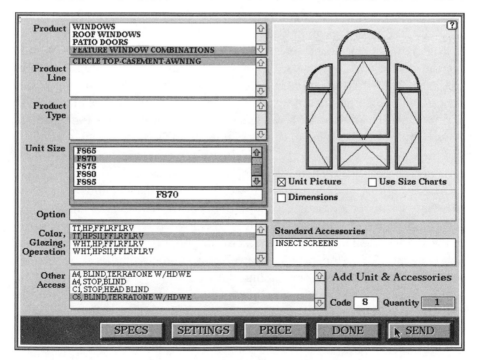

I print out for contractors a lot of rough opening schedules and graphics reports that show the windows in the project to scale. The professionalism and the visual aspect of being able to do this on the spot is key. Customers like having a picture to represent their ideas."

Organizations throughout the world are placing an increased emphasis on value-added selling. As Dave Steele of the Window Gallery in Augusta, Georgia notes, "Manufacturers and distributors are always emphasizing value-added services, but rarely does a consumer really perceive that value." The Window of Knowledge System gives retailers a set of tools, a vehicle, that allows them to sell Andersen Windows products more professionally and more profitably. It also allows them to provide services that they were unable to provide before. As Jay Lund of Andersen Windows says, "With this performance system, there's no doubt that customers perceive the value. People come in, they see what we can do for them, in terms of generating quotes, in terms of showing them different configurations and graphics. Contractors walk out of here wondering why anyone would ever want to buy a window any other way."

Certainly the system is one of the most visually impressive performance systems now in operation. But here again, the visual presentation only adds value because of the undeniable aesthetic dimension of the product. Andersen Windows is selling a *look,* not just a panel of glass, so the system must have the facility to present options to the customer in an aesthetic manner as well. Retailers report that the system draws a crowd. "When our staff isn't using the system with customers," reports one retailer, "we let it run in presentation mode. The most surprising thing to me was that it's the first thing in our showroom people gravitate toward. A lot of dealers may not realize that, in addition to what Window of Knowledge™ can do for them, it's fun to watch, as well. Many of our customers enjoy playing with the system. Their kids love it. Often, customers will bring their kids back to the store just to use it—future customers in the making."

The system network automates a wealth of information about Andersen Windows products at a central location to provide quick updates and to transfer information easily to every Window of Knowledge™ location across the United States. Dealers set up their systems in a nightly processing mode to receive updates from Andersen Windows' central processing location. For security purposes, all communications with dealers are initiated within the network, using an electronic "mailbox" capability. If an Andersen Windows distributor wants to access information in the system, the distributor places a call to the network. The network answers the call, records the distributor's identification number, then terminates the call. Using its memory information, the mainframe calls the distributor back to ensure that the transfer of information is made to a qualified distributor.

Future capabilities of the system are enormous, including the development of a kind of knowledge network or knowledge exchange. At some point, for example, dealers should be able to communicate through the network to their distributors. Dealers also should be able to gather inventory information from their distributors at the time of a sale. Leads also could be sent directly from Andersen Windows or from the distributor to the dealer.

The information deluge affects customers as well as workers; customers, too, want assistance in turning information into knowledge. As one Andersen Windows retailer puts it, "Customers want to make informed decisions. They don't want to be told what to do, but they have to have the support to decide. With this performance system, we can work together. We can start with options: 'Here are three different ways of doing the feature window in the back of your house, and here's exactly how it will look in all three of those ways.' We can show them the prices for all options, change the configurations, and then show those prices. We can make instant changes and get instant answers."

CASE EXAMPLE:
CONNECTICUT NATURAL GAS

The design and installation of new information systems can sometimes create information overload problems for workers. As we discussed in Chapter 4, technological innovations can sometimes give people so many options, so much information and functionality, that they cannot take full advantage of any of it very well. The modern phone system is a good example of this problem. Traditional phones may have been limited in their functionality, but people always knew how to use them for their primary function: to make a phone call. Anyone who uses a phone in the contemporary office environment knows that the powerful functionality of new systems can make even simple tasks difficult. Workers must be trained in even the basics: how to get a dial tone, how to place an outside call, how to put someone on hold. Try it yourself: go into an unfamiliar venue and experience the trauma of making a long distance phone call.

Connecticut Natural Gas in Hartford, Connecticut, faced a similar "good news, bad news" situation. The good news was that they were installing two new powerful information systems. The bad news was that workers were now faced with a much more complex work environment—and the problem was not going to be solved by traditional methods of user training. The answer for Connecticut Natural Gas was a performance-centered interface designed to connect workers with the two traditionally-designed systems. The story of the Connecticut Natural Gas performance system is instructive for two reasons: first, it shows the benefits of real performance-centered design, implemented in a short period of time to address business challenges being faced right now; second, it shows how organizations can deal with their legacy systems. Not all organizations can replace all of their legacy systems simultaneously, and many workers will need to access a combination of centralized legacy applications and new cooperative processing applications. IPS and the concept of performance-centered design can ensure that workers can efficiently and productively use this mixed set of applications. With IPS, organizations can begin at one level of performance support and then eventually migrate to a fully functional integrated performance system.

BUSINESS CHALLENGES

Connecticut Natural Gas is a medium-size, multidivision gas utility that distributes natural gas, steam, and chilled water. It serves over 147,000 customers in the greater Hartford/New Britain and Greenwich areas in Connecticut and employs over 650 people. Already a respected customer service leader in the Northeast United States, Connecticut Natural Gas elected to enhance this reputation by building two information systems: a Distribution Construction Information System (DCIS) and a Customer Information System (CIS). CIS is a 3270-based mainframe system; DCIS is an OS/2 client/server system. Integrated Performance Support concepts were applied to design a complementary performance support system—called CUSTOMER/1-IPS—to provide a seamless interface between the two systems.

The utility industry faces a significant period of change due to pending deregulation, increased competition, and the more sophisticated demands of customers. Connecticut Natural Gas employees must understand increasing amounts of rapidly changing information and then perform a wider variety of tasks. They must quickly and accurately answer customer questions, and they must grow and learn within their positions while they are working. Faced with these challenges, Connecticut Natural Gas management established several goals:

- To provide one-stop shopping for employees and customers of Connecticut Natural Gas.
- To reduce training costs for customer service representatives.
- To empower workers to make informed decisions.
- To ensure consistent and timely responses to customers.

To meet these goals, Connecticut Natural Gas elected to rebuild and integrate the two systems we have just described. Together, these two systems provide a single source for all customer information, covering any request from initial service through billing inquiries and routine service calls. These systems are also being integrated with a computer-aided dispatch system. This allows for future expansion to a facilities management system, which will provide an enterprise view of each customer and of related data.

Management's decision to build the new systems was made with an eye on the future. Going forward, they knew their existing mainframe hardware and software would be increasingly expensive to support. They wanted to move on instead to a leading-edge technical environment that would eliminate information systems backlogs, would be easy to maintain, and would allow for a continued migration to new technology. They envisioned developing integrated systems with real-time interfaces that could capture the full power of the system software.

THE TWO PRIMARY SYSTEMS

The Customer Information System, or CIS, is a mainframe, full-function customer system. CIS includes the following functions fully integrated and supported within one core system: billing, accounts receivable, credit and collections, service orders, meter reading, marketing, and meter management.

The Distribution Construction Information System, or DCIS, is a work management system in a fully cooperative, client/server environment. The system supports all functions necessary to plan and manage distribution construction activities including work initiation, planning, scheduling, tracking, closing, and preventive maintenance.

The two systems share customer address data, thus defining the same locations to both systems. Although functionality is rich within these systems, users now were faced with the prospect of having access to over 250 screens loaded with data; each screen was accessible only by entering a four character code.

The Integrated Performance Support solution to the integration of these systems, and to the performance problems engendered by the increased functionality, began with a challenge issued within the development team. As one designer remembers it, "We were using a product to build the Customer Information System that had been used many times before. But we were determined to improve on it. What scared us, almost, is how easily we could do that—how easily we could find more efficient ways for the system to work, how easily we could come up with a user interface that was truly performance-centered."

The team worked with a Senior Manager of Consumer Services who, although officially retired, was brought back in as the expert, the person with the most experience with the information systems. From interviews with him, the team determined that up to 40% of customer service questions could be grouped and made accessible from one screen—called a "Super Window." "That one simple step turned out amazing results. All of us said, 'Why hasn't this been done more often?' Well, all of us are guilty to a certain degree—all of us trained in traditional systems design. I spent 10 years designing systems where all you're looking for was getting the data onto the screen—not really

THE SUPER WINDOW FOR CONNECTICUT NATURAL
GAS SERVICE REPRESENTATIVES

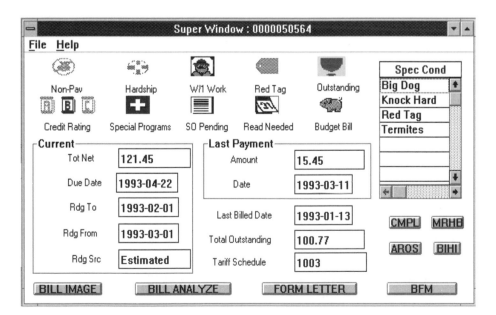

looking at how that data was to be used, what was important, and how it supported (or didn't support) the workflow and job processes."

"The senior utility people looked at the Super Window and told us we had made a quantum leap in usability here. Because of the new systems, workers went from thirty computer screens to 250 screens—that's an intimidating increase. Workers were dreading the possibility of having to remember separate four-digit transaction codes to get to every single screen. What were we going to do, train them for two weeks and get them to memorize all of the codes?"

A CONNECTICUT NATURAL GAS REPRESENTATIVE AT WORK

The Connecticut Natural Gas employee begins by logging on to the Customer Information System and can immediately access the Super Window. When a customer calls—let's say in this case that the customer is questioning a high monthly bill—the representative enters the customer name and accesses Super Window to get summary information about the customer's account. Instead of having to navigate to many different screens within the Customer Information System to locate data, Super Window provides an instantaneous picture of the person's account, which can answer most of the routine customer inquiries.

The Super Window's top line is an iconic "scoreboard." Each icon represents an account status or condition. If the icon is bright, it is enabled, meaning that that particular condition is true for this account. For example, the money bag icon represents the status "Shut Off for Nonpayment." These icons are helpful in alerting workers to preexisting account conditions. Other icons represent credit rating, status of pending construction work in a customer's area, service orders pending, budget bill, and unresolved customer issues.

In the upper right-hand corner of the Super Window is a Special Condition List Box. Premise conditions and special notations appear here. A premise condition alerts the worker to some existing building condition that personnel need to be aware of—a dangerous staircase, for example, or a watchdog on the premises. Special notations provide important information about a customer—perhaps the customer speaks only a particular language or has some other special need.

The middle section of the window provides commonly accessed billing and payment data. In the lower right corner of the screen are hot keys to frequently used functions, called "conversations." The Job Aids on the bottom line provide hot keys to the Integrated Performance Support services of the system. These keys save on navigation time and make the Super Window the home base for the entire Customer Information System. After reviewing the customer snapshot on the Super Window, the worker can launch into another screen or function.

Let's continue with the customer conversation. The Super Window has alerted the worker that this customer has previously called with a concern about a high bill, and the system alerts the worker that a service order has been executed for a visit to the customer's house to investigate. As the customer continues to struggle with the interpretation of the bill, the worker can call up the image of the customer's bill, which looks exactly like the copy the customer received in the mail. This is another example of good performance-centered design. Prior to the installation of the performance system, workers had to look at a traditional green-on-black display of the billing information, which was not formatted like the actual bill. This made even the simplest questions about the bill difficult for the representative to answer. With this system, workers can also print the bill at a nearby laser printer, rather than having to issue a work order to a separate department to have the customer's bill reissued.

The performance system includes a function called "Heating Usage Analysis," which allows workers to compare a particular month's bill with the bill from that month for the previous year. Variances are calculated by the system and displayed using a traffic light analogy. A variance below a predetermined value would appear green, indicating no alarming change. A variance above another predetermined value would appear red, indicating a drastic change had occurred. Values in between these upper and lower bounds would appear yellow.

The development of the Heating Usage Analysis function is an interesting part of the Connecticut Natural Gas project. Prior to the installation of the performance system, this analysis was almost always handled by the "super user," the representative who became the expert consultant to the design and development team. The experienced representative had invented a method to analyze customer bills to determine if something unusual was going on. But try as he might, he could never quite get all the representatives to learn his method: it was complicated to almost everyone except him. Developers met with him, had him explain it, and built that functionality into the system. That is one of the key goals of Integrated Performance Support: to find the special expertise within your company and then distribute it to all your workers. That's part of delivering an inexpensive solution to real performance problems.

Within the Heating Usage Analysis function, an Advisor prompts the worker with certain points that might help the customer determine why a bill might be higher than normal. Has the customer had any change in living habits? (More people living in the house, perhaps?) Might there be old or faulty heating equipment? Has the meter been misread? The worker can use one of the hot keys from the Super Window to access the screen showing the customer's meter readings for the past year. When the problem has been determined, the worker can generate a letter to that customer summarizing their conversation and indicating any additional work that is to be performed.

LESSONS FROM THE CONNECTICUT NATURAL GAS PERFORMANCE SYSTEM DEVELOPMENT

The development of a performance system, even one that builds upon existing legacy systems, must begin with the redefining and reengineering of the relevant business processes. One systems developer reports, "We began by looking at how the customer service representatives worked and then consulted with management and a select group of representatives to determine how they *wanted* to work. What did they want to support with this performance system? What are the challenges being faced? What support is needed to overcome that challenge?"

The Connecticut Natural Gas performance system also shows what can be done—and done impressively—by a relatively small organization. Not all organizations, of course, can look realistically at voice and video on workstations. Not all organizations will have the storage capabilities right away. CIO and IS executives from other companies who have heard of this project look at this performance system now and say, "This is real; it's doable. We can extend our mainframe and get some pretty impressive functionality by incorporating IPS concepts into our design." This is a way that organizations can use some of the newer technology to address specific performance problems.

The Connecticut Natural Gas project shows that Integrated Performance Support is a resource for organizations of any size—that performance systems are within reach for anyone. Especially as mainframe hardware enters its sunset period in the world of information technology, it will be important to many organizations to get as much out of their hardware as they can. There are a great number of middle managers in corporations today who cannot just go to their bosses and tell them that they need a whole new technical architecture. They tell us, "Look, I went to my boss eight years ago and said we needed this big mainframe system. If I say we need something else now, I'll lose my job." What these organizations are looking for is a way to extend the life of their mainframe systems, their legacy systems. IPS provides the means to begin with what an organization has in place. Then, because of the inherent flexibility of the system design, the organization can eventually migrate to newer technologies and architectures that can tap them into the greater power of client/server architectures and cooperative processing.

CHAPTER 7

ATTAINING AND SUSTAINING PROFICIENCY

"Informed and intelligent action," philosopher John Dewey once wrote, is "the aim of all educational development."[1] For Dewey, the flaw in most educational theories of the day could be found in their separation of mind and body, of thought and action. The result: either an academic and pedantic education, "aloof from the concerns of life," or an industrial and manual education, which teaches about "tools and means" without conveying a larger sense of purposes and ends. True education, the "supreme art" of education, engages thought toward the ultimate end of *action.*[2] And action connotes all sorts of human doings that involve the growth of power—especially, says Dewey, "power to realize the *meaning* of what is done."[3]

Dewey's seminal work on educational philosophy, particularly his emphasis on *activity* as an important educational principle, was an important influence on organizational training programs. As we shall see, several important thinkers today are carrying on Dewey's emphases in slightly different ways. But much of the training that occurs within some companies today continues to maintain the separation between thought and action that Dewey was attempting to bridge back in the early years of this century. Consider the characteristics of those things Dewey excluded from the category of true education: actions done under constraint, random reactions to random occurrences, actions that are merely routine, mechanical, and habitual. For many workers today, in many organizations, these sorts of actions may seem all too familiar. But they are, says Dewey, the sorts of actions where an education is definitely *not* taking place.[4]

Can information technology help this situation? Computers are becoming increasingly important as adjuncts to formal training programs, but there is still resistance in some circles to technology as an educational and performance enabler. Some executives may harbor the idea that "real" learning takes place only from human contact, from mentoring, from soaking in the wisdom of more experienced people. Personal contact is important to professional de-

- Today's and tomorrow's winning organizations can no longer focus on the *amount* of training for their knowledge workers or on the methods of *delivering* training. The focus must be on *performance outcomes* of that training.
- The critical success factor for knowledge workers is for them to *attain proficiency* quickly, and then to *sustain* that proficiency continuously.
- Traditional corporate training has often emphasized: (1) passive class-room-based and self-study techniques that take the worker away from the point of performance; and (2) "on-the-job" training that is often un-structured and unproductive.
- As a consequence, workers are often given too much training, too soon, before they are able to absorb the material; then, later, they are given too little training, too late to support them during actual job perfor-mance.
- Training should not be seen as a precondition for performance. The train-ing and learning principles of Integrated Performance Support empha-size getting the worker performing as quickly as possible.
- Training should not be the first resort to support knowledge worker per-formance, but the last resort.
- If organizations see the necessity of supporting knowledge worker per-formance throughout the continuums of their task and job progression, traditional distinctions among "training," "learning," and "education" will begin to blur.
- Training and educational support within Integrated Performance Sup-port is based on the principle of "learning by doing," or action learn-ing. Support is also "granular"—that is, designed and delivered in short segments relevant to specific performance situations.

velopment, but there are limitations to human resources: organizations have to consider whether they have enough experienced people to go around, es-pecially since in today's market "around" could mean any place on the globe, any time of the day. Resistance to technology-enabled training and learning may also be based on the presumption that workers have to know all sorts of *things*—facts, procedures, rules—before they can take action. The fact is, if an organization's corporate training programs are founded upon these kinds of assumptions, its workers may not be able to keep pace with the rapidly changing demands of the workplace today.

Consider two extremes of training that take place within many organizations today: (1) a classroom or self-study method, which supplants the normal workday for employees, requiring them either to sit passively and listen to lectures, or to work with printed workbooks; and (2) an experiential mode of on-the-job training, which in fact often turns out to be little more than "follow Joe around." The skills that result from passive, classroom learning are narrow, and retention rates are abysmally low; and on-the-job training does not necessarily produce workers who can absorb new situations, new responsibilities, and new modes of working.[5] Time-to-proficiency for some on-the-job training can be as high as eighteen months.[6]

Technology can help here. For years now, many organizations have taken advantage of computer-based training (CBT) and interactive video instruction (IVI) to supplement their traditional training programs. Instructional designers were quick to seize on the power of technology to deliver more powerful kinds of training experiences in a corporate setting. As we noted in Chapter 2, Instructional Design has been one of the fields whose work has merged with Artificial Intelligence and Systems Integration into the concept of Integrated Performance Support. But for some time, the primary focus of many discussions of electronic training has been on the new computer-based *delivery methods* for training. Now that these methods have become more common, attention is rightfully turning to the *performance outcomes* of that training. A recent article on future directions for corporate training predicts, insightfully, that trainers will increasingly be held accountable by management not just for the delivery of training, but for improved performance of workers that is supposed to result *from* that training.[7]

The amount of training, or the number of hours spent in training, then, is not the primary issue here. The primary issue is, rather, how do organizations get their workers to attain proficiency quickly, and then to sustain best performance continuously? In this chapter we examine the facility of performance systems to provide learning experiences, and to serve as a form of training focused primarily on real performance needs taking place at the location where employees do their work. Because of its focus on *performance proficiency,* an Integrated Performance Support strategy promises to lower dramatically the often hidden costs of traditional formal training programs: the costs of mistakes, of poor customer service, of rework, of trial and error, of on-the-job training that often makes two people do the work that one could do, and of training that may not be immediately applicable or pertinent.

IPS: REDUCING THE TIME TO PROFICIENCY

The graph below is an illustration of where we believe significant savings will be realized from performance systems. By reducing the lead time before workers can actually be on the job, performing effectively, IPS can significantly reduce the upfront training time for a new worker or for workers taking on a new task or new knowledge. Then, IPS allows workers to reach and maintain proficient levels of performance much faster. Although this is a theoretical representation, we are already seeing data from a number of clients to support the IPS proficiency curve and, therefore, the significant projected benefits from performance systems.

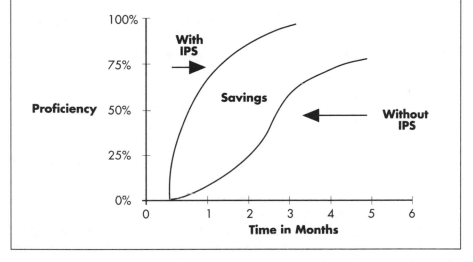

TRAINING AND EDUCATIONAL SUPPORT FOR DIFFERENT PERFORMANCE NEEDS

Consider the etymology of the word "training": the English verb "to train" derives from a word originally meaning "to draw" or "to drag." Thus, to train someone would mean to pull them along a predetermined course; the noun form of the word, meaning a set of railroad cars or the part of a bridal gown that trails back away from the bride, follows directly from that meaning.

At the heart, traditional understandings of training thus presume a high degree of *intentionality* on the part of management about what they want workers to be able to know and to do (as with a train: here are the tracks, just follow them and you'll get to where you want to go). They also presume a high degree of *predictability* about what the performance of a particular task within a job will entail (when the train rounds this curve, it will go up a steep incline: send more power to the engine). Gloria Gery notes other implicit assumptions behind the "training program paradigm":[8]

- Training is an event that occurs at a particular time and a particular place.
- The audience is relatively homogeneous, and the training must be consistent for all of these learners.
- The job situation is fairly static.
- Learners require someone who knows better—someone who can impose structure.
- Certain kinds of training, and certain kinds of information, are a precondition for performance.
- Teaching people facts *about* things will translate into their being able to *do* things.

Again, *intentionality* and *predictability* are the primary underpinnings of many of these training assumptions. But herein lies the paradox for work in the knowledge economy: predictable and routine tasks, jobs, and processes will increasingly be automated and offered directly (that is, transferred) to the consumer, thereby increasing the sales base and eliminating unnecessary personnel. True "knowledge workers" will be those whose work is only partly predictable: whose work involves some combination of the predictable and the unpredictable, and whose careers increasingly move them toward higher strategic levels where performance systems must do more than provide application- or task-specific support. Here, a performance system must enable what we may call a "learning environment": an environment where resources and networks are provided to ensure that continuous learning can take place. In this kind of environment, "training" will inevitably become more self-directed.

We can look at different kinds of performance needs for knowledge workers in terms of a "work pyramid" (see figure on the next page). From an enterprise perspective, work within an organization may be seen as a continuum with three primary levels:

- *Operational.* At the base of the pyramid, organizations must provide operational support. Work here is application centered and procedures are relatively fixed. Actions performed are often repetitive, like data entry, so support is often screen-based.

THE WORK PYRAMID

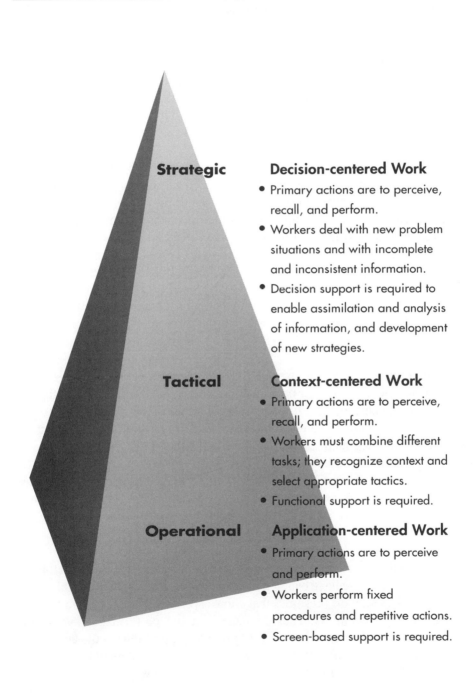

Strategic

Decision-centered Work
- Primary actions are to perceive, recall, and perform.
- Workers deal with new problem situations and with incomplete and inconsistent information.
- Decision support is required to enable assimilation and analysis of information, and development of new strategies.

Tactical

Context-centered Work
- Primary actions are to perceive, recall, and perform.
- Workers must combine different tasks; they recognize context and select appropriate tactics.
- Functional support is required.

Operational

Application-centered Work
- Primary actions are to perceive and perform.
- Workers perform fixed procedures and repetitive actions.
- Screen-based support is required.

- *Tactical.* In the mission of the pyramid, work is more context-centered, and organizations must provide functional support. Workers must recognize context, combine different tasks, and then recall and apply tactics in line with strategy and operational needs.
- *Strategic.* At the top of the pyramid, work is decision-centered, and organizations must support workers who are dealing with new problem situations and with incomplete or inconsistent information. They must assimilate and analyze information to create and apply solutions with long-term consequences.

The pyramid does not imply that any particular job involved *only* tactical work, or only strategic or operational work. Jobs may emphasize one type over another, but are usually comprised of degrees of all three. The issue here is that performance must be supported at *all* levels of the pyramid; the ability to provide that support is a distinctive feature of Integrated Performance Support. A performance system supports all levels of work. It starts at the lowest level with platform training (use of mouse and windows, for example); operational training (how to use an application); application training (what are the concepts behind an application?); job training (what are my tasks?); to even higher levels like company training (corporate culture), industry training, and professional development. These different levels of training and education reflect workflow and workflow support. With a performance system, one can go seamlessly from a higher workflow level to a lower level, and vice versa, and one is able to ask for (or be pointed toward) related training and other resources. In supporting these levels, workers build up a complete and, for them, relevant body of knowledge and related skills. This makes their working environment an integrated supportive environment.

The pyramid is, we have said, a view of work from an enterprise perspective. What about a view of work from the worker's perspective? These are not, we should emphasize, mutually exclusive kinds of views. But from a human-centered point of view, work may be conceived within a slightly different continuum.

- *Tasks.* At the lowest or most common level, a worker has *tasks* to perform— a series of what we have called potential "moments of value." At this level, performance support presumes that some aspects of a job have a fairly high degree of predictability. Thus, management and performance system designers can with some intentionality provide support during the actual performance of particular tasks—as we have said, "on demand, at point of need." Management may also require, however, that workers achieve a level of basic competence before the performance of a higher-risk task or series of tasks. In this case, training can still be found upon performance, but it will use simulation and testing techniques to ensure that proficiency is attained before going "live," as it were.

- *Job.* A complex and, in most cases, unique combination of tasks and responsibilities makes up a worker's *job.* From the knowledge worker's perspective, a fulfilling sort of job will be one where responsibilities increase as experience and skills grow. (Indeed, the traditional idea of a "job" as a predictable and constant thing is increasingly giving way to the idea of a "role," which changes depending on need and enhanced abilities.) Here, intentionality and predictability fall to lower levels. Management may have general ideas about the trajectory of training and education necessary as a worker's job continues, but this trajectory will necessarily be altered by market conditions and, hopefully, by the creativity of the knowledge worker as he or she improves the processes that make up that job. Here, again, the intentional or planned training of an organization must be supplemented by opportunities made available through the organization's learning environment. Self-directed training and education must occur that will enable the worker to develop skills and acquire knowledge necessary for continued proficiency.
- *Career.* At the highest level, a knowledge worker will be concerned about how a particular job fits into his or her career trajectory. Statistics show here, of course, that the average knowledge worker will change organizational affiliations many times over the course of a career, but this fact can hardly define the opportunities that an organization provides to its workers. An organization that says, "We know you're just going to leave anyway, so why bother?" will not be in business long enough to test that particular approach to training and education. Organizations must provide their knowledge workers with opportunities for long-term education and professional development. Here, however, intentionality and predictability about tasks and jobs are quite low. Organizations must rely ever more on the learning environment they have created. (See, for example, the discussion of a knowledge management system in Chapter 11.) Within this environment, workers grow in knowledge and skill; in turn, they become key providers and creators of new product and service ideas, of new knowledge capital.

If organizations begin to see the necessity of supporting the performance of their workers throughout these sorts of continuums—either from the enterprise perspective or from the worker's perspective—they will notice that the traditional distinctions among "training," "learning," and "education" will begin to blur. This is already happening. Todd Kutches of McCaw Cellular noted in Chapter 5 that the ability to provide context-sensitive reference information with a performance system really ends up becoming a kind of training. We have seen this same facility in the scenario in Chapter 3 speaking of the Total Information Management (TIM) system. Think of a commercial lender about to have lunch with a potential customer in, say, the printing industry. The lender knows next to nothing about the printing business. Without a performance system, the alternatives available to the lender are not very positive ones: go to the lunch and try to fake it; try to ask basic questions and risk being perceived as too busy to care about that customer; try to find a colleague who knows something about it; or hope that the pile of business magazines in the office might have an article on the printing business. The bank's research department could certainly help, but that would take days; the lender needs information in the next two hours. Using the performance system, the lender can immediately access information about the printing industry where, with a combination of text and multimedia elements, he or she can receive an effective overview of that industry. The performance system also allows the lender to retrieve articles about the customer that might have appeared recently in the press. You can imagine the impression that this lender will create in meeting the customer for the first time. The lender will be able to talk more intelligently about some of the issues facing the industry and will be able to know something about the interests of that specific customer as well. In a traditional sense, the support that the system gave the lender was a form of training support.

TOO MUCH, TOO SOON; TOO LITTLE, TOO LATE: SUPPORT ALONG THE CONTINUUM

What do organizations want their workers to know, what do they want them to do, and what is the link between knowing and doing—between thought and action, mind and body? What capabilities and skills do workers need, not only to achieve best performance, but also to grow in capabilities, and to ensure that their careers are rich and rewarding? If we can answer those questions, we need to ask how we are going to deliver the kind of training that *supports* the development of that knowledge and those skills. Ask this question of yourself: think about the skills that you have right now that you believe to be critical to the best performance of your work. Now, what percentage of those skills did you acquire through formal, corporate-sponsored training? One six-year study of managers at Honeywell Corporation, completed in 1985, put the figure at about 20%. It follows that 80% of critical job skills—an amazing figure—are acquired on the job.[9]

We have said that early theories indicating that technology would lead to the "deskilling" of the workforce have not proved to be true. In fact, workers today need more skills, not fewer, and higher-order skills, at that. Consider, for example, Anthony Patrick Carnevale's list of sixteen job skills crucial to success in today's workplace (see box on p. 190). Among the types of skills are "learning to learn" skills, academic basics, communication, adaptability, personal development, group effectiveness, and influencing skills. The list is insightful and comprehensive. Implicit within the list, however, is also the following: the ability to do the tasks a worker is assigned to do, and to do them well. This need cannot be ignored. Yes, we want to create lifelong learning opportunities. Yes, we want workers to be creative. Yes, we want to create an empowering learning environment. But we also want workers to be able to *perform specific assigned tasks well.* We want them to meet or exceed customer expectations. We want them to be able to complete an assignment with no errors. We want them to be able to make improvements to the procedures by which they complete tasks so that tasks can be done better next time. This is the training challenge: on the one hand, how to create an environment in which training and learning are taking place all the time—the learning environment. On the other hand, we want workers to be supported with services and facilities tailored to a specific performance need at the moment it is needed.

This distinction has been difficult to maintain with traditional approaches to training. The usual pattern of training has been to concentrate it at the early stages of a new job or new responsibility, and to see it as a precondition to performance. When conditions have been met, supervisors set the worker loose, as it were, trusting that whatever additional skills need to be learned will be acquired through experiential osmosis on the job. Many organizations today continue to give their workers too much training, too soon—before they have any real need or experience to absorb the material. And then, when it is needed, they give them too little training, too late to make a difference when job performance really matters to the workers and to their companies. Organizations need training that is available on demand, at the point where it is needed, in a form that is tailored to the particular performance need of that moment. They also need to create learning environments. Meeting both these kinds of training demands is a major goal of Integrated Performance support.

In the accompanying box (p. 192), we summarize the characteristics of training and learning experiences that a performance system can make available. We want now to provide more detail on each of these points.

CARNEVALE'S SIXTEEN JOB SKILLS FOR THE CONTEMPORARY WORKFORCE

Learning to Learn

1. *Foundation Skills:* learning how to learn—how to collect, know, and comprehend; how to give and receive feedback, and how to learn collaboratively.

Academic Basics

2. *Reading Skills:* basic literacy; reading in order to learn; reading in order to do.
3. *Writing Skills:* preparing and organizing information; writing, editing, revising.
4. *Computational Skills:* quantification, computation, measurement and estimation, quantitative comprehension, quantitative problem solving.

Communication

5. *Speaking Skills:* nonverbal skills, vocal skills, verbal skills.
6. *Listening Skills:* assigning meaning to aural stimuli.

Adaptability

7. *Problem Solving Skills:* the ability to bridge the gap between what is and what ought to be.
8. *Creativity Skills:* the ability to produce a novel idea, and then to turn it into a practical one.

Personal Development

9. *Self-Esteem Skills:* the ability to maintain a realistic and positive self-image.
10. *Motivation and Goal-Setting Skills:* the ability to translate work into an instrument for the development of the self.
11. *Personal and Career Development Skills:* the ability to adapt to changing work requirements to ensure employment security and to fulfill personal potential.

**CARNEVALE'S SIXTEEN JOB SKILLS
FOR THE CONTEMPORARY WORKFORCE (*CONTINUED*)**

Group Effectiveness

12. *Interpersonal Skills:* the ability to judge appropriate behavior, to absorb stress, to share responsibility, to deal with ambiguity.
13. *Negotiation Skills:* the ability to overcome disagreements by compromising and accommodating.
14. *Teamwork Skills:* the ability of groups to pool human talents to pursue common goals.

Influencing Skills

15. *Organizational Effectiveness Skills:* the ability to work productively in the context of explicit and implicit organizational cultures and subcultures.
16. *Leadership Skills:* the ability to influence others to serve the strategic purposes of an organization or the developmental needs of an individual.[10]

---

1. LEARNING BY DOING

Speaking of the training capabilities of the performance system at McCaw Cellular, CIO Ingvar Petursson says, "One way we make sure that all of our employees are getting the best use of our systems is to try *not* to send them to a training class every time something new happens in the system or in our business. Now, when we deliver a new product or a new capability in the system, we also deliver to them, through the system, all of the training, the tutorials, the help-me, show-me, assist-me, advise-me kinds of capabilities inherent in the system."

One of the primary productivity features of performance systems is their facility to get people working at their jobs better and faster. IPS and the actual performance systems built from an IPS strategy aim to minimize the amount of training away from the place where the work will actually be done. They aim to eliminate the assumption that, at the operational and tactical levels, training must always be a precondition for performance; instead they try to put the worker in a performance situation as quickly as possible. Why? The model that says people should learn first and then take action is not fast enough. *Can-do* and *know-how* have to happen at the same time for a

TRAINING AND LEARNING FROM A PERFORMANCE SYSTEM

There are many distinctive philosophical presumptions behind the approach to training and learning within Integrated Performance Support.

1. Effective training and educational support should be based on the principle of "learning by doing," or action learning.
2. Training and educational support at the task level should be "granular"—designed and delivered in short segments relevant to specific performance situations.
3. Support should be specific to the unique tasks being performed and to the unique person performing those tasks.
4. Learning takes place continuously, often in ways that trainers and educators least expect.
5. An effective learning environment is geared toward helping workers discover and construct knowledge; it does not merely attempt to fill workers with facts and information.
6. Training and educational support should be available on demand; it should be learner-driven, self-paced, and nonlinear.
7. Effective training and learning is one-on-one.
8. Learning is exploratory and interactive—opportunities for discovery and creative linking must be provided.
9. Training and education must be multisensory, employing a variety of media appropriate to the subject or task to be performed.
10. Training and education must be continuously updated so that workers always have access to up-to-date information and the latest innovations.

worker, if the organization is truly focused on performance.[11] Proficiency requires that people get significant practice in performing the task. As Gloria Gery notes, people must have sufficient practice in actually doing the task in order to become proficient at it. It's not enough to talk about the task or to listen to a lecture about it. It also isn't enough to watch someone do the task, whether the person doing it is standing next to the worker, on videotape, or within a computer-based training module. Passive learning is still passive learning, even if it happens in front of a computer. Without practice, without doing, knowledge rarely eventuates in proper actions and in best performance.[12]

IPS presumes that the most effective learning takes place for workers while they are doing their work—so it follows that the goal should be to get them doing that work as quickly as possible. There is a growing body of research to support the argument that increased retention results from learning that is action-based. Workers are more likely to retain information provided in the context of their work because more parts of the brain become involved in the cognitive acquisition of that information. Some research suggests that traditional training in the workplace has only a 10–15% retention rate[13]—a figure that suggests that corporate training dollars are leaking out of the organization at an astonishing rate.

"Learning by doing" is now an accepted concept in corporate training, and one of the ways in which John Dewey's educational philosophy continues to have an impact. Under the leadership of Roger Schank, the Institute for the Learning Sciences at Northwestern University is developing many innovative programs about adult learning that relate to workforce learning. Learning by doing has become, for example, a full-fledged teaching architecture, and a number of applications based upon this architecture have been developed. We will discuss a couple of them later in this chapter.

Schank bases much of his work on what he calls "natural learning." Natural learning, says Schank, can be seen by observing young children—those younger than school age. Instruction to that child, if the parent is a good teacher, is always available when the child wants it; it's personal, tailored to the ability of the child, and under no performance pressures. Observe a toddler learning to walk and talk. There, learning takes place by performing the action. The inevitable early failures are simply part of the learning process. Each time they perform the action, they do better.[14]

Repeatedly, researchers such as Schank are finding, as Dewey found, that the model for learning should *not* be the traditional education model from schools and universities. On the subject of nurturing genius in children, for example, Schank says that the way *not* to nurture it is by the traditional methods of schools. Intelligent children want only limited guidance; they don't want to be told answers or to sit passively and drink in facts. They want to discover answers for themselves. Most educational systems can't accommodate such a learner—indeed, many teachers will be frightened by the sorts of questions these children ask and may intentionally or unintentionally discourage the child and try to bring that natural creativity under the control of some preconceived methodology. Truly creative people, says Schank, work at their own pace at subjects that interest them. To make this happen in organizations and in systems, one has to create a learning environment that supports that sort of behavior.[15] While recognizing that there are some important distinctions between adult and child learning, we believe that Schank's notion of natural learning has validity in both domains.

Now that learning by doing has become more accepted, the next step is to move it beyond its present state, which all too often does not extend past a verbal commitment to the idea. Practical implementation in the training program has not always followed, beyond, perhaps, a few modules of traditional computer-based training. The link between computer-based training and "learn by doing" is most often made through the technique of simulation. Flight simulators, for example, allow pilots to develop and test their skills without jeopardizing the lives of passengers. Performance systems use simulations as well. Consider, for example, the aerospace industry example discussed in Chapter 6. Between repairs of engines, technicians can use the performance system to build their skills. Basic concepts training uses on-screen multimedia elements—full-motion video, photos, diagrams, graphs, audio, and text—to describe basic operations, as well as detailed maintenance procedures. Technicians can hone their diagnostic skills, or even practice actual repairs. With full case simulation, technicians can practice an actual diagnose-and-repair operation. On-screen functions allow parts to be rotated and examined, and then placed, so technicians can practice correct positioning during a repair and then test the repair for correctness.

But learning by doing can go beyond simulated performance to actual performance. Here is where Integrated Performance Support represents a significant advancement for workforce performance and for the attainment of proficiency in less time. Because of the variety of support services available at a performance system, workers can in many instances begin the actual performance of a new job or responsibility, relying during the initial period on the advisory, job aid, reference, and training facilities of the system. Here, again, traditional understandings of training begin to blur. Consider the analogy of taking an automobile trip. With traditional understandings of training, we would give the driver the entire information about how to reach the destination before the trip was actually made, hoping the driver could retain that information long enough to complete the trip successfully. With an IPS understanding, we would just tell the driver to get into the car and go; whenever the driver reached a point of uncertainty, the "system" would provide the support necessary to keep the driver performing until the destination was reached. From one point of view, we have eliminated the entire need for training for that task. But from another point of view, the entire experience of making the trip has become a kind of training. In effect, training and performance have merged into one experience. If one wants to maintain a traditional view of training, then a performance system will mean that that kind of support will be a last resort, not a first resort. Only when the advisory, job aid, and reference facilities of the system have not been able to provide the necessary support for the performance will the knowledge worker turn to a training tutorial.

2. GRANULAR DELIVERY OF TRAINING FOR TASK SUPPORT

The support provided to the driver of the car in the above example is based upon what is called the "granular" delivery of support. Rather than give a worker the entire training content for a job or series of tasks at the beginning, we want to provide that worker only with the training content relevant to the task being performed at the moment. This piece of training content is called a "granule." One might think of this idea of granularity by comparing it to the way we often look something up in the index of a box. Traditional training delivers the whole book to the worker; granular training delivers just those pages that are relevant to what the worker is trying to understand or to find out at the moment. One of the reasons people don't use documentation very easily, and why traditional training often fails, is because too much unnecessary and irrelevant information is included for each worker, since, by definition, it must cover all types of workers in work situations.[16] Workers become overwhelmed when developers include everything that the abstract category "worker" might want to know. With Integrated Performance Support, there is no abstract category "worker," but rather this person right here who has a performance need. To meet this need, performance systems can layer and structure the training so that workers can access only the part needed to perform the task at hand. Conversely, one of the reasons why traditional help screens fail is that they are structured at the lowest common denominator of knowledge. Consequently, they usually lack context for the worker. Layering and structure are the critical assets of instructional design in a performance system.

Not everyone has been convinced about the importance of "granularity" as the basis for training delivery. Ruth Clark, for example, believes that workers need a "wholistic" schema—they need the big picture, not just the small portion of the picture delivered by the task-specific method. Workers may not take the time to engage in this training and may ignore it or never stumble across it.[17] But granular delivery of training is only one part of the goal of Integrated Performance Support. The other half, as we have said, is to provide that wholistic picture, a picture of the entire job, and the place that job has within the entire company. Within this learning environment, workers will be able to enlarge their own knowledge base and that of the whole organization.

Granularity and wholistic training are not, after all, an either/or situation. In fact, performance systems permit workers to access training content in a variety of ways. In the North West Water case study we will look at later in the chapter, workers receive basic training at a high level about a certain procedure, and they learn the entire procedure through simulation and other interactive, multimedia delivery techniques. But then, as they actually perform the procedure, that same training is broken down into granules and made available to the worker at critical moments during actual performance.

We cannot say that every performance situation is like the driver taking the automobile trip; not every worker in every job can go "live" immediately. As we have indicated, some jobs require that a level of proficiency be achieved before entering into actual performance. Few of us, we suspect, would want our surgery performed by a first-year medical student just learning to use a scalpel. But most of us would be relieved if support was at all times available to that surgeon at any point during the performance of the surgery, particularly if the surgery involves procedures rarely encountered or practiced.

3. TRAINING TAILORED TO UNIQUE TASKS PERFORMED BY UNIQUE PEOPLE

In Chapter 5 we noted that in today's competitive environment, organizations must move beyond generic notions of customers to a specific orientation toward *this* customer, right here. The corollary in the training environment is that there are no workers, just *this* worker right here needing support; there are no "learners," there is only *this* learner. Organizations must not drive their training programs only by the facts that they want their workers to acquire, or by the convenience of scheduling. Training must be driven by the actual performance needs of the learner, who has unique needs, capabilities, experience, and educational background; unique responsibilities and work profiles; and unique ways in which knowledge, training, and work profile combine to bring forth actual performance.

Performance systems reach their fullest potential when Knowledge Worker Services and Work Profile Services are included as part of the system design. With these two services, all other support, especially training, can be customized and tailored to the work to be performed and to the particular worker performing it. But this is only part of what we mean by saying that training is geared toward the individual. It also means that each person *learns* in different ways. Traditional training has presumed a homogeneity in the workforce that was based on a more stable work environment and workforce. Training cannot be delivered the same way to everyone today and have the same effectiveness. The dynamic of today's work environment requires different people to learn different jobs in different ways and under different conditions.

_____ GRANULAR TRAINING: A BANKING PERFORMANCE _____
SYSTEM FROM THE NETHERLANDS

The concept of granular training can be seen in a prototype performance system designed by Andersen Consulting's Educational Computing Consortium (ECC) in the Netherlands.

This performance system demonstrates a number of IPS services to support the work of bank employees as they do cash withdrawals and as they assist clients with savings plans and mortgages. In this demonstration, the worker calls up the basic profile of a customer who wishes to do a cash withdrawal. A photograph of the customer, an image of the customer's signature, and all account information is immediately accessible.

The system alerts the worker if the requested withdrawal exceeds the customer's current balance and then provides advice as to the circumstances that might permit the worker to approve the withdrawal anyway. If the customer shows a high balance in a low-interest account, the worker may be advised to suggest other types of accounts. If the customer is interested, the worker receives support to gather the necessary customer information, to forecast the future earnings potential of various accounts

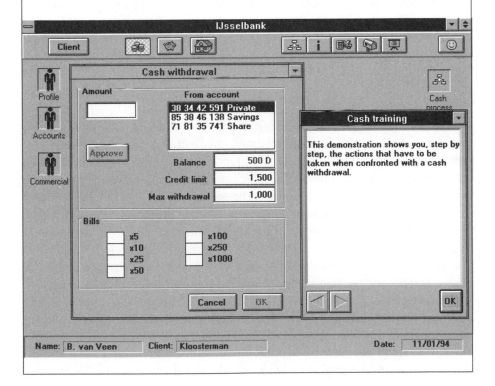

──────── Granular Training: A Banking Performance ────────
System from the Netherlands (*Continued*)

given the customer's savings plan, and ultimately to establish the new savings account.

During any of these procedures, a brief training tutorial may be accessed at the touch of a button. The screen pictured is from the tutorial demonstrating the procedure for cash withdrawals.

The worker moves through any of the tutorials at his or her own pace and can practice at any point within the session. As the tutorial progresses, the cash withdrawal window demonstrates the correct manner of completing the procedure. The granular delivery of training in this case permits the worker to complete this training either as a new employee or as a "refresher" during the first weeks of employment—even, if necessary, during an actual transaction with a customer.

Some people learn best by reading texts; other people need more varied media—graphics, pictures, sound. Some people learn well in a group setting, others do not; they may need to move at their own pace, faster or slower than the group. Performance-centered training means that we must be attuned to the variety of methods and conditions for learning.

4. CONTINUOUS LEARNING

One writer calls for the reengineering of corporate training by beginning with a design for the "100% learning event." This includes some traditional elements of formal training, as well as a great deal of support for people while they apply new skills on the job.[18] "Design" is perhaps the wrong word here, implying a control over the learning process that no one has in today's learning environment—or should wish to have. Even computers, no matter how sophisticated, will not be able to provide all things to all people and must at some point provide *access* to knowledge sources in addition to specific support for tasks. Roger Schank has written that it is unlikely that we could put even a fraction of the knowledge available to people into the computer. "It would take several generations of thousands of workers in different areas just to obtain all the information and determine how it should be represented. In the meantime, knowledge would be changing and new discoveries being made. It is simply unrealistic to contemplate doing this, even if we had built a system that could organize and store all the materials properly."[19]

The very word "training" may be the wrong word, even obsolete in certain cases, at least as it has been traditionally understood—as one person delivering information to another person, in a "train" so to speak. One of the key characteristics of the Integrated Performance Support training paradigm is the transfer of the responsibility for the training event to the worker. This transfer parallels, in fact, the transfer of work to the consumer that is characterizing today's marketplace. (Today, the consumer is a bank teller, telephone operator, airline reservation agent, service station attendant, and so forth.) In the training area, when we move beyond the intentional support for predictable tasks, organizations must make available a body of knowledge relevant to the worker, but the worker initiates and drives the training process in response to the task to be done or in pursuit of the opportunity to be gained.

Just as important, the organization enables learning and self-training to occur almost constantly. We noted in the last chapter the importance of "conversation" to the learning process on the job. Through conversation, workers discover knowledge, share it with colleagues, create relationships with themselves and with their customers as well. Tom Peters' book, *Liberation Management*, describes one company as a place where "conversations rewire the company to leverage its knowledge base—so much so that the conversation *is* the organization."[20] Performance systems encourage the conversing of workers through the network and will continue to enhance that conversation as video mail and other technologies like knowledge management systems increasingly become a part of the workplace.

This sharing of knowledge expands the knowledge base of the entire organization. Knowledge is an intellectual asset of an organization that grows as it is shared. As a worker shares knowledge with a colleague, the colleague learns, but in turn gives feedback—questions, clarifications, amplifications—which then increase the value of the knowledge to the worker. Each person's knowledge base grows, and the knowledge base of the entire organization grows.[21]

5. HELPING WORKERS DISCOVER AND CONSTRUCT KNOWLEDGE

A number of prominent educators are directing their research toward the manner in which human beings learn not merely by acquiring information, but by participating in the construction of meaning. Stephanie Pace Marshall, executive director of the Illinois Mathematics & Sciences Academy in Aurora, Illinois, notes that part of the task of educators is to facilitate constructive learning *by* the learner. Marshall refers to research from the American Psychological Association (APA) into something they call "Learner-Centered Psychological

Principles." Says Marshall, "Several premises derived from the APA principles are particularly important: learning is an individual and goal-directed process. It is a process of constructed meaning, and that meaning is constructed from both information and experience. Learners construct representations of knowledge that make sense to them. They associate and connect new information with what they already know, and they use higher-order thinking skills to enhance their creative and critical thought."[22]

This conclusion is also supported by William J. Clancey of the Institute for Research on Learning in Palo Alto, California. Clancey argues that human learning is not based upon a model that says that the brain simply receives and stores external representations, which can then be retrieved, modified, and stored again—to remain unchanged until their next use. Instead, the meaning is not inherent in the form of a representation, but is rather constructed when humans comment on the form. That is to say, humans construct meaning from their perceptions. "A major error in cognitive science has been to suppose that the meaning of a representation is known prior to its production. It's the person perceiving the representation who determines what it means." Learning is not a separate process, says Clancey, but an integral part of every perception and movement.[23]

We might illustrate this concept with a figure used in cognitive psychology. In the figure below, note that the symbol in the middle is ambiguous; we provide the "correct" reading based upon the context in which we perceive the symbol.[24]

From Robert E. Ornstein, *The Psychology of Consciousness.* San Francisco: W. H. Freeman and Company, 1972, p. 41.

6. WORKER-DRIVEN TRAINING

If we want to support workers as they not only discover but construct meaning, we must, as we have noted, transfer much of the responsibility for the training experience to that worker. Traditional corporate training and education have been based upon the trainer being in control. But that model has sometimes failed. One reason for this is that, as Clancey and others argue, the idea of control has always been sort of fiction. The second reason is that the belief in control has sometimes impeded rather than facilitated real learning. Placing the locus of learning in the worker, not in the classroom, is more faithful to the actual human cognitive process. It's also more productive. It is difficult to keep the attention of workers when information is forced on them out of context. In context, during performance and at the moment of need, workers can internalize the cognitive components of the training.[25]

Is everyone in the workplace ready for this kind of learning experience? Probably not. In countries like the United States, where instructor-driven learning has been the norm, employees may come into the workplace expecting to be told what to do and when to do it. Craig Mindrum, who teaches business ethics at a university in the United States, laments that many students are poorly prepared for his more Socratic teaching methods, where students are expected to contribute to the learning experience of the class. "I actually had one student one time tell me that he was going to demand a refund from the university— that 40 students don't learn together, but riot together. That's an extreme example, but many, many students come into the classroom with contradictory notions: on the one hand, they expect to finish the class with an ordered set of class notes containing the 'truth' about the subject. On the other hand, they're clearly bored during those times when I do give brief lectures. Many have never learned what learning is. When professors are presenting information with an obvious structure—like, 'the author makes three points about this subject'—it's all being written down in the notebooks. But when the real learning is taking place, when we are critiquing things and coming up with new ideas, they appear bored and nothing gets written down."

With a performance system, job-specific training is available at the moment when workers need it to support their performance. One education director calls this kind of on-demand training the "mass customization" of education. "What I learn will be different from what other people learn. We each learn what is needed—[it's] the customization of what we need to do our jobs. It's more efficient and it's more motivating."[26] Learner-driven training is the area where technology plays its most important role. Many organizations fear, however, that such interactive training is extremely costly to develop. This does not always have to be true. Todd Kutches of McCaw Cellular notes that the first version of their performance system, which included splices of context-sensitive training, impressed management, because they simply hadn't thought it could be done within the budget. "They didn't expect any training in the system; they thought that was a black hole that was really expensive. Their preconceived notion was that developers were going to have to stay away from computer-based training, but we proved that notion wrong."

The point is well taken that organizations with an installed base of workstations at workers' desks are going to be able to implement on-demand training faster than other companies. Nevertheless, we believe that a system of distributed learning—on-demand training and education at employee workstations—is inevitable. Greg Kearsley, a professor at George Washington University and author of *Training and Technology: A Handbook for HRD Professionals,* argues that in the near future, trainers will need to justify a decision to do traditional, classroom training, rather than to deliver training via advanced information systems.[27]

One often-overlooked benefit of on-demand training is that certain kinds of employees can make more productive use of downtime—time when they are not actively helping a customer, for example, or when they are waiting for work to come in. The technicians from our aerospace industry case study, for example, are sometimes waiting in the hangars for jets to return from test runs. With their performance systems, they can use this time to build their skills and, better still, to come up with improved maintenance procedures.

7. ONE-ON-ONE LEARNING

We have dubbed the Training Services facility of a performance system the system's "tutor" with good reason. If we had called it a "teacher," that might have called to mind the image of a person standing at the front of a room, delivering the same information to many people, each of whom actually has different educational backgrounds and needs. And learning is most often effective when it is delivered as a tutor would: one-on-one. Gloria Gery makes the interesting point that traditional training in companies is the result of the mass industrialization of modern society. The numbers of people who had to be trained simply got too large for old methods of teaching, which were based on apprenticeship, one-on-one coaching, and tutoring. "No one could possibly handle the number of apprentices and entry-level people that entered the workplace during modern industrialization. The training program was the new paradigm that replaced one-to-one instruction when it became ineffective."[28]

Can a computer possibly imitate the intimacy and effectiveness of one human teaching another human? The answer depends on what you mean. Certainly, as one writer notes, the "warm fuzzies" of personal interaction cannot be duplicated, and that's an important issue to remember. People appreciate the chance to get together with co-workers, especially those they rarely see. Informal conversations are crucial to the learning experience of an organization. And, while voice mail and electronic mail can bring people together technologically, that sort of interaction cannot duplicate face-to-face contact.[29]

But here again, we should not confuse different modes or forms of training: one is task or job specific, the other is person specific. As human beings, workers need contact with other human beings; that is part of the learning environment of the organization, and Integrated Performance Support presumes that those contacts must take place. But performance systems *can* duplicate the attention to the needs of the worker and the worker's tasks that a human tutor or coach can provide. Indeed, they can improve on it because the system doesn't need a break—it's always available. Only the worst Orwellian doomsayers would point to computer training and see the end of person-to-person contact. Unless electronic training takes place within the larger context of a learning organization, where conversation and sharing of knowledge is always taking place between people, it is likely to fail. We should not confuse the issue by saying that ineffective classroom methods should continue because they get workers together. If that's the only time that an organization is getting its workers together, its problems are bigger than just training-related ones.

Given the real problems with traditional approaches to learning—the approach founded on written texts supplemented by classroom lectures—will there be a future for classroom teaching in the workplace? Perhaps we could say that classroom, lecture-based training should be a part of the workplace, as long as it is properly conceived and executed. The key is to base it on the proper model. In the United States, university lectures are most often driven by a structured environment: there is a syllabus for a class, the professor is in charge, and the students are led through the material like tour buses driven through cities. At universities like Oxford or Cambridge, on the other hand, students choose from a range of available lectures on any given day. Students are in charge of their educations, and they attend a lecture or do not attend based on whether the subject matter is appropriate to what they are trying to learn and to accomplish. In the workplace, a good lecturer can be inspirational and can teach more in an hour than some workers learn in a month. But a bad lecturer can be deadly. One might, in fact, see a performance system as a simulation of the role of an Oxford don. The meetings with the don are student initiated; they are one-on-one, exploratory, and tailored to the interests and abilities of the student. Conclusions and assumptions are challenged, feed-back is given, and new areas to explore are recommended.

8. EXPLORATORY AND INTERACTIVE LEARNING

Interactive learning is hardly a new concept. It was the basis of instruction in ancient Greece, for example (hence, the "Socratic method"), and has formed the basis for discussion-oriented instruction for some time. Performance systems are designed to provide interactive learning experiences.

Interactive learning is important to organizations not simply because it can be more interesting or more entertaining. The issue is retention of knowledge. Studies have shown that, in appropriate learning situations, student retention is 30% to 50% better with interactive systems than with most instructor-led learning.[30] With a well-designed interactive program, students are continually engaged an average of every two or three minutes instead of perhaps only a few times a day, or perhaps not at all, with instructor-led training.[31] Logic paths are complete and distinct, allowing students to access information as needed and to discard or bypass information that is not pertinent or is already understood. Learning becomes more personal and tailored.

9. MULTISENSORY LEARNING

Here we come to the issue of multimedia and its role in the workplace. Some of the more impressive technological developments of the past decade have been in the area of multimedia delivery of information at computer workstations. It seems certain that its presence will grow, even become a natural part of the workplace, especially as children raised on sophisticated computer games enter the workplace with high expectations of what computers should be able to deliver.

An Integrated Performance Support strategy presumes that information will be delivered through performance systems in a variety of media. These systems offer more sensory stimulation than is provided by traditional class-room methods; they use visuals, audio, touchscreens, voice activation, full-motion video, graphics, animation, as well as text, to increase knowledge. But multimedia is not the end; it is only the means. There has been a great deal of excitement in recent years as the generation of computer users accustomed to dumb terminals suddenly began to see color, graphics, and movement on their screens. But these capabilities are hardly going to impress anyone in five years. Ask any ten-year-olds if they're impressed right now. They'll most likely yawn and tell you how great the graphics are on Super Nintendo.

What's the point? The point is that multimedia is just the means to an end; it must take a back seat to the training, learning, and performance ends that it serves. As an end in itself, multimedia's great promise will come to nothing unless it can be designed and integrated, from a performance-centered perspective, into the overall learning process that takes place within organizations. Multimedia is not always the right medium for a training or learning need; virtual reality, when it becomes a *real* reality, will not always be the right medium, either. But then again, sometimes it will be—and those will be exciting moments. The key is not to let the breathless excitement of whiz-bang technology get in the way of the real performance needs of the workforce. And when the technology is all but invisible, omnipresent, ubiquitous, it will become fully integrated with our living and working—a line that continues to blur with twenty-four-hour global time zones, voice mail, and electronic knowledge exchange.

10. LEARNING BASED ON UP-TO-DATE INFORMATION

The ease with which McCaw Cellular can now get updated product and service information to employees is a powerful feature of performance systems. Workers have available to them the most recent training, when they need it, in the context of their work. Training should be designed so that it serves the purposes of actual workers today, not workers in circumstances that were accurate twelve or eighteen months ago. The marketplace is changing far too quickly for training to have the shelf life it once had.

CASE EXAMPLE:
NORTH WEST WATER

North West Water is a recently privatized water utility in England, with central offices in Warrington. It is among the largest companies in the United Kingdom by market capitalization and is the fourth largest water and waste water organization in the world. North West Water serves a population of nearly seven million people, over an area of some 14,500 square kilometers, using almost 500 water sources and reservoirs. Acquisitions in other parts of the United Kingdom, Ireland, and the United States, together with an increasing number of international contacts, have strengthened the market position of North West Water worldwide.

This is a time of great change for the company, in terms of both business and technology. North West Water is moving toward its strategy for the year 2000, a strategy built around the needs of the company's four stakeholders: customers, shareholders, employees, and the community. This initiative, called "North West Water 2000," will have profound effects on all business functions, affecting over 5,000 employees. Major new information systems are being implemented to support the new organization. In this new environment, there will be intensified demands on the company's people: demands to increase the quality of customer service, to learn new jobs and skills, while organizational changes are altering traditional support networks and sources of knowledge.

North West Water is implementing a significant training program to support the substantial changes being introduced as part of North West Water 2000. As part of the work, North West Water with the help of Andersen Consulting undertook a research project into Integrated Performance Support. The project looked at the costs, benefits, and implementation issues relating to the introduction of IPS into one particular area of North West Water's business: the management of work on the water distribution network.

One aspect of the project was the development of a prototype system called "Learning Manager," designed around one of the existing on-line applications at the company. The application, called the Work Management System (WMS), is an on-line Windows™-driven application, used to manage work on North West Water's assets through the entire life cycle from the initial request for work through definition, scheduling, execution, reporting, and completion. The type of work managed by this system includes installing new mains and services (as a result of property development), installing commercial and domestic water metering systems, and replacing or repairing existing assets in the system due to faults or customer requests.

OVERVIEW OF LEARNING MANAGER

The performance support functions of the prototype system's Learning Manager are represented to the worker in a manner similar to the "guides" metaphor discussed in Chapter 4. As an extension of the "human metaphor," Guides provide nonintrusive active support that is specific and context-sensitive. The support functions of Learning Manager include Coordinator, Coach, Librarian, Historian, and Assistant. (Note: the features described here relate to the prototype system and not to the existing work management application.)

Coordinator. Coordinator contains information on the jobs of the people in the work management function. These are presented in the form of workflows that describe job tasks, inputs, outputs, and decision points. The job-related information contained in Coordinator can be accessed directly from the Work Management System or from the overall support main menu. Main menu access to Coordinator provides an overview of the Work Management System and the detailed workflows and tasks relating to specific jobs. Information is presented textually or in the form of audio and still images. It is possible to drill down below workflows to lower levels until detailed job steps are presented.

Accessing Coordinator from within the Work Management System application provides context-sensitive information on how the specific system task being performed is related to the job. Some work steps involve simple decisions to be made (for example, assigning a work category). At these points, decision support is provided by Coordinator in the form of a "decision tree" that takes the worker through the decision-making process.

Coach. Coach provides on-line training in two modes, which could be described in a variety of ways. Developers have termed the modes "at-the-job training" (general, high-level) and "on-the-job training" (specific, task-based). They actually represent two of the methods by which performance systems support the continuum of work: one mode is an educational mode, the other a doing mode; one mode is passive, the other active; one is based upon the traditional CBT form of training modules; the other is based upon granular, point-of-need support. The traditional computer-based training approach consists of training modules that make up training courses. The training modules are available at different training levels: "summary," "walkthrough," and "detailed." A training plan is established for individuals depending on their role, experience, training, and performance history. Traditional features of computer-based training (such as simulation and testing) enable workers to achieve specific learning objectives.

On-the-job training is provided during actual job performance and provides granules of appropriate training to a worker in the context of the work being performed. This is accessed directly from the Work Management System. Coach also holds a training history for employees.

Librarian. Librarian contains on-line reference information relevant to work management personnel. Information can be accessed through different searching and browsing techniques and is presented in appropriate formats: text, video, audio, and still images. Librarian contains information on the North West Water 2000 initiative, current policies and procedures, Work Management System information, legal requirements, and local information. Local information may be particularly relevant in the future as more centralization takes place within North West Water. Centralization of personnel could conceivably place existing local knowledge at risk of being lost—for example, understanding the impact of local market days in a particular town on maintenance work.

Historian. Historian records and displays historical information on the performance of different organizational units against defined key performance indicators, such as work order performance, customer care appointments, levels of service, and aborted jobs. These indicators are set up for different jobs for the work management function (that is, works controllers, systems controllers, distribution services management estimators, and work management center personnel).

Performance history data is displayed graphically by week for the current quarter. Specific information can be obtained by drilling down through levels of windows. For example, the menu window for a works controller allows the worker to view average key performance indicator data for teams in comparison with the area and region or to drill down to individuals' key performance indicator information. Feedback is provided by Historian and is triggered if certain warning thresholds are reached. In addition to recording and analyzing performance, Historian also records user interactions with the support facilities themselves as a way of identifying individual performance issues. Care is taken within Historian not to make individual performance judgments based on quantitative data. As we have noted, it is vital that organizations focus on *effectiveness* of workers, not just efficiency.

Assistant. Assistant acts as a personal agent for the worker in Learning Manager. Assistant highlights when there have been changes to the on-line system or to the surrounding job procedures and requirements (for example, the new legal requirements of the New Roads and Street Works Act, implemented in the United Kingdom in 1992). Assistant filters out information that is irrelevant to particular employees, although workers can update their work profiles to ensure that the Assistant keeps track of new areas of interest. Assistant draws on information held in other parts of the performance system—for example, detailed reference information in the Librarian or workflow and job information contained in Guide.

LEARNING, TRAINING, AND PERFORMANCE
WITH LEARNING MANAGER

Let's now consider an imaginary, future scenario of people at North West Water who execute a series of tasks with the help of Learning Manager. The scenario begins at the Customer Service Center, where a representative takes a call from a customer who is having difficulty with low water pressure. The representative accesses Guide and, by clicking on "Walkthrough," receives a step-by-step presentation of the workflow for this task. When the task is complete, the system automatically schedules an inspection and prints an inspection note for a systems controller, who goes out to determine the cause of the low pressure.

Under current conditions, systems controllers perform these inspections and must then manually perform the follow-up recording and reporting based upon the inspection. Learning Manager supports the performance of this task on-line. When the systems controller logs on, the Assistant icon is immediately highlighted, indicating that there is an important update for the systems controller to read. Assistant alerts the systems controller to any recent procedure changes, new legal requirements, or policy changes that are relevant.

Using Assistant, the systems controller completes the write-up of the inspection notes following the on-site inspection of the customer's residence. Because the format of the document has recently changed, the performance system helps the worker understand the update. The systems controller views the inspection note, which is in four parts and segmented into areas. By clicking on an individual area, the system displays help at a detailed or a summary level, depending on the worker's needs and preferences. Assisted by the performance system, the systems controller recommends that the service pipe be replaced at the customer's residence. When this further work has been defined on the system, the process passes on to the work management center where the work must be scheduled.

For purposes of this scenario, let's presume that the employee at the work management center who is to work on this scheduling task happens to be relatively new on the job, and so will need to take full advantage of the training facility of the performance system. As it happens, the Coach of the Learning Manager recommends the "Basic Scheduling" course for this worker, based upon his experience and work profile. The worker accesses this course and, following its completion, has his or her training history automatically updated. Having completed the required initial training, the worker is now ready to schedule work. The worker enters the work management scheduling function and starts the scheduling dialogue. Upon reaching a complex work scheduling window, the worker becomes uncertain and asks Coach for help. The relevant unit of the "Basic Scheduling" course is automatically displayed, showing him how to complete this task. A video case history is provided from an experienced worker who talks about typical problems encountered in scheduling work.

The latter parts of this scenario effectively demonstrate two modes of training within a performance system: training tailored to specific tasks at hand,

_____ TRAINING FROM "LEARNING MANAGER" AT NORTH WEST WATER _____

and training tailored to the overall performance requirements of a job. In both cases, however, Learning Manager demonstrates the power of training that is delivered at the work location rather than training that interrupts the normal workday or, worse, takes the worker away from the regular work location to participate in classroom courses. The training within Learning Manager is always appropriate to the particular worker: to his or her ability level, experience, and performance requirements.

The IPS work at North West Water is at the research stage. However, the prototype Learning Manager highlights some of the potential ways in which the approach to training and learning within performance systems can help organizations. An IPS strategy can:

- Reduce the up-front delivery costs by moving training from the classroom to the workplace. Set training courses often interrupt ongoing work or occur at the wrong time. Some workers may miss certain training programs altogether, or they may forget the skills learned away from the work location.
- Reduce the time to proficiency for workers, minimizing the period during which people feel uncomfortable with new roles, procedures, and technologies—a period when many performance mistakes are frequently made.
- Reduce costs of inadequate performance by minimizing rework, and by meeting the challenges of customer care and quality initiatives, all of which may result from a lack of skill and knowledge at the point of need.
- Offer greater access to organization expertise by capturing and disseminating knowledge throughout the organization.

The research at North West Water provides a glimpse into the business solutions of the future. These solutions synchronize technology, strategy, and processes, as well as the people-centered aspects of change. It's in this area that IPS can help businesses change to be more successful.

CASE EXAMPLE:
GUIDED SOCIAL SIMULATION (GuSS)

Guided Social Simulation or GuSS is one of the innovative learning projects coming out of the Institute for the Learning Sciences at Northwestern University. GuSS is a general architecture for building systems that help people to perform complex social tasks more effectively—tasks such as interacting well with prospective customers. We have already noted the importance of *simulation* in the training approach of Integrated Performance Support. In a "learn by doing" educational environment, simulation of actual performance can dramatically reduce the time to proficiency for workers in a wide variety of jobs. Flight simulators are one of the most well-known kinds of training environments where technology plays a particularly important role. Flight simulators allow inexperienced pilots to practice their skills in an environment that mimics the real world, except that the simulator makes it possible to make mistakes without dramatic consequences. The purpose of GuSS is to accomplish in the social world what a flight simulator can accomplish in the physical world. Using the GuSS general architecture, a number of applications have been built to allow people to gain a variety of business skills founded upon the ability to interact socially.

In their Technical Report on GuSS, Institute researchers note that the process of teaching someone a complex skill is a demanding proposition. Certain methods of teaching are fairly effective at conveying abstract principles, but are not effective in teaching how those principles apply in practice.[32] In formal schooling, knowledge and skills are often removed from their practical application in the real world.[33] In contrast with traditional apprenticeships, where learning is grounded in the actual use of skills—in real hands-on experience—classroom teaching often fails to connect with the practices for which the instruction is the basis. As a result, motivation of learners is low, and much of what is learned is quickly forgotten or fails to be integrated into the experience of the learners. On the other hand, some other methods of teaching leave out the abstract principles, the higher-order knowledge, and merely teach by rote. These methods offer little improvement in the actual performance of the job. Learners following this method may memorize the steps they need to take, but they may be unable to adapt to new situations.[34] If you have ever had a conversation with a customer service representative who has been trained by rote, you know the limitations of that approach. Knowledge workers who act as the primary interface with customers are becoming increasingly important to organizations, one reason why a number of performance systems and prototypes already exist for that function.

In order to become proficient in performance, the learner must learn the abstract principles behind a task, as well as how those principles apply in practice. When instruction and practice are combined effectively, a synergism occurs. As Roger Schank notes, the student can reflect on his or her experiences in the practice environment with the guidance of an instructor, and the abstract principles described by the instructor are motivated, operationalized, and made memorable by the experience.[35]

As usual, timing issues often prevent the synergism from occurring. If the complementary interaction between practice and instruction is to be exploited, the instructor must be available to deliver the appropriate instruction at the moment the student needs it. In an apprenticeship, this often happens; when the student-to-instructor ratio is high, the instructor cannot always be present at the right moment. Furthermore, because many activities cannot be performed in the classroom, there is often a physical separation between the location of instruction and that of practice.[36]

Computer simulations that incorporate tutorial guidance provide an environment that can achieve integration between instruction and practice. The Institute for the Learning Sciences is developing a class of systems, called "Intelligent Learning-By-Doing Environments," or ILDEs, to provide such integration. ILDEs provide both (1) an interactive task environment, and (2) a suite of teaching modules.

1. The task environment lets a learner practice a target skill without any of the risks that might be associated with the task in the real world. The simulated environment is participatory, requiring the learner to make decisions and to take actions like those required by the actual task.
2. The teaching modules monitor the learner's interaction with the task environment and interject their expertise at the appropriate time. Their role is to guide the student, and to teach abstract principles in a meaningful and memorable way by delivering instruction at just the moment when its relevance will be obvious to the learner. The teaching modules can coax the student. They can stop the simulation to tell a story about a relevant experience or explain the principles currently at work. Or they can manipulate the situation itself to provide a timely challenge to the learner.[37]

The principles behind GuSS, to provide timely instruction integrated with practice in a simulated environment, are the same general principles guiding the entire approach to training and learning within Integrated Performance Support. IPS seeks to integrate instruction and practice at each "moment of value" during worker performance. As we have already argued, there are different kinds of performance within any worker's job. In some cases, basic levels of proficiency must be attained before going "live." There, simulation experiences like GuSS would be made available through the performance system. For other, less risky tasks, training and performance merge into one experience. In this respect, as we have already noted, IPS treats "training"—at least in the sense it has meant traditionally—as a last resort. Ideally, a worker needing performance support would first have access to advice from the performance system; if that were not available, or if it did not meet the particular performance challenge, a job aid would be provided; if that were not sufficient, the worker could access reference information. Only when all those avenues failed to support the particular task would the worker interrupt the natural performance flow to ask for training.

A GuSS APPLICATION: AMERITECH PAGES PLUS™ SALES TRAINING

One application currently in development based upon the GuSS architecture is a joint project between the Institute for the Learning Sciences and Ameritech.

The system permits workers to practice techniques for effective selling of advertising in Ameritech's "Pages Plus."™ As the learner begins the simulation, the introduction and set-up are provided. There are three parts to the primary GuSS window: the activity display, the action constructor, and the guidance monitor. The activity or scene display provides the learner with a "window into the simulated world." Pictures of the locations and characters within the simulation are displayed. For example, in the first scene, the learner is found in his or her office at Ameritech. The learner is then asked to go to a small business owner, Ed Swain of Swain's Roofing, to discuss his next advertisement in Pages Plus™. Because the Swain business is usually conducted within the kitchen of the Swain's home, this view appears in the activity display.

The action constructor that appears in the lower left-hand corner of the window provides the learner with options for interaction: things the learner may say, places the learner may go, and props that the learner may manipulate (for example, the learner may view a customer file containing information about Swain Roofing). The options available to the user vary based upon the circumstances of the situation.

The learner arrives at the Swains and at first finds only Mrs. Swain at home. Various options for what to say to Mrs. Swain are presented and, as the learner makes these choices, indicators below Mrs. Swain's picture reflect her outward reaction—what the learner would see if face to face with Mrs. Swain. The indicators track whether Mrs. Swain is interested in the conversation or not, whether she is calm or nervous, contented or angry. Mrs. Swain tells the learner to wait just a bit, that Ed will be back in a minute. Here, the learner again has options: should the learner assume that Mrs. Swain has an active interest in the business or not? If the learner presses Mrs. Swain and tries to talk to her about the ad, she becomes increasingly disinterested and then, if pressed, irritated.

If, however, the learner ignores Mrs. Swain altogether, another of then interesting features of the Pages Plus™ system comes into play. Across the top of the main GuSS window is the guidance monitor. Guidance related to what the learner has just done is provided by expert Ameritech Pages Plus™ salespeople. For example, if the learner does not interact much with Mrs. Swain, the guidance monitor alerts the learner to a relevant story. If the learner chooses to display the story, a full-motion video clip is played in which another sales representative tells a story. It seems that this representative once went to the house of a small business owner. Both husband and wife were at home, but the wife appeared disinterested and was, in fact, watching TV through much of the interaction. It eventually turned out, however, that the

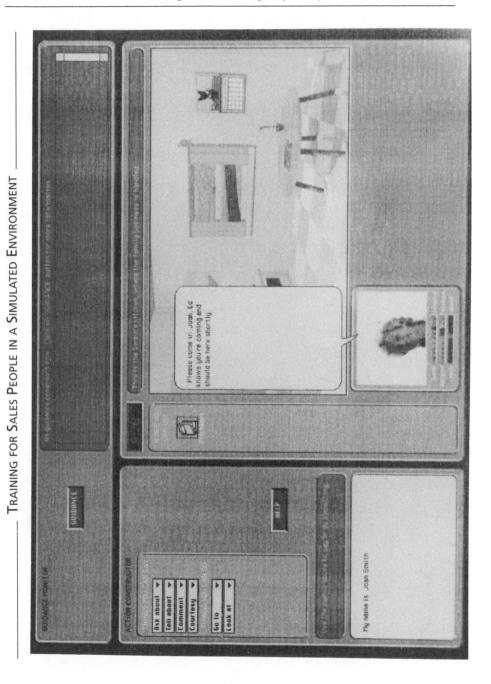

wife had equal responsibility for approving the ad. If the representative had simply ignored her, the sale might have been jeopardized.

At the conclusion of the simulation, the learner can go back and run through the scenario again, to see the difference any other responses would make in the interaction. To review what they have done, learners may view a "Transcript" of their simulated conversation. The Transcript includes the dialogue of the simulation as well as scene and prop changes. It is interesting in this environment to recall the work pyramid we introduced earlier in the chapter. The Pages Plus™ simulation is a crucial form of training support for work near the top of that pyramid, work where a person often encounters new problem situations and may be asked to revise assumptions based upon actual performance needs as they are encountered. Providing training support at this level has been a challenge to organizations, and it is one of the challenges that Integrated Performance Support can meet.

CHAPTER 8

DOING MORE WITH LESS

The history of warfare is rife with lessons that a smaller foe that is able to be nimble, to move swiftly and strike quickly, can overcome a much larger adversary. Think of David and Goliath, the Soviets in Afghanistan, the Americans in Vietnam, or the British in colonial America. The lesson of "lean and mean" is becoming increasingly important for businesses today, as well, and organizations in general are getting smaller. In recent years, U.S. companies in particular have found themselves losing ground in the global marketplace to smaller competitors who can move products to consumers faster and more efficiently. One reason: leaner organizational structures.

Reductions in workforce are also caused, of course, by cutbacks and downsizing done for reasons of pure economic survival. But for whatever reason, organizations today find themselves challenged to do more with less. Here, information technology can play a vital role. For downsizing efforts, performance systems can reshape the work and provide additional support for those workers who remain following organizational cutbacks. For companies restructuring to achieve flatter organizational structures, these systems can encourage worker self-management and the efficient interaction of workgroups.

WHY SMALLER AND LEANER MAY BE BETTER

In his book, *The Next American Frontier,* Robert Reich tells the following story about the effect of excessive layers of management upon an organization's ability to respond quickly to marketplace pressures:

A salesman hears from a customer that the firm's latest bench drill cannot accommodate bits for drilling a recently developed hard plastic. The customer suggests a modified coupling adapter and an additional speed setting. The salesman thinks the suggestion makes sense but has no authority to pursue it directly. Following procedures, the salesman passes the idea on to the sales manager, who finds it promising and drafts a memo to the marketing vice president. The marketing vice president also likes the idea, so he raises it in an executive meet-

---

KEY MESSAGES: CHAPTER 8

- The challenge for organizations to "do more with less" may be rooted in pure economic survival, or in efforts to reconstitute the organization along leaner and more horizontal management structures.
- It is vital that organizations provide intensified support for their knowledge workers who remain following a downsizing initiative. Performance systems become a crucial part of this support, ensuring that overall organizational performance is not put at risk by the downsizing.
- For companies moving toward horizontal management structures, performance systems encourage employee self-management and facilitate cooperation among members of workgroups.
- Performance systems will make use of new collaboration tools, such as "groupware," to support the timely sharing of information, to make communication and collaboration among group members more profitable, and to improve the ability to coordinate and manage workflows.

ing of all the vice presidents. The executive committee agrees to modify the drill. The senior product manager then asks the head of the research department to form a task force to evaluate the product opportunity and to design a new coupling and variable-speed mechanism.

The task force consists of representatives from sales, marketing, accounting, and engineering. . . . After months of meetings the research manager presents the group's findings to the executive committee. It approves the new design. Each department then works out a detailed plan for its role in bringing out the new product, and the modified drill goes into production.

If there are no production problems, the customer receives word that he can order a drill for working hard plastics two years after he first discussed it with the salesman. In the meantime, a Japanese, West German, or South Korean firm has already designed, produced, and delivered a hard-plastics drill.[1]

The bloated layers in the middle of this organization are on their way out, and we can see everywhere the trend toward horizontal structures that can help organizations move their products to market faster and make decisions more efficiently. The size of the workforce, the way labor is organized, and the manner in which it is managed are all going through a major period of transition for companies around the world, particularly in the United States.[2] As we move past the turn of the century, the following trends will be felt by many companies:

- The average company will have a smaller workforce than it does today.
- The traditional notions of corporate pyramids or hierarchies will be replaced by a variety of organizational forms.
- The vertical division of labor will be replaced by a horizontal division.[3]

Small Is Beautiful was the title of an early E. F. Schumacher book, and it appears that he was right, though perhaps not in exactly the way that he thought at that time. Small is not, of course, always beautiful to everyone. Indeed, "doing more with less" may sound only negative at first, conjuring up dispiriting organizational movements that take place under equally dispiriting titles like "demassing."[4] To many workers, doing more with less suggests only the latest incarnation of traditional worker exploitation, a painful overreaction to temporary problems.[5] But downsizing, the need to be more productive with fewer workers, is an economic reality today. Many organizations, in fact, find themselves simply trying to "make do with less" or "get by with less." In the throes of worldwide recession, some organizations find the need for smaller and leaner organizations thrust upon them as an economic survival tactic.

But a growing body of evidence and research suggests that management techniques and organizational forms geared toward smaller worker groupings are far more efficient. Service companies, for example, are discovering new and more effective organizational models in order to achieve not only technological efficiency and flexibility, but also more effective modes of customer service.[6] James Brian Quinn argues that technology naturally supports the movement toward worker empowerment and flatter organizations,[7] and this is our primary point in this chapter as well. Performance systems support the current movement toward "the small" and "the lean," whether that move stems from economic necessity or from advanced thinking about more efficient organizational forms. IPS enables such movements by:

- Supporting workers who remain after downsizing and rightsizing reorganizations, giving them the ability to do their jobs more effectively, despite a reduced workforce;
- Encouraging and facilitating self-managed workers and workgroups; and
- Facilitating communications along flatter and wider reporting spans.

SUPPORTING A DOWNSIZED WORKFORCE

All business and technological innovations that are aimed at improving efficiency engender certain degrees of fear and misunderstanding. Michael Hammer and James Champy reveal in their book on reengineering that even business process reengineering is often misunderstood as something else: "Oh, I get it," people will say, "Reengineering is another name for downsizing." The authors' counterargument is instructive, because it reveals the flaw in many downsizing efforts that have taken place over the past few years. "Reengineering," they write, "is not restructuring or downsizing. These are just fancy terms for reducing capacity to meet current, lower demand. When the market wants fewer GM cars, GM reduces its size to better match demand. But downsizing and restructuring only mean doing less with less. Reengineering, by contrast, means doing *more* with less."[8]

It would be more accurate to say that reengineering *can* mean doing more with less. Workers *can* do more, but only if they are empowered and supported in the performance of their jobs following the reengineering of the business processes.

One thing is certainly true: without reengineering and without consequent use of technology to provide performance support, downsizing can have negative rather than positive effects on organizations. In the United States, fewer than one-half of those companies that have gone through formal downsizing programs since 1988 have improved their profits; only one-third of these companies have shown an increase in productivity.[9] Why such mediocre results? Because organizations did not change the *work* for those employees who remained. Instead, they just added responsibilities to employees without supporting that work.

Make no mistake: there are profound cultural and moral issues at work in any organizational restructuring movements that involve technology in efforts to increase efficiency and productivity. Executive intent is the crucial factor here. One of G. B. Trudeau's "Doonesbury" cartoons has captured the worst extreme of efficiency movements: a CEO is looking down from his executive suite at his workers, all of whom stare intently at their computers. Turning to one of his vice-presidents, he says, "See the guy with the glasses? He's a temp. He's an experienced creative director, and he's working on a small, in-house publishing project for us. His salary is low, he gets no training, no health benefits, no vacations, and no sick days. In short, he's the perfect employee. And he's inspired me to rethink the future. I've decided to fire everyone—all 6,500 employees of Universal Petroleum—and then re-hire the core players on a consultant basis. I figure the move will cut operating expenses by at least a third, maybe even 40%! What do you think?" "What do I think?" replies the vice-president, "It's brilliant, big guy! It's a simple but bold, visionary strategy for the 21st century! Naturally, I love it! When do we start?"

"We?" answers the CEO.[10]

Trudeau's cartoon is exaggerated, but lurking behind it are real organizational attitudes toward the workforce. Economist Lester Thurow is extremely critical of these attitudes, comparing them with the treatment of "chattel serfs" in medieval Europe. "Not much loyalty can be expected," writes Thurow, "if one can expect to be treated as a slave and sold to the highest bidder."[11] With a series of striking comparisons between U.S. and Japanese firms, Thurow shows that concern for the workforce can have positive bottom-line implications, as well. Contrasting the money-making firms of the United States with the empire-building firms of Japan, Thurow argues that empire-building firms see the workforce as a strategic asset to be nurtured. If you're fighting a battle, you want the best soldiers. Some revealing comparisons: the ratio of average CEO salary to average worker salary in the United States is 119 to 1; in Japan it is 18 to 1. In the United States, the chief financial officer is second in command, while the person in charge of human resource development is relatively unimportant, making 40% less than the CFO. In Japan, this is reversed. It is more fitting, concludes Thurow, for the officer in charge of the troops to outrank the officer in charge of the money.[12]

Most striking is Thurow's comparison of the effects of *automation* on Japanese and U.S. firms. Research has shown that when automation increases in America, wages decrease. In Japan, increases in automation are accompanied by complementary increases in wages, because technological investments are used to enhance the productivity of labor. In the United States, where lower wages equal higher profits, technology is used to replace skilled labor with unskilled labor.[13]

We believe that Integrated Performance Support, and the resulting performance systems that it makes possible, represent the future of workforce-centered technology—automation that has a human face and technology that can be used to enhance productivity without diminishing the importance of those who are using the technology. For those organizations forced to reduce workforce numbers, performance systems can more effectively support those who remain, ensuring that organizational performance is not put at risk.

PRODUCTIVITY, EFFICIENCY, DOWNSIZING, AND TECHNOLOGY

Although $862 billion has been spent on information technology in the service sector in the United States over the past decade, there has been little improvement in workforce productivity until very recently.[14] This failure extends far beyond corporate America; it has been, in fact, an international problem.

Why haven't there been enormous productivity increases to accompany the enormous new power of computing?

The accepted and now well-known answer to this question is that corporations threw technology at people's work, but didn't change the work itself. Some technological improvements, in fact, worsened productivity by increasing the volume of work to be done. The photocopying machine, for example, made one part of staff work easier. But then once organizations knew how easy it was to make copies of documents, workers at all levels increased their requests for copies, inundating staffs and, at times, lowering their overall productivity. Real productivity increases are beginning to happen now, largely because downsizing activities in the face of the recession forced organizations finally to reengineer the work. This reengineering is now beginning to create the expected efficiency and productivity gains from technology that were expected all along. A large company doesn't necessarily want to lay off workers unless absolutely necessary. Thus, productivity benefits of information technology are not realized until companies are forced by economic conditions to make the cost-cutting moves they should have made earlier.[15]

To what extent does this technology-enhanced movement toward efficiency threaten the real people who make up an organization? Doubtless there will be layoffs for some companies as technology and reengineering finally begin to work in tandem. But some economists and analysts argue that this is not a doomsday scenario for workers. As Esther Dyson writes, "Change is often unpleasant. The layoffs make people worry that the economy is going downhill. This is hardly a new phenomenon. In the last century the Industrial Revolution put millions of farmers out of work in England; pundits worried that the country was losing its agricultural base, . . . much as we're worried about our manufacturing and services base."[16] In fact, however, when the effects of increased productivity become widespread, demand should grow for knowledge workers. Moreover, this work should be more rewarding than clerical and filing work. A new breed of knowledge worker should be able to use information technology to move beyond routine work to more creative endeavors.[17] Performance systems will play a key role in this movement, helping to create an environment where more important and creative work can be done efficiently.

Even a human-centered technology positioned to enable the workforce could be used in ways that do not serve the best interests of an organization or its workers. There could be organizations that may attempt to use technology merely as a means toward workforce reduction and then as a means to control and monitor the workers who remain. We believe these organizations miss the point and will have difficulties, especially as opportunities ultimately grow for educated and talented knowledge workers in a knowledge economy.

The valuing of human capital over financial capital—and the understanding of workers as assets to be developed, rather than as costs to be cut—will be vital to the survival of organizations in the global economy. This will take a massive movement toward understanding anew the priorities of the workplace today and some of the moral dilemmas that accompany new technological capabilities.

BALANCING PRODUCTIVITY AND DIGNITY

Faced with the problem of economic survival, organizations are compelled to maximize the productivity of their workforce. The implication is usually that productivity improvements through reengineering and technological innovation will lead to downsizing. How is one to maintain a balance between, on the one hand, maximizing returns to shareholders and, on the other hand, engaging the workforce to generate those profits?

Providing employees with purpose, dignity, and a secure working community is not unrelated to workforce productivity.[18] The development, capabilities, and morale of the workforce are extremely valuable to an organization. It is revealing, for example, that in the Japanese language the word for education, "kyo-iku," is built from two characters: "kyo" means "to teach" and "iku" means "to nurture." Author Kenji Muro notes that in Japan, "The purpose of education is to teach a Japanese identity, to teach the skill of living harmoniously together in a group, to teach how to develop the group spirit so the group goes forward and up, and very importantly, to educate to give the means to the individual for upward mobility in the society."[19] Certainly there are important cultural differences here between Japanese society and other societies around the world. But organizations seeking to emulate Japanese productivity and efficiency cannot hope to succeed without some measure of commitment to their workers as people, and without a commitment to the nurturing of those people as organizational assets.

Downsizing is not always synonymous with immediate lay-offs. For those organizations not faced with an immediate economic threat, there are alternatives: buy-outs and early retirement; hiring freezes coupled with natural attrition.[20] During times of more radical and immediate downsizing, organizations must be prepared to cope with the weakened commitment of the workforce that accompanies lay-offs. This is a real loss of energy, a loss of value, that is in everyone's interest to minimize.[21] One way to anticipate and cope is to commit to an equality of sacrifice, an equality that can manifest itself in different ways. Well known, for example, is former Chrysler chairman Lee Iacocca's decision to cut his salary to $1 a year during the years when

Chrysler was working its way back from near-bankruptcy. Other organizations have also come up with innovative policies. Hewlett-Packard, for example, led by founders Bill Hewlett and Dave Packard, responded to a downturn in the electronics industry by ordering, not a 10% lay-off, but a 10% pay cut across the board. Everyone from the President on down stayed home every other Friday.[22]

A similar policy has been followed at Nucor Steel in Charlotte, North Carolina. During slow economic periods, Nucor reduces the work week to four days. Chairman and CEO F. Kenneth Iverson calls it a "share the pain program." "The average hourly employee will have his compensation drop 20–25 percent because he drops from five to four days. The department head's compensation drops 35–40 percent, and the total compensation of the officers drops 60–70 percent. So, we never get any questions from employees about, 'Why isn't my pay better' or something like that. All they ask is, 'When do we get back on five days?' I'm a great believer in that because I think that management's pay should drop more because they have more responsibility for the decisions that mean success or failure of the company."[23]

Many companies such as Nucor have committed themselves to no-lay-off policies because of the belief that you can't get good people if you're always laying them off and then trying to rehire them.[24] Not every organization is in a position to make such a commitment. However, every organization *is* in the position to treat with dignity those who must leave an organization. "Dignity must be a watchword for the entire process. There needs to be a clear, explicit and open logic to any redundancies. Employees need to participate in the process and use their creativity to take responsibility for themselves and for the company. To discover dignity is a process of learning for most people in these circumstances."[25] The performance-centered, human-centered perspective we are advocating here is an important part of maintaining the dignity of the workforce, because it takes seriously the real capabilities, performance needs, and potential of an organization's workforce.

SUPPORTING, NOT CONTROLLING

As technological capabilities in the workplace increase in power, a growing concern is the fine line between *supporting* the knowledge worker and *monitoring* the knowledge worker: between enabling and controlling. The Integrated Performance Support environment is a performance *support* environment, a *facilitation* environment, not a performance *control* environment. Unless that is kept in mind, performance enhancement will be either illusory or temporary. Information technology will doubtless continue to pose dilemmas for organizations and their workers in terms of privacy. Recall from our narrative in Chapter 3 that Sue Peters could access a real-time snapshot of how her performance compared to that of other commercial lenders at her bank. Should other lenders be allowed to see that information? What will organizations do with their increased ability to gather information about individual knowledge workers? These are moral, rather than technological, issues. Systems are morally neutral; systems design is not. Here again, human dignity must be the primary consideration.

It must be said that the onus of future technological moral dilemmas does not rest solely at the organization level. As workers are increasingly tapped in to information networks, the possibility for abuse will grow there, too. Why not take a couple of hours to use the Reference Services facility of my performance system to do some research for one of my M.B.A. classes? Why not play a couple of interactive, virtual reality games at my desk? It appears certain that there are enough moral issues arising from the coming knowledge economy and its technological capabilities to shelter those who teach business ethics, at least, from any downsizing movements.

INTEGRATED PERFORMANCE SUPPORT AND ORGANIZATIONAL TEAMWORK

The need to do more with less leads naturally to the idea of encouraging group and team work, and this is one of the many benefits of a performance system. Interestingly, this benefit may grow during times of organization adversity. Reed Powell, a professor at California State Polytechnic University, argues that some of the Japanese success in the world economy can be traced to what he calls the "survival mode" mentality of Japanese corporations. "The concept of a continuing survival mode seemed to me to provide a basic stimulus to do more with less. . . . I am convinced that doing more with less is a positive concept at the individual, company, and national level because it focuses on developing additional capacity. The growth of this capacity is what education strives to generate—whether it is to increase skills in the application of knowledge or to develop insights for the creative expression of emerging abilities."

Powell's point is that by encouraging teamwork and a community-based approach to overcoming challenges, organizations can incent the workforce to meet higher goals. Powell has found that a dominant influence in the careers of executives has been the sense of fulfillment that resulted from accomplishing goals that required new levels of capability, "and the satisfaction that results from doing things they were not sure they could do. As for overall morale within organizations, more often than not territorialism, counter-productive work patterns, and negative attitudes result when people are underemployed in their current jobs and feel they must protect what they have."[26]

Here we find the paradox of the technology-efficiency link. Technological change must be embraced by the workforce to succeed. But workers know that by embracing the technology, the resulting increase in efficiency may cost them their jobs. Performance systems can help to overcome this inherent stand-off by encouraging the sort of teamwork necessary to be innovative and creative in today's marketplace. If this spirit of teamwork is accompanied by an entrepreneurial system of rewards for teams that find ways to be more efficient and productive, the organization should find growth and efficiency occurring with less threat to the workers. The trick is to demonstrate clearly, at the worker level, how the excess capacity is converted into customer demand.

Several sterling examples of this approach already exist. Arden Sims, CEO of Globe Metallurgical Inc. (the first small company to win the Malcolm Baldrige Quality Award), notes, "I felt that the commitment [to full employment] was important if Globe was going to continue cutting costs. I made it clear that if an employee suggested a change that meant the loss of a job, no one would get laid off."[27]

Such a commitment may not be possible in every industry. At the least, however, organizations must be honest and open about the effect that technology and efficiency movements are having on the company. As Robert Hass, CEO of Levi Strauss, notes, "You can't promise employment security and be honest. The best you can do is not to play games with people."[28] Levi Strauss has an open policy of closing down production plants when they are no longer competitive, a policy driven by openness and honesty. Here, the kind of open communication enabled by performance systems will really dictate management candidness. If there are difficulties, employees will generally hear about them through the internal grapevine, and organizations do themselves damage by being less than candid. Workers will know or suspect the truth anyway, so it is always best for management to articulate problems clearly and then face up to them.

Another success story built on teamwork and community building is Quad/Graphics—the largest privately held printing company in North America. From eleven employees and a single press in an abandoned factory in Pewaukee, Wisconsin, the company now has sales in excess of $500 million. "What's different about the firm is its ironclad commitment to breaking down differences between management and workers. Teamwork is sacred. It includes workers in administrative offices and on the production floor. By en-

---

IPS INITIATIVES IN SPAIN

Many different drivers are moving organizations today toward performance systems. Some organizations, for example, are challenged to improve the performance of their sales workers. IPS can meet that challenge by ensuring that support is always available, and by getting "old style" workers to perform better in the new performance environment. In retail banking this often means moving back-office functions out to the front office, closer to the customer. By eliminating the non-value-added tasks and then integrating the selling process at the point of need, a bank can establish a reputation for customer service that can be a major competitive edge. This point-of-need process must be supported technologically.

Major initiatives to support the retail banking industry are currently under way at two major savings banks in Spain. One savings bank in the north of Spain, with more than 250 branches and 1,500 employees, is sharpening its client focus, driving toward more aggressive service and sales to customers. The new systems that will enable knowledge workers to provide this service have been designed from an IPS perspective.

- The system was designed based upon various scenarios workers typically encounter as they provide services to customers.
- Advisory services and context-sensitive help are provided on-line, both for system support and job performance support.
- On-line procedures are designed to link to other IPS elements using hypertext.
- Training is provided at the system, either as CBT training modules or as granular training support. A "learn by doing" environment is established by providing simulated performance environments where workers can complete basic processes under conditions that mimic an actual customer encounter.

Another IPS initiative is taking place at Caja España, a major savings bank institution with about 450 branches and 2,500 employees. Caja España in its present form is a merger of five other savings banks. After the merger, the bank needed a single information system that ensured that uniform service would be provided to customers at all its branches. Caja España has undertaken a very large and global technological effort to support its new business approach.

_____ IPS Initiatives in Spain (CONTINUED) _____

Performance-centered design principles have guided those designing the system, as well as those managing change for the workers who will be performing new business processes. The IPS structure of the system ensures that workers can easily access on-line help and advisory services. The system will also deliver training using simulation techniques, and both modular and granular support.

---

trusting key decisions to staff and encouraging creativity, the company has moved at a lightning pace in response to opportunities. Meanwhile, quality stays high and project work time is lowered."[29]

Motorola Corporation, in Schaumburg, Illinois, also has been innovative in rewarding teamwork. At the request of employees, thousands of worker teams are set up each year. In 1992, more than 4,000 of these teams submitted entries to Motorola's annual problem-solving competition at all of its worksites. Its quality programs increasingly involve teamwork, and the company estimates that it saves $2.2 billion annually from these programs.[30]

FACILITATING COMMUNICATIONS IN THE NEW HORIZONTAL ORGANIZATION

Empowered teamwork is an important goal of organizational restructuring today, a restructuring that moves companies toward what is most often called the "horizontal organization." A flattened organizational structure is cited, for example, by the authors of *Workplace 2000* as a hallmark of successful companies in the next century. For example, at Nucor Steel, an $850 million company, the central corporate staff is comprised of only seventeen people, which includes office support staff. The rest of Nucor's 3,700 employees are workers. Nucor has only four management levels, and workers are thus given an extraordinary sense of responsibility for the jobs they are performing.[31]

In the last decade, the inherent problems of managing large companies became increasingly apparent as corporations began to face competition from firms that could change and seize opportunities faster than they could. Big companies could not be as agile as their smaller competitors. Big became bigger: the larger companies built up layer upon layer of bureaucracy, leading to managers and employees who had insufficient numbers of customer contacts, and thus a poorer quality of service to those customers. As one analyst wrote of one large American corporation struggling at the end of the 1980s, these behemoths are like "a 2,000-pound centipede. The antennae work poorly, so the creature is directionless. When some of the 101 legs try to move ahead, others interfere and even move backward."[32]

In response to the problems of "too big and too slow," organizations are now shifting gradually away from the strict vertical and hierarchical approach to management. The purpose of such structures was to keep power, information, and decision making under the control of higher-level management. (It was better, after all, to control than to be controlled.[33]) The horizontal organization has fewer managers, especially in the middle of the traditional pyramid. It emphasizes teamwork, self-management, employees with cross-disciplinary skills, and coaching. Done right, a horizontal restructuring leads not only to higher productivity, but to more satisfied workers.[34]

One company in the midst of an already successful restructuring is IDS Financial Services in Minneapolis, Minnesota. The VP of transaction services for this American Express Co. unit says that the movement toward the horizontal organization began fairly innocently: "We began by saying, 'Let's redraw the boxes in the organization.' This led to the creation of a design team to see how the company might improve its delivery of services." Their goals were, first, "to organize around their financial planners—the front line of service. This led them to geographic teams." Other goals included the desire to be a multiskilled organization and to use self-managed work teams "with increased decision-making at the bottom of the organizational ladder." Results have been extraordinary, including a 1990 survey indicating that overall customer satisfaction with IDS has jumped from a low of 25% to 95%.[35]

Much of James Brian Quinn's book, *Intelligent Enterprise*, is devoted to discussions of how the movement of information and knowledge is facilitated by new organizational structures. Quinn argues, in fact, that there appears to be no limit to the potential reporting span—the number of people reporting to a single supervisor or center. Quinn calls this potential the "infinitely flat" organization. "While spans of 20–25 have become relatively common, spans of hundreds exist in some service organizations. Even the term 'span of control' seems an anachronism. Perhaps a better term would be 'span of communication' or 'span of coordination.' In most of these 'very flat' organizations, few orders are given by the line organization to those below. Instead, the central authority becomes an information source, a communications coordinator, or a reference desk for unusual inquiries. Lower organizational levels more often connect into it to obtain information for the purpose of performing better rather than for instructions or specific guidance from above."[36]

The implementation of performance systems, linked by networks throughout an organization, will be vital to the success of the "infinitely flat" company. Some examples of this power already exist. In some chain restaurants, for example, information systems are able to monitor sales at fifteen-minute intervals. Based upon this data, the systems suggest changes to the product mix, promotional moves, or operational changes to improve the response to customers.[37]

Technology also eliminates the time lag that management has traditionally faced just in getting basic operating information. The president of one electric utility, for example, now has a Windows™-based PC on his desk. Each morning when he comes in, he calls up the information about the power plant units that were on-line during the night. That simple information-gathering tool now means that the president doesn't have to wait for some middle manager to tell him how efficiently the plants are running.[38]

Flatter structures encourage self-management and a heightened sense of personal responsibility for performance at all levels of the company. One company that incorporated end-users into the design of its software, for example, found that moving decision making out along the organizational structure moved personal responsibility out as well. "When something goes wrong, no one asks why MIS gave us software that didn't work right."[39]

Some analysts point to a future in which efficiency and creativity—perhaps even spin-off companies—will come directly from the impetus of self-managed teams within an organization. An intrepreneurial "feel" will be attained within larger companies by encouraging "intrepreneurial" ventures. Colgate-Palmolive, for example, created Colgate Venture Company in the late 1980s, "a small, entrepreneurial 'oasis' where people with a flair for risk-taking could pursue the development of specialized, innovative, and nontraditional products as various as a deodorizing pad for cat litter boxes and a cleaning solution for teenagers' retainers."[40]

But what exactly is the link between technology, the horizontal organization, and the team approach vital to organizational success today? The performance-centered enterprise will continue to find innovative ways in which performance systems can link workers together and support them in their common endeavor. One promising category of software is specifically addressing the unique needs of groups and teams at work. This software is called, appropriately, "groupware."

THE POWER OF GROUPWARE

Groupware emerged out of frustration with the inability of traditional software to directly support the work performed by teams.[41] Team and group work has its own set of challenges. Organizations rely on teams and groups to accomplish tasks that usually require expertise from many areas and that are too large for individuals to accomplish alone. Every work group is unique. Its approach to work depends on the nature of its task, the group size, and the roles of its group members. The technology that supports group work must recognize and support these essential elements, many of which evolve informally and implicitly, by capturing the essence of the group task and by providing flexible support for group processes.

The multidisciplinary research community studying the potential of technology to meet the demands of team work coined the term "Computer-Supported Cooperative Work" (CSCW) to describe this emerging field. Groupware is the term most often used to describe the software products that support group work. (Other names for CSCW technologies include "coordination technology," "group decision support systems," "multiuser applications," and "computer-mediated communication.") Groupware promises many benefits by changing how teams work together. (We should note that increasingly, people like our colleague Hugh Ryan are using the term "teamware." "Groups grope," says Ryan. "Teams produce.") It supports the process that team members use to contribute to collaborative projects, and it enables teams to share information more effectively. In fact, introducing groupware into an organization is an opportunity to evaluate and to change, if necessary, current organizational practices.

Today's technologies, including those that empower performance systems, provide the tools that translate research about computer-supported cooperative work into practical applications. These software applications support five primary needs of groups and teams within organizations:

1. *Effective communication among group members.* Effective communication within a group or organization depends on choosing an appropriate channel. That choice is based on several factors: the nature of the information to be communicated; the group to be addressed; the level of interaction required within that group; and the need to keep the communication timely.

   Technology is increasingly used as a communications vehicle: electronic mail and electronic bulletin boards, for example, are the most common choices for informal, nonurgent communication.

2. *Timely sharing of information.* Teams function better when they can draw on their organization's accumulated knowledge and experience. Libraries and filing systems are familiar examples of materials that encourage information exchange. Effective use of information repositories relies on two key questions: "How do I find what I need?" and "How useful is the information to the problem I'm working on?"

Lotus Notes™ is an example of a groupware product that promotes information sharing across large organizations. Operating in networked environments, this PC-based product is an integrated set of applications and tools for circulating documents, exchanging ideas, and communicating through electronic mail. Products like Notes allow team members to work from many locations at different times. The software collects each person's contributions and makes them available for others to access and use. For example, Andersen Consulting's Global Management Council, made up of partners from around the world, routinely uses Notes to work on strategic issues.

3. *Profitable collaboration.* Collaboration is the act of working jointly to produce such products as decisions, documents, software applications, or tangible goods. Individual contributions can be a key component of collaborative work, since groups often divide a project into subtasks, assign them to individual members, and then merge the results to produce the final product. Examples are a paper-based delphi session, reviews of funding proposals, or team development of a proposal to a major client.

The role that each individual plays within a group, and the skills each contributes, affect the way a group functions. More than that, groups change over time as the members become comfortable working together, as the nature of the task changes, and as individual skills and preferences emerge. These evolutions, as much as task content and goals, can drive group work.

Collaboration tools, therefore, support the dynamic nature of the group process by:

- supporting individual participation and ways for individuals to view and manipulate contributions to the group product;
- supporting the collection of information about the task and other information relevant to the group's work (such as pending issues and decisions); and
- providing mechanisms for tracking the status of an emerging product (for example, versions of the product under development and histories of the group's activities).

4. *Productive meetings.* Meetings are a type of group work suited to face-to-face interaction. Usually, the main goals of meetings are to make decisions, solve problems, and craft solutions for organizational issues that are not

routine. To make meetings more productive, groups often rely on formal techniques designed to facilitate decision making. The technology-based techniques, sometimes referred to as Group Decision Support Systems, support domain-specific, group problem solving and decision making. They structure the discussion of a problem, provide the framework for brainstorming, establish criteria for evaluating proposals, and provide the tools for analyzing the constraints on a business model. Each member of the meeting uses a computer to contribute ideas, vote on ideas, and view the group's work.

These tools enhance group effectiveness because they support the process the group follows, and because they promote the capture and manipulation of key information—including intermediate results and outcomes—that is difficult to capture with generic software such as spreadsheets and outlines.

5. *Improved ability to coordinate and manage workflow.* Finally, groupware can help teams meet the major business challenge of managing workflow, projects, and schedules. People who work in fast-paced environments find it difficult to effectively process paperwork (such as purchasing requests) and coordinate team members' schedules. These products improve the procedures for scheduling meetings, setting deadlines, establishing procedures for carrying out work, and keeping group members informed of project status.

Key features of workflow products are methods for defining workflow processes and using these workflows within teams, creating work groups, and establishing access rights for creating, modifying, and using shared materials. Users can create customized forms and workflows that can improve the processing of claims, purchases, or documents that require approval by many people. They can also provide project status, show how a project flows through the organization, and highlight information that may have an impact on schedules already in place.

The benefits of these systems extend beyond the needs of a single work group. By sharing calendars, schedules, documents, and project materials, and by recording project histories, many organizations streamline their business processes and develop effective procedures for work that involves multiple groups.

CASE EXAMPLE:
OMNI COLLABORATION SYSTEM

OMNI is a model for structuring the collaborative process for complex tasks. This class of tasks usually depends on large information bases, which require the collaboration of numerous experts and which occur over an extended time period. Examples include:

- Hiring and employee promotion decisions
- Evaluation of proposals
- Design work

Each of these tasks can be described by a set of underlying issues that drive the outcome. By addressing the important issues relevant to any given situation, a group structures its decision process. The OMNI model provides the mechanisms for group members to submit positions on issues and conduct conferences on any controversial or unresolved issues. A system built from the OMNI model allows group members to contribute positions on issues, view the state of the decision process, interact through conferences, and reach closure on tasks. OMNI seeks to strike a balance between the needs for individual work, access to the group work, and ways for team members to interact.

Using OMNI, group members can work at different times, and even different locations, while having the tools for remaining in contact with their colleagues. A group member has immediate access to all of the work contributed by team members and has a number of tools to use for reaching colleagues. These capabilities allow group members to identify the likely outcome of the task, determine the key areas of disagreement and the issues of importance, and use the conference tools to initiate the deliberation process for resolving conflicts.

One prototype system built from the OMNI model supports the venture capital funding process.[42] Venture capital firms make complex decisions in the face of uncertainty about risky ventures. Handling hundreds of proposals each month, venture capitalists turned to technology to improve their process. OMNI changed how the team members work by bringing attention to key issues. The traditional face-to-face approach treated all issues as equal, and groups wasted time over unimportant issues or issues for which there was already consensus.

Decision making for venture capitalists is driven by the "due diligence" process, a process that ensures fair evaluation of each proposal. Proposal review is based on the consideration of hundreds of issues, often stated as questions about the proposed venture. The OMNI system permits each member of the team to submit positions on the issues, and it lets them view all the positions. Issues can be ranked by the degree of disagreement. Positions include statement of opinion plus an indication of the issue's rela-

SUPPORT FOR A VENTURE CAPITAL WORKGROUP

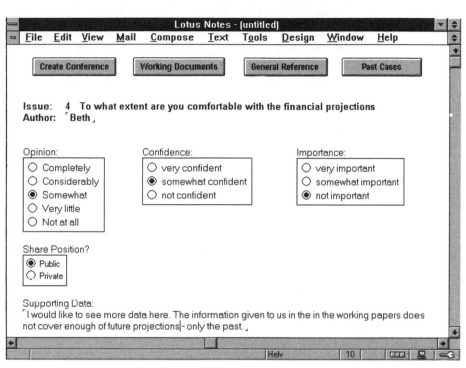

tive importance to the overall assessment. Each team member indicates a confidence in the position submitted. Positions cannot simply be tallied for an outcome. Group members can hold electronic conferences on the issues to discuss positions, share available information, and influence others' positions.

When the group meets face-to-face to make a decision, the group members already know what the key issues are. There is less need for the group to take time to sense how each member "really" feels, since the technology-enabled group process will already have made that abundantly clear.

Future enhancements to OMNI will be intriguing. For example, researchers are building tools that support the use of icons for conveying "tone of voice" in conference inquiries regarding opinions, and creativity prompters for determining the sources of disagreement. This support includes the use of guidance and suggestions for discovering and resolving disagreement.

Groupware tools such as OMNI will be vital components of performance systems and thus will need to be designed from an IPS perspective. The six IPS components for OMNI would be:

1. *Work Profile Services.* These services can provide task structuring support and provide guidelines on the types of expertise needed to accomplish a task. In the venture capital domain, group members are all responsible for making assessments of a proposed business plan, but one person is usually assigned the role of primary investigator, and someone may be assigned the task of validator, to look over the conclusions and rationale of the group. These services would outline the tasks of these two roles and the areas of expertise required of anyone assuming these roles, and would describe how these group members should use the applications for optimal performance.
2. *Knowledge Worker Services.* A key aspect of the OMNI model is the communication and interaction of team members. For example, when a team member is uncertain about an issue, the best way to work may be to talk

---

Center for Strategic Technology Research (CSTaR)

The goal of Andersen Consulting's Center for Strategic Technology Research (CSTaR) in Chicago, Illinois, is the development of solutions to today's and tomorrow's business problems through innovation, advanced thinking, and research. In contrast to the technology-driven approach of many research organizations today—an approach that begins with specific technologies and then searches for problems that those technologies can solve—CSTaR's scientists and researchers are guided by a different principle: begin with the business problem and then create a technological solution.

The Center is divided into three areas of expertise: the Human Systems Integration Laboratory (HSIL), Technology Transfer (TT), and the Software Engineering Laboratory (SEL). Much of the research currently being conducted at CSTaR has direct implications for Integrated Performance Support. Within HSIL, for example, research focuses on the new generation of systems applications designed from a human-centered, performance-centered perspective. These applications, highly knowledge-based and collaboration-intensive, will support both knowledge workers and consumers. Creating such applications involves integrating new technologies such as multimedia, visualization, groupware, and intelligent agents. In addition to designing applications and system prototypes (see Chapter 9 for the example of the Electronic Shopping Mall), HSIL is conducting research to assess the usability of such systems. CSTaR's Software Engineering Lab is focusing on how to incorporate Integrated Performance Support concepts into software development.

with a colleague who is well versed in the subtleties of the issue. These services can be used to help team members get in contact by utilizing the expertise and interest information contained in the worker profile.

3. *Advisory Services.* When a worker is confronted with hundreds of issues and reams of information about a proposed business venture, choosing which issues to examine can be a critical first step. These advisory services can offer insight by examining similar past cases and determining which issues were key to those decisions.

   Likewise, team members can be advised on the use of techniques for resolving conflicts. Given that these decisions are consensus-based, the group members need to resolve disagreements. Choosing the appropriate method for identifying differences and finding a resolution is important.

4. *Job Aid Services.* These services are at the heart of the OMNI process. Although individuals can begin an evaluation by independently making assessments of the issues, the difficult work begins when they collectively evaluate all the stated opinions on the issues. Teams rely on the use of job aid services to propose solutions, discuss the issues, and communicate. Telepresence tools (such as teleconfcrencing) can be used for team members who want to engage in lively discussions in real time. These services are instrumental to improving the quality of the process.

5. *Reference Services.* Access to previous cases is a key benefit of using technology for these tasks. By indexing the issues, rationale, and work objects (such as business plans), the groups have ways to easily access information about their prior evaluations of business proposals. They can rely on the materials rather than simply make assessments by relying on their memory of those cases and the key issues.

6. *Training Services.* The job of the primary investigator includes closely monitoring the progress of the evaluation and the level of contribution of the team members and collecting additional materials needed for the evaluation. If someone has not previously assumed this role, these training services can be used to give the investigator experience and an opportunity to learn about the important factors to monitor as a business plan evaluation progresses.

CASE EXAMPLE:
AGT LIMITED

We have noted that the capability to be self-directing is vital to the success of knowledge workers in the new economy. But what does that mean, exactly, and how do organizations begin to support those workers so that they have the ability to act independently, to serve customers well with a minimum of supervision, and to cope with complex working environments?

Senior management at AGT LIMITED, the telecommunications provider for the Canadian province of Alberta, had an innovative idea: why not transform their customer service representative role from one of passive information gathering to one of proactive sales? Customer service representatives are, after all, the primary point of customer contact for the company. It makes sense, therefore, to give the representatives the support needed so that they can analyze the communications needs of a customer or potential customer and then match existing products and services to those needs.

But providing this support is a challenge to every organization. As the telecommunications industry has become increasingly competitive, companies have intensified their customer focus and expanded their offerings of products and services. Through modernization of equipment, for example, AGT has been able to offer now-familiar services such as call waiting and three-way calling. They have also offered more options for toll packages to accommodate customers with different types of phone usage. These expanded offerings have been wonderful for the company and wonderful for the customers, but a challenge to the customer service representatives. AGT went from offering just six basic services in 1986, to over thirty services in 1992. Management at AGT began to see the effects of this information overload on their representatives: errors in some types of order entry by the representatives had increased to almost 20%. Representatives were finding their work increasingly stressful because of the need to remember and to be an expert at so many things: sales, customer service, calculation, credit assessment. As a consequence, the turnover rate for representatives was beginning to rise.

Why was all this happening? First, because of the limitations of existing information systems, representatives had no on-line support for pricing information. The existing system centered on several discrete mainframe applications, augmented by tools like pocket calculators and various kinds of paper-based support. As new services were offered to customers, the representatives added supporting documentation to their service binders: added, indeed, until the binders exceeded 1,000 pages in length. Navigating through these binders required a great deal of experience and patience; sometimes it required a fair bit of luck, as well. Each worker had to turn to paper manuals to get information. And paper manuals often meant that natural human error intervened—either by the representative looking up the information, or by the workers charged with ensuring that each representative's manual contains up-to-date information.

The communications infrastructure of any telecommunications provider is also complex. Not every area or every neighborhood is served by identical equipment and facilities. Certain services might be provided in one part of a town, but not in another. Information like this was not available to the representative; occasionally, then, representatives would sell a service to a customer, only to find later that the company's or customer's equipment could not support that service. This complex working environment also had training ramifications. Committed to excellence in customer service, AGT management was also committed to training its customer service representatives to ensure that this level of excellence was sustained. Representatives went through a formal thirteen-week training period, including four weeks of training just on how to enter an order. But the on-the-job learning curve continued to be long; representatives worked eighteen months before they were considered to be "experienced."

As should be quite clear by now, this kind of working environment is tailor-made for a performance system. AGT management was not, after all, beginning with system types of issues: that is, here is a system, now we need to train our users. Instead, the starting point was a business need: we want our customer service representatives to be sales people as well as resource people; we want them to be *knowledge workers*. Now, how can they be empowered technologically not only to perform in a complex environment, but also to move beyond the capacities of their current roles?

The project team established to design support for the new customer service representative role at AGT set out to create a system to handle one of the more frequent and complex customer service requests: the residential install order. As a part of that system, a knowledge-based "assistant" was developed to facilitate the sales process. The resulting system, called "Customer Service Representative (CSR) Advisor," thus contains two major components: an order entry component and a marketing component.

ORDER ENTRY

By designing and automating this component, developers intended to increase the effectiveness of customer service representatives, and thus to increase the level of customer satisfaction. This has been accomplished in a number of ways. First, the process of taking orders was simplified, and the number of interfaces required for any one representative was drastically reduced. All resources are now available to the representative at a single work-station. The new system masks the complexity of the technology, allowing representatives to devote more attention to their customers and less time to locating information resources. The order entry component is a series of graphical user interface screens designed to capture all information relevant to the customer's request for service. Service location, billing information, and directory details are received from the customer and entered by the representative.

The system eliminates manual calculations (previously done by handheld calculators) and puts information about pricing, network services by location, service charges, and other customer reference information at their fingertips. When a customer places an order, the representative need only select the designated product or service from a roster of available items. The system then calculates the appropriate charges and creates an itemized record of the transaction. At the same time, the system verifies the selected configuration, making certain that the chosen products or services can work together.

System support reduces the number of errors in order entry, lessening the need for rework, and reducing the chance of customer dissatisfaction. The system also ensures that company policies are applied consistently from one representative to another, and from one region to another. Government regulations pose additional challenges for telecommunications companies and their workers, and a performance system can ensure that all workers are performing in compliance with these regulations. As the representative proceeds with the customer transaction, information about prior service is retrieved from mainframe files, credit information is obtained from the customer, and a credit assessment is calculated by the system. One of the benefits of CSR Advisor is improving the objectivity and accuracy of the credit assessment procedure. These risk assessments were occasionally marred by subjective factors and carried out inconsistently across business offices. With the new system, automated risk assessment has become a built-in component of the sales process.

Finally, the representative captures a number of other physical installation details such as winter installation, trailer home installation, or type and number of jacks required. The system guides the novice representative through the order entry procedure with context-sensitive help, available on every screen and for every item. On selected items, expanded help also is available. Entry validation ensures that the representatives receive instant feedback when an error is made. Simple data entry validation is performed as well as complicated business logic evaluation using additional data residing on the local workstation. In addition, the CSR Advisor ensures that items such as names are consistently capitalized through the entire order and between different orders. All data is entered in plain language; special formatting for use by other systems is maintained in the background.

MARKETING COMPONENT

To transform customer service representatives into a potent sales force, designers of CSR Advisor intended the marketing component to provide a broad range of support services to the representatives. Workers must be able quickly to match the company's existing products and network services to customer needs, and the system must leverage the knowledge of the company's marketing experts, delivering that expertise in real time, at point of need, to every representative. Part of the power of the marketing component of CSR Advisor comes from the simple fact that the order entry component has reduced the complexity of the service order, giving the customer service representative more time to take advantage of the customer contact to market services and products. Marketing strategies in today's competitive environment must be flexible; they may change at a moment's notice. With CSR Advisor, every representative has access to the latest sales/marketing statistics and support for performance according to current strategy.

To provide continual feedback regarding service and product offerings that can meet customer needs, information gathered during the order is maintained. The information is gathered from the order-taking process and from questions posed directly to the customer. The representative also is supported to gather facts picked up in the background during the conversation; these facts are recorded on a checklist that is displayed on the application desktop. Information gathered during the customer's credit assessment, such as occupation type, estimated toll usage, and residence type, is used to compile a profile of the customer. As the representative moves into the marketing stage of the conversation, the system supports the worker with a series of standard questions that can determine a customer's needs. More specific follow-up questions can then be asked to streamline recommendations and to identify calling patterns. Novice customer service representatives are especially supported at this point in the process. They are literally guided though the set of questions to establish the customer profile and to recognize sales opportunities. Representatives also are taught, and then supported, as they gather additional information during the call: perhaps there is a child in the background, or the customer indicates he or she frequently works at home. This information is entered on a checklist, and CSR Advisor can use this information to suggest additional products and services.

To assist the representative in selling, a sales script is automatically generated, ready to be read to the customer, and tailored to the responses to the previous questions. If the representative is more experienced, a full script is not required, and instead the system provides an abbreviated list of the reasons for, and benefits of, a particular recommendation. CSR Advisor also provides screens that list all the available products and services in the event that the customers indicate they would like a service or product that has not been recommended. Descriptions of the products and services and their rental rates, service charges, and retail prices are available for every product and service. When a customer has decided to make a purchase, the system offers customized guidance to help the representative complete the sale.

BENEFITS OF THE CSR ADVISOR

Initial data from implementation of the CSR Advisor supports the intuitive expectation that sales would increase for the average representative. In the month studied, average sales performance increased 166% for representatives at the trial location compared to the same month in the previous year. In addition, a comparison of representatives at the trial site with representatives

_____ Advice from the CSR Advisor at AGT Limited _____

Services: Recommendations/Summary

? Based on the needs you have identified, the following AGT services are recommended:

S	Service	Base Rate	Benefit/Reason
	CALL DISPLAY	4.95	know who's calling|before you answer
A	CALL WAITING	3.00	calls get through|on busy telephone
	IDENT A CALL	4.95	know who call is for|teen or adult

[Script]   [Accept]   [Not Accept]   [Description]

? Would you like any additional AGT services?   [Services]

The following NETWORK SERVICES will be added to the order:

Service	Rental Rate	Svc Chg
CALL WAITING	3.00	0.00

[Change]   [Delete]

[HELP]   [DONE]

from another location not supported by CSR Advisor showed the study representatives besting their colleagues by 372%. Revenue generated per minute of representative time with customers also increased 137%.

A number of other tangible benefits of CSR Advisor are being realized. Average number of keystrokes per order has dramatically decreased. The amount of rework on orders also has gone down precipitously: sales order errors, for example, dropped from 18.2% to 0%. Because the risk assessment procedures have been automated, errors on the credit classification portion of the order have also dropped to zero. In addition, documentation necessary to support the work of customer service representatives at AGT has also fallen, because the CSR Advisor incorporates most of the infrastructure data that the representative must reference during an install order.

Finally, AGT management expects to realize tangible savings on training costs for their representatives and also expects its employee turnover rate to fall quickly. CSR Advisor lets the representative to be knowledge worker, not a system "user." The system's complexity is shielded from the representative by the graphical interface, so workers require less time away from the site of performance to take part in passive learning. With the old system, the thirteen-week initial training period involved four weeks of classroom training, followed by nine more weeks of hands-on experimentation. With CSR Advisor, customer service representatives are navigating the system by the end of the first day of training.

Most important in all of this, however, is the more intangible, but also more crucial, aspect of customer satisfaction. In a recent annual report, AGT notes that "satisfied customers will provide a strong foundation in an increasingly competitive marketplace, and in a society that is increasingly reliant on high-quality telecommunications." As organizations are challenged to give their workers the power to be self-managing and self-directing, and to represent the entire company to every customer, performance systems like CSR Advisor will link knowledge worker performance to the performance of the entire organization.

PART THREE

Preparing for Tomorrow

CHAPTER 9

INTEGRATED PERFORMANCE
SUPPORT FOR EVERYONE

What do the following two stories have in common?

1. Hotel service workers, who do not yet read or speak the native language of a country adequately, use a touch screen terminal to track the status of their work: which rooms have been cleaned and which have not, what supplies need to be ordered, and what repairs need to be made.
2. Customers at the Berlin airport wait in line to purchase tickets on Lufthansa airlines to Duesseldorf. When it's their turn, they step up to a machine much like a banking automatic teller. On the video screen in front of them, they can examine flight schedules, make reservations, select seats, and pay for their tickets in a matter of minutes.

Answer: in both cases, the information system must be designed to accommodate a person who is working with little, if any, knowledge base about the system or the work itself. These are not workers like those who are using the systems at McCaw Cellular or Connecticut Natural Gas, and who become, over time, expert performers. Both kinds of systems stretch to the limit the idea of user friendliness and intuitive interface design. With a minimum of training, or even with no training at all, people must be able to step up to these workstations and transact their business.

At the heart of these scenarios are two major challenges of the future marketplace:

1. A workforce that will increasingly include workers with diminishing basic skills, inexperienced workers, and workers who are still learning the language native to the country in which they are employed.
2. The continuing effort by organizations to automate certain business processes in such a way that more and more of the work of the organization can be transferred to the consumer.

- Usability—the ease with which workers and consumers can interact with technology—will become increasingly vital to organizations over the next decade.
- Two major trends indicate that Integrated Performance Support will increasingly play a vital role in the workplace and in the entire knowledge economy: (1) the influx of workers with inadequate literacy, computational, and communications skills, who will need special kinds of support from the systems with which they work; and (2) the effort of organizations to transfer work directly to the consumer (as banks have done with automatic teller machines), necessitating systems that are quickly and easily navigable.
- Performance systems can lessen the performance gap for workers with less developed basic skills by tailoring system interaction to their abilities, and also by providing remedial training and education to bring them more effectively into the workforce.
- Integrated Performance Support principles can mean the difference between success and failure for organizations that are transferring work to the consumer, or that are offering interactive services. Ease of use will be a key competitive edge. If a consumer has to struggle with the technology, the moment of value may be lost forever.

In this chapter we examine the manner in which performance systems can meet these two formidable challenges. The future will bring advanced information technology into everyone's lives. The promise of IPS is to provide support so that workers can perform and so that consumers can consume, enabled rather than restricted by the systems being used. In the future, IPS will be for everyone.

CLOSING THE SKILLS GAP OF THE TWENTY-FIRST CENTURY WORKFORCE

Will the workforce be up to the challenge of the marketplace in the twenty-first century? As we have seen, those analysts who predicted that technology would permit the "deskilling" of the workforce were wrong. True knowledge workers will require more skills, more education, more training; they will need to be more creative and innovative, and more willing to take risks in the manner in which they search for and introduce new ideas and new applications for knowledge. It is doubtful that educational systems in many parts of the world, particularly in the United States, are up to this challenge. It remains to be seen how these nations will cope with the need to produce workers who not only must know more information, but must also be creative in the application of that information, in transforming that information into knowledge, and in utilizing this knowledge for productive means.

The basic make-up of the workforce will change in many ways in the twenty-first century. In the United States, for example, the following major demographic trends will be in evidence, according to the well-known report from the Hudson Institute, *Workforce 2000.*[1]

1. *Slower growth in overall workforce numbers.* Because of slow population growth (only 0.7% by 2000), the labor force will expand by only 1% each year. This means, obviously, fewer numbers of workers entering the workforce each year, requiring organizations to find more ways to increase their productivity with their existing workforce.
2. *An aging workforce.* The average age of a worker will increase from thirty-six in the late 1980s, to thirty-nine by the year 2000. The number of young workers (aged sixteen to twenty-four) will drop by almost two million. This will increase pressure on technology to be adaptable to older workers, who are more resistant to change and less likely to undergo wholesale retraining.
3. *More women in the workforce.* About two-thirds of new entrants into the workforce by the year 2000 will be women. This will certainly continue to cause changes to societal structures and increase the importance of products and services geared to convenience for busy households. From a technological point of view, information systems will most likely link together workers who are not necessarily in a central office. The so-called "virtual office" will become increasingly prevalent, with people working from home several days a week. The need will grow for systems that manage group work and facilitate the exchange of information from off-site workers.
4. *A more culturally diverse workforce.* The number of minorities entering the workforce will double by 2000, and immigrants will make up the largest share of the increase in the overall workforce population. Here the

need for flexible and adaptable information systems will become most important.

In addition, current assumptions about educational backgrounds of the workforce in the United States may not hold, in terms of basic literacy skills, communications skills, motivation levels, and problem-solving abilities. Here, too, systems will have to accommodate a wide range of skills and abilities.

When one combines two of these trends—a shrinking labor pool and a labor pool with declining basic skills—it seems clear that the educational "minimum entrance requirement" for new workers at many organizations is going to drop. Universities have already been through this development, forced to lower admissions standards to maintain student populations, and businesses—the school of last resort—may have to follow suit, if they are not already doing so.

But how are we to reconcile this development with the predictions that jobs in the next century are not going to be able to be deskilled? In the past, a few people at the top of an organization did the thinking, and the rest of the people did the doing. In the future, everyone will have to think in order to do. The Hudson Institute report indicates that new jobs in the service industries will require higher levels of skills than today's jobs. There will be few new jobs for workers who cannot read, compute, follow directions. Demographic trends, combined with higher skill requirements, seem to point to one inevitable conclusion: lower unemployment for those with strong educations, and higher unemployment for the less skilled.[2] Our contention is that IPS may help narrow this gap.

This great educational divide is already in evidence. Consider one study that compared increases in real income of workers before and after the dawning of the information age. For 1968 to 1977 in the United States, real (inflation adjusted) income grew 20%, an increase that did not depend on the education of workers. High school dropouts gained 20%, college graduates 21%. But during the next decade, educational differences were crucial. From 1978 to 1987, overall income increased 17%, but high school dropouts actually declined 4% while college graduates grew 48%.[3] The number of low-skilled jobs is declining dramatically, and there will be no turning back from that trend.

The challenge for organizations is how to use technology to keep productivity high even in the face of lower skill levels among the workforce. In this respect, performance systems offer organizations a clear advantage. The facility to support the worker at every moment, to make advice, tools, reference, and training available on request, will close much of the performance gap for

THE EASY LEASING SYSTEM

We have called Work Profile Services the "workflow coordinator" of a performance system. One interesting and powerful example of this facility is the "Easy Leasing" performance system, a prototype developed for Italease, a leasing company in Milan, Italy. Like all performance systems, Easy Leasing enables a new worker to perform at a higher proficiency level more quickly.

One of the ways the system does this is by presenting the worker with a graphical depiction of the workflow for a given task.

The workflow representation shows the clerk the four main activities for this task. Color coding indicates the responsibilities, as well as tracking what work has been completed. Because the system knows the competency level of the worker, steps out of competence are shown in white. Red indicates a step to be done, yellow a step in progress, and green a completed step.

By clicking on a particular step, the worker is shown a to-do list. At any point, a worker can get advice on any step by dragging the question mark icon from the tool set on the right side of the screen over to any part of the to-do list.

these workers. Interfaces and basic human-computer interaction that can be tailored to the employee, based on the profile of both work and worker and how the worker wants the interface to look, will permit people with a wide range of abilities to use performance systems.

But we cannot ignore the greater social challenge of the coming knowledge economy. Peter Drucker, for example, foresees a new kind of class conflict in the twenty-first century, one between knowledge workers and service workers. The social challenge for nations around the world, not just the United States, will be in maintaining the dignity of the second class—the service workers— in what Drucker calls the "post-capitalist society." Service workers will lack the necessary education to be knowledge workers, but in even the most highly advanced countries, these workers will make up the majority of the population.[4]

Is this the only path into the future? Will this gap widen into a new kind of caste system? Are companies in the knowledge economy doomed simply to take the best of those workers that the educational system gives them, leverage these intellectual assets, and let the rest fall where they may? This is perhaps the route that many think technology will take over the next twenty years: empower the skilled and smart people coming into the workforce and downfunction the technology so that the rest of the workforce—the service workers—can at least get by. However, this does not have to be the only scenario for technology in the knowledge marketplace.

Economic progress in the new economy depends on learning: on the formative and formal education that a worker receives before entering the workforce, and then on opportunities for continuous learning while employed. *Workforce 2000* estimates that of all the new jobs that will be created by the year 2000, more than half will require some education beyond high school, and nearly one-third will be filled by college graduates.[5] But unless basic educational programs in the United States and, presumably, elsewhere can be improved, we will continue to see companies and entire nations at risk. At 29%, the high-school-dropout rate in the United States is, as Lester Thurow writes, "positively Third World." Japan's dropout rate is 6%; Germany's, 9%. But lowering the dropout rate is not the only step needed. "Getting people through a system that does not provide them with usable skills," says Thurow, "isn't an achievement."[6] Jack Bowsher has written that illiteracy is not just a minor problem in the U.S. workforce, but something affecting thousands of workers in every major company.[7]

What is the role of business given the problems of basic education? A number of companies, including Ford, GM, Polaroid, and Prudential, have, says Bowsher, "turned themselves into educators of the last resort, providing the basic instruction that in an ideal world would be found in the schools."[8] Technology will affect the manner in which basic instruction is provided both by the state and by corporations. In Chapter 12 we will look at one view of the technological future, a view that sees the entire world linked together through information networks, making more information and knowledge accessible to consumers at home and at work than ever before. In this environment, new modes of education will inevitably develop, and it is likely that public education will encounter more competition from the private sector. On-demand, point-of-need, at-home, interactive learning enabled by IPS is on the way, and it is still unclear what the cultural and educational fallout will be from this technological development. In the meantime, certainly one role people and organizations could take is to become more vocal in calling for the reform of public education, and to develop apprenticeship programs and other educational approaches that can bring business and industry into the educational picture. Such programs would be wonderful for the next generation. But what about this one?

The human-centered technology of performance systems could help. Because the goal of Integrated Performance Support is to get people from various backgrounds and educational abilities actually *performing* their jobs, as quickly as possible, other kinds of remedial training could easily take place during the course of this person's job.

Why should businesses play the role of remedial educator? There are two possible reasons. The first forces us finally to face up to the most important trend of the late twentieth century regarding the role of business in society. That trend is that, in an unprecedented way, the business enterprise system has become the dominant institution both in America and in the world. This dominance extends far beyond mere economic matters, and into areas traditionally occupied by the family, the church, and the schools. The institution of business, one writer notes, "has become a major determiner of social values, of personal and family priorities, readily observable in our own society. Business values seem to have filled the vacuum left in recent years by the withdrawal of much of the educational system from the value-development area."[9] Drucker argues, in a chapter on the "responsibility-based organization," that the new knowledge society demands that organizations take social responsibility. No one else in the society of organizations seems capable of taking care of society itself, though businesses must take such action responsibly and without endangering their own capacity to perform.[10]

The second reason why organizations must take responsibility for remedial education of workers is more practical. They may have to. If the supply of talented and educated workers remained high, even in the face of generally declining educational fortunes generally, one could argue that intervention by corporations would be optional. But more and more corporations will find themselves the school of last resort, bringing people with marginal educations into their workforce, people who are perhaps functionally illiterate, and most certainly lacking in the more important creative skills necessary to thrive in the knowledge economy.

REMEDIAL PERFORMANCE SUPPORT

Recall that the approach to training that undergirds Integrated Performance Support has two separate, though related, dimensions. The first is to support real performance needs right now for workers wherever they need it. The second is to create an environment in which learning takes place continually. Both these aspects, working in tandem, can support the needs of an organization and its workforce. The organization gets optimal performance; workers get to grow and learn and better themselves.

Without the creation of a learning environment, workers risk exploitation, and organizations may focus only on their worth in the near term. Certainly this is destructive to the worker as a human being; it is also damaging to the organization, which loses the ability to have its employees grow to meet the needs of an ever-changing marketplace. A learning environment presumes that workers change and grow, that their skills and capabilities become enhanced as they learn on the job.

Performance systems and related technologies can support the work of undereducated workers by supporting them in their work immediately. This is the hallmark of the performance-centered approach: to tailor support to the needs of the real worker—this worker right here, not some hypothetical construct of what the "ideal" worker should be. Here, some who have written on the use of computers and other technologies by illiterate or functionally illiterate workers misunderstand the issues. The object of performance support in this case is not to be a crutch for the worker, or to make it easier for the worker to remain illiterate or otherwise poorly educated. The object is to provide a base from which to begin, a base that allows the worker, even an illiterate one, to begin to perform a job immediately, and then to grow in the job to become an even more productive worker. As we have seen, only by getting workers to perform real job tasks as quickly as possible can they begin to reap the benefits of the "learning by doing" approach to education and training.

In the future, the gap between knowledge workers and service workers may intensify. If there is to be hope that people can bridge that gap—that they can begin as service workers and increase in knowledge and skill to the point that they become knowledge workers—remedial performance support will play a key role. If touch screens and pictures must at first drive the service worker's performance at the system, so be it. That worker is also empowered concurrently, however, to take advantage of computer-based training in basic skills such as reading, mathematics, and critical thinking.

Some promising research into literacy training in the workplace has been conducted. One project was the Workplace Literacy System Project (WLS), sponsored by the U.S. Department of Education's Office of Vocational and Adult Education, and by the National Workplace Literacy Program. Although the focus of the project was on learning outcomes, not performance outcomes, we think it is useful to note its performance-*based* approach to literacy training.

The WLS project prepared interactive CD-ROM discs containing about fifty hours of instruction and drill in basic skills presented within the context of the textile/apparel manufacturing industry. The project was conducted at a Sara Lee knit products plant in North Carolina. During the project, literary task analyses were completed for all occupations at the plant, documented for each job position, and organized into a curriculum outline. A total of 376 employees were recruited, and a comprehensive workplace literary curriculum for the textile industry was developed and recorded on CD-ROM discs.

On-site instructional programs using both group instruction and computer-based programs were in operation during the eighteen months of the project. Instruction was made available in a high school equivalency program, a job enhancement skills program, a metric mathematics program, and the comprehensive curriculum on the interactive computer disks. The Sara Lee Company was pleased with the program and its benefits to the company in terms of increased skills.

Courseware designed by the project is self-paced and developed around the tasks of the textile industry. It has both reading and math components, and both tracks are designed to help employees develop the critical thinking skills necessary to be better prepared for changes in the workplace.

The reading component is grouped into five modules:

1. Preparing Cotton Fibers for Spinning
2. Spinning of Wool and Cotton Yarn
3. Knitting Fabric
4. Wearing Fabric
5. Fabric Finishing and Color Application

A short article (four paragraphs) introduces each topic and is used throughout the module to teach a variety of important reading comprehension skills.

The math component consists of four levels of word problems dealing with specific math skills. Workers apply known math and critical thinking skills to problems a textile employee would find on the job or in everyday life. Each level is broken down into three or four programs covering whole numbers, fractions, decimals, and percentages. Each program includes problems that review skills from previous levels.

The Sara Lee Company clearly has expectations for this project that go beyond the needs of the individual workers. They expect that the program will enhance their ability to respond to additional training needs as they arise. Management also believes that those workers who have committed their energy to improving their skills will also be more productive and energetic and more committed both to their job tasks and to the work of the entire organization.

THE CUSTOMER AS CO-WORKER

One of the major trends in the marketplace today, one that will intensify over the next decade or so, is the transfer of work to the consumer. That is, whenever organizations reengineer and automate business processes in the future, they will look more and more toward "hiring the customer"—taking the customer on as a co-worker and letting the customer handle many of the tasks currently done by an organization's employees. Our colleague Rudy Puryear refers to this trend as extending the moment of value out to the customer base. Business in the twenty-first century will not necessarily, or not always, be conducted at certain fixed locations—offices, shopping malls, grocery stores. Business may be transacted at any time, at any place. If this is to happen efficiently, information systems of the future must be accessible by those who are using the system for the first time. Customers, too, must have performance support; indeed, their need is probably more intense than anyone's. But one more competitive variable comes into play here: ease of system use and the ability to provide customer performance support will be a vital determinant of profitability for organizations in the future. If a customer cannot easily transact business with that organization's computer system, the customer will simply, and quickly, go elsewhere.

Hiring the customer is already happening, of course. You are already, in many cases, your own bank teller, your own telephone operator, your own airline reservations clerk, your own service station attendant. Hallmark Cards has recently allowed you to be your own greeting card designer. Computerized kiosks with touch screen capabilities are being installed in Hallmark stores and other locations that allow customers to design and print their own customized greeting cards. Buyers are presented with the image of a salesperson, who walks the customer through the process of designing the card by asking a series of questions: "What is the occasion?" "Is the recipient male or female?" Buttons on the touch screen offer a series of design suggestions. About 800 card designs are available, but because customers can write their own messages, there are an infinite number of customized possibilities. When the card is complete, an ink-jet color printer produces the finished product.

Hallmark's choice of traditionally user-friendly Macintosh machines reinforces the importance of natural human-computer interaction in providing customer performance support. Hallmark's technical development manager, Mike Vandemark, notes, "We're dealing with a very not-computer-literate consumer, so we really needed to make it easy to use."[11] The focus is on doing the job, not using the computer.

CASE EXAMPLE:
LUFTHANSA SALES SERVICE TERMINALS

Competition in the airline industry continues to intensify, and the major carriers are looking for ways to increase efficiency and streamline their business processes. As part of an overall effort to redefine the manner in which they deal with customers, Lufthansa identified the following goals:

- Reduce nonvalued-added time by eliminating long lines at ticket counters.
- Provide Lufthansa ticket sales and check-in staff with more time to deal with difficult or complex passenger issues and spend more time delivering service to customers.
- Accommodate the continued growth in the numbers of passengers traveling on Lufthansa.

Lufthansa's customer service organization began six major initiatives to redefine processes and to automate wherever possible. One of these initiatives was a project to design and install a network of self-service kiosks within Germany. These kiosks provide customers with immediate access to flight information. Customers can make reservations and pick up tickets; they can select seat assignments and check in for individual flights; and they can print their own tickets and boarding passes. Each network of machines is linked directly to Lufthansa's host for passenger check-in and to the European-based computerized reservations consortium, AMADEUS.

Lufthansa's initiative chose a perfect candidate for a process that could be transferred to the customer. Passenger check-in is a routine procedure, and personal contact at this point adds little, if any, value to the majority of fre-

LUFTHANSA'S SELF-SERVICE TICKETING SYSTEM

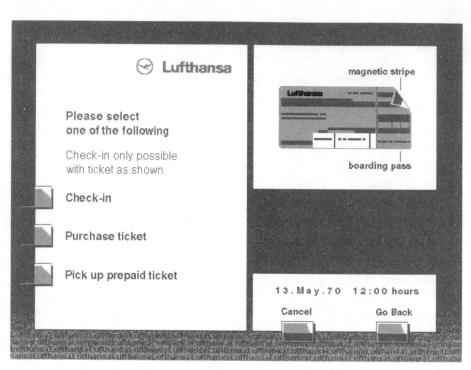

quent flyers. Personal service is still available, of course, to persons more unfamiliar with flying or those having some other special needs.

Organizations will continue to find processes like this one and offer it back to the consumer. In Rudy Puryear's phrase, this process electronically "colocates the moment of value with the place of the event." In each case, providing performance support to that customer during the transaction will be vital to the success of the newly automated process.

CASE EXAMPLE:
THE ELECTRONIC SHOPPING MALL

One of the biggest challenges for information systems in the twenty-first century is to make human-computer interaction natural and easy enough to allow anyone at home to access public information networks and interactive computer buying services. Here, as we have said, the ease with which a consumer can maneuver and navigate through a system will be a big determinant of financial success for companies in the future who seek to offer their services via public networks. And few companies will want to pass up the enormous buying public who, through years of practice, understand how to watch television. Why not have people buy things at the same time?

Those who follow the comic strip "Doonesbury" have already seen such interactive computer shopping lampooned as a female character in the strip floated through a virtual reality shopping mall, unable to contain her excitement as she racked up several thousand dollars of purchases. Readers may have seen humor in it, but it's no joke. Such systems, as you will see shortly, are ready to go now, waiting only for the information superhighways of the next century, which we discuss in Chapter 12.

One particular innovative system is called the "Electronic Shopping Mall," a research prototype under development at Andersen Consulting and a test bed for a number of ideas in interactive consumer-oriented services. This system is a three-dimensional, virtual reality environment designed to be accessed by buyers at home through their television sets. The primary interface of the system places the customer in a realistic graphical depiction of a three-dimensional shopping mall. Using a joystick, the customer can turn and move in any direction. Several stores are available, including a grocery store, a sports store, and a video store.

Entering the grocery store, the customer has two immediate choices: to shop for basic foods, or to shop for "solutions"—particular events that require special menu planning. Available to the shopper at all times are several guides or agents (concepts discussed in Chapter 4), which serve as resources for the shopper during this experience. A nutritionist will help choose healthy foods; a young parent will help shoppers who need advice about menu planning for young families; a gourmet food expert helps those needing some haute cuisine assistance; and a slightly rumpled-looking bachelor type is ready to assist people who need some advice on "quick and easy meal preparation."

In one example, shoppers stop at one of the displays within the grocery store, where they can choose from a number of types of entertainment, or entertaining events. Choosing "picnic," for example, shoppers then provide information about numbers of people and types of food wanted. Menus are displayed, and detailed shopping lists are provided depending on choices entered. The system also displays choices for related products. Because this event is outdoors, the system suggests insect repellent, for example. If the shoppers want, they can ask the system to take them to that product, and they will be whisked to that part of the store, allowing them to see other products on the way there.

While the shopper is transacting business, a moving set of images scrolls past at the bottom of the screen, representing other products and services that might be of interest, based on an evolving set of "psychographics" that cor-

"WALKING THROUGH" THE ELECTRONIC SHOPPING MALL

respond to a shopper's purchasing history. The system tracks the shopper's interest and can suggest other buying options that it thinks might be of interest. If the shopper often purchases microwave meals, for example, the system might infer that the shopper is a young professional working outside the home and might make other shopping suggestions: a discount professional clothing store elsewhere in the mall, for example, or certain travel bargains being offered by the mall's travel agency. If the shopper is interested in any of these options, clicking on them will take him or her directly to that store.

Merchandisers identified five different shopping styles that represent most consumers, and designed the system to be tailorable to any of those styles:

1. *Casual browsing.* The system facilitates browsing by allowing the shopper to jump from one virtual store to another. Future enhancements to the system will allow the person to interact with other shoppers within the virtual store, adding a social element to this type of shopping.
2. *Cross-shopping.* By capturing a shopper's purchasing history, the system can offer related products to a potentially receptive buyer. Buyers of char-

_____ SPECIAL SHOPPING SOLUTIONS AT THE MALL'S GROCERY STORE _____

coal will be asked if they need charcoal lighting fluid. Certain meat purchases in the butcher part of the grocery store will automatically present
the shopper with alternative wines appropriate to that meat selection.
3. *Directed search.* Shoppers who know what they want can go directly to
   that item.
4. *Solutions shopping.* Through the availability of the shopping agents or
   guides, the Electronic Shopping Mall offers shoppers their own personal
   consultant to assist with particular entertaining situations.
5. *Impulse shopping.* The Mall enables impulse shoppers to buy anything,
   anytime, and it isn't afraid to make intelligent suggestions based on their
   buying habits. If you have rented several videos over the past year in a certain category, the system may make similar suggestions. If you have a favorite author or recording artist, the system will let you know when that
   person has a new book or CD available.

The Electronic Shopping Mall is at the leading edge of a logical development or evolution of IPS: performance support for the consumer. Indeed, many

of the services of IPS are present in this example: a service similar to Knowl-edge Worker Services keeps a profile of the purchasing habits of the customer; advice and reference are available to the customer through the agents; at the grocery store, granular training is available to help shoppers needing infor-mation about certain foods or food preparation methods. "Performance" in this case is the performance of a shopper, and supporting that performance can mean not only a more satisfying experience for the consumer, but a more satisfying bottom line for the organization offering this interactive shopping experience.

CHAPTER 10

MAKING CHANGE WORK

"If you build, they will come," said the semimystical voice from the well-known movie *Field of Dreams*.[1] The phrase might also serve as the motto for some corporate efforts over the past several decades to create new information systems, new strategies, new management techniques, new organizational structures. If you build new computer systems, your workers will be more productive. If you reengineer business processes, your employees will automatically work better. If you institute quality programs, your workers will be empowered. If you build, they will come. They'll embrace these new systems and processes, right?

The stories we hear and witness in the field tell us it is hardly a field of dreams. Sometimes organizations build but no one comes. Consider, for example, one state government agency in the United States that was reengineering its processes and installing new computer systems. The officials were extremely encouraged by this initiative and were quickly caught up in the excitement about workforce empowerment. Through these new information systems, workers would have access to more information, could serve their customers better, and could really begin to think about ways to improve their workflow and to manage their work. The officials hadn't counted on one important problem, however: the employees had little interest in being empowered. Most of them were quite content to come in each day, be told what to do, and to do it.

Or consider the fate of the international oil company that adopted a diversification strategy because of political threats and because its current business would not support long-term growth. Five years after announcing the diversification, it was back in the oil business, having found that the new strategy was being resisted and even sabotaged by its own employees. The strategic change being directed by top management so violated the employees' basic values and beliefs about their roles, as well as the traditions implicit in the culture, that no amount of leadership could overcome it.[2]

There are numerous examples like these: examples not just of making change *happen,* which is relatively easy, but making change *work,* which is very difficult. We believe that technology can be the catalyst for making change work, rather than the change inhibitor it has sometimes been in the past. Because organizations have rarely taken sufficient time to reorient their workforce to the new processes accompanying technological change, and then

263

KEY MESSAGES: CHAPTER 10

- Making change happen is easy; making it *work* is extremely difficult.
- The pace of change in the business and economic environment around the world will only intensify in the coming years, and organizations must take advantage of the ability of performance systems to facilitate change management.
- "Technology assimilation" is frequently a challenge during times of change. But a human-centered technology like a performance system represents a symbiosis between technology and knowledge worker. Embedded within the system is the capability to respond to change, and to support the worker during those times of change.
- Because of the performance orientation of IPS, organizations are able to concentrate not only on high, strategic levels, but also on the level of the individual knowledge worker, where one really makes change work.
- Performance systems can also support change in more specific ways. Within a performance system are definitions of, and support for, competencies necessary to produce desired outputs. During times of change, management can use the information from the system to determine which competencies it possesses, which need to be recruited, and which need to be trained in the new environment. The mobility of competencies across jobs and processes makes an organization more responsive to change.
- Performance systems are vital to the success of reengineering efforts. They provide the crucial support for knowledge workers as they begin to perform new processes. More specifically, the analysis of existing workforce competencies can help an organization determine which of several workflow options it can realistically support. The ability to implement a new process workflow quickly is a huge competitive advantage.

---

have not supported the performance of the workforce following the change, they have encountered stiff resistance. Sometimes, as the oil company saw, the result has been total surrender. This cannot take place in the twenty-first century marketplace. There, successful organizations will have to be resilient and be able to recover quickly. In response to competitive forces, government regulation, and technological innovation, companies must be able to change direction quickly, and to push that change through their organizations. Better still, they must have their workforce own and pull the change through themselves.

In this chapter, we want to look at ways in which an Integrated Performance Support orientation, and an increased reliance on performance systems, can quicken the pace of cultural change. Because technology has been seen as something separate from, and sometimes foreign to, the worker, efforts to manage change generally speak of the need for "technology assimilation" by the workforce. But a human-centered technology like a performance system is already an assimilated technology. Worker and technology function together naturally, in symbiosis, to perform job tasks and to learn continuously, worker and system. The facility to tailor support to the worker, and to provide additional support when necessary during times of organizational change, is inherent within Integrated Performance Support and embedded within the performance system.

CULTURE AND STRATEGY: THE TORTOISE AND THE HARE

Our colleague Robert Laud has noted in a recent article that the problem for organizations during times of change is the "tortoise and hare" relationship of culture and strategy: cultures move much more slowly than strategies do.[3] Change management, helping an organization navigate the change process during times of strategic and technological change, is a fairly young field. Laud notes that as recently as 1980, organizational consciousness about culture had not been raised enough for Michael Porter to note the strategic impact of culture in his seminal work *Competitive Strategy,* itself a significant contribution to the process of change. Since that time, however, a number of important works about organizational culture have been published, and more organizations are at least familiar with the idea and the importance of nourishing and growing their corporate culture. When Peters and Waterman published their book *In Search of Excellence,* they affirmed the belief that a strong culture is essential for market leadership and long-term success. "Without exception," they wrote, "the dominance and coherence of culture proved to be an essential quality of the excellent companies."[4]

The irony, however, is that a culture that is such a source of strength during times of stability can become a major obstacle for organizations trying to implement a new strategy. The president and chief operating officer for one major corporation put the problem well: "I am confident," he said, "that we will develop the right technical solutions. Our greatest obstacle will be changing the culture." Statistics over the past decade justify his concern. According to one recent study, for example, a poorly planned change program led to overall failure in implementing strategy 70% of the time.[5] The inability to sustain the intended change for these organizations meant not only was there no overall improvement; it also meant an actual performance decline of as much as 4%.[6]

Organizations that have been successful in accomplishing large-scale cultural change report that the process can take from six to fifteen years.[7] This is hardly a comforting time frame. What sorts of strategies could possibly endure such a long cultural implementation period? Like the tortoise and the hare in the classic fable, the slower-moving culture in these cases will surely win out in the end, defeating the flashier antics of even the best strategic thinking.

The goal must be to quicken the pace of cultural change. But what exactly are we changing? What is culture, exactly? Efforts to accelerate the pace of cultural change and to bring it into alignment with corporate strategy are likely to fail unless one fully understands the dual nature of corporate culture: that it is comprised of both formal and informal elements. Laud, for example, defines corporate culture as:

1. the *informal* and collective values of the people of an organization; and
2. the *formal* methods and systems by which management reinforces corporate values and behavior encompassing these values.[8]

By including both informal and formal elements, we can avoid two common extremes. On the one hand, people sometimes define culture so narrowly that it becomes something imposed on the organization from above. On the other hand, people sometimes emphasize the "fuzzy factors" of an organization's people, defining culture so broadly and vaguely that it begins to resemble some sort of metaphysical entity. The first extreme is common among those who hold to the position that a culture is "the way we do things around here," implying that culture is a static possession of the organization and its workforce that can be manipulated to certain strategic ends. The result of this understanding is usually a negative one: distinctions between management and employee become exacerbated, and even the finest mission, vision, or credo statement is perceived by the worker as just another sort of behavioral modification program.

In fact, a culture conceived in this fashion can never be anything more than a facade covering the *real* culture, which is something generated by members of the organization through collective enterprise and activity. A culture is not something an organization *has;* a culture is what an organization *is.*[9] The employees help build the firm; as they do, they are in fact collectively generating meaning. This helps us understand better the slow pace of cultural change. A culture does not come into being overnight, but is shaped gradually over time. In addition, the collective activity of the workforce is taking place within the larger culture from which the workforce is drawn. The culture's value orientation is reinforced through a number of other systems over which the organization has no real control: the educational, social, and economic systems. Change programs must take into account this greater societal context in which change takes place.

But to speak of this collective whereby culture is generated may lead to error at the other extreme. We cannot conceive of corporate culture as some amorphous life form, uncontrollably moving through time like a creature from a science fiction movie. This is why we emphasize both formal and informal elements. A culture is a living entity; it cannot be controlled without killing it. But it can be *shaped* by management practices and by the gradual sorts of change facilitation enabled by performance systems and led by the active participation of people.

Consider once again the Performance Model we introduced in Chapter 1:

_____ PERFORMANCE MODEL _____

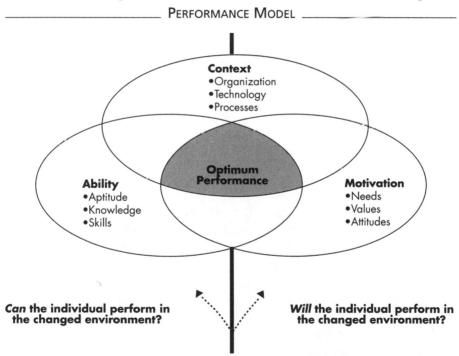

We want now to look at this model from the standpoint of strategic and cultural change. Thus we have changed the central questions driving the performance model. They are not merely "Can the individual do it?" and "Will the individual do it?" but rather "Can the individual perform in the new work environment?" and "Will the individual perform in the new work environment?" As an organization responds to competitive pressures, anticipates future needs, expands its markets, or engages in any of the multifarious activities that cause change to occur within the organization, how might an Integrated Performance Support strategy enable organizational change by ensuring that workers *can* perform and *will* perform?

CONTEXT

ORGANIZATION

The informal and formal components of our definition of culture correspond nicely to the two orientations of Integrated Performance Support that we have stressed throughout this book. That is, on the one hand, IPS is focused on representing an overall environment in which continuous learning and conversation among workers takes place, supporting the informal aspects of corporate culture. On the other hand, IPS allows for the design of systems that support the performance of each worker, supporting the formal aspects of culture, and helping management emphasize those aspects that will best push strategic change through the organization.

The technological or systems aspect of Integrated Performance Support is actually a subset of a more global kind of thinking and a particular organizational self-understanding. That is, from the technological standpoint, we would ask companies to what extent performance support is integrated into their application systems. But from a higher, strategic standpoint, we would ask companies to what extent performance support is integrated into the mindset of the organization. To what extent are you focused on performance—on the moment of value of every action taken by your workers? To what extent are you willing to ensure that your workers have the intellectual firepower of your organization behind the tasks they perform? In this respect, we can see that Integrated Performance Support is, in fact, a strategic approach in itself. In a practical way, it causes an organization to think in terms of more fully integrating technology toward workforce support. This, in turn, forces a change in the technical architecture: from systems that process transactions to systems that let workers transact business. But more important, it encourages organizations, and then makes it possible, to think *wholistically.* No thinking about strategic direction can be adequately done without considering its impact on the organization as a whole, especially the people who really *are* the organization. Thinking at the macro level must be linked to its impact at the

MARKETING SUPPORT: MOBIL OIL AUSTRALIA

Once one begins to think of working environments that can benefit from performance systems, the possibilities seem endless. One fascinating example of the creative application of the Integrated Performance Support concept comes from Australia, where Andersen Consulting's Melbourne office has developed a performance system prototype for the oil industry, called "Right Hours of Operation," or RHO. RHO has been developed as a proof-of-concept prototype for Mobil Oil Australia.

The business need for Mobil in this case is to increase the profitability of the entire organization by maximizing the hours of operation of all Mobil service stations worldwide. To make this happen, Mobil marketing personnel must be able to determine the optimum hours of operation for any particular service station; then they must be able to convince the dealers, who run their stations independently, of the value of staying open for the recommended number of hours. The marketing personnel needing support for these activities are located all over the world and are on the road most of the time.

Currently, marketing personnel are taught how to analyze shop hours for service stations as part of a four week introductory marketing course taught in Melbourne. The training delivered to marketing personnel with the RHO system helps them analyze the optimum hours of a service station and then helps them sell the benefits of extended hours to the dealer. The support services of the prototype assist the worker to collect and analyze data, and to make a recommendation. Then, based upon those findings, RHO provides the worker with a powerful and interactive on-line marketing presentation development tool. With this tool, the worker can use the results of the shop hours analysis to make a persuasive case to the particular dealer.

micro level, because it is at the micro level where one makes change work. An orientation to performance means that organizations are constantly thinking not only at high and abstract levels, but also at the level of the individual worker. This is the strategic power of Integrated Performance Support: the construction of a *knowledge infrastructure* within the organization, which not only supports individual performance at the moment of need, but which also supports the organization as it pushes change throughout various levels to shape and respond to the forces of the marketplace.

TECHNOLOGY

Implicit within the understanding of performance-centered systems design is the notion that organizations now can not only support the real-time performance needs of their workers, but can also help enable their workers toward higher performance and proficiency levels. During times of change, it is particularly important to maintain high levels of performance and to get workers quickly to proficiency on new tasks that they must perform in the new strategic or competitive environment. Until the advent of Integrated Performance Support, technology could only rarely support this latter goal.

The key to moving the workforce toward proficiency in new tasks is what we call the "common currency of competencies."[10] Competencies are the "currency" exchanged between employees and the organization. Traditional understandings of job classifications are on their way out, to be replaced by classifications based upon competencies and roles. Ideally, the organization should be able to manage and account for competencies as it manages and accounts for capital. During times of market and competitive change, organizations that can respond quickly will obviously have the advantage, and a flexible workforce is vital to quick response. Management of competencies is a critical success factor. To move the workforce in a new direction, the objective is to identify a number of moving targets: competencies the new work requires, competencies the current workforce possesses, and the gap between the two.

Recall that within a performance system are the definitions of, and the support for, the competencies necessary to produce required job outputs and required process outputs for the organization. Because IPS defines required competencies for the outputs that achieve job, process, and, eventually, strategic objectives, IPS provides one more factor for management decision making. With IPS, an organization can quickly define what competencies are needed in a new competitive environment or for a new strategic direction. Knowledge Worker Services can identify which competencies are currently employed within the organization, which competencies have to be recruited from the outside, and which competencies must be developed through training and other forms of professional development. It also provides an inventory of preexisting performance support: that which can be utilized and that which needs to be developed. This can help to identify the true costs of change.

The mobility of competencies across jobs and processes makes an organization more responsive to change. This mobility also allows organizations to assemble cross-functional workteams to respond to new customer demands or other marketplace developments. Again, the "infobase" of Knowledge Worker Services can help determine the make-up of such teams. Selection decisions can be based not only on assumptions of what potential team members can bring to the table, but on the fit of their competencies, and how the team's composite competency set can contribute to meeting business challenges.

PROCESSES

The ability to reengineer business processes, and then to support workers in those new processes, is vital to future organizational success. Reengineering, of course, is on everyone's lips these days. The cover of a recent *Fortune* magazine says it all: "Reengineering the Company: It's Hot, It's Happening, It's Now." As opposed to many business fads, however, there is great truth and power in the reengineering movement. It represents a forward-thinking, forward-looking approach to business that has real teeth to it. Done well, reengineering can deliver dramatic gains in speed, productivity, and profitability.[11]

But there are inherent dangers in the reengineering movement as it is most frequently described. First, to ask companies to begin with a clean sheet of paper, to redesign processes in a radical fashion is, of course, an extremely demanding request. For example, the two-year reengineering effort of AT&T Global Business Communication Systems included the following: "Rewrite job descriptions for hundreds of people, invent new recognition and reward systems, revamp the computer system, retrain massively, and make extensive changes in financial reporting, writing proposals and contracts, dealing with suppliers, manufacturing, shipping, installation, and billing."[12] Sometimes the effort may work brilliantly, but will fail to bring benefits because it has not been directed, or has been misdirected. One computer company, for example, reengineered its selling operations so that its sales force could provide more expertise to customers. Only after spending tens of millions of dollars did they realize that customers only cared about price; the ongoing training expertise of the sales people was tangential, at best, at least in the customers' minds.[13]

Second, unless specific details can be worked out by an organization as to how actually to go about the reengineering effort, how to assess and benchmark along the way, and what the ultimate goal is, reengineering risks the same fate as some TQM initiatives: that is, people will be saying all the right things, but there will be no assurances that anything concrete will come of it.[14] Already there are signs that this is happening. One survey of CIOs, for example, has shown that reengineering projects consistently fall short of their expected benefits. On a scale of 1 to 10, CIOs gave reengineering projects targeted at customer service only a score of 5. Projects targeted at increased revenue averaged a score of 2. Even Michael Hammer estimates that 70% of reengineering projects fail.[15]

The higher-level goal for organizations is not reengineering, but what we call *enterprise transformation.* Organizations seek the proper alignment and integration of their strategy, people, technology, and business processes, which we accomplish through a process Andersen Consulting identifies as *business integration.* Reengineering of processes is part of the procedure by which these components are aligned. The crucial question organizations must ask themselves is this: "What assurance do I have that I won't have to *re*-reengineer in a few years, after spending perhaps millions of dollars on this effort?" Reengineering that results in an integrated organization means that the process for incorporating and dealing with change has been designed into every aspect of the business, particularly the workforce, thus enabling continuous reengineering. Here is where the intelligent use of performance systems—that is, innovation at the intersection of technology and the workforce—provides the mechanism for continuous improvement, and for more rapid deployment of new strategies.

Reengineering, too, has effects on corporate culture, especially since it is usually conceived of as a radical procedure. Recall that Michael Hammer's original article in *Harvard Business Review* was "Reengineering Work: Don't Automate, Obliterate."[16] In their book, Hammer and Champy again stress this all-or-nothing characteristic. Reengineering "doesn't mean tinkering with what already exists or making incremental changes that leave basic structures intact. . . . It does mean abandoning long-established procedures. . . . Reengineering a company means tossing aside old systems and starting over. It involves going back to the beginning and inventing a better way of doing work."[17]

So what's the problem? The problem is that reengineering must address properly how to help the workers change, help them perform their reengineered jobs, and help them to interact powerfully with each other. Recall from Chapter 6 that one of the characteristics of knowledge is that it has a *past,* a history. In the same manner, an organization will only become a knowledge organization over time, by being what we called a "community of memory" and a "community of practice." And that memory—that habitual manner of working, "the way we do things around here"—becomes an impediment to new strategy implementation, particularly during times of radical or dramatic change. It does little good to inform the workforce, following or during a reengineering project, that they will be "empowered." Some workers have little desire for empowerment. More important, without performance support that is integrated into the work of the reengineered processes, employees will find themselves with *less* power, not more.

There is perhaps a bit too much optimism among the leading spokespersons for reengineering about how workers will respond. "Teams, of one person or several," Hammer and Champy write, "performing process-oriented work are inevitably self-directing."[18] Are they? Or are they occasionally perplexed and bewildered, scared, insufficiently prepared and supported? "Empowerment," the authors go on to say, "is an unavoidable consequence of reengineered processes; processes can't be reengineered without empowering process workers."[19] This may be true, but the question remains: how? There is a great difference, after all, between *telling* people they are empowered and having those people actually *perform* as empowered. Empowerment may mean, not obliteration, but the transfer of *some* skills, competencies, and approaches to work inherited from the old job or process. Integrated Performance Support, thus, could support what we may call a "continuity of performance": the transfer of some elements from the old environment to the new, as well as measures to influence behavior and rewards to assure persistence.

The knowledge infrastructure envisioned by Integrated Performance Support facilitates change by supporting *workers* during the change. Moreover, that same infrastructure will provide the means for cushioning the effect of change on the workforce during subsequent periods of growth. Infrastructure development must precede growth and strategic change. Many firms have been defeated by launching products and services before their infrastructures could support them. In one much-discussed example, Atari sent products out onto the market and then had to play catch-up with sales training, distribution center development, and distributor selection. The machine wasn't quite ready, the sales force wasn't adequately supported, and distributors were poorly chosen. When this happens to a company, not only does the product launch go poorly, but the organization's reputation will be set back immeasurably, perhaps irreparably.[20]

How can Integrated Performance Support help here? Organizations should consider, first, an approach to reengineering that does not proceed monolithically. That is, one should not presume that there is only one new process flow possible. Work first with several flows; build a few scenarios; and recognize that knowledge workers are integral to this flow, not simply add-ons. Then, as with other types of organizational change, see what competencies are going to be required for each possible flow. By matching current competencies, as determined by Knowledge Worker Services, to each scenario, an organization can choose a workflow that its competencies can realistically support, while minimizing time and training investment. This lowers the learning curve during the transition to the new process workflow. More important, it ensures that organizations can more quickly perform optimally in the new process. The ability to implement a new process workflow quickly is a huge competitive advantage.

ABILITY

The next part of the performance model, Ability, provides the most obvious way in which Integrated Performance Support can hasten organizational change. We have already noted the facility of a performance system to track workforce competencies, helping an organization to identify those competencies that it must buy externally or develop internally.

Training to enhance the abilities of the workforce is a vital part of managing strategic change. Organizational change is impeded when the workforce does not possess the basic skills and capabilities necessary to propel the strategy of the organization. But organizations must bear in mind that they place themselves at a severe disadvantage if they wait only for times of change to upgrade their training. As we have noted, this notion of training cannot keep pace with the demands of the twenty-first century marketplace. As an organization evolves along its natural life cycle, it must also engage in *continual upgrading of skills and knowledge,* in anticipation of change. An organization that provides a range of training and learning opportunities stands a much better chance at achieving a workforce with the flexibility to adapt at any stage in its evolution. Here, Hammer and Champy's emphasis on education over skills training may be troublesome if misunderstood. "In companies that have reengineered, the emphasis shifts from training to education—or to hiring the educated."[21] They stress the need for continual education as well, but as we have seen, changing workforce demographics make it increasingly difficult to hire the educated, since "educated" is not necessarily synonymous with "graduated." Further, implicit in a shift to an education emphasis is a presumption that skills training is in some way being accommodated. And we agree: accommodated through an increased use of performance support facilities. Organizations must take advantage of the ability of performance systems to accommodate a wide range of capabilities, to support workers based upon those capabilities, and then to support (lead, motivate, reward, enable) workers to attain ever higher levels of proficiency.

In his book, *Thriving on Change,* Tom Peters writes that basic skills/capabilities development must precede growth:

- Lead with upgrading the skills of the workforce. Teach factory people to be flexible; invest in equipment that abets that flexibility *before* you need it.
- Upgrade the skills of the sales force continuously—*before* the need arises; provide that sales force with tools ahead of the market need.
- Engage in distribution system/distributor upgrading *before* the specific market requirement arises.

- Emphasize in budgets ongoing skill/capability development as the essential strategy.

In short, says Peters, "The firm should be looked at as an ever-improving packet of necessary capabilities. If this conception becomes second nature, then the company will indeed be ready to take advantage of almost any market opportunity that comes along, with foreknowledge that it can execute to support the idea."[22] Here too, then, IPS and its continuous learning facilities make this theory a reality by empowering a worker to engage in the kind of continuous improvement that leads to easier organizational change.

What about times of radical change, however? What about support for those who remain in an organization after a downsizing or rightsizing movement? What about support for new initiatives? What about support following a merger or acquisition, or following a new strategic initiative? Here the granular approach to training in a performance system facilitates the rapid development of new training programs. If an organization has a fully-developed performance system, it probably already has granules of training that can be lifted from their current context and placed into new performance contexts. New on-demand support will certainly have to be developed, but because a context or framework can be adapted from elsewhere, this can dramatically reduce the development time for the new training support.

MOTIVATION

A workforce enabled by Integrated Performance Support, we have noted, is one that knows more, can do more, and *will* do more. The latter point, obviously, relates to the motivational components of our performance model: needs, values, and attitudes. Motivating workers is a complex and subjective dimension of organizational success, one that often relates most closely to the *informal* elements of corporate culture discussed above. The question here is to what extent a performance system can embody those cultural values and attitudes involving many different components such as appraisal and rewards. One's first reaction is justifiably one of suspicion. How can values be inherent in a system?

But it is not so apparent that values are absent, even in the performance systems discussed and demonstrated earlier. We believe that cultural values are embedded within the integrated support of a performance system. Consider, for example, the kinds of questions organizations must ask as they develop and implement a performance system:

- What performance is expected and how is it rewarded?
- What sorts of mastery are valued?
- What kinds of knowledge exchange are enabled?
- What communications from management are delivered to knowledge workers at their work location?

In fact, these questions carry with them many motivational and cultural assumptions about needs, values, and attitudes. And the resulting system cannot help but reflect those assumptions. Indeed, as an organization responds to change, the cultural values embedded within the system become a competitive advantage, because they are extremely difficult for a competitor to copy.

As we noted in Chapter 8, technological capabilities within the knowledge economy will create some moral dilemmas for companies and for knowledge workers. If misused, the facility of systems to track performance could become "Big Brother-ish." But intelligently, morally, and sensitively implemented, an IPS strategy can aid in motivation in some specific ways. Currently, for example, organizations frequently risk losing their high-potential employees simply because there is no consistent way to identify these individuals and to nurture them. Because a performance system will create an "infobase" of performance and competencies, organizations can better incent top performers and reward them well.

Furthermore, these top performers can be a significant factor in defining new job roles after strategic or business process change. Again, because of the capabilities of the performance system, top performers can be identified through general evaluations or through performance at critical incidents. Organizations can determine what those employees do and what they know that makes them top performers. They can develop the support to replicate that knowledge and enable that performance in other employees. Thus, organizations can let those employees help define the job performance requirements. Certain kinds of approaches to the work can even be identified and embedded within Job Aid Services, leveraging knowledge and skill throughout the entire organization.

CASE EXAMPLE:
ORGANIZATION CHANGE ADVISOR (ORCA)

Based upon what we have said about the relationship between performance systems and organizational change, virtually any of the systems we have discussed to this point could be seen as supporting cases. But we want to highlight one interesting and promising system currently in development that helps organizations manage change: it is called the Organizational Change Advisor, or "ORCA." The system, a joint project of Andersen Consulting and the Institute for the Learning Sciences, is an adaptation of the "Ask Systems" we have described previously. The prototype was designed to support Andersen Consulting Change Management Services professionals, but it also shows potential as an aid to organizations from virtually any industry. ORCA is an advice-giving program that helps an organization analyze its current situation and then provides analogous stories and descriptions to help it learn from the experiences of other organizations. ORCA gathers information about an organization by posing a series of questions to the user. The answers to these questions build up a description in the system's memory, which, in turn, reminds ORCA of previous, similar cases, whose features provide expectations that translate to additional questions to ask. This elaboration leads to several different retrievals of past cases, and these are used to build a description of the organization's situation through a series of follow-up discussions that incrementally contribute to the further elaboration and building of the case base of organizational experiences.[23]

Organizational change is an uncertain area of knowledge, what some call a "weak-theory" domain. Such a domain, which includes business and law, for example, is characterized by a lack of reliable general principles. Knowledge is incomplete, uncertain, and sometimes contradictory. Expert problem solving in such contexts often involves more than simply gathering data and then using it to generate answers. Here, problem solving involves interpreting a complex problem situation in many ways. Experts often solve problems by hearing and telling stories, by asking and answering questions. They explore alternative hypotheses and implement intermediate solutions. They also gather further data and revise their assessments and then produce new and improved solutions to partially solved problems.

ORCA, like other "Ask Systems," operates through the technique of case-based reasoning. A particular case, or story, serves as an example for interpreting a situation and tells the problem solver which features to attend to (out of a potentially huge range of possibilities) and how important their presence or absence might be. Case-based interpretation means retrieving a seemingly appropriate case on the basis of certain similar features to the situation at hand.

ORCA's cases are gathered by interviewing experts and by searching professional journals. At this stage in prototype development, because the system would first support Andersen Consulting professionals, the experts are Andersen Consulting managers and partners from Change Management Services who have experience in organizational change. The cases are recorded, stored, and then made available to help the worker consider realistic problem-solving alternatives; the system familiarizes the user with the cases in memory most closely related to the organization's situation. As the worker answers questions about the relevance of certain case elements to that organization's situation, ORCA uses the answers to manage a queue of possibly relevant stories and, when sufficiently reminded of a particular story, shows it to the worker as a related case. As new information is gathered, either from worker input or as a consequence of the worker revising his or her assessment of the organization's case, the reminding network of ORCA considers other types of problems and proposes further stories.

ORCA AT WORK

Consider a hospital renowned for its innovation; we'll call it "Mercy Hospital." It currently faces the challenges of reengineering its processes in anticipation of major government initiatives in the area of health care. The hospital

_____ RETRIEVING A STORY USING ORCA _____

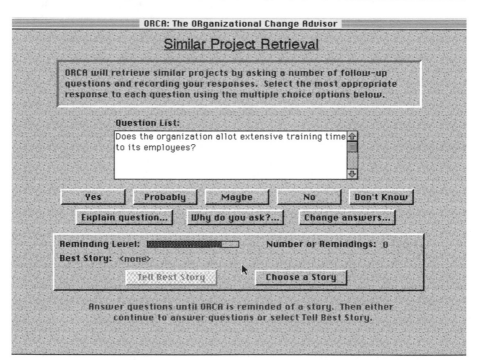

has to get its costs under control, and it has to improve its service to its customers—its patients as well as its doctors.

The team charged with the reengineering and change management effort begins its work with ORCA by having the worker-analyst select the relevant change drivers, the most important high-level problems that are driving the need for change: new technology, strategic planning, merger/acquisition, business relocation, market changes, political crises, competitive threats, and reorganization/restructuring. In this case, the worker chooses competitive threats and reorganization. These change drivers are the initial entry points into ORCA's memory. The worker is then prompted to choose the appropriate type of industry, the annual sales, and the number of employees.

Choosing this background information reminds ORCA of related surface features and anticipated organizational change problem types. ORCA then asks the worker a number of questions to confirm or disconfirm the anticipated features and problem types. For example, "Is it time that the organization consider updating its processes?" To each question, the worker responds on a scale of answers, from a certain yes, to maybe, to a definite no, or an "I

_____ AN EXPERT TELLS A RELEVANT STORY FROM ORCA'S INFOBASE _____

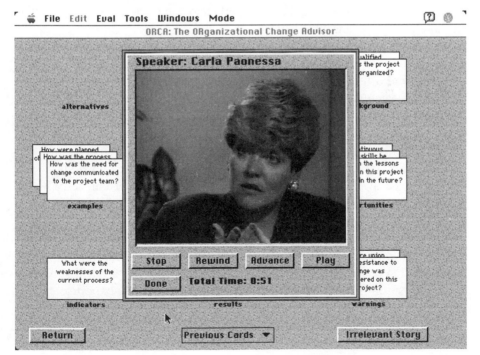

don't know." Additional buttons on the screen allow the worker to get additional information about the question. As the questions are answered, the "reminding level" indicator on the screen lets the worker know how close ORCA is to retrieving a relevant case story. When ORCA finds a story, the worker can call it up for review.

A story in ORCA is represented in the form of a small "Ask Network." The central point of the network provides a summary of the problem that ORCA has anticipated and the worker has confirmed by answering questions. The worker can view the summary by playing the video of an expert. Follow-up questions related to the same study appear as peripheral nodes of the Ask Network. Using the Ask System arrangement already seen in the Total Information Management system in Chapter 3, the worker can ask questions that are grouped according to how someone might ask questions in an ordinary conversation. The worker can move a particular question into the middle of the screen, and then request that a relevant story be shown answering or illuminating that question.

Let's say that the story played at this point is an interesting case about problems that an organization faced in getting middle management to go along with strategic change. The worker can then change the focus of the questions and make "problems with middle management" the primary focus. Now, the worker has access to all of ORCA's experts and can choose one of them who has additional relevant information.

At the end of the session with ORCA, the worker can generate a report, showing how the worker answered ORCA's questions, the stories that were accessed, and a listing of relevant articles that might assist the worker with his or her particular organizational challenge.

One more powerful feature of ORCA is that each worker's interaction with ORCA adds to the system's knowledge base. When the Mercy Hospital worker is done, the hospital's story is entered into the case base of the system. ORCA is also interested in how the worker feels about the questions asked. Through a Knowledge Base Refinement Tool, the worker can tell ORCA whether a particular question or story was irrelevant. The system can then use this information to make future refinements.

Part of ORCA's strength comes from the fact that it makes expertise available to everyone. Experts are expensive to organizations. Their time is costly, they are often unavailable, and there is no guarantee that they will stay with the organization for a lifetime. With a system like ORCA, expertise can be captured and added to the organization's knowledge base and maintained there for as long as it continues to add value.

CHAPTER 11

LEARNING ORGANIZATIONS AND GROWTH ORGANIZATIONS

What does the future hold for your organization? We mean this as a real question, not as some empty rhetorical flourish. What is going to happen to your organization, do you think, over the course of the next five years? ten years? twenty? The evolution of organizations, products, and industries is often discussed in terms of the familiar life cycle theory, predicting four major phases or stages of development: Introduction, Growth, Maturity, and Decline.[1]

—————————— PRODUCT LIFE CYCLE CURVE ——————————

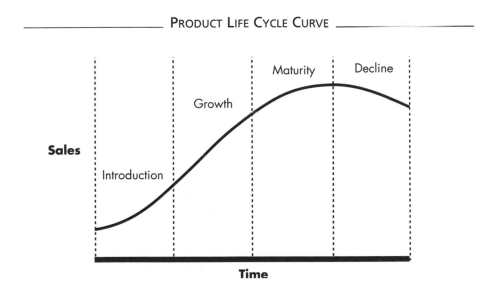

A product, for example, will have a relatively flat introductory phase as a company tries to convince people to try it. When the product has become successful, a steep period of growth occurs until sales level off in the mature phase. Finally, when imitators come onto the market and competition stiffens, the product will enter a period of decline. Is this evolutionary pattern inevitable? Is every company fated to an inexorable movement toward decline,

---

_____ KEY MESSAGES: CHAPTER 11 _____

- Successful organizations in the future will be "growth organizations": those which create a learning environment for their workforce, but which also direct that learning toward measurable improvements in organizational performance.
- The ability to innovate constantly, to transform learning into new opportunities in the marketplace, will become increasingly important to organizations.
- Integrated Performance Support can be a primary enabler for organizations wanting to provide opportunities for continuous learning, but which also want those opportunities directed toward actual performance needs of knowledge workers, and toward innovations that will create and sustain growth.
- Growth organizations have the following characteristics:

  1. They encourage "big picture" thinking.
  2. They support each individual within the organization with knowledge gleaned from the entire organization.
  3. They aim high in their long-term goals and communicate those goals to all employees.
  4. They also communicate short-term goals, or intermediate targets, and support their workers to achieve those goals.
  5. They measure _effectiveness_ of their knowledge workers, as well as efficiency.
  6. They provide workers with immediate feedback on their job performance.
  7. They give workers control over their jobs and create structures that make personal mastery a possibility for all workers.
  8. They communicate not only across the organization, but also across time.
  9. They are open to new ideas, from both inside and outside the organization.

- An important technology that will be a part of performance systems is a "knowledge management system," a system that collects knowledge and experience from workers, organizes and stores it, and then delivers it at point of need to support future work.

or is the life cycle theory a kind of self-fulfilling prophecy? Can't organizations have an effect on the shape of the curve through innovation?

We think they can. Companies *can* prolong the growth phase of their life cycle, but as we have already seen, we must rethink what we mean by "growth." Corporations are not forecast to get bigger, at least not in the foreseeable future. Small is beautiful today, and leaner, flatter organizations appear to be the rule for now. Organizations in some industries may be looking at the same situation with their customer base. The challenge recently faced, for example, by one telecommunications company is a good example of new understandings of growth. Company executives were looking at a flat rate of growth in their customer base; the most effective way for them to compete, given that restriction, was to enable their workers to be more productive with each customer. Growth in that case meant sales growth, certainly, but it was based upon the growth in the capabilities and power of their workforce.

We believe that similar sorts of responses will be the norm in the future—that the performance-centered use of technology embodied within Integrated Performance Support will be the way organizations become what we will call "growth" organizations. Traditionally, organizations have worked backward, as it were, from strategic thinking about how to increase profits, back to how to get the workforce to achieve those goals. Increasingly, organizations will find themselves also working in the opposite direction: how can they grow their workforce in terms of the skills, knowledge, character, and values of each human being—and then how does that lead to new, and sometimes unforeseen, kinds of organizational growth?

A "growth" organization enlarges itself in manifold ways. Its people grow in knowledge, in power, in ability. Its relationships with suppliers and with its surrounding community grow. Above all, profits grow, since without that kind of growth no other kinds of growth are possible. The constant renewal possible in a growth organization is rooted in several characteristics:

- The organization is led by men and women with vision, people who can learn from their successes and their failures, and who are not afraid to take risks.
- The organization is truly committed to strengthening the links between organizational performance, process performance, and workforce performance.
- Because of this performance link, everyone is also committed to the overall human network of the organization; the relationship between worker and infrastructure is the same, and as critical, as that between individual neurons and the brain of a human being.

- The organization is utilizing a human-centered set of technologies to ensure the efficient operations of both worker and human infrastructure, of both neurons and brain.

This chapter looks in more detail at the manner in which Integrated Performance Support serves as the "brain food" of the growth organization.

LEARNING, PERFORMANCE, GROWTH

We welcome and encourage current thinking that emphasizes the *learning* facets of organizational life. Our emphasis on both the neurons and brain of an organization parallels what is most commonly called the "learning organization."[2] But discussions of learning bring out both the best and the worst in people. On the one hand, in a world of business often dominated by number crunching and abstruse economic theory, these softer subjects open up the discussion into the realm of human needs and capabilities. On the other hand, the discussion sometimes gets out of hand. No amount of educational, psychological, or sociological analysis about an organization and its people can make that organization profitable. The test of any theory is in its effect on measurable individual and organizational performance.

One way to understand this is to compare current thinking about learning organizations with some trends found in the U.S. public education system. Some influential educational psychologists today preach a version of student empowerment. That is, they want students to "learn how to learn," to be open to continuous learning. All of this sounds very good. The problem is that as this theory becomes translated into practice, too many schools are equating self-empowerment with a sort of "feel good" approach to measuring student achievement. Too few of those putting theory into practice want to hold students to any objective standards of performance. To suggest that there is any such thing as a "failed" performance, one is told, would interfere with the delicate psyches of students—would mean that some students are better than others, would diminish the capacity of these students to accept themselves and feel good about themselves.

There are several consequences of this approach, the most obvious being the downward spiral of college preparatory testing scores. Parents, justifiably, are beginning to say that empowerment is great, but what I really want is for my children to be able to calculate 9 times 7, or discuss John Quincy Adams, or describe in writing what the Magna Carta represents. The "feel good" approach to education is hardly the proper preparation for students for life in the marketplace, where a Darwinian "survival of the fittest" more commonly reigns.

We can easily criticize this educational approach—except that business has frequently fallen prey to the same kind of thinking. Quality programs, reengineering, employee empowerment: all will fail unless they can withstand the real practical tests of everyday business life—the equivalent of "What's 9 times 7?" Any organization can *claim* to be a learning organization—one which, as one article defines it, is "able to sustain consistent internal innovation or learning, with the immediate goals of improving quality, enhancing customer or supplier relationships, or more effectively executing business strategy, and the ultimate objective of sustaining profitability."[3]

But what good is all that learning unless it can be directed at sustaining profitability, at least in the broadest sense? unless it can be supplied at the place where it is needed, at the moment of need, to generate the moment of value? Take the example of one global organization: our own firm, Andersen Consulting. Andersen Consulting has offices around the world and provides solutions to thousands of clients each year. But how do we capture the expertise that comes out of those solutions, package it, and make it available so that in the future, we won't be reinventing the wheel every time situations are encountered that someone else has already addressed in an elegant and creative manner? When you stop to think about it, it's a huge task: the information is grouped differently, written in different languages, in different formats. But making that information available to our professionals is the essential requirement today and into the next century. Later in this chapter we will provide more detail on the progress of Andersen Consulting in creating a knowledge infrastructure, and in delivering performance support to our own employees around the globe. We, too, of course, wish to sustain our identity as a "growth organization."

THE GROWTH ORGANIZATION

A growth organization is a learning organization whose learning environment—whose capacity for internal innovation and expanding its knowledge base—is being translated into *measurable performance enhancements*. As we have said, "growth" means something different than growing in size. Companies are forecast to become smaller as we head toward the year 2000.[4] Either they will employ fewer people or they will organize themselves in such a way that they will "feel" smaller. If this is so, then our notions of what "growth" means will change. For a growth organization, market share is improving, earnings are growing steadily each year, and customers are being served better. Employees are growing, too: becoming more competent, more innovative, better able to manage their own work.

Integrated Performance Support can be a primary enabler for the growth organization. The measurable effect of a learning environment upon the overall organization stems from the fact that knowledge is accumulated, disseminated throughout the organization, and made available to employees at the point of need. With this knowledge, they can provide services more efficiently, with fewer errors. Customers are more satisfied and, just as important, the workers are satisfied. Growth organizations realize that knowledge and motivation go hand in hand. That is, the more that workers know about their organization, about their own performance, and its relationship to overall organizational performance, the better they perform.[5] They also obviously perform better when the organization's mindset is focused upon supporting their performance needs.

Growth organizations have the following characteristics:

1. They encourage "big picture" thinking. Rather than giving workers a picture only of their own small piece of the enterprise, they encourage a view of the entire system of that organization.
2. They support each individual within the organization with the knowledge gleaned from the entire organization.
3. They aim high in their long-term goals and communicate those goals to all employees.
4. They also provide short-term goals, or intermediate targets; they support workers, challenge them to meet the goals, and reward them when it happens.
5. They measure effectiveness as well as efficiency.
6. They provide workers with immediate feedback on their job performance.
7. They give workers control over their jobs, encouraging personal mastery, and they create structures that make this mastery a possibility for everyone.
8. They communicate not only across the organization, but also across time.
9. They are open to new ideas, from both inside and outside the organization.

1. "BIG PICTURE" THINKING

In Michael Crichton's novel, *Jurassic Park,* secrecy dominates the development of the ill-fated dinosaur amusement park. The head of information systems development, for example, is never told how the application he is developing will contribute to the overall project. He is just told what kind of application to write, and what functions to give it. No one, in fact, is given the big picture of the project; the result, as readers of the novel and viewers of the movie version know, is total system breakdown. As predicted by the mathematician consultant in the story who specializes in chaos theory, the overall system of the park is unstable and eventually disintegrates into violence and terror.[6]

Each person within an organization must be a part of the overall mission of that organization. Each person must understand what the company is doing, where it is going, and how his or her performance contributes to the performance of the entire company. Peter Senge, in his book, *The Fifth Discipline,* calls this kind of thinking "systems thinking," the fifth of the learning disciplines or component technologies of the contemporary organization. Although the development of all five disciplines is important (the five according to Senge are: personal mastery, mental models, building shared vision, team learning, and systems thinking), the ability to think in big-picture, systemic terms is the sine qua non for the growth organization. One of the unfortunate offshoots of the development of modern science has been the tendency for humans to see themselves as separate from, detached from, their environment. We analyze our environment through science and manipulate it through technology. But reality is not that simple. We also help *construct* our environment through our modes of perception and *affect* our environment through our manipulations. The system doesn't make us; we make the system. But if we do not continue to understand *how* we have made the system, the system will turn on us and, like the feature attractions of Jurassic Park, consume us.

An organization's system, its structure, can tend to *cause* certain behaviors in those people working within the system—behaviors over which they may have little control. Sometimes this is good, and sometimes it is not so good. Senge's extended example to illustrate this point is the "beer game," a game played in classrooms and in management training seminars for a number of years. In this game, players divide into three groups: one plays a beer retailer; another plays the wholesale distributor; another plays the brewery itself. An accidental event that causes demand for one brand of beer to increase dramatically triggers a number of behaviors among all people playing the game. The retailer begins by doubling his order for the particular beer. This causes shortages at the wholesaler, who doubles his orders. The brewery itself goes out of stock and increases its production. But there is a four-week delay between ordering and receiving the beer. This lag time eventually causes all three players to have a "beer glut." All end up with large inventories that they cannot sell. If, says Senge, thousands of players from different backgrounds all end up with the same results, the cause of their behavior must go beyond the individuals.[7]

Structure influences, even causes, behavior. Another well-known illustration of this fact is the elementary school experiment where a classroom is divided into two groups, blue-eyed children and brown-eyed children. The children are told that brown-eyed people are more intelligent, better behaved, and socially superior. Within hours, the children are displaying behavior in line with those predictions. The blue-eyed children are unruly and dispirited; the brown-eyed children are confident and performing well and, moreover, will have little to do with their blue-eyed classmates except to mock them.

How many "blue-eyed children" do organizations create today? How do we help people understand how their actions can influence the system of which they are a part? Part of the Integrated Performance Support orientation involves giving workers a sense of the end or purpose to which their performance is being directed.

2. SUPPORT FOR EACH INDIVIDUAL WITHIN THE SYSTEM

Once we are clear that we need to understand an organization from the systemic point of view, and that individuals can influence that system, we must become practical about *how* individuals are to gain a systemic perspective and about how they are to influence the system. Within the modern organization, it is inconceivable that this can happen without advanced information technology and systems that are focused on supporting individual performance. We do not mean to overemphasize the place of technology within the human condition. Certainly, if one moves to a level beyond information and knowledge to the level of, let us say, wisdom, one would probably want to acknowledge that wisdom advances only very gradually, and independently of technology. But within the modern organization, technology is, as we have said, the power boost for the organization's brain power.

Indeed, once technology is placed within a systemic understanding of the organization, it also becomes a major determinant of behavior. The structural influence on behavior can become particularly pernicious as structure is reinforced throughout the information systems of an organization. As we wrote in the chapter on making technology work, science and technology have done marvelous things for humankind. Our lives today would be inconceivable without them. But as one particular instantiation of technology came to dominate the development of information systems—an orientation to processing transactions—this structure fated companies to particular kinds of business processes, particular types of behaviors from workers using that technology, and a particular understanding of the relationship between information systems, people, and organizational goals.

Growth organizations see information technology as a means to an end. Integrated Performance Support, and those systems designed around that concept, enable workers to move beyond the particular structure embodied in their present technologies, and to create their own structures. What is the job I wish to do? What knowledge do I need in order to accomplish that job? These are the questions driving the development of performance systems. With these systems, organizations can deal with the dynamic nature of the marketplace into the next century and with the demands placed on workers in that marketplace.

3. COMMUNICATING POWERFUL LONG-TERM GOALS

The growth organization aims high in its strategic vision. Growth organizations realize that demanding goals are the fertilizer of excellence—that knowledge and performance grow most when they are challenged. James Brian Quinn calls this type of challenge a "frontier vision"—the method whereby intellectual dominance can be led onward into a continuously growing competitive edge.[8]

The word "vision" was appropriated several years ago by politicians and so has lost much of its power. Yet a number of companies have successfully set for themselves challenges that are visionary and yet real. The common denominator for these companies is that their goal is to be the best. The corporate goal of Intel, for example, is "To be, and to be recognized as, the leader in meeting our customers' needs for delivery, reliability, quality, and service."[9] "To be second is to die," reads one statement from Motorola. What these companies realize is that the advantage of first place grows quickly. Those organizations in the lead attract better people, which increases the knowledge base, which in turn increases the lead over the also-rans considerably. "Too few companies have recognized that, in intellect, the alternative to excellence is mediocrity, failure, and death."[10] World-class performance will be needed in the next century to be successful. The definition of quality goods and services will be much more demanding in years to come: quality must be closer to perfect than an organization's competitors can achieve; the long-range goal for numbers of defects in a manufacturing process will be zero.[11] Clearly, these goals cannot be achieved without powerful performance systems.

4. THE CHALLENGE AND REWARD OF SHORT-TERM GOALS

It is often difficult for long-term goals, even powerfully stated visions, to be motivating forces to the entire range of an organization's employees. Here, the establishment of intermediate, short-term goals is crucial. Much of the research into goal-setting theory derives from Edwin Locke's work in the late 1960s. Locke argued that there was a clear correlation between goal setting and employee motivation. Research has suggested that "specific and difficult goals led to higher employee performance—provided the goals were accepted by those who had to attain them."[12] The key factors here are:

- Ensuring that workers participate in the setting of those goals.
- Providing feedback that lets them know that they are moving toward the goals.
- Providing appropriate rewards once the goals have been reached.

Setting short-term goals provides a target that is challenging, yet is perceived by the workforce as attainable. These goals, then, are consistent with goal-setting theory, but also with other research on motivation that suggests that "shaping" is an important tool for teaching employees new kinds of behavior and new ways of working.[13]

Short-term goals are a key component of the self-managed workgroups that will increasingly become crucial to organizational success. Enabled by performance systems, workers have both increased power over their workflow and increased responsibility for their performance. Intermediate goals are vital to the performance of these groups, as is an awareness of specifically how these intermediate goals link up to the achievement of the higher goal or vision of the organization. Again, for most organizations, it is inconceivable that this link can be made without information technology.

5. EFFECTIVENESS AS WELL AS EFFICIENCY

One computer industry executive, Richard Dalton, tells the story of touring a modern insurance company in the late 1960s and seeing a woman pounding away at her keyboard, entering policy data into the computer database. As he watched, the mainframe went down and her terminal screen went blank. "Thank goodness," she said. "I thought I was never going to get a break." The computer, writes the executive, "had brought an inexorable, factory-style production line feeling to the office."[14]

Dalton's article in which this story appears is entitled, fittingly, "Lose the Sweatshop Mentality." We, too, recall that keystrokes per hour was the stock in trade of companies at the advent of the Information Age. With this kind of productivity measurement, the heads-down data entry clerk became the computer-age equivalent of the Depression-era garment district worker or the factory worker and child laborer in the Industrial Age sweatshops. Even today, those who speak of productivity often appear to be using models of factory-based measurement and control. As Dalton notes, this begs the question of what it is, exactly, that knowledge workers produce, and what it means to produce "more" of it. "Being able to make the same decision badly and twice as often in the same amount of time doesn't sound much like progress."

The goal of performance systems is to produce *improved* performance, more effective performance; to produce applicable knowledge, not just chaotic information. Although the Information Age is less than fifty years old, it is already apparent that knowledge workers, those who wield the intelligent terminal of the future, will and must be measured by their effectiveness, not merely their efficiency. The sweatshop mentality was the natural outcome of a transaction processing mode in systems design. A system operator knew only one system and one function. Today, with a new generation of knowledge workers, one person knows which systems are available and, thus, will be aware of the knowledge domain of the organization.

6. PERFORMANCE FEEDBACK

Neither long-term nor short-term goals of an organization can be met without feedback on performance. Here, the limitations of recent information technology become apparent. How are workers to link their daily activities with the goals of their group or their organization when the best that some organizations can do is to print out monthly or weekly reports? One of the goals of growth organizations is to implement performance systems that provide immediate feedback to workers.

We have seen this capability in several systems already examined. The Total Information Management system, for example, provides a commercial lender with a snapshot of his or her performance at any time, in relation to other lenders within the bank, and in relation to previous performance levels. With the Business Marketing with IPS (BMIPS) prototype system, a customer service representative logging out of the system at the end of the day can request a snapshot of how his or her sales performance stacks up to personal goals and to the performance of co-workers. The Knowledge Worker Services component of Integrated Performance Support is the key enabler here. The type of feedback provided by the performance system matches information from Knowledge Worker Services with the work profile as contained in Work

Profile Services, comparing current performance to performance goals, and highlighting trends in performance over time. As one analysis has it, the message from this feedback is, "Here is where you were before, here is where you are now, and here is how far you have to go."[15]

7. PERSONAL CONTROL AND PERSONAL MASTERY

The feedback available with performance systems will be demoralizing to workers if they have not participated in the setting of goals, and if they are not provided with the means to achieve a level of competence and mastery over their work.

A growth organization must grow from within: its growth is tied to the personal and professional growth of each of its employees. An organizational models for many companies today need to be in tune with *individual* needs—with what makes work meaningful to us as human beings. Senge quotes Bill O'Brien, president of Hanover Insurance, who seeks organizational models "that are more congruent with human nature. When the industrial age began, people worked 6 days a week to earn enough for food and shelter. Today, most of us have these handled by Tuesday afternoon. Our traditional hierarchical organizations are not designed to provide for people's higher order needs, self-respect and self-actualization. The ferment in management will continue until organizations begin to address these needs, for all employees."[16]

As human beings, we crave a sense of control over our lives. And we crave having that control extend into the work we do, especially as the lines between working and living continue to blur. Unless we feel we have the ability to improve, to increase our understanding and competence, we are likely to lose interest, to spend the better part of our careers just going through the motions. Organizations cannot afford to have people fulfilling the lowest expectations for any position. Senge and others refer to this feeling of achievement as "personal mastery." Personal mastery "goes beyond competence and skills, though it is grounded in competence and skills. It goes beyond spiritual unfolding and opening, although it requires spiritual growth. It means approaching one's life as a creative work, living life from a creative as opposed to reactive viewpoint."[17]

Lest talk like this degenerate into "feel good" theories, we must add that by enabling personal mastery, or peak performance as the optimum, an organization also enables *itself* to become a growth organization. We believe that people whose performance is supported by the technologies and the performance-centered approach we are advocating are more committed, more creative (because they have time to be so), and more apt to take initiative. They learn faster and take a deeper sense of responsibility for their work.[18]

The support of personal mastery must be accompanied by efforts to build the community of the organization itself. An organization risks a sort of incoherence, a lack of direction, unless each person achieves mastery within the context of shared visions and models of the overall picture of the organization, its goals, and its place within society. Here, the complexities of modern life—the demands of the marketplace, of home life, of social and political pressures—dictate enabling technologies that support, advise, coach, and instruct workers. Without a knowledge infrasture within the organization, personal mastery can lead to an overemphasis on individualism that could undermine the system itself.

8. MOVING KNOWLEDGE THROUGH SPACE AND TIME

Knowledge grows only as it is shared. But sharing knowledge is difficult for today's organizations, especially those with a global reach. Finding and recognizing knowledge is only part of the battle; then it must be placed in context, captured in some storable form for others to use, and applied practically to real tasks. Knowledge, we have already said, is both individual and communal. It has no power in the abstract, but must be appropriated and owned by a worker. On the other hand, it cannot help the organizational knowledge base except as it is captured, stored, and retrieved by others. For a growth organization, its infrastructure must aid in the identification of knowledge, and then empower workers to apply it and to enter it into the organization's knowledge base. This is the basis of the exponential growth capability of knowledge. Writes James Brian Quinn, "As one shares knowledge with colleagues and other internal organizations, not only do these units gain information—linear growth—they usually feed back questions, amplifications, and modifications, which instantly add further value for the sender. . . . Exponential growth occurs in the value of each sharing group's knowledge base. As the groups share solutions with each other, the interactive potentials of their knowledge grow at an even steeper exponential."[19]

9. AN OPENNESS TO NEW IDEAS

Finally, growth organizations sustain growth only as they are open and receptive to what lies outside their company boundaries. Certainly, the new ideas generated from within are the primary fuel, but outside influences are crucial. Performance systems at their best will capture knowledge from outside the

"ASK TOM" AND OTHER INNOVATIVE LEARNING PROJECTS AT THE INSTITUTE FOR THE LEARNING SCIENCES (ILS)

Researching and designing applications that reflect how people think are the cornerstones of the Institute for the Learning Sciences (ILS) at Northwestern University, where Andersen Consulting is the founding sponsor. The focus of Andersen Consulting's sponsorship is to create innovative, breakthrough approaches to learning using artificial intelligence, case-based reasoning, and other state-of-the-art technologies.

Under the direction of Dr. Roger C. Schank, the ILS has become a premier research organization with an ambitious mission: to make profound changes to the future of human learning. The Institute's primary goal is to pursue research in learning strategies that use computer technology. By joining sophisticated hardware and software with computer-based learning systems, the ILS seeks to improve how people learn.

To enhance the powerful asset of an organization's knowledge capital, the ILS has developed a number of applications based on key teaching architectures. These architectures address the way people actually think and learn, and emphasize that learning involves such intrinsic values as interest and curiosity. Institute architectures such as Learn By Doing, Case-Based Teaching, Incidental Learning, and Responsive Questions reflect a different approach to learning and allow the student to reach higher levels of performance.

Based on these architectures, the ILS has created over thirty prototypes of systems that can make radical and substantial improvements in corporate learning. The Institute's long-term strategy is to apply these teaching architectures to public education, thus improving the learning process.

"Ask Tom" is an example of how an innovative application can contribute to the development of learning organizations, or what we have called "growth" organizations. Imagine that your employee is about to tackle a new and difficult task for the first time. As a good mentor and coach, you probably want to discuss the task before initiating the assignment. You may want to review examples, issues, lessons learned, and so forth. But in today's hectic business environment, these personal conversations between experts and novices are seldom possible. "Ask Tom" provides the technical architecture to hold a personal conversation with an expert via a computer.

"Ask Tom" is a conversationally based index that catalogs video inter-

---

"ASK TOM" AND OTHER INNOVATIVE LEARNING PROJECTS AT THE INSTITUTE FOR THE LEARNING SCIENCES (ILS) *(CONTINUED)*

views. It was created to relieve the bottleneck that exists between experts and apprentices trying to learn from them. "Ask Tom" allows learners to ask questions and gather information at their own pace, without the pressure and expense that usually accompany such interactions. Each story is contained in a very short video clip, organized by theme. The clips are connected in a network of generic links: warnings, background, results, indicators, examples, alternatives, context, and opportunities.

"Ask Tom" was designed to teach trust banking, and simulates a conversation with a trust banking expert. Using the multimedia system, learners make paths through the material to learn about the details of trust banking, deregulation, or how trust banking relates to their careers.

Learners may also ask a direct question of the video database in the same way that they tap the knowledge of an expert. For example, the learner chooses, "What are the effects of deregulation on tier III trust banks?" The program responds with a story from the expert that directly addresses the question. With this system, knowledge that exists primarily in the minds of experts is captured and made available to everyone in the organization. Consequently, people have access to the information they need, when they need it, and in a format that is as natural and comfortable as having a conversation with the expert in person.

---

organization as well, placing it into the context of the organization's knowledge base—even, perhaps, challenging that base to confront information that seems to be at odds with the historical assumptions or bases by which that knowledge was gathered and organized.

Only an openness to the outside world will ensure that an organization can be responsive to the changes and demands coming from that world. Access to new developments in different fields is vital; learning from customers and suppliers will shape the workflow of employees; awareness of the changing business environment will shape long-range visions and short-term goals.

Often, the capacity for renewal will come to an organization only through its attention to what lies outside of it. There is a natural tendency for human endeavors to become rigid and bureaucratic. Departments or divisions that were created to improve efficiency can become impediments over time if they cease to adapt and learn.[20] At their best, growth organizations gain their power because they are rooted in history while simultaneously being open to the future. The word "base" is appropriate here: the knowledge base gives a company stability. Like a strong tree, the organization sinks its roots deep into history and experience, from which one source of knowledge comes; it does not blindly follow the latest management fad. At the same time, the growth organization extends its branches into its environment, from which new knowledge will come.

CASE EXAMPLE:
ANDERSEN CONSULTING'S KNOWLEDGE XCHANGE™ KNOWLEDGE MANAGEMENT SYSTEM

We imagine a certain reader who has gotten this far in the book and is thinking the following: "OK, you've given us this vision of the performance-centered enterprise, of the theory behind Integrated Performance Support, and some specific examples of the performance systems that are helping other organizations meet today's marketplace challenges. What about you? What about Andersen Consulting? What are *you* doing to support *your* workers?"

Fair enough. There is an old saying to the effect that "the shoemaker's children always have the poorest shoes," so it is only fitting that we prove otherwise here, that we be asked to demonstrate our own efforts to use technology to gather knowledge, and to make it available to our consultants at their point of need.

Recall from Chapter 6 our discussion of how an Integrated Performance Support strategy enables organizations to turn information into knowledge. Knowledge, we said, is information with several additional characteristics. It is:

• Applicable or Practical
• Contextual
• Experiential
• Historical
• Communal or Social
• Individual

Like many organizations, one of Andersen Consulting's primary assets is its people and the combined knowledge that they represent. This knowledge is built up over years of experience working with organizations from all over the globe, with companies representing every industry. We continually gather knowledge from our history, our experience, our community; then we seek to deliver it to individuals, in context, on demand, and at point of need, so it can be applied to real performance challenges.

Our organization, too, faces many of the same performance challenges we have discussed earlier. We seek to meet and exceed our customer expectations, to enable our consultants to reach levels of high proficiency faster, to empower self-managed workgroups, and, above all, to turn information into knowledge. The business and technological marketplace has become much more complicated; many more options are available to organizations today in terms of programs, products, and service lines. Our overall mission, which is to help clients change to be more successful, means that a broad base of current knowledge and latest experience must be available to our consultants at all times. The type of solution that is configured and delivered to help organizations realize their ultimate goal of business integration will almost always cross traditional organizational boundaries and involve not just people with systems integration skills, but also people with skills in such areas as instructional design, change management, strategic planning, and human resources.

There is a lot of information out there, in the form of other consultants' experiences, electronic and paper-based reports and presentations, external articles and books, and so forth. The difficulty here is twofold: either there will be so much information that people cannot cope with all of it, or there will not be enough of the right *kind* of information available when a particular consultant needs it. If we are to turn information into knowledge for our professionals, we must have a feedback mechanism permitting people's experience to accumulate and then permitting that experience to be disseminated to people all over the world. Recall, though, that a mere database of experience will hardly meet the real performance needs of a knowledge worker. These workers must also be given the tools to apply that experience to their own personal environment. Here is where Integrated Performance Support and knowledge management systems unite in a powerful way.

Andersen Consulting's internal initiative to meet today's knowledge and performance challenges is the "Knowledge Xchange™ knowledge management system."[21] The Knowledge Xchange system is a vehicle for the capture, storage, enhancement, and dissemination of our firm's knowledge capital. Pilot projects of the system started in 1992, and parts of the Knowledge Xchange system began to be rolled out to our global organization late in 1993.

We see the Knowledge Xchange system as a virtual community, a marketplace for the exchange of this new form of capital—knowledge—through a network that crosses geographical and organizational boundaries. As a state-of-the-art knowledge management and delivery system, the Knowledge Xchange system has several tangible benefits:

1. *It provides a communications infrastructure for our firm.* On a basic level, the Knowledge Xchange system architecture connects all Andersen Consulting employees to one another, a connection that facilitates rapid communication and knowledge sharing.
2. *It fosters a sense of community.* The groupware capability of the electronic mail and database management system within the Knowledge Xchange system allows our consultants to create an electronic virtual relationship with other Andersen Consulting personnel working on similar kinds of projects. Within this virtual relationship or community, they can exchange ideas, tips, and even documents such as work plans or presentations.
3. *It enables a new horizontal form of organizational structure.* The limitations of geographical boundaries and hierarchical management structures are lessened in an electronic community. Conversations need not take place in real time, and each consultant can now communicate directly with the most appropriate subject expert, so there is less need for rigid reporting structures to control process.
4. *It improves responsiveness to our clients.* Most important, the Knowledge Xchange system benefits our clients. Our professionals can get rapid access to a knowledge base and a wealth of specialists, to address particular client needs. Each specialist, after all, is also serving his or her own clients, so the Knowledge Xchange system means that one person's specialized knowledge can be made available to everyone without taking him or her away from responsibilities to clients.

WHAT DOES THE KNOWLEDGE XCHANGE™ SYSTEM LOOK LIKE?

The high-level picture of the Knowledge Xchange system (see figure on the next page) depicts its primary components. On the outside are the consultants themselves, organized into "communities of practice," meaning groups of people who deal with similar issues and with similar kinds of knowledge—industry, technology, marketing, and so forth. Whether a particular community is formally defined within Andersen Consulting or is informal in nature, each will have certain responsibilities:

- Support the Knowledge Xchange system as the primary mechanism for sharing knowledge.
- Encourage teamwork within their local initiatives and business unit initiatives.
- Develop applications relevant to their community of practice, following the guidelines for the Knowledge Xchange system.
- Acknowledge the roles and responsibilities of knowledge management.
- Make knowledge contributions.

_____ PRIMARY COMPONENTS OF THE KNOWLEDGE XCHANGE™ SYSTEM _____

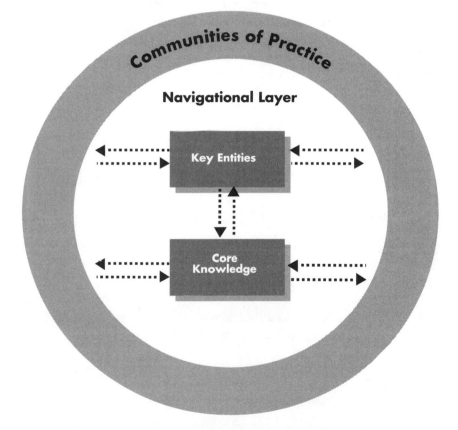

At the center of the Knowledge Xchange system are two primary kinds of applications, termed "Key Entities" and "Core Knowledge." Key Entities provide basic information about three data entities that are relevant across our entire practice: our business relationships with external organizations, our engagements, and our people. Because these entities are so central, all offices and communities of practice have a need for related information. Application design in this case will accommodate a base set of attributes that are common across all groups and shared locally, but that also allow for easy integration of additional attributes specific to any given office or community of practice.

Core Knowledge is the central, most stable, and most valuable knowledge capital of the firm: our industry and technology visions, best practices, core methodologies, and lessons learned. Core Knowledge is made up of four key components:

- *Methodology*. An integrated set of methodology "building blocks" derived from all of Andersen Consulting's service offerings.
- *Industry*. A storehouse for collective best thinking relating to each of the industries in which Andersen Consulting does business.
- *Technology*. A collection of synthesized information about technologies and architectures critical to Andersen Consulting and our clients.
- *Reference*. Reference and marketing information materials necessary to supplement the other three areas.

Finally, the Navigational Layer of the Knowledge Xchange system provides several tools to aid in the navigation through the system and in delivering the appropriate knowledge to the consultant at point of need.

MANAGING THE KNOWLEDGE XCHANGE™ SYSTEM

One of the implications for all organizations that will deal with knowledge capital in the new economy is the *management* of that knowledge. Knowledge, like many kinds of capital, depreciates over time; it must be kept current or it loses its usefulness. Toward this end, we have highlighted "Knowledge Management" as a function within Andersen Consulting to ensure the overall quality of our knowledge capital. At this time, different roles

---

THE KNOWLEDGE XCHANGE™
KNOWLEDGE MANAGEMENT SYSTEM IN ACTION

The following screen re-creations represent an actual conversation on the Knowledge Xchange™ system. Note how professionals from diverse locations, who may never have met in person before, are able to support one another with their knowledge, informing colleagues of their experiences, or directing them toward other resources.

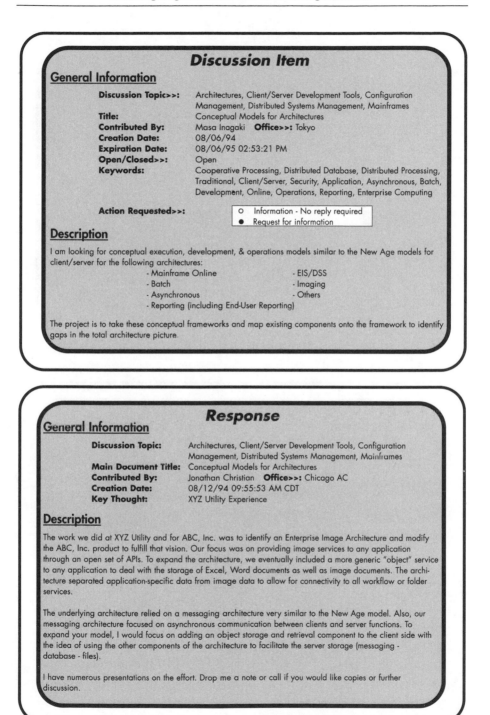

Discussion Item

General Information

Discussion Topic>>:	Architectures, Client/Server Development Tools, Configuration Management, Distributed Systems Management, Mainframes
Title:	Conceptual Models for Architectures
Contributed By:	Masa Inagaki **Office>>:** Tokyo
Creation Date:	08/06/94
Expiration Date:	08/06/95 02:53:21 PM
Open/Closed>>:	Open
Keywords:	Cooperative Processing, Distributed Database, Distributed Processing, Traditional, Client/Server, Security, Application, Asynchronous, Batch, Development, Online, Operations, Reporting, Enterprise Computing

Action Requested>>:

- ○ Information - No reply required
- ● Request for information

Description

I am looking for conceptual execution, development, & operations models similar to the New Age models for client/server for the following architectures:

- - Mainframe Online
- - Batch
- - Asynchronous
- - Reporting (including End-User Reporting)

- - EIS/DSS
- - Imaging
- - Others

The project is to take these conceptual frameworks and map existing components onto the framework to identify gaps in the total architecture picture.

Response

General Information

Discussion Topic:	Architectures, Client/Server Development Tools, Configuration Management, Distributed Systems Management, Mainframes
Main Document Title:	Conceptual Models for Architectures
Contributed By:	Jonathan Christian **Office>>:** Chicago AC
Creation Date:	08/12/94 09:55:53 AM CDT
Key Thought:	XYZ Utility Experience

Description

The work we did at XYZ Utility and for ABC, Inc. was to identify an Enterprise Image Architecture and modify the ABC, Inc. product to fulfill that vision. Our focus was on providing image services to any application through an open set of APIs. To expand the architecture, we eventually included a more generic "object" service to any application to deal with the storage of Excel, Word documents as well as image documents. The architecture separated application-specific data from image data to allow for connectivity to all workflow or folder services.

The underlying architecture relied on a messaging architecture very similar to the New Age model. Also, our messaging architecture focused on asynchronous communication between clients and server functions. To expand your model, I would focus on adding an object storage and retrieval component to the client side with the idea of using the other components of the architecture to facilitate the server storage (messaging - database - files).

I have numerous presentations on the effort. Drop me a note or call if you would like copies or further discussion.

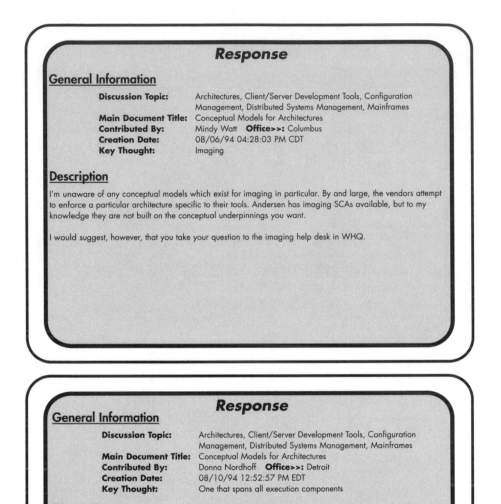

Response

General Information

Discussion Topic: Architectures, Client/Server Development Tools, Configuration Management, Distributed Systems Management, Mainframes
Main Document Title: Conceptual Models for Architectures
Contributed By: Mindy Watt **Office>>:** Columbus
Creation Date: 08/06/94 04:28:03 PM CDT
Key Thought: Imaging

Description

I'm unaware of any conceptual models which exist for imaging in particular. By and large, the vendors attempt to enforce a particular architecture specific to their tools. Andersen has imaging SCAs available, but to my knowledge they are not built on the conceptual underpinnings you want.

I would suggest, however, that you take your question to the imaging help desk in WHQ.

Response

General Information

Discussion Topic: Architectures, Client/Server Development Tools, Configuration Management, Distributed Systems Management, Mainframes
Main Document Title: Conceptual Models for Architectures
Contributed By: Donna Nordhoff **Office>>:** Detroit
Creation Date: 08/10/94 12:52:57 PM EDT
Key Thought: One that spans all execution components

Description

A few architects from EIS, Chicago, Detroit and FOUNDATION spent three days in St. Charles in June, creating the "Ideal Technical Architecture" conceptual model. It's really intended to be the launching point for a Financial Services initiative, but does present some interesting ideas. It supports migration to C/S computing and the key standards in the industry (CORBA, WOSA). If anyone would like a copy of this 50+ page PowerPoint doc, click here: ☐ . It's been compressed using PKZIP, so you'll need that, which you can get from the Tech Attachment library.

have been identified within the overall function of knowledge management, such as Knowledge Sponsor, Knowledge Integrator, Knowledge Developer, Knowledge Xchange Sponsor, Knowledge Base Integrator, and Knowledge Base Developer/Administrator. The strategy for assigning these responsibilities will depend on the type of knowledge base and the unique character and configuration of that repository. One of the most important knowledge management roles for us is maintaining the confidentiality of client information and establishing guidelines for what is appropriate to be shared. Such confidentiality is a matter of professional trust, without which there would be no knowledge to share in the first place.

We believe that Andersen Consulting's Knowledge Xchange knowledge management system will lead to new kinds of growth not only for our firm, but for our clients as well. Internally, our people now have access to a vast realm of knowledge and experience, provided to them where and when they need it. But our clients grow as well, because the Knowledge Xchange system means that every contact with one of our consultants is fueled by the knowledge firepower of our international organization.

There are important human dimensions to the Knowledge Xchange system, too. Indeed, among those phrases we are using internally to describe the Knowledge Xchange system—a virtual community, a knowledge marketplace, a global information village—one of them is a knowledge community or "neighborhood." The latter word is especially fitting and powerful. A neighborhood implies certain things about the relationships of the people who live and work there. They know each other—if not personally, then as a "friend of a friend." A different kind of friendliness characterizes their interactions. Lives are intertwined, contacts are informal, people pass on information about one person to another, and soon, everyone can share in everyone else's experiences, both successes and setbacks. This is our goal with the Knowledge Xchange system: to give our people a sense of this neighborhood of knowledge sharing, in spite of the immense distances that separate us in reality. We experience what others experience, learn what they learn. As colleagues and neighbors we become, together, a growth organization.

CHAPTER 12

Working and Living in the Infocosm

In 1989, a fledgling democratic movement stirred briefly in communist China. Thousands of students gathered in Tiananmen Square in Beijing, and an anxious world watched—connected by satellite communications and cable television. Most communications channels within China were under the control of the communist regime, but students were still getting messages out of the country and were receiving incoming messages of strategy and exhortation. How was it happening? By electronic networks and facsimile machines.

We are already a part of a huge, global information network—a system of communications that takes no heed of geographical or national boundaries, and that can alter the manner in which world events unfold. Telephone, radio, and television already link us together in ways that would have been foreign to people only a generation ago. Electronic mail, electronic bulletin boards, Internet: these are harbingers of what is to come. But as sophisticated as today's global network sometimes seems, it is nothing—mere child's play—compared to what is on the way: an electronic knowledge network that will connect homes, industries, schools, universities, and anyone or anything else one might think of. Though the construction of these networks (which some people are now calling "information superhighways") will begin within each nation, the ultimate vision is of nothing less than a *digital, virtual world of knowledge*—a world where computers, communication, and information merge into a single entity.

We believe that we are witnessing in the United States today the creation of a fundamentally new universal utility, an "Information Utility," which will become as important as electricity. In the same way that cheap, ubiquitous electricity made possible the Industrial Age, cheap, ubiquitous information and knowledge will make possible the advent of the true "knowledge economy." This information utility will eventually unite computers, television, radio, and telephone. From the information consumer point of view, individuals and industries will have various kinds of "information applications" that they plug into the information grid to pull off whatever they need, whenever they need it. Presumably, they would then get a regular bill from the information utility for the

304

_____ KEY MESSAGES: CHAPTER 12 _____

- Various companies and agencies in the United States and around the world today are involved in the creation of a fundamentally new universal utility: an information utility.
- The utility is made possible by the construction of an information supernetwork: an electronic knowledge network connecting homes, industries, libraries, and schools.
- The vision of this network is of a digital, virtual world of knowledge: an "Infocosm," an electronic cosmos or world teeming with information and knowledge.
- Depending on one's point of view, there can be five different views of the Infocosm: (1) residential consumers will see the Infocosm as a public information service; (2) knowledge workers will see it as a performance system linking them with all the support they need to do their jobs; (3) workgroups will see it as computer-supported collaboration; (4) organizations will see it as process automation; (5) various knowledge users will see it as a knowledge management system.
- From all these perspectives, Integrated Performance Support will play an important role in ensuring that all those within the Infocosm can find and use information and then supporting whatever performance needs they may have.

---

amount of the utility used. From the information provider point of view, they would hook their information cogeneration facility into the information grid and then get paid regularly for the amount of information delivered into the grid.

Clearly this will be a mega-industry, and its prospect is the source of many of today's business headlines. Regional Bell companies are moving into cable service; the largest cable TV companies are making commitments to build telephone-friendly networks. The dizzying array of deals in this area among cable, telephone, and media companies highlights the mad scramble to prepare for the coming changes. These companies know what is at stake here: a piece of what some project will be a $3.5 trillion industry in just a decade.[1]

The revenue figures point to the larger social and cultural issues at work here. The digital, interactive knowledge network of the future will affect our lives and the lives of our children in ways that are still unclear. It will shape how we work, where we work and live, how we engage in recreation, where and when we entertain ourselves, and how our children are educated. Most important, in an economy where access to knowledge is also the key determinant of wealth and power, it will affect who prospers and who does not. In 1843, having convinced the U.S. Congress to spend $30,000 on a telegraph line between Washington and Baltimore, Samuel Morse sent these first words along the wire: "What hath God wrought!" A century and a half later, and for a tad more than $30,000, we can imagine the first message coming over the global broadband information network: "What hath the telecommunications industry wrought!"

But to call such a development merely another network, or a couple of new technologies, or to call it an information "highway" or "railroad," is to risk missing the point. We are speaking of an entire world, a way of life, shaped by communications and computing. We are speaking of the technological infrastructure of the knowledge economy. Thus, the somewhat grander word we and our colleagues are now using is *Infocosm*—an electronic cosmos or world teeming with information and knowledge.[2]

It is appropriate, as we begin to close our discussion of Integrated Performance Support, to step back to this more comprehensive view of the technologies that will empower the knowledge economy of the next century. Integrated Performance Support, and the performance systems that IPS brings into being, are an important part of this Infocosm. IPS will have an effect on the modes of interaction within the Infocosm: the manner in which people and organizations interact with one another, with information systems, and with the component parts of the Infocosm. The Infocosm can only be effective with the right techniques for creating knowledge content, delivering that knowledge, and then accessing and interacting with it. IPS will be a key enabler within the Infocosm; it will be one of the means by which the Infocosm can enrich our lives at work, at home, or in a myriad of activities anywhere in the world. The Infocosm will be the ultimate proving ground for human-centered technology and for the performance-centered design and delivery of knowledge.

FIVE VIEWS OF THE INFOCOSM

At Andersen Consulting's Center for Strategic Technology in Palo Alto, California, researchers are exploring five different views of the Infocosm and thus five slightly different approaches to how technology can be configured to deliver knowledge effectively within the Infocosm. (See figure, "Five Views of the Infocosm.")

1. *The Personal Consumption View*. From the point of view of the consumer, the Infocosm looks like a public information services vehicle, where one can get entertainment and education on demand, access to government services, home shopping, and so forth.

2. *The Work Group View*. If you are a group of knowledge workers, your view of the Infocosm is Computer-Supported Collaboration, support for multiple knowledge workers collaborating across time and space on a subset of your work.

3. *The Organizational View*. From an organizational perspective, the perspective of the entire enterprise, the Infocosm looks like process automation. It would provide the ability to automate a business process from front to back, across all of the knowledge workers who are involved in the process.

4. *The Knowledge Management View*. From the point of view of *anyone* wanting access to knowledge, the Infocosm represents the entire process of gathering, packaging, and distributing what is probably a limitless variety of forms of knowledge: training, case histories, technical documents, rules and regulations—even good old common sense. One could take a video camera and tape experts in a given area talking about a particular subject, then index the videotape and put an interface on it so an individual could have a pseudo-conversation with those experts. The result would be similar to the "Ask System" we have seen several times before. You can't explicitly encode that kind of knowledge in a conventional program or database, but you can capture it, package it, and deploy it using the knowledge management technologies available in the Infocosm.

5. *The Knowledge Worker View*. From the point of view of the knowledge worker in the workplace, the Infocosm looks like the performance systems of which we have been speaking in this book. And, more important, IPS links the worker into the other views or components of the Infocosm. The Infocosm provides the worker with links to consumers who are interacting with public information services, links to colleagues for computer-supported collaboration, links to the entire business process through automation, and links into any kind of knowledge to which one wants access. A consumer may be engaged in interactive home shopping through the Electronic Shopping Mall and order a suit from a manufacturer; the manufacturer's customer services representative can directly interact with that consumer via the public information service and assist the consumer with questions and configuration. The consumer then places an order, which gets routed by a process automation system to other knowledge workers at the appropriate times. If the representative needs assistance from, say, a designer, he or she signs on to the collaborative system provided by the Infocosm. At any point that the worker needs information—product information, delivery, availability, troubleshooting assistance—it can be found by tapping into the knowledge management facilities provided by the Infocosm.

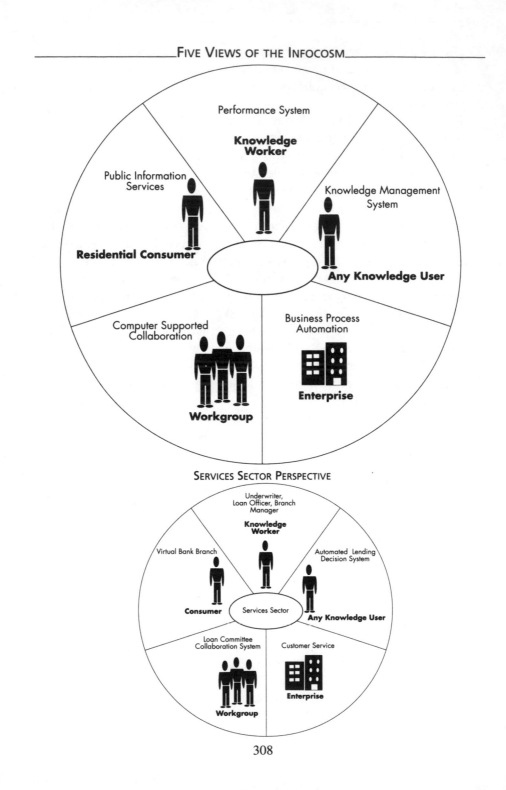

Performance System

Knowledge Worker

Public Information Services

Knowledge Management System

Residential Consumer

Any Knowledge User

Computer Supported Collaboration

Business Process Automation

Workgroup

Enterprise

Services Sector Perspective

Underwriter, Loan Officer, Branch Manager

Knowledge Worker

Virtual Bank Branch

Automated Lending Decision System

Consumer

Services Sector

Any Knowledge User

Loan Committee Collaboration System

Customer Service

Workgroup

Enterprise

PRODUCT SECTOR PERSPECTIVE

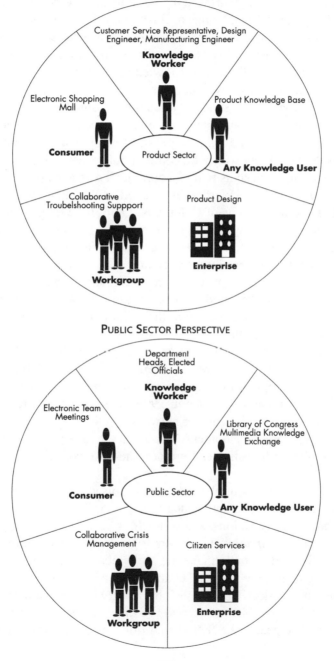

PUBLIC SECTOR PERSPECTIVE

WHY NOW?

Parts of the Infocosm have surfaced in academic and creative visions for many years. As long ago as 1945, Vannevar Bush, who was Director of the Office of Scientific Research and Development, wrote an article entitled "As We May Think."[3] In it, he envisioned a desktop computer that would give instantaneous access to the entire world's store of knowledge. This capability was not seen as an obvious advancement by everyone. Just three years later, the dark side of this technological capability was incorporated into George Orwell's novel *1984:* a government using the capabilities of a kind of "Infocosm" to monitor and control individuals. Later, some of the technology to support these preliminary ideas really was delivered, but was not a commercial success. In 1968, with much fanfare, AT&T introduced its first videophone: it was not a success. In the late 1970s, Warner (now Time Warner) introduced a fully interactive cable system called QUBE to the citizens of Columbus, Ohio. It never generated a profit.

So what's different now? To begin, some of the resistance to technology of which we spoke in Chapter 4—resistance due to culture, to generational differences, to habit—has been lessened greatly as the technology generation has come of age. Moreover, people of all ages have now grown accustomed to instantaneous access to news and information; in the marketplace, standards of customer service have been raised to the point that consumers are now puzzled by companies that cannot respond quickly to their requests. From a hardware point of view, the price-to-performance ratio has dramatically improved over the past decade, and we are now seeing multi-billion-dollar investments by infrastructure suppliers in jump-starting these markets. In the United States, the administration that took office in 1993 includes a Vice President who is committed to high-speed computer networks.[4]

Together, all these developments mean that the time is right for all three of the players of the Infocosm (see figure on the next page):

- *Content Providers.* Major players are now poised for the creation and packaging of Infocosm content: education, television, movies, publications, video games, conversations, and so forth.
- *Infrastructure Companies.* The technological capabilities of the infrastructure or delivery/distribution channel have increased a thousandfold in the past decade. One network being championed by the National Research and Education Network (NREN) envisions, by 1995, a 3-gigabit delivery channel—that's 3 billion bits per second, 66 times larger than current capacity. What does that mean? The NREN coalition compares this capacity to send-

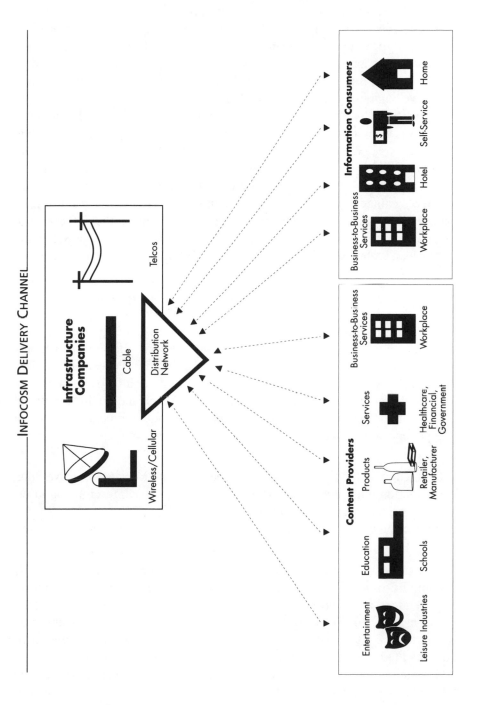

ing 100 three-dimensional X-rays and CAT scans every second for 100 cancer patients, or sending 1,000 satellite photographs to researchers.[5] In terms of typed pages of information, it amounts to 100,000 pages per second: meaning an entire encyclopedia could be transmitted in the blink of an eye. In short, the Infocosm itself is being enabled by relatively low-cost, massive computing power and bandwidth.

• *Information Consumers.* Interest in interactive network services by consumers is growing. Traffic on Internet and other on-line public information services, for example, has grown dramatically. Internet has grown from 9,800 U.S.-only subscribers in 1986 to 4.7 million international subscribers in 1993. Current usage is over 4 trillion bytes per month.[6] CompuServe gained a quarter of a million members in 1992 to reach 1.1 million subscribers, and America Online was predicted to reach the 500,000 subscriber mark in mid-1994.[7] Average annual revenues for CompuServe and American Online grew 25 and 21%, respectively, between 1987 and 1991.[8]

REMOVING CONSTRAINTS ON CONSUMPTION

The removal of traditional constraints on consumption has been happening gradually, and the astonishing growth rates in network services show that consumers and knowledge workers are catching on to the possibilities. We can only access, of course, what comes to us through our senses, and the Infocosm really only assumes the ability to virtualize consumption through the audio and visual senses. Within those constraints, there are three categories of interaction that can be experienced or consumed primarily through the auditory and visual senses:

1. Interaction with *people:* conversations, lectures, advice, gossip, storytelling.
2. Interaction with *places:* classrooms, museums, events, foreign countries, shopping malls, arcades, concert halls.
3. Interaction with *things:* movies, books, data, money, nonphysical games.

The consumption of these entities is constrained, or has been constrained, by *time* and by *space.* That is, it is difficult at best for someone in Columbus, Ohio to attend a concert in Berlin; a student in Tokyo cannot easily attend a lecture at Harvard. There have also been *form* constraints on consumption. Access to an encyclopedia, for example, meant that someone or some institution had to have physical access to a multiple-volume set of books.

Constraints on auditory consumption began to be removed years ago by radio and the telephone, because these are relatively low-bandwidth activi-

CENTER FOR STRATEGIC TECHNOLOGY

The Center for Strategic Technology is a working technology center in Palo Alto, California: a showcase for new and emerging technologies, and a proving ground for assessing and developing these technologies. The Center presents an integrated environment where many technologies work together to solve real business problems. Its mission is to be an ongoing influence on the technology strategy of the technology community and of business organizations worldwide.

For several years, Andersen Consulting has spoken of the "four pillars" of its technology vision: smart systems, the human metaphor, new age (client/server) architectures, and universal networks. Adding to these four pillars the new and powerful solution delivery methods, we have five important categories for emerging technologies.

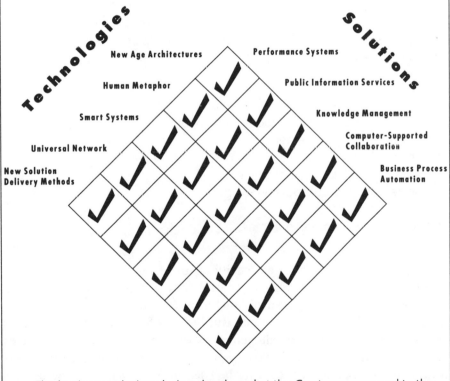

The business solutions being developed at the Center correspond to the five views of the Infocosm discussed in this chapter: performance systems, public information services, knowledge management systems, computer-supported collaboration, and business process automation.

Center for Strategic Technology (*Continued*)

More specifically, the Center is working with all leading edge technologies, including:

- Broadband Networking
- Case-based Reasoning
- Character Recognition
- Compression
- Desktop Video Conferencing
- Document Imaging
- Groupware
- HDTV
- Inference Engines
- Intelligent Agents

- Massively Parallel Computers
- Multimedia
- Object Orientation
- Personal Digital Assistants
- Virtual Reality
- Visualization
- Voice Recognition/Synthesis
- Wireless/Mobile Computing
- Workflow

Visitors to the Center for Strategic Technology can see demonstrations and videos of innovative technology solutions and participate in seminars and discussions of leading-edge alpha, beta, and commercial technology. Showcase locations at the Center include:

- Knowledge Worker Performance Support
- Executive Management Performance Support
- Process Automation Center
- Software Factories and Reinventing Systems Building
- Hands-on Hardware Demonstrations
- Telepresence and Collaborative Work
- Home Media Center
- Home Kitchen Command Center

---

ties: basic voice only requires a capacity of fifty-five bits per second. Visual processing, however, is a relatively high-bandwidth activity: still pictures, even at low resolution, require a million bits per second; full-motion video requires thirty million bits per second. But in the Infocosm, these constraints will be eased, if not removed altogether, as vast amounts of our visual lives will be "virtualized": movies, live theater performances, lectures, artwork, illustrations, books, charts, and so forth. The reason why this can be done is partly due to the capacity of fiberoptic cable, which could carry 25,000 channels, each with a possible *billion* bits per second capacity.

How soon will the Infocosm become a reality? We can try to answer that question by looking at the amount of time it took for existing utilities to pen-

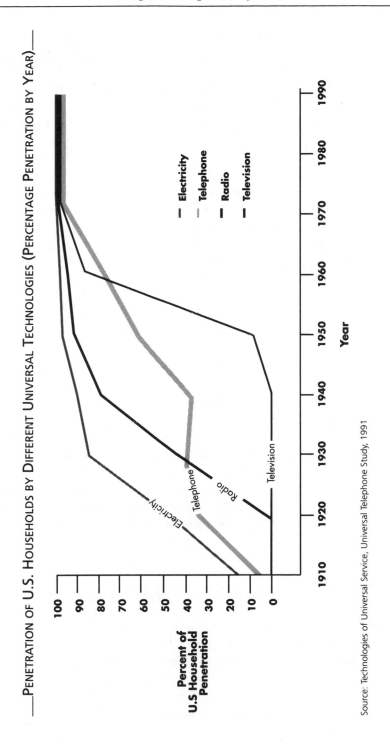

PENETRATION OF U.S. HOUSEHOLDS BY DIFFERENT UNIVERSAL TECHNOLOGIES (PERCENTAGE PENETRATION BY YEAR)

Source: Technologies of Universal Service, Universal Telephone Study, 1991

etrate the home. (See figure on the previous page.) As a rule, those utilities that require extensive terrestrial infrastructure have moved relatively slowly. Electricity, for example, took 70 years to reach 50% of the households in the United States. Telephone required 50 years to reach 70% of households; cable television took over 40 years to reach the 60% level. On the other hand, utilities not dependent on an extensive terrestrial infrastructure move much faster. Radio reached 70% of U.S. households within 10 years; television reached that level in 15 years. Because of the mixed bag of delivery methods of the Infocosm, different portions of it will reach maturity faster than others.

We can expect the same sort of uptake curve for the Infocosm as was experienced with other utilities, but that doesn't necessarily mean we have a long time to wait. Future historians may report that the uptake curve for the Infocosm started out in the early 1950s with the first commercial implementations of computers. In the 1990s the Infocosm is most likely at the same stage as electricity was in 1920, the telephone was in 1940, or the television was in 1950; that is, poised to penetrate a majority of the market in a few years' time after a long, slow incubation. Finally, organizations will start to see some real payback from the billions invested to date in computing resources.

It is certain that most companies and industries will ultimately be affected by the Infocosm, and many industries and jobs will be permanently displaced, or even eliminated. At least 75% of industries in the United States alone have some potential for new high-bandwidth "virtual" alternatives. Physical activities, needless to say—materials extraction, transformation, or handling—are nonvirtualizable. But if your company involves the sale, display, transformation, or aggregation of information, however, you will most likely be doing some of your business within the Infocosm in the relatively near future. It is no exaggeration to say that for many people, the rest of their lives, starting now, will be spent adjusting to what the Infocosm hath wrought.

HOW WILL THE INFOCOSM COME ABOUT?

We can break down a discussion of the development of the Infocosm over the next five years or so into traditional supply-and-demand components. That is, on the one hand we find that the infrastructure providers will largely supply or push the market; on the other hand, corporate and residential customers (knowledge workers and information consumers) will have varying levels of demand to pull the market for specific applications.

SUPPLIERS

Four types of infrastructure providers will supply the market in pursuit of new sources of revenue: content (the "stuff"); communications (the "pipes"); computing the ("boxes"); and context (the "glue"). (See figure on the next page.)

1. *Content* providers will make their money by providing valuable, copyrighted aggregates of information that will be available through the Infocosm. Here entertainment, education, shopping/trading, and remote-site working are the primary components. Major players in the entertainment business will include the major movie studios, cable channels, and the major television networks. The education component will most likely be driven by major research institutions and editorially strong newspapers. Various alliances will drive the home shopping component, such as the one between Spiegel and Time Warner.
2. *Communications* companies will survive by providing the most efficient and flexible transport from the digital source to the place of use. Transport mediums include:

   - Interexchange carriers (long-distance companies)
   - Local exchange carriers (regional Bells, major independents)
   - Cable companies (Top ten multiple system operators)
   - Competitive access providers
   - Public networks (Internet, NREN)
   - Digital broadcast satellite
   - Cellular/personal communications networks

3. *Computing* companies are seeking revenue sources to replace their shrinking hardware margins and to control access from the home. We now see such devices as set-top boxes, digital video servers, and personal data assistants coming from these companies.
4. *Context* providers will supply the "glue" of the Infocosm—the software and services to facilitate the creation, delivery, and support of the digital content. Integrated Performance Support is certainly a major component of this "glue." Context providers here would include:

   - Digital service bureaus
   - Content factories
   - Systems integrators
   - Gateway providers

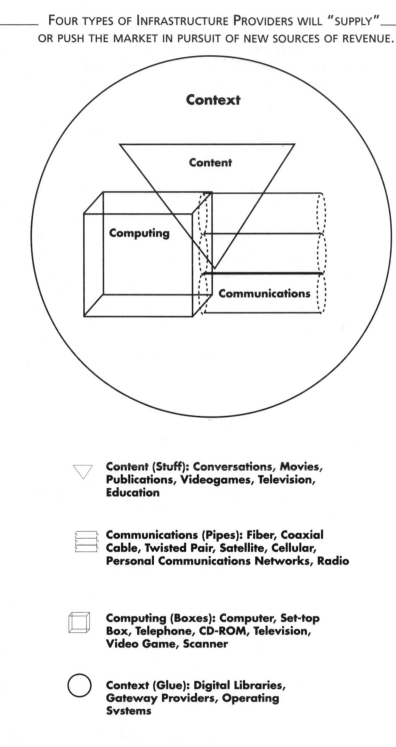

FOUR TYPES OF INFRASTRUCTURE PROVIDERS WILL "SUPPLY"
OR PUSH THE MARKET IN PURSUIT OF NEW SOURCES OF REVENUE.

Content (Stuff): Conversations, Movies, Publications, Videogames, Television, Education

Communications (Pipes): Fiber, Coaxial Cable, Twisted Pair, Satellite, Cellular, Personal Communications Networks, Radio

Computing (Boxes): Computer, Set-top Box, Telephone, CD-ROM, Television, Video Game, Scanner

Context (Glue): Digital Libraries, Gateway Providers, Operating Systems

CUSTOMERS

Residential and corporate customers will pull specific applications into the marketplace. Traditionally, only applications that significantly exceed existing methods of operation are pulled by the market. How can one determine what those applications will be? Andersen Consulting researchers recently set out to answer this question by taking a demand-based approach. By identifying visually and auditorially intensive activities and their potential substitutes, they were able to generate a rough estimate of market demand for specific information services applications. The questions driving the research were as follows:

- What current human activities require substantial auditory and visual inputs?
- Can one create electronic, "virtual" alternatives to these current information inputs?
- What added utility do these virtual alternatives offer? Who is likely to purchase them? How much will they spend?

Researchers found that residential customers will eventually reallocate their scarce time and money across the following selected Infocosm applications that provide high utility:

- *Entertainment.* Auditory and visual input presented to entertain, divert, and stimulate the individual.
- *Education.* Investment in individual human capital.
- *Shopping/Trading.* Auditory and visual input gathered to allow the consumer to make educated, optimized buying and selling decisions.
- *Interacting.* Auditory and visual input gathered and exchanged through the course of day-to-day interaction with other people.
- *Working.* Using Auditory and visual input in the consumer's role as a worker outside of direct work responsibilities.

The box on page 322 provides more detail on each of these categories. (Note that not all of the activities listed in the chart can be virtualized.)

The next step in determining the applications most likely to be successful is to identify audio/visual-intensive activities and their potential substitutes within the Infocosm. Here the following questions are the main drivers:

1. What information resources are currently available to enable these activities? What are their strengths and weaknesses?
2. What are the virtual alternatives to these information resources? Because consumers resist fundamental change, any new product must be a so-called

"10X" improvement. That is, it must be ten times better, faster, or cheaper than what exists.

3. Which potential customer segments will most value these virtual alternatives? For what reasons?
4. What are the key buyer values for these high-potential customers? What level of product, price, and performance are they looking for?
5. Given these buyer values, how many dollars can one expect consumers to reallocate from other activities for this new service?

Corporate customers within the Infocosm—companies and their knowledge workers—have different needs than do the residential customers. Important applications for companies will include:

- Training
- Interacting/collaborating
- Managing relationships with suppliers and alliances
- Managing relationships with customers and distributors
- Reducing time to market

For these corporate customers, Integrated Performance Support will play a major role within the Infocosm.

THE ROLE OF IPS IN THE INFOCOSM

Each facet of the Infocosm has been addressed at some point in our discussion of Integrated Performance Support. Public Information Services and Knowledge Management resources, for example, are important sources for the content delivered by the Reference Services facility of a performance system. We discussed the capability of IPS to enable group work in Chapter 8 and looked at one powerful example of groupware or computer-supported collaboration. Knowledge Management was an important aspect of our discussion of learning organizations and growth organizations in Chapter 11, and we briefly described the knowledge management system at Andersen Consulting. Business Process Automation was the subtheme for that portion of Chapter 9 that dealt with the transfer of work to the consumer; there we noted that every instance of process reengineering will henceforth always try to determine those processes that can be automated—either totally, or redesigned to allow transfer to the consumer. These areas of overlap within the general picture of the Infocosm point to the continuing importance of Integrated Performance Support principles as knowledge workers and information consumers learn to operate powerfully within this new world of information.

EASE OF INTERACTION IN THE INFOCOSM

As an example of IPS principles at work within the Infocosm, let's consider the kind of performance system that now supports the work of a customer service representative taking a new order or changing an order for a customer. It is likely that this process of gathering information from customers and simply inputting it to the system will change drastically in the Infocosm. There will be little reason then for having an intermediary between the customer and the system. Indeed, even today some companies are making software available to their customers and allowing them to interact, browse, and place orders directly to the company's information system. If this is the case, then the principles we touched on in Chapter 9, "Integrated Performance Support for Everyone," will become vital to the success of companies in the Infocosm. Ease of access to information, the ability to navigate through a system, to understand quickly what is available and how to buy it, will mean the difference between success and failure for the content providers to the Infocosm.

Current activity and current planning for the Infocosm continue to take place mostly on the supply side of the pipeline. We believe that a similar level of activity needs to be focused on the demand side, and this is where IPS principles come into play. The closer we get to meeting basic human and business needs, resulting in a clear economic benefit, the more likely it is that the content of the Infocosm will be successful. Performance-centered, human-centered technological principles should guide the development of the content, as well as the delivery and interaction methods within the Infocosm.

REFERENCE SERVICES IN THE INFOCOSM

The Knowledge Management component of the Infocosm will be different for different sectors of the economy. In the public sector, for example, consumers will have access to major research libraries and other kinds of university and educational knowledge bases. In the services and products sectors, knowledge management will take different forms. But in every case, the IPS approach to providing knowledge on demand, at point of need, will

High Utility Consumer Applications in the Infocosm

Entertainment

Passive Entertainment (demands only the subject's attention):

- On-demand viewing of entertainment (TV, movies) at home
- Passive viewing of entertainment (TV, movies) at home
- Viewing movies at theater
- Viewing live performances (theater, music, opera, dance)
- Reading
- Listening to music

Active Entertainment (requires active participation in the event):

- Group games (card games, board games, interactive TV games)
- Solo games (solitaire, jigsaw puzzles)
- Group sports
- Solo sports
- Hobbies, arts, crafts
- Personal travel

Education

Reading Activities:

- Homework or drill. Individual practice either at home or in class, with an emphasis on ensuring understanding through practical application and repetition.
- Research. Independent study of a single topic. The goal is, through self-directed learning, to gather enough information on a topic to form an independent conclusion about it.
- Self-study. Completely self-driven study, relying on drill, research, and practical application without the benefit of a teacher.

Speaking Activities:

- Lectures. Presentation of a subject by a teacher to a class. Although there may be the opportunity for some questions, the main goal is one-way information transfer by an expert to a relatively passive audience.
- Discussion. Discussion/exploration of a topic in a small group, with the main goal being interactive sharing of ideas and perspectives to better inform the whole through the opinions of many.

HIGH UTILITY CONSUMER APPLICATIONS IN THE INFOCOSM *(CONTINUED)*

Doing Activities:

- Hands-on Practice. Practical or lab work. The physical manipulation of elements, equipment, or objects to allow practical application of classroom learning on the actual subjects under study.

Shopping/Trading

Shopping/trading includes any and all buying and selling of goods and services:

- Gathering product information
- Shopping for necessities and sundries
- Shopping for big-ticket items
- Shopping for services
- Shopping for fun
- Investing and money management
- Selling used goods

Interaction

Interaction includes all forms of day-to-day contact with people. Interaction may be with individuals—those we know or don't know, communicating ideas and concepts, or communicating emotions and beliefs. Interaction could also be with groups—identifying affinity groups and communicating with them.

Working

From this consumer perspective, working includes those activities that occur in the home or in the course of getting to work. These activities would include commuting, working at a remote site (home or elsewhere), and looking for work.

determine whether information can be located and applied to real needs. We can presume that what we now think of as the information explosion will some day be a mere firecracker compared to the atomic blast of information available in the Infocosm. If that is so, then the ability to "turn information into knowledge" will become increasingly vital to both corporate and personal success, and IPS design principles will help guide the development of ongoing applications.

JOB AID SERVICES IN THE INFOCOSM

It is perhaps difficult to conceive of "job aids" or performance tools within the Infocosm, since the Infocosm itself will act as the biggest job aid of all. But one could well imagine that certain services to ease the ability to communicate, interact, and learn along the network will inevitably arise in ways as yet undetermined. Job aids presume a level of repeatability and consistency: when a job or task comes up again, it can be accomplished by the aid already in place. The knowledge worker or consumer could proceed uninterrupted to complete a repeated task.

TRAINING SERVICES IN THE INFOCOSM

Training and education are the areas that may be most profoundly affected by the Infocosm, with some potentially dramatic social and cultural effects. George Gilder, a leading writer on this subject, foresees a renaissance in education provided by the universal knowledge base. "The telecomputer could revitalize public education by bringing the best teachers in the country to classrooms everywhere. More importantly, the telecomputer could encourage competition by making home-schooling both feasible and attractive. . . . The competition would either destroy the public school system or force it to become competitive with rival systems."[9]

But merely bringing good teachers into a classroom, if they are still teaching in the old methods, would be akin to automating outdated business processes within a corporation. Crucial to the success of new training and education methods within the Infocosm are the IPS principles we discussed in Chapter 7. There we noted that effective training and education are based on the principle that people "learn by doing"; effective training is also one-on-one, interactive, exploratory, multisensory. We cannot take old teaching methods, methods which have not been able to keep up with today's needs, and simply import them wholesale into the Infocosm.

VIRTUAL RECORDS FOR THE HEALTH CARE INDUSTRY

In their book, *The Virtual Corporation,* authors Davidow and Malone predict that the winners of the knowledge economy will be those who can "virtualize" their products and services. A virtual product or service is one that probably did not exist before it was produced. Its concept, design, and production exist rather in the minds of teams and in performance systems. It is produced instantaneously and customized in response to customer demand.[10]

More accurately, the virtual corporation or industry is one that has transcended the traditional limitations of time, place, and form and is operating powerfully within the Infocosm. By and large, this is accomplished with the aid of the powerful technologies described in this book: communications technologies and systems that deliver information and knowledge at the precise time and place it is needed to accomplish a particular business objective. But many technologies in use today are inherently "Infocosmic." Your ATM card, for example, overcomes the old restriction of having to drive to a bank, park your car, and wait in line to deal with a teller.

The drive to virtualize transactions in this way will become vital to all industries. The health care industry, for example, finds itself facing intense scrutiny and will be challenged over the coming years to deliver high-quality service at lower cost. An "Infocosmic" capability can revolutionize the efficiency with which the vast array of players in health care come together to perform their services. The potential of performance systems in this environment can be seen in one prototype system developed by Andersen Consulting for a major insurance company in the United States.

Of particular interest within the system is its "Eligibility Verification" function. Eligibility Verification gives external health care providers the ability to determine if a patient is currently eligible for medical insurance benefits from the company. Information provided by the system includes:

- the member's current coverage with the company, including "as-of" dates and expiration dates
- the member's contractual deductibles, copayments, and coinsurance levels, as well as contractual benefit limitations
- indicators of Other Carrier Liability information
- authorized referrals for the member including physicians' names and locations of service
- contacts within the insurance company if additional information is required

---

VIRTUAL RECORDS FOR THE HEALTH CARE INDUSTRY (*CONTINUED*)

The intent of this system is to "virtualize" the member's contract, making it accessible at any time, and from any location, even when a representative of the insurance company is not present. The value to all the players involved here is immense. Ultimately, the greatest value is to the patients, who now can be assured that all physicians can obtain the real-time status of their contracts in case any doubts arise as to what services may or may not be covered under a policy.

A second system, an implemented system for a major American teaching hospital, automates and integrates the hospital's medical records department. The system lets many people—physicians, nurses, medical records technicians, utilization review coordinators, and healthcare managers—look at the same medical records from different locations at the same time. This improves the flow of the medical record, which ultimately improves the efficiency of patient care.

The system combines microcomputer-based workstations with a data server running a relational database management system. It uses an open information management tool that lets the medical records department capture, index, store, view, manipulate, retrieve, and print critical information. In effect, the system integrates the medical record—now a "virtualized" medical record—into the flow of the department.

WORK, WORKER, AND ADVICE IN THE INFOCOSM

Finally, you can be sure that companies serving as suppliers in the Infocosm will constantly be compiling profiles of the types of consumers, if not consumers themselves, within the Infocosm. The buying habits and tendencies of those who frequent an electronic shopping mall, for example, will be well known to the mall's merchants. This inevitably leads one to considerations of privacy, and other moral issues like intellectual property rights, that will arise within the Infocosm. Certainly, steps will need to be taken to ensure that private information may be kept private by those interacting within the Infocosm, but this will be a challenge, both morally and technologically. If someone is buying prescription medication via the network, will that record be kept private? Will cagey information pirates intercept or steal content provided within the Infocosm? As we noted earlier, the twenty-first century will bring with it difficult ethical matters. One can only hope that humanistic and moral innovation will accompany technological innovation.

Depending on the constraints that are eventually put into place, then, the

Infocosm will certainly have a "Consumer Services" facility, akin to the Knowledge Worker Services facility of the IPS model. It will also perhaps include something similar to Work Profile Services. Certain customers would most likely be authorized for certain kinds of interaction within a company's product and databases, and these profiles could be altered to suit the circumstances. Based upon these profiles, parts of the Infocosm would be able to tailor a set of advisory services to each knowledge worker or residential consumer to serve their information needs optimally.

The ability to provide advice is already apparent in systems like the Electronic Shopping Mall discussed in Chapter 9. There, a set of guides are present to answer questions and give advice to shoppers as they proceed through the mall. Advice will be a crucial aspect of the friendliness that must characterize consumer interactions within the Infocosm. Indeed, whole units of content in the Infocosm could be based upon advisory principles. If virtual bank branches are a part of the Infocosm, there is no reason why, for example, virtual brokers will not be present as well. Here, for a modest price, consumers could expect investment counseling and the development and management of portfolios based upon their incomes and unique investment goals.

"Performance" will mean many different things within the Infocosm. But whatever it means, whatever the need is, the basic tenets of Integrated Performance Support will still hold true. A knowledge worker and consumer within the Infocosm will need to be supported at the moment of value, the moment of interaction and decision within this new electronic world. IPS will both receive value from, and give value to, the Infocosm.

Epilogue: The Hunter-Gatherers of the Knowledge Economy

Watch children working with building blocks. They put them together slowly and a tower goes up until, finally, they knock it down or it falls of its own accord. Then they start again: same child, same blocks, but what they create the next time is never exactly the same as the time before.

Societies go through similar cycles of building, tearing down, and rebuilding. We spend years, even centuries, building a certain configuration of institutions, political and social structures, economic assumptions, nations, ethnic groupings, social classes, arts, values—and then it all falls apart and we put the pieces together in new ways. When the new structure is in place, we recognize parts of it—as the child recognizes that the same building blocks are being used—but the structure itself is unrecognizable. After a time, we cannot remember what the old one looked like.

The new economic structure—what we are calling, with others, the "knowledge economy"—is only partly built. Today, we cannot yet recognize which pieces are vestiges of the old structure and which are parts of the new. But it seems certain that a new understanding of *knowledge* as the capital of the future is on the ascendancy. As a result, our entire world will change. The technologies and movements of which we have spoken in this book are not passive aspects of the changes taking place today, but active forces helping make this change happen. But where is it all headed? What are the consequences of the events going on around us today, events over which most people feel they have little control? We have argued that only an awareness of the big picture, only systemic kinds of thinking, can give us any power *over* that system. Today we are all participants in the creation of new structures and new systems; unless we understand them and anticipate as best we can, we will become their victims.

As computers began to take hold in the 1960s, many analysts were concerned that automation would put large numbers of people out of work. At the time, defenders of automation argued that the reverse was true: that automation would bring job creation. From our perspective today, we can see that automation *did* put people out of work, pushing them into new sectors of the

329

- To this point in history, automation has completely revamped the three major sectors of the economy: agriculture, products, and services. The question today is where workers will go from the overbloated services sector.
- In the coming knowledge economy, technology must evolve to make the new capital—knowledge—and the knowledge worker must become the driver for the functioning of the information system.
- The new economy will be a return to a "hunter-gatherer" society. The hunt will be for knowledge; the fields and forests will be the Infocosm, the global telecommunications network.
- Smaller organizations, as small as one person, will attempt to find new forms of knowledge through innovation, creativity, and efficiency. They will find new ways to sell that knowledge and new ways to provide products and services.

---

economy. This is a pattern that has occurred before. In agriculture, for example, the application of automation moved farmers from the fields to the factories. The automation of the factories, in turn, moved those workers into the banks and other places in the service sector. Today, the overbloated service economy includes over 70% of the workforce. Automation will certainly move these people somewhere else, as well: but to where? As we turn over a new century, we will have completely revamped the three major sectors of the economy: agriculture, products, and services. Now what?

THE GLOBAL VIEW OF THE INFORMATION ECONOMY

It may be difficult to reconcile the contrasting messages of two major recent books. The first, Lester Thurow's *Head to Head,* assesses the prospects of the coming economic battle among the United States, Japan, and Europe. The second, Robert Reich's *The Work of Nations,* argues that the economic battle lines of the future will no longer correspond to national boundaries. More typical, says Reich, will be what he calls a "global web." Here, a company's headquarters may be in the United States, but research and design facilities may be spread throughout Japan, Europe, and North America; more production facilities might be located in Southeast Asia and Latin America; lenders and investors in Taiwan, Japan, West Germany, and the United States. All companies, says Reich, are becoming part of an international labor market. And competitiveness is coming to depend not on the fortunes of a particular corporation or industry, but rather on the functions the workers perform and the value they add to the global economy. "In a very few years, there will be virtually no way to distinguish one national economy from another except by the exchange rates of their currencies—and even this distinction may be on the wane."[1] No longer are citizens of a country rising or falling together in a unified national economy; instead, they are grouping together into smaller entities. It's a small world, after all, and the worlds within worlds are getting smaller, too.

How does information technology contribute to these developments? More important, what will information technology look like in this global economy, and what will it do to the work we perform, and to the people who perform the work?

Peter Drucker argues that we are now living through a period of profound transformation—a period akin to earlier transformations such as the rise of the medieval city, the invention of the printing press, and the dawn of the Industrial Age. The transformation began when information and knowledge started to become central to the workings of national economies and to the world economy. In the United States, the computer had much to do with this, of course, though Drucker insightfully points out that the G.I. Bill was just as central—giving thousands of young people the money to attend college, in return for having served their country. Whatever reason or reasons are at the heart of it, by midcentury we were already well past the industrial age, on our way toward a service-based economy and an information economy.

But how long will this economy last? We can try to make a prediction here by looking at the life cycle of the former economy, the industrial economy. There were four distinct stages. In stage 1, or start-up, core technologies were introduced, such as electricity and the internal combustion engine. In stage 2, or the growth phase, demand developed as companies found ways to employ the new technologies. During maturity, or stage 3, the surrounding support infrastructure—housing, communication, transportation—changed to accommodate a new business environment. Not until stage 4, the aging phase, did new organization and management models emerge.[2]

Stan Davis and Bill Davidson argue in their book *2020 Vision* that we are somewhere between growth and maturity, around the midpoint of the information economy life cycle. But a number of events lead us to believe that we will witness a compression of the maturity and aging phases in the information economy. Technology strategies like Integrated Performance Support have, embedded within them, implications for infrastructures and management models. These may hasten the transition from the information economy to the knowledge economy. New businesses are emerging in all economic sectors. The support infrastructure is changing to support the new business environment, just as happened in the maturity phase of the industrial economy. The growth of services and the decline in manufacturing is a natural outcome of this phase. The last decades have seen a transformation in how we work—from an emphasis on land and labor to an emphasis on knowledge and skill; from corporate understandings based upon a division between management and the workforce to a new division: between knowledge workers and service workers.

Data both for the United States and for other developed nations clearly show this trend. In 1975, the services sector of the economy in the United States accounted for 62% of gross national product.[3] Today that figure is 74%. 77% of all jobs are in the service industry, a figure projected to rise above 80% by the end of the decade. Other countries show parallel development: the industrial sector is falling and the services sector is rising. As services have expanded, they have restructured entire industries, the relationship among these industries, and, indeed, the entire economy. Traditional boundaries between industries have also broken down: a company's competitors may no longer come just from a company in the same industry. Airlines compete now not just with other airlines, but with rental car companies, travel agents, communications companies, and financial service companies.[4] It is in this environment—a service-based economy that is global and more competitive than ever before—that new organizational models are already emerging to cope with new challenges. The move to a knowledge-based organization, the encouragement of self-directed work teams, the emphasis on traditionally "fuzzy" areas like empowerment, learning, creativity: all these are attempting to respond to a business environment where we aren't *making* things, but *doing* things, only some of which result in things being made.

INTEGRATED PERFORMANCE SUPPORT AND THE NEW KNOWLEDGE ECONOMY

Integrated Performance Support and the performance systems that this concept brings into being are harbingers of the knowledge economy. As an economy evolves to a point where knowledge is the most important capital an organization has, the technology must evolve to make that knowledge, and the knowledge worker must become the driver for the functioning of the information system. Performance-centered design, or knowledge worker–centered design, is what now must drive all systems and all applications developed for organizations who want to stay alive during this transformational period.

We have spoken at some length about what "knowledge" is. One short definition that can serve us here is that knowledge is "the accumulating value of individual experience, shareable throughout the organization." That is, knowledge is more than information; it is information that has been sifted through our experience and has been acted upon. It would make no sense to say, "I have read this book about airplanes; now I know how to fly a plane." Knowledge grows only from having flown the plane. Knowledge also grows as it is shared with others; through conversation we enrich our own understanding of what we are talking about—and hopefully we enrich others at the same time. When we give it away, we still have it, and both sender and receiver enrich their respective knowledge capital. This understanding of knowledge drives the development of performance systems.

Performance systems, as we have argued throughout this book, answer two vital needs for organizations moving from the information economy to the knowledge economy. First, they support the actions of knowledge workers *right now;* they meet today's real performance challenges: serving customers, coping with excessive information, learning new skills. But these systems also prepare organizations and knowledge workers for tomorrow's challenges. By virtue of the knowledge infrastructure they help to create, they act as the primary means by which knowledge is accumulated, acted upon, shared, and delivered to the point of need.

THE HUNTER-GATHERER ECONOMY

But technology has its unintended effects, as well. As it makes its way through the services sector, just as it moved through agriculture and manufacturing, it is helping to cause what some people are calling "the jobless recovery." While GNP is modestly increasing, and while productivity is increasing, unemployment is also increasing. Growth and productivity are not translating into new jobs.

No one yet knows how knowledge will behave as an economic resource, and it is vital that theories emerge quickly to try to predict the manner in which knowledge can serve as the center of the wealth-producing, job-producing process.[5] Most people whom we would call knowledge workers today grew up in a business environment with planned retirements and pensions, health

programs, merit increases, an assurance (more or less) of lifetime employment. It is doubtful that these things taken for granted today will be a part of
the next economy. The move to learner organizations will not reverse itself;
indeed, we may see such things as "just-in-time" workers—part-time help,
outsourcing for all but the most vital activities of an organization. The movement to transfer work to the consumer, through such innovations as banking
ATMs and self-service airline ticketing terminals, will dramatically increase
as technology is put into the hands of consumers. After all, why pay someone
to perform a task that customers can do better themselves?

The past is prologue. Ancient hunter-gatherer economies gave way to agriculture. Agriculture gave way to the industrial era; industry gave way to information and services. In the knowledge economy, we will have moved full
circle, back to another kind of hunter-gatherer society. In primitive cultures,
people moved and lived in small groups, searching for what food they could
find among the flora and fauna of their environments. The next economy will
look something like that; this time, though, the hunt will be for knowledge,
and the fields and forests of the hunt will be the global telecommunications
network, the Infocosm. Smaller organizations—as small as one person—will
attempt, through innovation, creativity, and efficiency, to find new forms of
knowledge, new ways to sell it, and new ways to provide services and products. But unlike their ancient ancestors, these hunter-gatherers will have access to potential customers around the globe. And they will be empowered by
technological networks that are only beginning to be built today.

The movement from the older hunter-gather societies to the agricultural society came when animals were domesticated. In the new hunter-gatherer economy, a similar domestication of certain activities, certain forms of knowledge,
will almost certainly occur as well. What these activities will be we can only
guess. What is certain, however, is that the coming economic and technological developments will underscore in an unprecedented manner the importance of defining what we want for ourselves—for our neighbors, our
communities, our nations, and our world. What are the deeper human values
underlying the work that we do? What are the relationships and forms of work
that give our lives meaning? What obligations do we have to those who share
this planet with us? The boundaries of today's nations are set according to geography, ethnicity, and common economic needs. Tomorrow, a nation may be
defined less by geography and more by common interest within the Infocosm.
Technology cannot tell us what those interests are, however, nor can it tell us
what the deeper interests are that we share with humans around the globe.

We can hope that the technology that is helping to create the new economy
can also better enable us to meet the challenges that this economy will create.

In theory, at least, human-centered technology and systems should give larger numbers of people access to important knowledge. The new economic structure, and the presence of the Infocosm, have the potential to unleash the intellectual potential of all who participate, generating whose new ways of thinking, new ways of working, new avenues of individual pursuit, growth, and contribution. The sources of job and economic growth within the knowledge economy are as unclear now as they were to people when the steam engine and electricity were first introduced.

But it is certain that in the knowledge economy, those who are knowledge workers—or what Robert Reich calls "symbolic analysts"—will have an advantage, if we want to conceive of the events about to unfold as a sort of battle or competition. Those most "in the know" can be confident of victory. But what about the losers? In the post-capitalist society, we can be sure that, if left to develop naturally, there will come into being ever larger disparities of wealth, even within nations. Now is the time to ask ourselves what we are doing and why, what a meaningful life is, and how economic developments can enrich our lives rather than diminish them. "We are no more slaves to present trends than to vestiges of the past," Reich concludes. "We can, if we choose, assert that our mutual obligations as citizens extend beyond our economic usefulness to one another, and act accordingly."[6]

As we develop ever more powerful technologies and focus our attention on the manner in which these technologies are integrated into the life of the organization and into the environment in which we exist, we must also ask how these technologies are to be integrated into the lives of people: the people who make up our organizations and our social communities, now electronically defined and geographically dispersed. The coming tests of the knowledge economy are not merely tests of ingenuity, but of character as well.

NOTES

Introduction

1. A group of blind men gathered around an elephant. Asked to describe what an elephant is like, each man responded based on whatever part was within his reach. An elephant is long and thin, said the man holding the tail. No, an elephant is rough and leathery, said the man touching the animal's flank. No, an elephant is huge and round like a tree, said the man by one of the elephant's feet. The moral of the tale is clear: what the men lacked was an understanding of the whole elephant.
2. Source: *U.S. News and World Report,* August 30–September 6, 1993, 16.
3. One article notes that in the United States, fewer than one-half of those companies that have gone through formal downsizing programs since 1988 have improved their profits; only one-third of these companies have shown an increase in productivity. Stephen Franklin, "Layoff Fever Spreads to Robust Firms," *Chicago Tribune,* September 12, 1993.
4. Richard Saul Wurman, *Information Anxiety: What to Do When Information Doesn't Tell You What You Need to Know* (New York: Bantam, 1990).
5. Michael J. McCarthy, *Mastering the Information Age: A Course in Working Smarter, Thinking Better, and Learning Faster* (New York: St. Martin's Press, 1991).
6. One of the first to use these human analogies to describe performance support services was Clay Carr in his article "Performance Support Systems: A New Horizon for Expert Systems," *AI Expert,* May 1992, 39–44.
7. Peter F. Drucker, *Post-Capitalist Society* (New York: HarperCollins, 1993), 83.
8. Chances are, a few companies will register the turn of the millennium as legacy systems using MM/DD/YY for calculations and process triggers reach 01/01/00.
9. Drucker, *Post-Capitalist Society,* 8.
10. James Brian Quinn, *Intelligent Enterprise: A Knowledge and Service Based Paradigm for Industry* (New York: The Free Press, 1992), 32.
11. Alvin Toffler, *Powershift: Knowledge, Wealth, and Violence at the Edge of the 21st Century* (New York: Bantam Books, 1990), 20.
12. Joseph H. Boyett and Henry P. Conn, *Workplace 2000: The Revolution Reshaping American Business* (New York: Plume, 1991), 47.
13. Anthony Patrick Carnevale, *America and the New Economy: How New Com-*

337

petitive Standards Are Radically Changing American Workplaces (San Francisco: Jossey-Bass Publishers, 1991), 216.

14. Matthew A. Baum, "Evolving Along with Our Technology," *Chicago Tribune,* 6/4/93.

15. Storer H. Rowley, "Knowledge the Wealth of Nations?" *Chicago Tribune,* May 17, 1993, Section C, page 1.

16. Rowley, page 5.

17. Donald A. Norman, *Things that Make Us Smart: Defending Human Attributes in the Age of the Machine* (Reading, MA: Addison-Wesley Publishing Company, 1993), 253.

18. Alfred North Whitehead, *Science and the Modern World* (New York: The Free Press, 1967 [1925]).

19. Norman, *Things that Make Us Smart,* 253.

Chapter 1: The Performance-Centered Enterprise

1. Carnevale, *America and the New Economy,* 152–54.

2. See Geary Rummier and Alan F. Brache, *Improving Performance: How to Manage the White Space on the Organization Chart* (San Francisco: Jossey-Bass Publishers, 1990).

3. On this point, see Steven M. Hronec, Arthur Andersen & Co., *Vital Signs: Using Quality, Time, and Cost Performance Measurements to Chart Your Company's Future* (New York: AMACOM, 1993).

4. See, for example, Gloria J. Gery, *Electronic Performance Support Systems* (Boston: Weingarten Publications, 1991), 187.

5. See C. Rudy Puryear and John D. Rollins, "The Moment of Value: Technology Evolves to Deliver Strategic Results," *Outlook,* Andersen Consulting, 1993.

6. Quoted in James C. Livingston, *Anatomy of the Sacred* (New York: Macmillan Publishing Company, 1989), 4.

7. This performance model was developed by Andersen Consulting researchers as part of Andersen Consulting's school in Technology Assimilation.

8. Quoted in Charles M. Madigan, "Going with the Flow," *Chicago Tribune Magazine,* May 2, 1993, 20.

9. Madigan, 20.

10. Donald A. Norman, *The Design of Everyday Things* (New York: Doubleday, 1988), 188.

11. Are you aware of the fact that you are using computers every time you drive your car? We hope not. We hope you're paying attention to the road.

12. Source: *Fortune* and Forum Corporation Study of Customer Expectations (1989).

13. *Workplace 2000,* 12.

14. *Workplace 2000,* 12.

15. *Workplace 2000,* 12.

16. *Workplace 2000,* 12.

17. Madigan, 16.

18. Robert N. Bellah et al, *Habits of the Heart: Individualism and Commitment in American Life* (New York: Harper & Row [Perennial Library], 1985), 207.

19. Madigan, 18.

20. Madigan, 18.

21. Clarence J. Ross, "Integrated Performance Support," unpublished manuscript.

22. Source: U.S. Department of Commerce.

23. Source: Conference of the Chicago Chamber of Commerce.

Chapter 4: Making Technology Work

1. Macintosh television commercial, dialogue paraphrased.

2. "The Technology Payoff," *Business Week,* June 14, 1993, 59.

3. "Technology Payoff," 58.

4. "Technology Payoff," 58.

5. As Donald Norman notes in *Things that Make Us Smart.*

6. For an even more mundane, but truly wonderful example, how about the self-cleaning service station bathroom, named by *R & D Magazine* as one of the 100 most innovative inventions of 1992.

7. Thomas Hobbes, *Leviathan,* in D. D. Raphael, ed., *British Moralists 1650–1800* (Oxford: Oxford University Press, 1969), 37.

8. We address this concern in the final chapter of the book.

9. Charles J. Fombrun, "Corporate Culture and Competitive Strategy," in *Strategic Human Resource Management,* ed. Charles Fombrun, Noel M. Tichy, and Mary Anne Devanna (New York: John Wiley & Sons, 1984), 204.

10. Bill Amend, "Foxtrot," 7/18/93, © 1993 Bill Amend/Distributed by Universal Press Syndicate.

11. Our brains predispose, but do not necessarily dictate. You *can* teach an old dog new tricks. See, for example, Morton Hunt, *The Universe Within: A New Science Explores the Human Mind* (New York: Simon & Schuster, 1982).

12. Source: Direct Marketing Association. Quoted in *Newsweek,* May 31, 1993, 44.

13. William M. Bulkeley, "Information Age: Computer Use by Illiterates Grows at Work," *Wall Street Journal,* June 9, 1992, B1.

14. See, for example, Thomas Bailey, "Jobs of the Future and the Skills They Will Require," *American Educator,* Spring 1990.

15. Bailey, 12.

16. Norman, *The Design of Everyday Things,* 188.

17. Howard Rheingold, "An Interview with Don Norman," in *The Art of Human-Computer Interface Design,* ed. Brenda Laurel (Reading, MA: Addison-Wesley Publishing Company, 1990), 10.

18. Norman, *The Design of Everyday Things,* 2.
19. Norman, *The Design of Everyday Things,* 2.
20. Hugh Ryan, "The Human Metaphor," *Information Systems Management,* Winter 1992, 72.
21. Ryan, 72.
22. Lakoff, G. and Johnson, M., *Metaphors We Live By* (Chicago: The University of Chicago Press, 1980). Quoted in Aaron Marcus, "Human Communications Issues in Advanced UIs," *Communications of the ACM,* April 1993, Vol. 36, No. 4, 103.
23. Quoted in Thomas D. Erickson, "Working with Interface Metaphors," in Laurel, 66.
24. Erickson, 66.
25. Tim Oren, Gitta Salomon, Kristee Kreitman, and Abbe Don, "Guides: Characterizing the Interface," in Laurel, 368.
26. Brenda Laurel, "Interface Agents: Metaphors with Character," in Laurel, 356.

Chapter 5: Satisfying the Customer

1. Fyodor Dostoevsky, *Notes from Underground,* tr. Andrew R. MacAndrew (New York: Signet Classics, 1961), 91.
2. We are indebted to Henry Conn, coauthor of *Workplace 2000,* for this anecdote.
3. Sidney Doolittle, quoted in Shirley Leung, "Job Training, Courtesy of Walt and Sam," *Chicago Tribune,* July 20, 1993, Section 3, page 4.
4. Quinn, *Intelligent Enterprise,* 342.
5. See, for example, Michael Treacy and Fred Wiersema, "Customer Intimacy and Other Value Disciplines," *Harvard Business Review,* Jan.–Feb. 1993.
6. Michael Hammer and James Champy, *Reengineering the Corporation* (New York: HarperCollins, 1993), 18.
7. Peter M. Senge, *The Fifth Discipline: The Art and Practice of the Learning Organization* (New York: Doubleday Currency, 1990), 333.
8. Source: *Fortune* magazine and Forum Corporation Study, 1989.
9. Quinn, *Intelligent Enterprise,* 345.
10. Senge, *The Fifth Discipline,* 333.
11. V. Zeithaml, A. Parasuraman, and L. Berry, *Delivering Quality Service* (New York: The Free Press, 1990). Cited in Quinn, *Intelligent Enterprise,* 344.
12. Gery, *Electronic Performance Support Systems,* 3.
13. Patricia Sellars, "Companies that Serve You Best," *Fortune,* May 31, 1993, 75.
14. Lester Thurow, *Head to Head* (New York: William and Morrow Company, 1992), 137.
15. Quoted in Leung, *Chicago Tribune,* Sec. 3, p. 4.
16. Leung, p. 1.
17. *Wall Street Journal,* July 6, 1993, A8.
18. Carnevale, *America and the New Economy,* 204.
19. C. W. Trim, "Zero Defect," *Mortgage Banking,* January 1987, 19–24. Cited in Robert G. Murdick, Barry Render, and Roberta S. Russell, *Service Operations*

Management (Boston: Allyn and Bacon, 1990), and in *Why Performance Support?* (Vienna, Virginia: Legent Corporation, 1992).

20. *Fortune* and Forum Corporation Study. Cited in Boyett and Conn, *Workplace 2000,* 13.

21. Robert L. Desatnick, "Service: A CEO's Perspective," *Management Review,* October 1987, 41. Cited in *Workplace 2000,* 12.

22. Frederick F. Reichheld and W. Earl Sasser, Jr., "Zero Defections: Quality Comes to Services," *Harvard Business Review,* Sept.–Oct. 1990, 105–11. Cited in *Why Performance Support?,* 22.

23. See Chapter 9, "Integrated Performance Support for Everyone," for a discussion of this kind of transfer of work to the consumer.

Chapter 6: Turning Information into Knowledge

1. Just for your information, we made these statistics up. But does it matter? Would anyone ever know the difference?

2. Peter Large, *The Micro Revolution Revisited* (Towata, NJ: Rowman and Allanheld, 1984).

3. Richard Saul Wurman, *Information Anxiety: What to Do When Information Doesn't Tell You What You Need to Know* (New York: Bantam Books, 1990).

4. William J. Clancey, "Practice Cannot Be Reduced to Theory: Knowledge, Representations, and Change in the Workplace," forthcoming in S. Bagnara, C. Zuccermaglio, and S. Stucky, eds., *Organizational Learning and Technological Change.*

5. Clancey, 13.

6. Shoshana Zuboff, *In the Age of the Smart Machine* (New York: Basic Books, Inc., 1988), 3-16.

7. We should not overlook the fact that some workers will not want to be brought up to a higher level. Ultimately, in spite of an organization's best efforts to get people to shape up, some may have to ship out. As Atok Ilhan, CEO of Philips Malaysia, says, "If you can't change the worker, change the worker."

8. See Zuboff, 62.

9. Zuboff, 5–6.

10. Cited in Simon Majaro, "Strategy Search and Creativity: The Key to Corporate Renewal," *European Management Journal,* Vol. 10, No. 2, June 1992, 230–38.

11. *Ibid.*

12. "A New Learning Agenda: Putting People First," Institute for Research on Learning, 1993.

13. Clancey, 12–13.

14. Bellah et al., *Habits of the Heart,* 152.

15. "A New Learning Agenda," 3–4.

16. Alan M. Webber, "What's So New About the New Economy?" *Harvard Business Review,* Jan.–Feb. 1993, 28.

Chapter 7: Attaining and Sustaining Proficiency

1. John Dewey, "Body and Mind," in Dewey, *Intelligence in the Modern World,* ed. Joseph Ratner (New York: The Modern Library, 1939), 605.
2. *Ibid.*
3. John Dewey, *Interest and Effort in Education,* in Ratner, 607.
4. *Ibid.,* 607–8.
5. Thurow, *Head to Head,* 275.
6. Stanley E. Malcolm, "Reengineering Corporate Training," *Training,* August 1992, 58.
7. Floyd Kemske and Nancy J. Weingarten, "A Memo for the Future: Computer Training in 1999," *CBT Directions,* December 1989, 29–32.
8. Gloria Gery, *Electronic Performance Support Systems,* 18–19.
9. Malcolm, 58. See also Charles D. Winslow and James C. Caldwell, "Integrated Performance Support: A New Educational Paradigm," *Information System Management,* Spring 1992, Vol. 9, No. 2.
10. Anthony Patrick Carnevale, *America and the New Economy,* 165–82.
11. Gerry Puterbaugh, Marc Rosenberg, and Robert Sofman, "Performance Support Tools: A Step Beyond Training," *Performance and Instruction,* Nov./Dec. 1989, 1.
12. Gery, *Electronic Performance Support Systems,* 21.
13. Source: Conference of the Chicago Chamber of Commerce.
14. Quoted in "Star Techs: The Next Generation," *Wall Street Journal,* May 24, 1993. On the importance of failure in learning, see Schank, *Dynamic Memory: A Theory of Reminding and Learning in Computers and People* (Cambridge, England: Cambridge University Press, 1982), especially Chapter 3.
15. *Ibid.*
16. Gery, *Electronic Performance Support Systems,* 35.
17. Ruth Clark, "EPSS—Look Before You Leap: Some Cautions About the Applications of Electronic Performance Support Systems," *Performance & Instruction,* May/June 1992.
18. Malcolm, "Reengineering Corporate Training," 59.
19. Roger C. Schank, with Peter G. Childers, *The Cognitive Computer: On Language, Learning, and Artificial Intelligence* (Reading, MA: Addison-Wesley Publishing Company, 1984), 186.
20. Cited in Alan M. Webber, "What's So New About the New Economy?" *Harvard Business Review,* 29.
21. Quinn, *Intelligent Enterprise,* 254.
22. Quoted in "Star Techs: The Next Generation," *Wall Street Journal,* May 24, 1993.
23. William J. Clancey, "Why Today's Computers Don't Learn the Way People Do," in P. A. Flach and R. A. Meersamn, *Future Directions in Artificial Intelligence* (Amsterdam: North-Holland, 1991), 53–62.

24. Source: Robert E. Ornstein, *The Psychology of Consciousness* (Penguin Books, 1972), 41.
25. Gery, *Electronic Performance Support Systems,* 20.
26. Quoted in Beverly Geber, "Goodbye Classrooms (Redux)," *Training,* January 1990, 28.
27. Geber, "Goodbye Classrooms," 29.
28. Gery, *Electronic Performance Support Systems,* 18.
29. Geber, "Goodbye Classrooms," 32.
30. See Winslow and Caldwell, "Integrated Performance Support," 77.
31. *Ibid.*
32. Alex Kass, Robin Burke, Eli Blevis, and Mary Williamson, "The GuSS Project: Integrating Instruction and Practice Through Guided Social Simulation," Technical Report #34, September 1992, The Institute for the Learning Sciences, Northwestern University, 1.
33. On this point, see Allan Collins, John Seeley Brown, and Susan E. Newman, "Cognitive Apprenticeship: Teaching the Crafts of Reading, Writing, and Mathematics," in L. B. Resnick, ed., *Knowing, Learning, and Instruction: Essays in Honor of Robert Glaser* (Hinsdale, NJ: Lawrence Erlbaum Associates, 1989).
34. Kass et al., 1.
35. See Roger C. Schank, *Teaching Architectures,* Technical Report #3, The Institute for the Learning Sciences, Northwestern University.
36. Kass et al., 2.
37. Kass et al., 2.

Chapter 8: Doing More with Less

1. Robert Reich, *The Next American Frontier* (New York: Times Books, a Division of Random House, Inc., 1983), 143–44. Robert M. Tamasko quotes this story as well, in his book *Downsizing,* noting that many companies have it even worse than this drillmaker. Six, seven, or eight layers of management between salespeople and the chief executive are common. And three- and four-year waits for products are common, as well. (*Downsizing: Reshaping the Corporation for the Future* [New York: Amacom, a division of American Management Associaiton, 1987], 7.)
2. An important research project into European human resources trends has recently been conducted by Andersen Consulting, led by our colleague Massimo Merlino from Milan. The project, published under the name "Europeople," was intended to provide a clear and comprehensive vision of the main factors governing the evolution of Human Resources Management in Europe over the next decade.
3. See Walter Kiechel III, "How We Will Work in the Year 2000," *Fortune,* May 1993, 39.
4. See Tomasko, *Downsizing,* especially Chapter 2.
5. Reed M. Powell, "A Point of View: Doing More with Less," *National Productivity Review,* Winter 1990, Vol. 9, No. 1, page 1.

6. Quinn, *Intelligent Enterprise,* 113.
7. *Ibid.,* 116.
8. Hammer and Champy, *Reengineering the Corporation,* 47–48.
9. Stephen Franklin, "Layoff Fever Spreads to Robust Firms," *Chicago Tribune,* Sept. 12, 1993.
10. G. B. Trudeau, "Doonesbury," Universal Press Syndicate, June 20, 1993.
11. Thurow, *Head to Head,* 137.
12. *Ibid.,* 138.
13. *Ibid.,* 139.
14. Interview with Stephen Roach, "The Redemption of the 'Inept,' " *Information Week,* April 19, 1993, 30.
15. Esther Dyson, "Job Losses Are Mounting: Good News?" *Forbes,* March 9, 1992, 104.
16. *Ibid.*
17. *Ibid.*
18. Steb Fisher, "Cutting Costs or Re-building Business?" *European Management Journal,* March 1993, 74–79.
19. Quoted in "Star Techs: The Next Generation," *Wall Street Journal,* May 24, 1993.
20. For a good discussion of alternatives to layoffs, see Tomasko, 199–215.
21. Fisher, *European Management Journal,* 74–79.
22. Tomasko, *Downsizing,* 191–92.
23. James E. Liebig, *Business Ethics: Profiles in Civic Virtue* (Golden, CO: Fulcrum Publishing, 1990, 1991), 113.
24. *Ibid.*
25. Fisher, 74–79.
26. *Ibid.* Stephen R. Covey speaks of this in terms of a "Scarcity Mentality." He sets forth an "Abundance Mentality" as a crucial trait of the "Win/Win" paradigm of human interaction. See *The 7 Habits of Highly Effective People* (New York: Fireside Books, 1990), 219.
27. Quoted in Steb Fisher.
28. *Ibid.*
29. Richard M. Krieg, "The New Era: Workers as Assets," *Chicago Tribune,* July 23, 1993, Section 1, page 15.
30. *Ibid.*
31. Boyett and Conn, 18.
32. Patricia Sellers, "Why Bigger Is Badder at Sears," *Fortune,* Dec. 5, 1988, 79.
33. Tomasko, 22.
34. Jon Pepper, "The Horizontal Organization," *Information Week,* Aug. 17, 1992, 32.
35. *Ibid.,* 32–33.
36. Quinn, *Intelligent Enterprise,* 113.
37. *Ibid.,* 118.
38. Pepper, "The Horizontal Organization," 37.

39. Quoted in Pepper, "The Horizontal Organization," 36.
40. Boyett and Conn, *Workplace 2000,* 37.
41. For much of the information contained in this discussion of groupware, we are indebted to Beth Marcia Lange, an Associate Scientist with Andersen Consulting's Center for Strategic Technology Research (CSTaR).
42. We are indebted to Jim Treleaven of Battelle Venture Partners as our content expert for this task.

Chapter 9: Integrated Performance Support for Everyone

1. *Workforce 2000: Work and Workers for the Twenty-first Century* (Indianapolis, IN: Hudson Institute, June 1987), xix-xx. We should note that there has been criticism of aspects of the Workforce 2000 study. Political economist Pat Choate has argued that U.S. companies will have less difficulty recruiting skilled workers than predicted in Workforce 2000 because there will be less demand for them, due to the decreased dominance of U.S.-headquartered companies. (See "What's Wrong with Workforce 2000?" *HR Magazine,* August 1991, 38–42.) The bulk of criticism, however, has centered on misleading interpretations of the study, not on the data itself. See "Debunking the Workforce 2000 Myths," *Human Resources Professional,* Winter 1992, 37–40; also, "A New Perspective for Tomorrow's Workforce," *Industry Week,* May 6, 1991, 6–11.
2. *Ibid.,* xiii.
3. Source: McKinsey & Co. Cited in Tom Peters, "Global Thoughts for Information Age Summer," *Chicago Tribune,* July 19, 1993.
4. Drucker, *Post-Capitalist Society,* 8.
5. William H. Miller, "A New Perspective for Tomorrow's Workforce," *Industry Week,* May 6, 1991, 6–11.
6. Thurow, *Head to Head,* 276–77.
7. Jack E. Bowsher, *Educating America: Lessons Learned in the Nation's Corporations* (New York: John Wiley & Sons, 1989), 184.
8. Bowsher, 184.
9. Liebig, *Business Ethics,* 2.
10. Drucker, 97.
11. Quoted in James Daly, "Hallmark Offers Do-It-Yourself Cards," *Computerworld,* June 14, 1993, 52.

Chapter 10: Making Change Work

1. Copyright 1989, Universal City Studios. Gorden Company Production, Executive Producer, Brian Frankish. Director by Phil Alden Robinson.
2. E. Huse and T. G. Cummings, *Organizational Development and Change* (St. Paul, MN: West, 1985), 351.
3. Robert L. Laud, "Cultural Change and Corporate Strategy," in *The Change Man-*

agement Handbook: A Road Map to Corporate Transformation, ed. Lance A. Berger and Martin J. Sikora, with Dorothy R. Berger (Burr Ridge, IL: Irwin Professional Publishing, 1993), 300.

4. Thomas J. Peters and Robert H. Waterman, *In Search of Excellence* (New York: Harper & Row, 1982), 75.

5. Sources: American Production and Inventory Control Society, Society of Manufacturing Engineers, Office of Technology Assessment.

6. M. Beer, *Harvard Business Review,* Nov.-Dec. 1990.

7. Huse and Cummings, 352.

8. Laud, 297.

9. Charles Fombrun, "Of Tribes and Witch Doctors: The Anthropologist's View," in Melissa A. Berman, ed., *Corporate Culture and Change: Highlights of a Conference* (New York: The Conference Board, 1986), 7.

10. For the discussion of the strategic and human resources implications of IPS, we are indebted to our colleague Donald M. Jastrebski.

11. Thomas A. Stewart, "Reengineering: The Hot New Managing Tool," *Fortune,* August 23, 1993, 41.

12. *Ibid.,* 42.

13. *Ibid.,* 43.

14. On this point see, for example, Richard Y. Chang, "When TQM Goes Nowhere," *Training and Development,* January 1993.

15. Jeff Moad, "Does Reengineering Really Work?" *Datamation,* Aug. 1, 1993, 22.

16. *Harvard Business Review,* Jul.-Aug. 1990, 104–112.

17. Hammer and Champy, 31.

18. *Ibid.,* 71.

19. *Ibid.*

20. Tom Peters, *Thriving on Change,* 621.

21. Hammer and Champy, 72.

22. Peters, 622–23.

23. For much of the description of ORCA, we are indebted to Brian M. Slator and Ray Bareiss, "Incremental Reminding: The Case-Based Elaboration and Interpretation of Complex Problem Situations," The Institute for the Learning Sciences, unpublished paper.

Chapter 11: Learning Organizations and Growth Organizations

1. See, for example, the discussion of the product life cycle theory in Michael Porter, *Competitive Strategy,* Chapter 8.

2. See most especially Peter Senge, *The Fifth Discipline.*

3. Daniel Quinn Mills and Bruce Friesen, "The Learning Organization," *European Management Journal,* June 1992, Vol. 10, No. 2, 146–56. Peter Senge's short definition of the "learning organization" is one "that is continually expanding its capacity to create its future" (Senge, 14).

4. See "How We Will Work in the Year 2000," *Fortune,* May 17, 1993.
5. Boyett and Conn, *Workplace 2000,* 50.
6. See Michael Crichton, *Jurassic Park* (New York: Alfred A. Knopf, 1990).
7. Boyett and Conn, *Workplace 2000,* 41.
8. Quinn, *Intelligent Enterprise,* 257.
9. Quinn, 257.
10. Quinn, 259.
11. Boyett and Conn, *Workplace 2000,* 72–73.
12. *Workplace 2000,* 73.
13. *Workplace 2000,* 74.
14. Richard Dalton, "Lose the Sweatshop Mentality," *Information Week,* July 5, 1993, 63.
15. *Workplace 2000,* 79.
16. Senge, 140.
17. Senge, 141.
18. Senge, 143.
19. Quinn, 254.
20. Mills and Friesen, 146–56.
21. For much of the information here on the Knowledge Xchange™ knowledge management system, we are indebted to Charles M. Paulk, Jr. and other colleagues in Andersen Consulting's CIO Organization.

Chapter 12: Working and Living in the Infocosm

1. See, for example, the interview with John Sculley in *USA Today,* Feb. 11, 1993.
2. For the major concepts and the details relating to Infocosm presented in this chapter, we are indebted to our colleagues Arnim E. Whisler III and Andersen Consulting's Strategic Services Group; Joe K. Carter, who heads up Andersen Consulting's Center for Strategic Technology in Palo Alto, CA; and Alan A. Burgess, Managing Partner of Andersen Consulting's Worldwide Telecommunications Practice.
3. In Irene Greif, ed., *Computer-Supported Cooperative Work* (San Mateo, CA: Morgan Kaufmann, 1988).
4. President Clinton himself has noted that Vice-President Gore is the only person holding national office who can talk about the "gestalt of the gigabit." See *Scientific American,* May 1993, 122.
5. Roger Karraker, "Highways of the Mind," *Whole Earth Review,* Spring 1991, 7.
6. *Washington Post,* May 25, 1993, D5.
7. George Gilder, "The Issaquah Miracle," *Forbes ASAP Supplement,* June 7, 1993, 122.
8. Source: Veronis, Suhler and Associates.
9. Quoted in Karraker, 8.
10. William H. Davidow and Michael S. Malone, *The Virtual Corporation: Struc-*

turing and Revitalizing the Corporation for the 21st Century (New York: Harper-Business, 1992), 4.

Epilogue: The Hunter-Gatherers of the Knowledge Economy

1. Reich, *The Work of Nations,* 171–72.
2. See Stan Davis and Bill Davidson, *2020 Vision* (New York: Simon & Schuster, 1991).
3. Quinn, *Intelligent Enterprise,* 3–4.
4. Quinn, 21.
5. Drucker, *Post-Capitalist Society,* 183.
6. Reich, 315.

GLOSSARY

Add-on. A type of IPS implementation where performance support functions are "added on" after business applications have been built and installed. An authoring system generally provides the vehicle for add-on implementation. See Chapter 3.

Advisory Services. One of the six IPS services: it functions as a coach or advisor. It interprets job activity and, when appropriate, offers alternatives and suggestions to meet the needs of the knowledge worker. See Chapter 3.

Affordances. The fundamental properties of an object that determine how the object should or can be used. If an object has clear affordances, people know intuitively what to do with it. A zipper, for example, needs no explanation. As the term relates to good interface design, it means that within a graphical user interface, or GUI, a particular sign or icon should clearly communicate the affordances; that is, it should clearly indicate what is to be done with it. If the worker is to click on a button to perform an action, the graphic must be designed so workers know they should click on it. See Chapter 4.

Agent. One who acts on behalf of another. In a computer-based environment, an agent is a software function programmed to perform certain tasks and make certain choices on behalf of the worker. Because the agent is often depicted graphically within the system interface in a human-like fashion, the interaction of worker with system becomes more natural and intuitive. See Guide.

Architecture. The organized collection of hardware and/or software components and their interrelationships that make up a business solution. Components might include servers, workstations, operating systems, database management system(s), communications software, application code, report writers, and so forth.

Ask System. A type of system that allows a person to ask a question, either by choosing from a list or by keystroke input; to this question, the system generates a possible answer in a variety of presentation modes, from text to a multimedia presentation with full-motion video. See Chapters 3 and 10 for examples of Ask Systems.

Bandwidth. The range of communications frequencies assigned to a service or over which a device can operate. See discussion of the Infocosm in Chapter 12.

Benchmarking. The process whereby one action, product, or service becomes the reference point from which similar actions, products, or services are measured.

BPS. Bits per Second. A measure of the amount of data that can be transmitted via a communications line or modem.

Built-in. A type of IPS implementation where performance support functions are developed or "built in" as an integral part of business applications with a common user interface. See Chapter 3.

Business Process Reengineering. The redesign of organizational operations or processes to accommodate or anticipate marketplace, workforce, or technological change and to achieve market leadership. See Chapter 10.

Case-Based Reasoning (CBR). A technique for solving new problems by adapting solutions that solved old problems. Cases are indexed and structured to present information including situation descriptions, similarities and differences of cases, and other unique attributes relevant to specific problems.

CBT. Computer-Based Training. An approach to workforce training that delivers traditional, modular training in an electronic form. Contrast with "granular" delivery of training in a performance system. See Chapters 5 and 7.

Center for Strategic Technology. A technology demonstration and educational center of Anderson Consulting, located in Palo Alto, CA. See Chapter 12.

Change Management. Managing the human dimensions of technological, strategic, workforce, and marketplace change.

Client/Server Computing. A type of cooperative processing: a requester-server message approach to computing. In client/server processing, the requester asks for some type of service. The server provides information or supports that request. The communication between the client and the server occurs through messages. The client is usually an intelligent workstation.

Cognitive Sciences. That branch of study that focuses on human knowing, awareness, judgment, and learning.

Computer-Supported Cooperative Work (CSCW). An interdisciplinary field of study focusing on the potential of technology to support the work of teams and groups. See also Groupware. Computer-Supported Cooperative Work is discussed in Chapter 8.

Context-Sensitive Help. Supporting information for a worker at an information system that is matched to particular aspects of an application or to particular actions being performed. The most powerful or desirable form of context-sensitive help is when workers do not need to go to a separate directory of help, but can access a particular granule of supporting information tailored to one specific action or item.

Cooperative Processing. A form of computer processing in which one particular application is partitioned between two or more hardware platforms. Computing that requires two or more distinct processors to complete a transaction, but that relies on mutual data and interaction. See Client/Server Computing and Distributed Processing.

Coordination Technology. Software that supports group work—allows teams to share information and coordinate schedules, and facilitates the process by which team members contribute to collaborative projects. See Groupware.

Courseware. The generic term used to describe training or educational software and its associated documentation.

CSTaR. Center for Strategic Technology and Research. A technology research organization within Andersen Consulting, located in Chicago, IL. See Chapter 8.

Customization. The extent to which performance support is tailored or "customized" based on the attributes of the work (work context) and the worker or workgroup profile.

Data. Symbols that serve as input and which, when acted upon by human beings, become information. A string of numbers can be "data," but these numbers need additional context before they can become "information." See Information and Knowledge.

Data Modeling. An activity that defines the organizational structure of data within a computer system.

Deskilling. A theory, first advanced in the 1950s, which argued that advanced skills are required when a new technology is introduced, but that the skills necessary to operate it will fall as the technology matures. The theory is now disputed.

Desktop Metaphor. In human-computer interface design, a metaphor that uses a human being's intuitive sense of how to order and operate on items and work priorities on a desktop to order and operate on system functions. See Chapter 4.

Distributed Processing. An approach to systems architecture in which the data for a single application's use are located on more than one computer. See also Cooperative Processing and Client/Server Computing.

Dumb Terminal. A nonprogrammable computer terminal that only accesses a host computer. Contrast with Intelligent Terminal.

Education. As opposed to "training" and "learning," education represents the symbiotic process whereby learner and teacher participate together in the advancement of knowledge. One of the effects of Integrated Performance Support is to blur some of the traditional distinctions among these words, however, as all three become more self-directed.

EPSS. Electronic Performance Support Systems. An electronic environment that supports knowledge workers in the performance of their jobs. EPSS is essential for Integrated Performance Support. The key difference is the emphasis of the IPS concept on integration of performance support services with business applications and the delivery of support based on work and worker attributes. See Chapter 2.

Expert System. A computer system design based on rules (e.g., "if-then" statements) to emulate a human expert to help knowledge workers solve problems. See also Rule-Based Reasoning.

Granule. A small chunk of reference or training targeted to provide support for a specific task or objective of a knowledge worker. See Chapter 7.

Graphical User Interface (GUI). A human-computer interaction style that uses icons, metaphors, and pictures instead of command words to represent objects and actions. Graphical user interfaces enable advanced interaction techniques such as direct manipulation and the use of metaphors. See Chapter 4.

Groupware. Software that is designed for use in a network and serves a group of workers on a related project. Examples include electronic conferencing systems, group editing, and workflow management. See Chapter 8.

GUI. See Graphical User Interface.

Guide. An autonomous software entity, generally represented in human-like form (as a cartoon drawing, for example), that supports worker performance at the computer system in a variety of ways. A guide may, for example, alert a worker to relevant supporting information or may aid the worker in navigating through the system. Guides are discussed in Chapter 4, and other examples are found in Chapters 7 and 9.

HCI. See Human-Computer Interaction.

Human-Computer Interaction. (1) The way in which people interact with computer systems. Human-Computer Interaction principles are applied to design systems with intuitive and transparent "user" interfaces. These principles are discussed in Chapter 4. (2) Within the IPS model, the Human-Computer Interaction layer focuses on making the interface between the human and the computer intuitive and transparent so that workers focus on performing the work, not on using the computer system. The HCI component of the IPS model is discussed in Chapter 3.

Human Metaphor. A philosophy of human-computer interaction that builds upon our intuitive understanding of the ways in which humans interact with each other. See Chapter 4.

Hypermedia. An associative, nonlinear means of navigating through information in more than one type of media—multimedia (e.g., text graphics, audio, video).

Hypertext. An associative, nonlinear means of navigating through information in textual media. Workers can navigate by means of links between related segments of text, usually by clicking on underlined text (which signifies that a link exists).

Icon. A small pictorial representation of an object, such as an application, file, business object, or disk drive, that is used in graphical user interfaces (GUIs). See Chapter 4.

ILS. See Institute for the Learning Sciences.

Imaging. The recording of pictures, signatures, forms, and so forth, into a machine format.

Infocosm. The electronic, interactive network of the future. Also referred to as the "information superhighway." See Chapter 12.

Information. Data that has been supporting context to transform it into intelligible symbols. "70%" is an example of data; "70% chance of rain" is an example of information.

Institute for the Learning Sciences (ILS). A research and educational institution affiliated with Northwestern University in Evanston, IL. Andersen Consulting is a founding sponsor. See Chapter 7.

Integrated Performance Support™(IPS). An organizational concept and a systems design strategy. As a concept, IPS focuses organizations at the level of knowledge worker performance, linking worker performance with overall organizational performance. As a systems design strategy, IPS results in performance systems that enable the workforce to do their work better by providing advice, tools, reference, and training on demand at the point of need. Integrated Performance, or IPS, is Andersen Consulting's response to address workforce performance challenges. See also EPSS. The logical model of Integrated Performance Support is discussed in Chapters 2 and 3.

Integration. In the IPS context, integration has three aspects: (1) integration of the IPS services, (2) integration of multiple technologies into one system (e.g., multimedia: text, graphics, audio, video, image), and (3) integration of IPS services and multiple technologies with multiple applications.

Intelligent Terminal. In contrast to the dumb terminal, the intelligent terminal can be programmed independently of the main computer and also operate to a substantial extent independently of the main computer. Instead of sending its data from the terminal to the computer for processing, the processing power is brought to the source of the data—that is, the terminal.

Interaction. (1) The dynamic process by which the worker communicates with a computer system in an intuitive and/or transparent fashion. (2) The dynamic process by which various IPS services and applications interact with each other. See Human-Computer Interaction.

Interaction Protocol. The limits or expectations that guide a worker's interaction within a system application. The idea of interaction protocols builds upon our natural understandings of the different ways we interact with people and things in our lives. For example, we expect a particular kind of interaction with a telephone operator, another kind of interaction with a service station attendant. See Chapter 4.

Interface. The primary point of contact between a computer system and a human being.

Job Aid Services. One of the six IPS services: it functions as an assistant to the worker. It provides access to automated tools and techniques that simplify and automate routine tasks performed by the knowledge worker. See Chapter 3.

Knowledge. The condition of awareness or understanding developed through education and experience. It is information or intelligence stored in memory that can be retrieved and applied. (Contrast with Data and Information.) See Chapter 6.

Knowledge-Based Systems. A development within the field of Artificial Intelligence, working from the point of the limitations of expert systems. Knowledge-based systems embody within them general forms of reasoning and rules (case-based and rule-based reasoning), which then permit the system to analyze a new situation or process, finding similarities to existing cases or relevance to existing rules.

Knowledge Economy. An economy in which the means of production is knowledge. See Introduction and Epilogue.

Knowledge Management System. A type of enterprise-wide system that facilitates communications within an organization. The system can capture, store, and deliver knowledge and experience to knowledge workers. See Chapter 11.

Knowledge Worker. Someone who interprets and applies information to create and provide value-adding solutions, and to make informed recommendations. A worker whose job depends on the processing and use of information in a continuously changing work environment. The responsibility to make recommendations and provide value-added solutions is what differentiates a knowledge worker from a "service worker." See Introduction.

Knowledge Worker Services. One of the six IPS services: it functions as a "human resources coordinator." It maintains information relevant to workers or workgroups to customize the support provided and adjust the performance system to meet the needs of knowledge workers. See Chapter 3.

Learning. "An enduring change in behavior or in the capacity to behave in a given fashion, which results from practice or other forms of experience." Source: D. H. Schunk, *Learning Theories: An Educational Perspective* (New York: Macmillan, p. 2). See Chapters 7 and 11.

Mainframe-Based System. A hardware environment in which many existing applications built in the 1970s and 1980s were designed and implemented using a dumb terminal (e.g., 3270) that has a display limited to text and numeric figures.

Manipulation. In human-computer interaction theory, direct manipulation is the ability to work with data and information, and to move that information around. This is also referred to as "drag-and-drop." GUIs have made direct manipulation easier and more intuitive. See Chapter 3.

Metaphor. Natural models allowing persons working with a system to extend the familiarity they have with concrete objects and experiences to the level of abstract concepts. See Chapter 4.

Moment of Value. (1) In the realm of customer service, the time when consumer and provider come together, and the provider delivers value to the consumer. (2) In terms of general performance philosophies, the optimal performance by a knowledge worker at any point in time. See Chapter 1.

Multimedia. The capability to display multiple forms of communicative mediums, such as data, text, photographs, images, graphics, animation, audio, and full-motion video. See Hypermedia.

Natural Categories. A concept popularized by psychologist Eleanor Rosch in the 1970s. There is an intuitive sense by which we group concepts and things: for example, a school, an office complex, and an apartment complex would naturally fall into the category of "building." In human-computer interaction theory, good interface design builds upon a worker's innate understanding of things, or upon "natural categories," to plan the interaction. See Chapter 4.

Navigation. The dynamic interaction process concerned with how the worker moves or navigates through the different parts of a computer system. See Chapter 3.

Organizational Change. The ability of a company or organization to take change in one area—in strategy, technology, processes, or workforce—and move that change with all its ramifications throughout the other areas. See Chapter 10.

Performance. When applied to a knowledge worker, performance is the complete accomplishment of specific job objectives by taking the right action(s) with no errors or defects. According to the "performance model," performance is dependent on worker ability, motivation, and context or environment. See Chapter 1.

Performance-Centered Design. Design of computer systems/software that supports the unique needs of each worker and provides support services (advice, tools, reference, training) at the time and the point of need. See Chapter 2.

Performance Gap. The disparity between optimal or desired knowledge worker performance and actual knowledge worker performance.

Performance Model. A model developed by Andersen Consulting to portray the elements that make up optimum performance by a knowledge worker. Optimum performance takes into account (1) context; (2) ability; and (3) motivation. See Chapter 1.

Performance Support Controller. A physical or logical architecture layer that serves as the steering mechanism that monitors, controls, and coordinates IPS services in a performance system. See Chapter 3.

Performance System. An implementation of the IPS concept in a system, built to transact business across multiple business functions by incorporating the IPS services. Performance systems are designed to support the dynamic relationships among the work, the worker, and the support needed to attain and then sustain high levels of organizational and workforce performance. See Chapters 1, 2, and 3.

Post-Capitalist Society. A term most closely associated with Peter Drucker's book of the same name. According to Drucker, industrialized nations have crossed a divide from a capitalist society to a "knowledge society." See also Knowledge Economy. See Introduction and Epilogue.

Presentation. The primary display of data and information within a system interface. Powerful and effective interfaces, such as those found in performance systems, provide an appropriate simulation of the overall picture of the work, represent access to multiple sources of information with a common look and feel, and provide a picture of the capabilities of the system. See Chapter 4.

Priming. In human-computer interaction, priming is related to the concept of "natural categories." An icon of a file drawer, for example, builds on our natural understanding of what we can do with files and a storage cabinet for those files. We are thus preprogrammed or "primed" to know what to do with that icon.

PS. Performance Support. See Integrated Performance Support (IPS).

PSS. Performance Support System. See EPSS.

Real Time. In a performance system environment, system facilities and functionalities that occur at the moment of need. Performance feedback within a performance system, for example, is always up-to-date, or "real time," not based upon figures from a previous month's report.

Reengineering. See Business Process Reengineering.

Reference Services. One of the six IPS services: it functions as a "librarian." It provides context-sensitive reference information and knowledge to help meet the needs of knowledge workers. It also serves as the basic reference resource by which knowledge workers can do self-initiated research. See Chapter 3.

Rule-Based Reasoning. A technique for solving problems by identifying "if-then" statements sequenced to represent knowledge. See also Expert System.

Seamless. Unnoticeable, transparent. Performance systems provide supporting services to knowledge workers without them being aware that they are moving from one service to another, or from one application or level of support to another.

Semiotics. The science that studies the relationships among signs, symbols, and the things represented by them.

Service Worker. Someone who interprets and applies information to complete assigned tasks correctly, and to make informed decisions. Contrast with Knowledge Worker.

Stand-alone. A type of IPS implementation where performance support functions are developed independently from business applications and provided as "stand-alone" support applications. See Chapter 3.

Tailorability. The ability within a performance system to customize aspects of interface presentation or aspects of performance support to the unique needs and desires of a particular knowledge worker.

Taylor, Frederick Winslow (1856–1915). A pioneer business thinker of the early 1900s, responsible for revolutionizing processes of the industrial economy. He espoused worker specialization as a means of gaining efficiency.

Technology Assimilation. The process by which the workforce accommodates continuous technological change into their performance environment. See Organizational Change.

TIM. See Total Information Management.

Time Compression. The elimination of non-value-adding time in task completion or business processes.

Time to Proficiency. The amount of time it takes for workers to learn the skills necessary to perform their jobs most effectively and efficiently. See Chapter 7.

Total Information Management. A prototype performance system for the banking industry, supporting commercial lenders. See Chapter 3.

Total Quality Management. A current strategy in the marketplace to focus the workforce on continuous improvement in quality of products and services, for the purpose of delivering customer satisfaction.

Training. Organizational-directed education aimed at improving and augmenting workforce skills. See also Education and Learning. See Chapter 7.

Training Services. One of the six IPS services: it functions as a "tutor." It helps the knowledge worker acquire new skills and knowledge in the context of performing a job or task. See Chapter 3.

Transaction-Based Systems. Traditional, usually mainframe-based systems designed around particular actions or transactions to be carried out by a system "user." The transaction is the object, rather than the business itself. Contrast with Performance-Centered Design. See Chapter 2.

Transparent Computing. Interaction with computer systems/software that is so natural that a person comes to forget that he or she is even working within a computing environment. In transparent computing, a worker does not need extensive system or application training.

Ubiquitous Computing. Computing that is omnipresent, supporting a variety of tasks, often in a manner such that it is not perceived as computing. The type of computing in the modern automobile is an example.

Usability. The ease with which a worker can interact with a system.

User-Centered Design. A systems design/development approach that focuses on the system user rather than system functionality. Similar to, but not as advanced as, Performance-Centered Design.

Virtual Reality. A computer interface that is a simulation of an actual spatial environment, of the real working or playing environment of a person.

Wizard. A software feature of Microsoft Excel that acts as an assistant, helping the worker create charts or perform other work by proceduralizing and simplifying the task.

Workforce 2000. A 1987 study done by the Hudson Institute in Indianapolis, IN, focusing on changing workforce demographics in the late twentieth century.

Work Profile Services. One of the six IPS services: it functions as a "workflow coordinator." It identifies workflows, job tasks, specific procedures, and other work-related information to provide customized support to knowledge workers. See Chapter 3.

Workstation. The term "workstation" is often used with two slightly different meanings: (1) Only high-performance computers that are usually targeted for scientific computing, complex graphics, or heavy analytical processing. (2) Any dedicated computer from a simple PC up to a high-end, high-performance machine. See Intelligent Terminal.

BIBLIOGRAPHY

**Performance, Integrated Performance Support, and Related Technologies
(Chapters 1, 2, and 3)**

Andersen Consulting. *Trends in Information Technology* (4th edition): *The Challenge of Business Integration.* Andersen Consulting, 1991.

Arenberg, Thomas. "Firms Trying New Ways to Increase Productivity." *Milwaukee Sentinel,* October 5, 1992, p. 11B.

Barletta, Ralph. "An Introduction to Case-Based Reasoning." *AI Expert,* August 1991, pp. 43–49.

Bentley, Trevor. "Performance Support Systems." *Management Accounting,* May 1990, p. 12.

Braasch, Bill. "Performance Support Systems Helping Business." *Computing Canada,* February 1990, p. 23.

Bramer, William L., and Ghenno Senbetta. "The New Wave of Performance Support." *Chief Information Officer Journal,* September/October 1993, pp. 16–17.

Brownsmith, Keith. "Improving Organizational Performance with Performance Technology." *Educational Technology,* May 1990.

Carlisle, Kenneth E., and Philip D. Coulter. "The Performance Technology of Job Aids." *Educational Technology,* May 1990, pp. 26–31.

Carr, Clay. "Performance Support Systems: A New Horizon for Expert Systems." *AI Expert,* May 1992, pp. 39–44.

———. "PSS! Help When You Need It." *Training and Development,* June 1992, pp. 31–38.

———. "Performance Support Systems: The Next Step." *Performance & Instruction,* February 1992, pp. 23–26.

Clark, Ruth. "EPSS—Look Before You Leap: Some Cautions About the Applications of Electronic Performance Support Systems." *Performance & Instruction,* May/June 1992, pp. 22–25.

———. "EPSS: A Book Review." *Performance & Instruction,* May/June 1992, pp. 36–37.

Diamondstone, Jan. "Performance Support: Let's Get Literal." *The CBT Digest,* Fall 1990, pp. 20–23.

Drucker, Peter F. "The New Productivity Challenge." *Harvard Business Review,* November/December 1991, pp. 69–79.

Druckman, Daniel, and Robert A. Bjork. *In the Mind's Eye: Enhancing Human Performance.* Washington, D.C.: National Academy Press, 1991.

Dublin, Lance. "Learn While You Work." *Computerworld,* August 30, 1993, pp. 81–82.

Dyson, Esther. "Performance Support: Worker Information Systems." *Release 1.0,* August 24, 1993.

Filipczak, Bob and Jack Gordon. "Electronic Performance Support: More Than User-Friendly." *Training,* October 1991, pp. 88–90.

Florian, Vicki, and Isabel Barros. "Using a Knowledge-Based System Shell." *CBT Directions,* July 1989, pp. 30–31.

Geber, Beverly. "Help! The Rise of Performance Support Systems." *Training,* December 1991, pp. 23–29.

Gery, Gloria. *Electronic Performance Support Systems.* Cambridge, MA: Ziff Institute, 1991.

———. "Closing the Gap." *Authorware Magazine,* First Quarter 1990, pp. 15–21.

———. "Issues in Computer-Based Reference." *CBT Directions,* March 1991, pp. 10–19.

———. "Electronic Performance Support Systems." *CBT Directions,* June 1989, pp. 12–15.

———. "The Quest for Electronic Performance Support Systems." *CBT Directions,* July 1989, pp. 21–23.

———. "Solve a Real Problem." *CBT Directions,* November 1990.

Hronec, Steven M. *Vital Signs: Using Quality, Time, and Cost Performance Measurements to Chart Your Company's Future.* New York: AMACOM, 1993.

Ku, Xian Hong. "Supporting Performance." *Business Times,* May 17, 1993.

Legent Corporation and Ziff Institute. *Why Performance Support?* Legent Corporation, 1992.

Lemmons, Larry. "PSS Design: Getting Past That First Step." *CBT Directions,* February 1991, pp. 32–35.

McCarthy, Michael J. *Mastering the Information Age: A Course in Working Smarter, Thinking Better, and Learning Faster.* New York: St. Martin's Press, 1991.

McConnell, Vicki C., and Karl William Koch. *Computerizing the Corporation: The Intimate Link Between People and Machines.* New York: Van Nostrand Reinhold, 1990.

Parker, Stephen. "The Performance Support System." *IT Training,* October/November 1991, pp. 25–27.

Puterbaugh, Gerry. "Performance Support Tools: Theory and an Example. The AT&T Training Consultant." *Journal of Interactive Instruction Development,* Winter 1990, pp. 23–25.

Puryear, C. Rudy, and John D. Rollins. "The Moment of Value: Technology Evolves to Deliver Strategic Results." *Outlook.* Andersen Consulting, 1993.

Raybould, Barry. "A Case Study in Performance Support." *CBT Directions,* October 1990, pp. 22–31.

———. "A Modular Approach to Electronic Support." *Data Training,* March/April 1992, pp. 24–26.

———. "Solving Human Performance Support Problems with Computers." *Performance & Instruction,* November/December 1990, pp. 4–14.

Rettig, Marc. "Cooperative Software." *Communications of the ACM,* April 1993, pp. 23–28.

Rosenberg, Marc. "Performance Technology: Working the System." *Training,* February 1990, pp. 43–48.

Rossett, Allison. "Electronic Job Aids." *Data Training,* June 1991, pp. 24–27.

Rummler, Geary, and Alan P. Brache. *Improving Performance: Managing the White Space on the Organization Chart.* San Francisco: Jossey-Bass Publishers, 1990.

Scales, Glenda Rose, and Chia-Shing Yang. "Perspective on Electronic Performance Support Systems." Paper presented at the Annual Meeting of the Eastern Educational Research Association, February 1993.

Senbetta, Ghenno. "Helping Workers Perform." *Stada News* (Singapore), March–June 1993.

Sisson, Gary R., and Richard A. Swanson. "Improving Work Performance." *Educational Technology,* May 1990, pp. 16–20.

Stevens, George. "Applying Hypermedia for Performance Improvement." *Performance & Instruction,* July 1989, pp. 42–50.

Swartz, Connie, and Lloyd Petrie. "Expert Systems." *CBT Directions,* October 1988, pp. 33–35.

Trim, C. W. "Zero Defect." *Mortgage Banking,* January 1987, pp. 19–24.

Wilson, Lois. "An On-line Prescription for Basic Skills." *Training and Development,* April 1990, pp. 36–41.

Zeigler, R. "Integrated Performance Support Systems: The Time Is Right Now." *Enterprise Computing,* November 1990, pp. 40–42.

Zuboff, Shoshana. *In the Age of the Smart Machine: The Future of Work and Power.* New York: Basic Books, 1988.

"Making Technology Work"—Human-Computer Interaction, Usability, and Interface Issues (Chapter 4)

Andersen Consulting. "Multimedia and the Metaphor." *The Spang Robinson Report,* August 1992, p. 7.

Bender, Eric. "Desktop Multimedia: You Ain't Seen Nothing Yet." *PC World,* March 1990, pp. 191–96.

Bijker, W. E., T. P. Hughes, and T. J. Pinch, eds. *The Social Construction of Technological Systems.* Cambridge, MA: MIT Press, 1987.

Bodker, S. "A Human Activity Approach to User Interfaces." *Human-Computer Interaction,* 4, pp. 171–95.

Carr, Clay. "Making the Human-Computer Marriage Work." *Training and Development Journal,* May 1988, pp. 65–74.

Carroll, J. M. *Designing Interaction: Psychology at the Human-Computer Interface.* New York: Cambridge University Press, 1991.

Corn, J. J., ed. *Imagining Tomorrow: History, Technology, and the American Future.* Cambridge, MA: MIT Press, 1986.

Lakoff, G., and Johnson, M. *Metaphors We Live By.* Chicago: The University of Chicago Press, 1980.

Laurel, Brenda. ed. *The Art of Human-Computer Interface Design.* Reading, MA: Addison-Wesley, 1990.

Norman, Donald A. *The Design of Everyday Things.* New York: Doubleday, 1988.
————. *Things that Make Us Smart: Defending Human Attributes in the Age of the Machine.* Reading, MA: Addison-Wesley, 1993.

Norman, D. A., and S. Draper, eds. *User-Centered Systems Design: New Perspectives in Human-Computer Interaction.* Hillsdale, NJ: Erlbaum, 1986.

Postman, Neil. *Technopoly.* New York: Alfred A. Knopf, 1992.

Pylyshyn, Z. W., and L. J. Bannon, eds. *Perspectives on the Computer Revolution.* Norwood, NJ: Ablex, 1989.

Ryan, Hugh. "The Human Metaphor," *Information Systems Management,* Winter 1992, pp. 72ff.

Schneiderman, Ben. *Designing the User Interface: Strategies for Effective Human-Computer Interaction.* Reading, MA: Addison-Wesley, 1987.

Suchman, L. *Plans and Situated Actions: The Problem of Human-Machine Interaction.* New York: Cambridge University Press, 1987.

"The Technology Payoff." *Business Week,* June 14, 1993, pp. 58ff.

"Users' Champion." *Computerworld,* July 6, 1993, pp. 71–72.

Zeldin, Anita E. "Technology and the Human Factor." *Wall Street & Technology,* May 1993.

Satisfying the Customer (Chapter 5)

Berry, Leonard L., Valarie A. Zeithaml, and A. Parasuraman. "Five Imperatives for Improving Service Quality." *Sloan Management Review,* Summer 1990, pp. 29–38.

Boyett, Joseph A., and Henry P. Conn. *Workplace 2000: The Revolution Reshaping American Business.* New York: Penguin Books, 1991.

Braasch, Bill. "Performance Support Systems Helping Business." *Computing Canada,* February 1990, pp. 23ff.

Desatnick, Robert L. "Service: A CEO's Perspective." *Management Review,* October 1987, p. 41.

Leonard, Stew. "Love That Customer!" *Management Review,* October 1987, pp. 36–39.

Leung, Shirley. "Job Training, Courtesy of Walt and Sam." *Chicago Tribune,* July 20, 1993, Section 3, pp. 4ff.

Reichheld, Frederick F., and W. Earl Sasser, Jr. "Zero Defections: Quality Comes to Services." *Harvard Business Review,* September–October 1990, pp. 105–11.

Schlesinger, Leonard A., and James L. Heskett. "The Service-Driven Service Company." *Harvard Business Review,* September–October 1991, pp. 71–81.
Sellers, Patricia. "Companies that Serve You Best." *Fortune,* May 31, 1993, p. 75.
———. "What Customers Really Want." *Fortune,* June 4, 1990, pp. 58–68.
Treacy, Michael, and Fred Wiersema. "Customer Intimacy and Other Value Disciplines." *Harvard Business Review,* January–February 1993, pp. 84–93.
Whiteley, Richard C. *The Customer-Driven Company: Moving from Talk to Action.* Reading, MA: Addison-Wesley, 1991.

Turning Information into Knowledge (Chapter 6)

Clancey, William, J. "Practice Cannot Be Reduced to Theory: Knowledge, Representations, and Change in the Workplace." Palo Alto, CA: Institute for Research on Learning, 1993.
Grice, Roger A. "Online Information: What Do People Want? What Do People Need?" in *The Society of Text,* ed. Edward Barrett. Cambridge, MA: MIT Press, 1989.
Large, Peter. *The Micro Revolution Revisited.* Totowa, NJ: Rowman and Allanheld, 1984.
Lucky, Robert W. *Silicon Dreams: Information, Man, and Machine.* New York: St. Martin's Press, 1989.
Madigan, Charles M. "Going with the Flow." *Chicago Tribune Magazine,* May 2, 1993, pp. 16–20.
McCarthy, Michael J. *Mastering the Information Age: A Course in Working Smarter, Thinking Better, and Learning Faster.* New York: St. Martin's Press, 1991.
A New Learning Agenda: Putting People First. Palo Alto, CA: Institute for Research on Learning, 1993.
Paulapuro, Hannu. "The Future of the Information Society." *The Electronic Library,* June 1991, pp. 135–43.
"A Plague of Numbers." *Business Week,* November 25, 1991.
Poe, Richard. "The Knowledge-Value Boom: Tomorrow's Consumer Thirsts for Wisdom-Based Products." *Success,* April 1992, p. 80.
Tufte, E. R. *Envisioning Information.* Cheshire, CT: Graphics Press, 1990.
Webber, Alan M. "What's So New About the New Economy?" *Harvard Business Review,* January–February 1993, pp. 28ff.
Wurman, Richard Saul. *Information Anxiety: What to Do When Information Doesn't Tell You What You Need to Know.* New York: Bantam Books, 1990.

Attaining and Sustaining Proficiency—Training, Learning, and Education in the Workplace (Chapter 7)

Booker, Ellis. "Training on Thin Ice." *Computerworld,* October 11, 1993, pp. 81ff.
Bowsher, Jack E. *Educating America: Lessons Learned in the Nation's Corporations.* New York: John Wiley & Sons, 1989.

Brechlin, Jeff, and Allison Rossett. "Orienting New Employees." *Training,* April 1991, pp. 45–51.

Carnevale, Anthony P., and others. *Training in America.* San Francisco: Jossey-Bass, 1990.

Chute, Alan G., Burton W. Hancock, and Lee B. Balthazar. "Distance Education Futures: Information Needs and Technology Options." *Performance & Instruction,* November/December 1991, pp. 1–6.

Doyle, John. "Innovations in Training." *Credit Magazine,* January/February 1991, pp. 10–14.

Ertmer, Peggy A., and Timothy J. Newby. "Behaviorism, Cognitivism, Constructivism: Comparing Critical Features from an Instructional Design Perspective." *Performance Improvement Quarterly,* Volume 6, Number 4/1993, pp. 50–72.

Geber, Beverly. "Goodbye Classrooms (Redux)." *Training,* January 1990, pp. 27–35.

Gery, Gloria. "Training vs. Performance Support: Inadequate Training Is Now Insufficient." *Performance and Improvement Quarterly,* 1989, Volume 2/Number 3, pp. 51–71.

Gross, Ronald. *Peak Learning.* Los Angeles: Jeremy P. Tarchar, 1991.

Heathman, Dena J., and Brian H. Kleimer. "Training + Technology: The Future Is Now." *Training and Development Journal,* September 1991, pp. 49–54.

Kemske, Floyd, and Nancy J. Weingarten. "A Memo for the Future: Computer Training in 1999." *CBT Directions,* December 1989, pp. 29–32.

Laud, Robert, and Max Dennis. "Providing IT Training for Workforce 2000." *Service News,* July 1993.

Lave, J. *Cognition in Practice.* Cambridge, UK: Cambridge University Press, 1988.

Malcolm, Stanley E. "Reengineering Corporate Training." *Training,* August 1992, pp. 57–61.

Minton-Eversole, Theresa. "Smart Training: The Manager's Guide to Training for Improved Performance." *Training & Development,* June 1993.

Newell, A. *Unified Theories of Cognition.* Cambridge, MA: Harvard University Press, 1991.

Norman, Donald A. *Learning and Memory.* New York: Freeman, 1982.

Pastore, Richard. "Training on Tap." *CIO,* June 1, 1993, pp. 56–62.

Perelman, Lewis J. "How Hypermation Leaps the Learning Curve." *Forbes ASAP,* October 25, 1993, pp. 77–90.

Puterbaugh, Gerry. "CBT and Performance Support." *CBT Directions,* June 1990, pp. 18–25.

Puterbaugh, G., M. Rosenberg, and R. Sofman. "Performance Support Tools: A Step Beyond Training." *Performance & Instruction,* December 1989, pp. 1–5.

Putman, Anthony O. "Computer-Based Coaching: The Trainer's Missing Piece." *Training and Development Journal,* March 1989, pp. 35–37.

Quinlan, Tom. "Andersen Builds Multimedia Training Program." *MIS Week,* March 1990.

Schank, Roger C. *Dynamic Memory.* New York: Cambridge University Press, 1982.

————. *Tell Me A Story: A New Look at Real and Artificial Memory.* New York: Scribner, 1990.

Schank, Roger C., with Peter G. Childers. *The Cognitive Computer: On Language, Learning, and Artificial Intelligence.* Reading, MA: Addison-Wesley, 1984.

Senbetta, Ghenno. "The Myth of One Hour of CBT." *CBT Directions,* October 1991, pp. 18–22.

"Star Techs: The Next Generation." *Wall Street Journal,* May 24, 1993.

Winslow, Charles D., and James C. Caldwell, "Integrated Performance Support: A New Educational Paradigm." *Information System Management,* Spring 1992, pp. 76–78.

Doing More with Less—Downsizing, Horizontal Management Structures, Cooperative Work (Chapter 8)

Dyson, Ester. "Job Losses Are Mounting: Good News?" *Forbes,* March 9, 1992, p. 104.

Fisher, Steb. "Cutting Costs or Re-building Business?" *European Management Journal,* March 1993, pp. 74–79.

Fitz-enz, Jac. "Getting—and Keeping—Good Employees." *Personnel,* August 1990, pp. 25–28.

Franklin, Stephen. "Layoff Fever Spreads to Robust Firms." *Chicago Tribune,* September 12, 1993.

Greif, I. *Computer-Supported Cooperative Work: A Book of Readings.* San Mateo, CA: Morgan Kaufmann, 1988.

Grudin, J. "Why Groupware Fails: Problems in Design and Evaluation." *Office Technology and People,* 4, pp. 245–64.

Ishii, H., and Miyake, N. "TeamWorkStation: Towards an Open Shared Workspace." *Communications of the ACM,* 34, pp. 37–50.

Krieg, Richard M. "The New Era: Workers as Assets." *Chicago Tribune,* July 23, 1993, Section 1, pp. 15ff.

Liebig, James E. *Business Ethics: Profiles in Civic Virtue.* Golden, CO: Fulcrum Publishing, 1990.

Noer, David M. *Healing the Wounds: Overcoming the Trauma of Layoffs and Revitalizing Downsized Organizations.* San Francisco: Jossey-Bass Publishers, 1993.

Pepper, Jon. "The Horizontal Organization." *Information Week,* August 17, 1992, pp. 32ff.

Powell, Reed M. "A Point of View: Doing More with Less." *National Productivity Review,* Winter 1990, p. 1.

Reich, Robert. *The Next American Frontier.* New York: Times Books, 1983, pp. 143–44.

Roach, Stephen. "The Redemption of the Inept," *Information Week,* April 19, 1993, pp. 30ff.

Schrage, M. *Shared Minds: The New Technologies of Collaboration.* New York: Random House, 1990.

Sellers, Patricia. "Why Bigger Is Badder at Sears." *Fortune,* December 5, 1988, pp. 79ff.

Tomasko, Robert M. *Downsizing: Reshaping the Corporation for the Future.* New York: AMACOM, 1987.

"Integrated Performance Support for Everyone"—Future Workforce Competencies, Transfer of Work to the Consumer (Chapter 9)

Bailey, Thomas. "Jobs of the Future and the Skills They Will Require." *American Educator,* Spring 1990, pp. 12ff.

Bulkeley, William M. "Information Age: Computer Use by Illiterates Grows at Work." *Wall Street Journal,* June 9, 1992, p. B1.

Carnevale, Anthony Patrick. *America and the New Economy.* San Francisco: Jossey-Bass, 1991.

Coffee, Peter. "Plan Now for Major Changes in the Labor Force." *PC Week,* January 6, 1992, p. 48.

Johnston, William B., and Arnold H. Packer. *Workforce 2000: Work and Workers for the Twenty-first Century.* Indianapolis, IN: Hudson Institute, 1987.

Kearns, David T. "The Business of Business Is Also Education." *Business Week,* November 25, 1991.

Kiechel, Walter. "How We Will Work in the Year 2000." *Fortune,* May 1993, pp. 39ff.

Kurland, Norman D., and others. "Role of Technology in the Education, Training, and Retraining of Adult Workers." Delman, NY: Kurland and Associates, October 5, 1984. Sponsored by the U.S. Congress Office of Technology Assessment.

Loden, Marilyn, and Judy B. Rosener. *Workforce America! Managing Employee Diversity.* Homewood, IL: Business One Irwin, 1991.

Miller, William. "A New Perspective for Tomorrow's Workforce." *Industry Week,* May 6, 1991, pp. 6–11.

Thurow, Lester. *Head to Head.* New York: William and Morrow Company, 1992.

Making Change Work—Organizational Change, Reengineering, Human Resources Issues (Chapter 10)

Belasco, James A. *Teaching the Elephant to Dance: The Manager's Guide to Empowering Change.* New York: Penguin Books, 1990.

Berger, Lance A., and Martin J. Sikora, with Dorothy R. Berger. *The Change Management Handbook: A Road Map to Corporate Transformation.* Burr Ridge, IL: Irwin Professional Publishing, 1993.

Fombrun, Charles, Noel M. Tichy, and Mary Anne Devanna, eds. *Strategic Human Resource Management.* New York: John Wiley & Sons, 1984.

Gould, Lawrence. "What About the Worker Who Doesn't Want to Be Empowered?" *Managing Automation,* September 1993.

Hammer, Michael, and James Champy. *Reengineering the Corporation.* New York: HarperCollins, 1993.

Huse, E., and T. G. Cummings. *Organizational Development and Change.* St. Paul, MN: West, 1985.

Kissler, Gary D. *The Change Riders: Managing the Power of Change.* Reading, MA: Addison-Wesley, 1991.

Moad, Jeff. "Does Reengineering Really Work?" *Datamation,* August 1, 1993, pp. 22ff.

Morton, Michael S. Scott, ed. *The Corporation of the 1990s: Information Technology and Organizational Transformation.* New York: Oxford University Press, 1991.

Naisbitt, John, and Patricia Aburdene. *Re-inventing the Corporation.* New York: Warner Books, 1985.

Stewart, Thomas A. "Reengineering: The Hot New Managing Tool." *Fortune,* August 23, 1993, pp. 41ff.

Learning Organizations and Growth Organizations (Chapter 11)

Carnevale, Anthony P. "The Learning Enterprise." *Training and Development Journal,* February 1989, pp. 26–33.

Dalton, Richard. "Lose the Sweatshop Mentality." *Information Week,* July 5, 1993, p. 63.

Miller, William H. "A New Perspective for Tomorrow's Workforce." *Industry Week,* May 6, 1991, pp. 6–11.

Mills, Daniel Quinn, and Bruce Friesen. "The Learning Organization." *European Management Journal,* June 1992, pp. 146–56.

Quinn, James Brian. *Intelligent Enterprise.* New York: The Free Press, 1992.

Rowley, Storer H. "Knowledge the Wealth of Nations?" *Chicago Tribune,* May 17, 1993.

Senge, Peter M. *The Fifth Discipline: The Art & Practice of the Learning Organization.* New York: Doubleday Currency, 1990.

Infocosm—Electronic Networks, Information "Superhighways" (Chapter 12)

Davidow, William H., and Michael S. Malone. *The Virtual Corporation: Structuring and Revitalizing the Corporation for the 21st Century.* New York: HarperBusiness, 1992.

Rheingold, Howard. *The Virtual Community: Homesteading on the Electronic Frontier.* Reading, MA: Addison-Wesley, 1993.

Targowsky, Andrew S. "Strategies and Architecture of the Electronic Global Village." *The Information Society 7,* no. 3, 1990, pp. 187–200.

The Knowledge Economy (Epilogue)

Barnet, Richard J., and John Cavanagh. *Global Dreams: Imperial Corporations and the New World Order.* New York: Simon and Schuster, 1994.

Davis, Stan, and Bill Davidson. *2020 Vision.* New York: Simon & Schuster, 1991.

Drucker, Peter F. *Post-Capitalist Society.* New York: HarperCollins, 1993.

Reich, Robert B. *The Work of Nations: Preparing Ourselves for 21st Century Capitalism.* New York: Alfred A. Knopf, 1991.

Toffler, Alvin. *Power Shift.* New York: Bantam Books, 1990.

INDEX

369

EDITORIAL BOARD

ACKNOWLEDGMENTS

Special thanks to those companies and organizations mentioned throughout the book who allowed us to share their working and research experiences with Integrated Performance Support™.

AGT LIMITED—Alberta, Canada
Andersen Windows—Bayport, Minnesota
Bell Atlantic—Arlington, Virginia
Caja España—Leon, Spain
Connecticut Natural Gas—Hartford, Connecticut
ICA Handlarna—Stockholm, Sweden
The Institute for the Learning Sciences, Northwestern University—Evanston, Illinois
Italease—Milan, Italy
Lufthansa—Koeln, Germany
McCaw Cellular Communications—Kirkland, Washington
Mobil Oil Australia—Melbourne, Australia
North West Water—Warrington, England
Rogers Cantel Mobile Communications—Toronto, Canada

This book has been made possible by the teamwork of Andersen Consulting professionals throughout the world. Many of these colleagues are listed as Contributing Editors and Case Study Editors. Others are acknowledged in footnotes throughout the book where our debt to their work is clear. There are a number of other individuals, however, who provided crucial support at varous times during the research and writing of *FutureWork*.

Sheri Browning, San Francisco
Kimberly D. Cantalupo, Chicago
Ron Chandler, Chicago
John E. Cisek, Chicago
Melissa K. Hale, Chicago
Susan M. Heiser, Chicago

Phyllis S. Kennedy, Chicago
Michelle L. Kilbourne, Chicago
Donna Lachapelle, Hartford
Muriel Lederer, Lederer Marketing Consultants, Inc., Winnetka, IL
Anthony G. Lombardo, Washington, D.C.
Eric Neinhaus, Enschede, The Netherlands
Ellen M. O'Dwyer, The Institute for the Learning Sciences, Evanston, IL
John P. Rogers, Chicago
John E. Salkeld, Chicago
Laura J. Schroeder, Chicago
Valerie A. Stone, Chicago
Lisa Szatkiewicz, Dallas
Olaf Tennhardt, Munich
Mindy J. Watt, Chicago
Gillian E. Wilson, Chicago